George Richmond. Del.   (From a drawing in the possession of the Earl of Carlisle.)   H. Wright Smith. Sc.

Very truly yours,

Wm H. Prescott

BIOGRAPHICAL

AND

CRITICAL MISCELLANIES.

BY

WILLIAM H. PRESCOTT,

AUTHOR OF

"THE HISTORY OF FERDINAND AND ISABELLA," "THE
CONQUEST OF MEXICO," ETC.

PHILADELPHIA:

J. B. LIPPINCOTT & CO.

1865.

TO

GEORGE TICKNOR, ESQ.

THIS VOLUME,

WHICH MAY REMIND HIM OF STUDIES PURSUED TOGETHER IN EARLIER YEARS,

Is Affectionately Dedicated

BY HIS FRIEND,

WILLIAM H. PRESCOTT.

ADVERTISEMENT

OF

THE AMERICAN PUBLISHERS.

As many of the pieces in this volume are the result of more care than is usually bestowed on periodical writing, and as they embrace a range of study very different from that by which Mr. Prescott has been hitherto known as an author, it is thought that the republication of them in this form will be acceptable to his countrymen. The publishers have taken care that the mechanical execution of the book shall be uniform with that of his historical works.

*** In addition to the matter published in the former editions of these " Miscellanies," will now be found an article of considerable length upon Spanish Literature, which appeared in the " North American Review" for January, 1850. It forms the last in the series of essays.

PREFACE

TO THE ENGLISH EDITION.

THE following Essays, with a single exception, have been selected from contributions originally made to the North American Review. They are purely of a literary character; and as they have little reference to local or temporary topics, and as the journal in which they appeared, though the most considerable in the United States, is not widely circulated in Great Britain, it has been thought that a republication of the articles might have some novelty and interest for the English reader.

Several of the papers were written many years since; and the author is aware that they betray those crudities in the execution which belong to an unpractised writer, while others of more recent date may be charged with the inaccuracies incident to rapid, and, sometimes, careless composition. The more obvious blemishes he has endeavoured to correct, without attempting to reform the critical judgments, which, in some cases, he could wish had been expressed in a more qualified and temperate manner; and he dismisses the volume with the hope that, in submitting it to the British public, he may not be thought to have relied too far on that indulgence which has been so freely extended to his more elaborate efforts.

Boston, March 30th, 1845.

CONTENTS.

CONTENTS.

BIOGRAPHICAL AND CRITICAL
MISCELLANIES.

MEMOIR OF

CHARLES BROCKDEN BROWN,
THE AMERICAN NOVELIST.*

THE class of professed men of letters, if we exclude from the account the conductors of periodical
journals, is certainly not very large, even at the
present day, in our country; but before the close
of the last century it was nearly impossible to meet
with an individual who looked to authorship as his
only, or, indeed, his principal means of subsistence.
This was somewhat the more remarkable, considering the extraordinary development of intellectual
power exhibited in every quarter of the country,
and applied to every variety of moral and social
culture, and formed a singular contrast with more
than one nation in Europe, where literature still
continued to be followed as a distinct profession,
amid all the difficulties resulting from an arbitrary
government, and popular imbecility and ignorance.

Abundant reasons are suggested for this by the
various occupations afforded to talent of all kinds,
not only in the exercise of political functions, but

* From Sparks's American Biography, 1834.

4   A

in the splendid career opened to enterprise of every description in our free and thriving community. We were in the morning of life, as it were, when everything summoned us to action; when the spirit was quickened by hope and youthful confidence; and we felt that we had our race to run, unlike those nations who, having reached the noontide of their glory, or sunk into their decline, were naturally led to dwell on the soothing recollections of the past, and to repose themselves, after a tumultuous existence, in the quiet pleasures of study and contemplation. "It was amid the ruins of the Capitol," says Gibbon, "that I first conceived the idea of writing the History of the Roman Empire." The occupation suited well with the spirit of the place, but would scarcely have harmonized with the life of bustling energy, and the thousand novelties which were perpetually stimulating the appetite for adventure in our new and unexplored hemisphere. In short, to express it in one word, the peculiarities of our situation as naturally disposed us to active life as those of the old countries of Europe to contemplative.

The subject of the present memoir affords an almost solitary example, at this period, of a scholar, in the enlarged application of the term, who cultivated letters as a distinct and exclusive profession, resting his means of support, as well as his fame, on his success; and who, as a writer of fiction, is still farther entitled to credit for having quitted the beaten grounds of the Old Country, and sought his subjects in the untried wilderness of his own. The particulars of his unostentatious life have been collected with sufficient industry by his friend, Mr. William Dunlap, to whom our native literature is under such large obligations for the extent and fidelity of his researches. We will select a few of the most prominent incidents from a mass of miscellaneous fragments and literary lumber with which his work is somewhat encumbered. It were to be wished that, in the place of some of them, more copious extracts had been substituted for his journal and correspondence, which, doubtless, in this as in other cases, must afford the most interesting, as well as authentic materials for biography.

CHARLES BROCKDEN BROWN was born at Philadelphia, January 17, 1771. He was descended from a highly respectable family, whose ancestors were of that estimable sect who came over with William Penn to seek an asylum where they might worship their Creator unmolested in the meek and humble spirit of their own faith. From his earliest childhood Brown gave evidence of his studious propensities, being frequently noticed by his father, on his return from school, poring over some heavy tome, nothing daunted by the formidable words it contained, or mounted on a table, and busily engaged in exploring a map which hung on the parlour wall. This infantine predilection for geographical studies ripened into a passion in later years. Another anecdote, recorded of him at the age of ten, sets in a still stronger light his appreciation of intellectual pursuits far above his years. A visiter at his father's having rebuked him, as it would seem, without cause, for some remark he had made, gave him the contemptuous epithet of "boy." "What does he mean," said the young philosopher, after the guest's departure, "by calling me boy? Does he not know that it is neither size nor age, but sense, that makes the man? I could ask him a hundred questions, none of which he could answer."

At eleven years of age he was placed under the tuition of Mr. Robert Proud, well known as the author of the History of Pennsylvania. Under his direction he went over a large course of English reading, and acquired the elements of Greek and Latin, applying himself with great assiduity to his studies. His bodily health was naturally delicate, and indisposed him to engage in the robust, athletic exercises of boyhood. His sedentary habits, however, began so evidently to impair his health, that his master recommended him to withdraw from his books, and recruit his strength by excursions on foot into the country. These pedestrian rambles suited the taste of the pupil, and the length of his absence often excited the apprehensions of his friends for his safety. He may be thought to have sat to himself for this portrait of one of his heroes. "I preferred to ramble in the forest and loiter on the hill; perpetually to change the scene; to scrutinize the endless variety of objects; to compare one leaf and pebble with another; to pursue those trains of thought which their resemblances and differences suggested; to inquire what it was that gave them this place, structure. and form, were more agreeable employments than ploughing and threshing." "My frame was delicate and feeble. Exposure to wet blasts and vertical suns was sure to make me sick." The fondness for these solitary rambles continued through life, and the familiarity which they opened to him with the grand and beautiful scenes of nature undoubtedly contributed to nourish the habit of revery and abstraction, and to deepen the romantic sensibilities from which flowed so much of his misery, as well as happiness, in after life.

He quitted Mr. Proud's school before the age of sixteen. He had previously made some small poetical attempts, and soon after sketched the plans of three several epics, on the discovery of America, and the conquests of Peru and Mexico. For some time they engaged his attention to the exclusion of every other object. No vestige of them now remains, or, at least, has been given to the public, by which we can ascertain the progress made towards their completion. The publication of such immature juvenile productions may gratify curiosity by affording a point of comparison with later excellence. They are rarely, however, of value in themselves sufficient to authorize their exposure to the world, and notwithstanding the occasional exception of a Pope or a Pascal, may very safely put up with Uncle Toby's recommendation on a similar display of precocity, " to hush it up, and say as little about it as possible."

4   A*

Among the contributions which, at a later period of life, he was in the habit of making to different journals, the fate of one was too singular to be passed over in silence. It was a poetical address to Franklin, prepared for the Edentown newspaper. " The blundering printer," says Brown, in his journal, " from zeal or ignorance, or perhaps from both, substituted the name of Washington. Washington, therefore, stands arrayed in awkward colours; philosophy smiles to behold her darling son; she turns with horror and disgust from those who have won the laurel of victory in the field of battle, to this her favourite candidate, who had never participated in such bloody glory, and whose fame was derived from the conquest of philosophy alone. The printer, by his blundering ingenuity, made the subject ridiculous. Every word of this clumsy panegyric was a direct slander upon Washington, and so it was regarded at the time." There could not well be imagined a more expeditious or effectual recipe for converting eulogy into satire.

Young Brown had now reached a period of life when it became necessary to decide on a profession. After due deliberation, he determined on the law; a choice which received the cordial approbation of his friends, who saw in his habitual diligence and the character of his mind, at once comprehensive and logical, the most essential requisites for success. He entered on the studies of his profession with his usual ardour; and the acuteness and copiousness of his arguments on various topics proposed for dis-

cussion in a law-society over which he presided,
bear ample testimony to his ability and industry.
But, however suited to his talents the profession of
the law might be, it was not at all to his taste. He
became a member of a literary club, in which he
made frequent essays in composition and eloquence.
He kept a copious journal, and by familiar exercise
endeavoured to acquire a pleasing and graceful style
of writing; and every hour that he could steal from
professional schooling was devoted to the cultivation of more attractive literature. In one of his
contributions to a journal, just before this period,
he speaks of " the rapture with which he held communion with his own thoughts amid the gloom of
surrounding woods, where his fancy peopled every
object with ideal beings, and the barrier between
himself and the world of spirits seemed burst by the
force of meditation. In this solitude, he felt himself surrounded by a delightful society; but when
transported from thence, and compelled to listen to
the frivolous chat of his fellow-beings, he suffered
all the miseries of solitude " He declares that his
intercourse and conversation with mankind had
wrought a salutary change; that he can now mingle in the concerns of life, perform his appropriate
duties, and reserve that higher species of discourse
for the solitude and silence of his study. In this
supposed control over his romantic fancies he grossly deceived himself.

As the time approached for entering on the practice of his profession, he felt his repugnance to it

increase more and more; and he sought to justify a
retreat from it altogether by such poor sophistry as
his imagination could suggest. He objected to the
profession as having something in it immoral. He
could not reconcile it with his notions of duty to come
forward as the champion indiscriminately of right and
wrong; and he considered the stipendiary advocate
of a guilty party as becoming, by that very act, parti-
cipator in the guilt. He did not allow himself to
reflect that no more equitable arrangement could be
devised, none which would give the humblest individual so fair a chance for maintaining his rights
as the employment of competent and upright counsel, familiar with the forms of legal practice, necessarily so embarrassing to a stranger; that, so far
from being compelled to undertake a cause manifestly unjust, it is always in the power of an honest
lawyer to decline it; but that such contingencies
are of most rare occurrence, as few cases are litiga-
ted where each party has not previously plausible
grounds for believing himself in the right, a question only to be settled by fair discussion on both
sides; that opportunities are not wanting, on the
other hand, which invite the highest display of eloquence and professional science in detecting and
defeating villany, in vindicating slandered innocence,
and in expounding the great principles of law on
which the foundations of personal security and property are established; and, finally, that the most illustrious names in his own and every other civilized
country have been drawn from the ranks of a pro-

fession whose habitual discipline so well trains them for legislative action, and the exercise of the highest political functions.

Brown cannot be supposed to have been insensible to these obvious views; and, indeed, from one of his letters in later life, he appears to have clearly recognised the value of the profession he had de serted. But his object was, at this time, to justify himself in his fickleness of purpose, as he best might, in his own eyes and those of his friends. Brown was certainly not the first man of genius who found himself incapable of resigning the romantic world of fiction, and the uncontrolled revels of the imagination, for the dull and prosaic realities of the law. Few, indeed, like Mansfield, have been able so far to constrain their young and buoyant imaginations as to merit the beautiful eulogium of the English poet; while many more comparatively, from the time of Juvenal downward, fortunately for the world, have been willing to sacrifice the affections plighted to Themis on the altars of the Muse.

Brown's resolution at this crisis caused sincere regret to his friends, which they could not conceal, on seeing him thus suddenly turn from the path of honourable fame at the very moment when he was prepared to enter on it. His prospects, but lately so brilliant, seemed now overcast with a deep gloom. The embarrassments of his situation had also a most unfavourable effect on his own mind. Instead of the careful discipline to which it had been lately subjected, it was now left to rove at large wherever

B

caprice should dictate, and waste itself on those romantic reveries and speculations to which he was naturally too much addicted. This was the period when the French Revolution was in its heat, and the awful convulsion experienced in one unhappy country seemed to be felt in every quarter of the globe; men grew familiar with the wildest paradoxes, and the spirit of innovation menaced the oldest and best established principles in morals and government. Brown's inquisitive and speculative mind partook of the prevailing skepticism. Some of his compositions, and especially one on the *Rights of Women*, published in 1797, show to what extravagance a benevolent mind may be led by fastening too exclusively on the contemplation of the evils of existing institutions, and indulging in indefinite dreams of perfectibility.

There is no period of existence when the spirit of a man is more apt to be depressed than when he is about to quit the safe and quiet harbour in which he has rode in safety from childhood, and to launch on the dark and unknown ocean where so many a gallant bark has gone down before him. How much must this disquietude be increased in the case of one who, like Brown, has thrown away the very chart and compass by which he was prepared to guide himself through the doubtful perils of the voyage! How heavily the gloom of despondency fell on his spirits at this time is attested by various extracts from his private correspondence. "As for me," he says, in one of his letters, "I long ago discovered that Nature had not qualified me for an actor on this stage. The nature of my education only added to these disqualifications, and I experienced all those deviations from the centre which arise when all our lessons are taken from books, and the scholar makes his own character the comment. A happy destiny, indeed, brought me to the knowledge of two or three minds which Nature had fashioned in the same mould with my own, but these are gone. And, O God! enable me to wait the moment when it is thy will that I should follow them." In another epistle he remarks, "I have not been deficient in the pursuit of that necessary branch of knowledge, the study of myself. I will not explain the result, for have I not already sufficiently endeavoured to make my friends unhappy by communications which, though they might easily be injurious, could not be of any possible advantage? I really, dear W., regret that period when your pity was first excited in my favour. I sincerely lament that I ever gave you reason to imagine that I was not so happy as a gay indifference with regard to the present, stubborn forgetfulness with respect to the uneasy past, and excursions into lightsome futurity could make me; for what end, what useful purposes were promoted by the discovery? It could not take away from the number of the unhappy, but only add to it, by making those who loved me participate in my uneasiness, which each participation, so far from tending to diminish, would, in reality, increase, by adding those regrets, of which I had been the author in them, to my own original stock." It is painful to witness the struggles of a generous spirit endeavouring to suppress the anguish thus involuntarily escaping in the warmth of affectionate intercourse. This becomes still more striking in the contrast exhibited between the assumed cheerfulness of much of his correspondence at this period and the uniform melancholy tone of his private journal, the genuine record of his emotions.

Fortunately, his taste, refined by intellectual culture, and the elevation and spotless purity of his moral principles, raised him above the temptations of sensual indulgence, in which minds of weaker mould might have sought a temporary relief. His soul was steeled against the grosser seductions of appetite. The only avenue through which his principles could in any way be assailed was the understanding; and it would appear, from some dark hints in his correspondence at this period, that the rash idea of relieving himself from the weight of earthly sorrows by some voluntary deed of violence had more than once flitted across his mind. It is pleasing to observe with what beautiful modesty and simplicity of character he refers his abstinence from coarser indulgences to his constitutional infirmities, and consequent disinclination to them, which, in truth, could be only imputed to the excellence of his heart and his understanding. In one of his letters he remarks, "that the benevolence of Nature rendered him, in a manner, an exile from many of the temptations that infest the minds of ardent youth

Whatever his wishes might have been, his benevolent destiny had prevented him from running into
the frivolities of youth." He ascribes to this cause
his love of letters, and his predominant anxiety to
excel in whatever was a glorious subject of competition. "Had he been furnished with the nerves and
muscles of his comrades, it was very far from impossible that he might have relinquished intellectual
pleasures. Nature had benevolently rendered him
incapable of encountering such severe trials."

Brown's principal resources for dissipating the
melancholy which hung over him were his inextinguishable love of letters, and the society of a few
friends, to whom congeniality of taste and temper had
united him from early years. In addition to these resources, we may mention his fondness for pedestrian rambles, which sometimes were of several weeks'
duration. In the course of these excursions, the circle of his acquaintance and friends was gradually
enlarged. In the city of New-York, in particular,
he contracted an intimacy with several individuals
of similar age and kindred mould with himself.
Among these, his earliest associate was Dr. E. H.
Smith, a young gentleman of great promise in the
medical profession. Brown had become known to
him during the residence of the latter as a student
in Philadelphia. By him our hero was introduced
to Mr. Dunlap, who has survived to commemorate
the virtues of his friend in a biography already noticed, and to Mr. Johnson, the accomplished author
of the New-York Law Reports. The society of

4   B

these friends had sufficient attractions to induce him to repeat his visit to New-York, until at length, in the beginning of 1798, he may be said to have established his permanent residence there, passing much of his time under the same roof with them. His amiable manners and accomplishments soon recommended him to the notice of other eminent individuals. He became a member of a literary society, called the *Friendly Club*, comprehending names which have since shed a distinguished lustre over the various walks of literature and science.

The spirits of Brown seemed to be exalted in this new atmosphere. His sensibilities found a grateful exercise in the sympathies of friendship, and the powers of his mind were called into action by collision with others of similar tone with his own. His memory was enriched with the stores of various reading, hitherto conducted at random, with no higher object than temporary amusement, or the gratification of an indefinite curiosity. He now concentrated his attention on some determinate object, and proposed to give full scope to his various talents and acquisitions in the career of an author, as yet so little travelled in our own country.

His first publication was that before noticed, entitled "*Alcuin*, a dialogue on the Rights of Women." It exhibits the crude and fanciful speculations of a theorist, who, in his dreams of optimism, charges exclusively on human institutions the imperfections necessarily incident to human nature. The work, with all its ingenuity, made little impression on the public : it found few purchasers, and made, it may be presumed, still fewer converts.

He soon after began a romance, which he never completed, from which his biographer has given copious extracts. It is conducted in the epistolary form, and, although exhibiting little of his subsequent power and passion, is recommended by a graceful and easy manner of narration, more attractive than the more elaborate and artificial style of his latter novels.

This abortive attempt was succeeded, in 1798, by the publication of *Wieland*, the first of that remarkable series of fictions which flowed in such rapid succession from his pen in this and the three following years. In this romance, the author, deviating from the usual track of domestic or historic incident, proposed to delineate the powerful workings of passion, displayed by a mind constitutionally excitable, under the control of some terrible and mysterious agency. The scene is laid in Pennsylvania. The action takes place in a family by the name of Wieland, the principal member of which had inherited a melancholy and somewhat superstitious constitution of mind, which his habitual reading and contemplation deepened into a calm but steady fanaticism. This temper is nourished still farther by the occurrence of certain inexplicable circumstances of ominous import. Strange voices are heard by different members of the family, sometimes warning them of danger, sometimes announcing events seeming beyond the reach of hu man knowledge. The still and solemn hours of night are disturbed by the unearthly summons. The other actors of the drama are thrown into strange perplexity, and an underplot of events is curiously entangled by the occurrence of unaccountable sights as well as sounds. By the heated fancy of Wieland they are referred to supernatural agency. A fearful destiny seems to preside over the scene, and to carry the actors onward to some awful catastrophe. At length the hour arrives. A solemn, mysterious voice announces to Wieland that he is now called on to testify his submission to the Divine will by the sacrifice of his earthly affections— to surrender up the affectionate partner of his bosom, on whom he had reposed all his hopes of happiness in this life. He obeys the mandate of Heaven. The stormy conflict of passion into which his mind is thrown, as the fearful sacrifice he is about to make calls up all the tender remembrances of conjugal fidelity and love, is painted with frightful strength of colouring. Although it presents, on the whole, as pertinent an example as we could offer from any of Brown's writings of the peculiar power and vividness of his conceptions, the whole scene is too long for insertion here. We will mutilate it, however, by a brief extract, as an illustration of our author's manner, more satisfactory than any criticism can be. Wieland, after receiving the fatal mandate, is represented in an apartment alone with his wife. His courage, or, rather, his desperation, fails him, and he sends her, on some pretext, from the chamber. An interval, during which his insane passions have time to rally, ensues.

"She returned with a light; I led the way to the chamber; she looked round her; she lifted the curtain of the bed; she saw nothing. At length she fixed inquiring eyes upon me. The light now enabled her to discover in my visage what darkness had hitherto concealed. Her cares were now transferred from my sister to myself, and she said, in a tremulous voice, 'Wieland! you are not well; what ails you? Can I do nothing for you?' That accents and looks so winning should disarm me of my resolution was to be expected. My thoughts were thrown anew into anarchy. I spread my hand before my eyes that I might not see her, and answered only by groans. She took my other hand between hers, and, pressing it to her heart, spoke with that voice which had ever swayed my will and wafted away sorrow. 'My friend! my soul's friend! tell me thy cause of grief. Do I not merit to partake with thee in thy cares? Am I not thy wife?'

"This was too much. I broke from her embrace, and retired to a corner of the room. In this pause, courage was once more infused into me. I resolved to execute my duty. She followed me, and renewed her passionate entreaty to know the cause of my distress.

"I raised my head and regarded her with steadfast looks. I muttered something about death, and the injunctions of my duty. At these words she shrunk back, and looked at me with a new expres-

4   B *

sion of anguish. After a pause, she clasped her hands and exclaimed,

"'O Wieland! Wieland! God grant that I am mistaken; but surely something is wrong. I see it; it is too plain; thou art undone—lost to me and to thyself.' At the same time she gazed on my features with intensest anxiety, in hope that different symptoms would take place. I replied with vehemence, 'Undone! No; my duty is known, and I thank my God that my cowardice is now vanquished, and I have power to fulfil it. Catharine! I pity the weakness of nature; I pity thee, but must not spare. Thy life is claimed from my hands: thou must die!'

"Fear was now added to her grief. 'What mean you? Why talk you of death? Bethink yourself, Wieland; bethink yourself, and this fit will pass. O! why came I hither? Why did you drag me hither?'

"'I brought thee hither to fulfil a divine command. I am appointed thy destroyer, and destroy thee I must.' Saying this, I seized her wrists. She shrieked aloud, and endeavoured to free herself from my grasp, but her efforts were vain.

"'Surely, surely, Wieland, thou dost not mean it. Am I not thy wife? and wouldst thou kill me? Thou wilt not; and yet—I see—thou art Wieland no longer! A fury, resistless and horrible, possesses thee: spare me—spare—help—help—'

"Till her breath was stopped she shrieked for help—for mercy. When she could speak no longer.

her gestures, her looks appealed to my compassion
My accursed hand was irresolute and tremulous.
I meant thy death to be sudden, thy struggles to be
brief. Alas! my heart was infirm, my resolves mu-
table. Thrice I slackened my grasp, and life kept
its hold, though in the midst of pangs. Her eye-
balls started from their sockets. Grimness and dis-
tortion took place of all that used to bewitch me
into transport and subdue me into reverence.

"I was commissioned to kill thee, but not to torment thee with the foresight of thy death; not to
multiply thy fears and prolong thy agonies. Hag-
gard, and pale, and lifeless, at length thou ceasedst
to contend with thy destiny.

"This was a moment of triumph. Thus had I
successfully subdued the stubbornness of human
passions; the victim which had been demanded
was given; the deed was done past recall.

"I lifted the corpse in my arms, and laid it on
the bed. I gazed upon it with delight. Such was
the elation of my thoughts that I even broke into
laughter. I clapped my hands, and exclaimed, 'It
is done! My sacred duty is fulfilled! To that I
have sacrified, O my God! thy last and best gift,
my wife!'

"For a while I thus soared above frailty. I
imagined I had set myself forever beyond the reach
of selfishness, but my imaginations were false. This
rapture quickly subsided. I looked again at my
wife. My joyous ebullitions vanished, and I asked
myself who it was whom I saw. Methought it

could not be Catharine. It could not be the woman who had lodged for years in my heart; who had slept nightly in my bosom; who had borne in her womb, who had fostered at her breast, the beings who called me father; whom I had watched with delight, and cherished with a fondness ever new and perpetually growing : it could not be the same.

" Where was her bloom ? These deadly and blood-suffused orbs but ill resemble the azure and ecstatic tenderness of her eyes. The lucid stream that meandered over that bosom, the glow of love that was wont to sit upon that cheek, are much unlike these livid stains and this hideous deformity. Alas ! these were the traces of agony : the gripe of the assassin had been here !

" I will not dwell upon my lapse into desperate and outrageous sorrow. The breath of Heaven that sustained me was withdrawn, and I sunk into *mere man.* I leaped from the floor; I dashed my head against the wall ; I uttered screams of horror ; I panted after torment and pain. Eternal fire and the bickerings of hell, compared with what I felt, were music and a bed of roses.

" I thank my God that this degeneracy was transient—that he deigned once more to raise me aloft. I thought upon what I had done as a sacrifice to duty, and *was calm.* My wife was dead ; but I reflected that, though this source of human consolation was closed, yet others were still open. If the transports of a husband were no more, the feelings

of a father had still scope for exercise. When re-
membrance of their mother should excite too keen
a pang, I would look upon them and *be comforted.*

"While I revolved these ideas, new warmth
flowed in upon my heart. I was wrong. These
feelings were the growth of selfishness. Of this I
was not aware; and, to dispel the mist that obscured my perceptions, a new effulgence and a new
mandate were necessary.

"From these thoughts I was recalled by a ray
that was shot into the room. A voice spake like
that which I had before heard, ' Thou hast done
well; but all is not done—the sacrifice is incom-
plete—thy children must be offered—they must
perish with their mother!'"

This, too, is accomplished by the same remorse-
less arm, although the author has judiciously re-
frained from attempting to prolong the note of
feeling, struck with so powerful a hand, by the recital of the particulars. The wretched fanatic is
brought to trial for the murder, but is acquitted on
the ground of insanity. The illusion which has
bewildered him at length breaks on his understanding in its whole truth. He cannot sustain the
shock, and the tragic tale closes with the suicide of
the victim of superstition and imposture. The key
to the whole of this mysterious agency which con-
trols the circumstances of the story is—ventriloquism! ventriloquism exerted for the very purpose
by a human fiend, from no motives of revenge or
hatred, but pure diabolical malice, or, as he would

make us believe, and the author seems willing to endorse this absurd version of it, as a mere practical joke! The reader, who has been gorged with this feast of horrors, is tempted to throw away the book in disgust at finding himself the dupe of such paltry jugglery; which, whatever sense be given to the term ventriloquism, is altogether incompetent to the various phenomena of sight and sound with which the story is so plentifully seasoned. We can feel the force of Dryden's imprecation, when he cursed the inventors of those fifth acts which are bound to unravel all the fine mesh of impossibilities which the author's wits had been so busy entangling in the four preceding.

The explication of the mysteries of Wieland naturally suggests the question how far an author is bound to explain the *supernaturalities*, if we may so call them, of his fictions; and whether it is not better, on the whole, to trust to the willing superstition and credulity of the reader (of which there is perhaps store enough in almost every bosom, at the present enlightened day even, for poetical purposes) than to attempt a solution on purely natural or mechanical principles. It was thought no harm for the ancients to bring the use of *machinery* into their epics, and a similar freedom was conceded to the old English dramatists, whose ghosts and witches were placed in the much more perilous predicament of being subjected to the scrutiny of the spectator, whose senses are not near so likely to be duped as the sensitive and excited imagination of the reader

in his solitary chamber.   It must be admitted, however, that the public of those days, when the

" Undoubting mind
Believed the magic wonders that were sung,"

were admirably seasoned for the action of superstition in all forms, and furnished, therefore, a most
enviable audience for the melo-dramatic artist,
whether dramatist or romance-writer.   But all this
is changed.   No witches ride the air nowadays,
and fairies no longer " dance their rounds by the
pale moonlight," as the worthy Bishop Corbet, indeed, lamented a century and a half ago.

Still it may be allowed, perhaps, if the scene is laid
in some remote age or country, to borrow the ancient
superstitions of the place, and incorporate them into,
or, at least, colour the story with them, without shocking the wellbred prejudices of the modern reader.
Sir Walter Scott has done this with good effect in
more than one of his romances, as every one will
readily call to mind.   A fine example occurs in the
Boden Glass apparition in Waverley, which the
great novelist, far from attempting to explain on
any philosophical principles, or even by an intimation of its being the mere creation of a feverish
imagination, has left as he found it, trusting that
the reader's poetic feeling will readily accommodate itself to the popular superstitions of the country he is depicting.   This reserve on his part, indeed, arising from a truly poetic view of the subject,
and an honest reliance on a similar spirit in his
reader, has laid him open, with some matter-of-fact

people, to the imputation of not being wholly untouched himself by the national superstitions.   Yet
how much would the whole scene have lost in its
permanent effect if the author had attempted an
explanation of the apparition on the ground of an
optical illusion not infrequent among the mountain
mists of the Highlands, or any other of the ingenious
solutions so readily at the command of the thorough-
bred story-teller!

It must be acknowledged, however, that this way
of solving the riddles of romance would hardly be
admissible in a story drawn from familiar scenes
and situations in modern life, and especially in our
own country.   The lights of education are flung
too bright and broad over the land to allow any
lurking-hole for the shadows of a twilight age.   So
much the worse for the poet and the novelist.
Their province must now be confined to poor human nature, without meddling with the " Gorgons
and chimeras dire" which floated through the bewildered brains of our forefathers, at least on the
other side of the water.   At any rate, if a writer,
in this broad sunshine, ventures on any sort of *dia-*
blerie, he is forced to explain it by all the thousand
contrivances of trapdoors, secret passages, waxen
images, and other makeshifts from the property-
room of Mrs. Radcliffe and Company.

Brown, indeed, has resorted to a somewhat higher
mode of elucidating his mysteries by a remarkable
phenomenon of our nature.   But the misfortune of
all these attempts to account for the marvels of the

story oy natural or mechanical causes is, that they are very seldom satisfactory, or competent to their object. This is eminently the case with the ventriloquism in Wieland. Even where they are competent, it may be doubted whether the reader, who has suffered his credulous fancy to be entranced by the spell of the magician, will be gratified to learn, at the end, by what cheap mechanical contrivance he has been duped. However this may be, it is certain that a very unfavourable effect, in another respect, is produced on his mind, after he is made acquainted with the nature of the secret spring by which the machinery is played, more especially when one leading circumstance, like ventriloquism in Wieland, is made the master-key, as it were, by which all the mysteries are to be unlocked and opened at once. With this explanation at hand, it is extremely difficult to rise to that sensation of mysterious awe and apprehension on which so much of the sublimity and general effect of the narrative necessarily depends. Instead of such feelings, the only ones which can enable us to do full justice to the author's conceptions, we sometimes, on the contrary, may detect a smile lurking in the corner of the mouth as we peruse scenes of positive power, from the contrast obviously suggested of the impotence of the apparatus and the portentous character of the results. The critic, therefore, possessed of the real key to the mysteries of the story, if he would do justice to his author's merits, must divest himself, as it were, of his previous

knowledge, by fastening his attention on the results, to the exclusion of the insignificant means by
which they are achieved. He will not always find
this an easy matter.

But to return from this rambling digression : in
the following year, 1799, Brown published his second novel, entitled *Ormond.* The story presents
few of the deeply agitating scenes and powerful
bursts of passion which distinguish the first. It is
designed to exhibit a model of surpassing excellence
in a female rising superior to all the shocks of adversity and the more perilous blandishments of seduction, and who, as the scene grows darker and
darker around her, seems to illumine the whole
with the radiance of her celestial virtues. The
reader is reminded of the "patient Griselda," so
delicately portrayed by the pencils of Boccaccio
and Chaucer. It must be admitted, however, that
the contemplation of such a character in the abstract
is more imposing than the minute details by which
we attain to the knowledge of it; and although
there is nothing, we are told, which the gods looked down upon with more satisfaction than a brave
mind struggling with the storms of adversity, yet,
when these come in the guise of poverty and all the
train of teasing annoyances in domestic life, the tale,
if long protracted, too often produces a sensation of
weariness scarcely to be compensated by the moral
grandeur of the spectacle.

The appearance of these two novels constitutes
an epoch in the ornamental literature of America.

They are the first decidedly successful attempts in the walk of romantic fiction. They are still farther remarkable as illustrating the character and state of society on this side of the Atlantic, instead of resorting to the exhausted springs of European invention. These circumstances, as well as the uncommon powers they displayed both of conception and execution, recommended them to the notice of the literary world, although their philosophical method of dissecting passion and analyzing motives of action placed them somewhat beyond the reach of vulgar popularity. Brown was sensible of the favourable impression which he had made, and mentions it in one of his epistles to his brother with his usual unaffected modesty: "I add somewhat, though not so much as I might if I were so inclined, to the number of my friends. I find to be the writer of *Wieland* and *Ormond* is a greater recommendation than I ever imagined it would be."

In the course of the same year, the quiet tenour of his life was interrupted by the visitation of that fearful pestilence, the yellow fever, which had for several successive years made its appearance in the city of New-York, but which in 1798 fell upon it with a violence similar to that with which it had desolated Philadelphia in 1793. Brown had taken the precaution of withdrawing from the latter city, where he then resided, on its first appearance there. He prolonged his stay in New-York, however, relying on the healthiness of the quarter of the town where he lived, and the habitual abstemiousness of his diet. His friend Smith was necessarily detained there by the duties of his profession; and Brown, in answer to the reiterated importunities of his absent relatives to withdraw from the infected city, refused to do so, on the ground that his personal services might be required by the friends who remained in it; a disinterestedness well meriting the strength of attachment which he excited in the bosom of his companions.

Unhappily, Brown was right in his prognostics, and his services were too soon required in behalf of his friend Dr. Smith, who fell a victim to his own benevolence, having caught the fatal malady from an Italian gentleman, a stranger in the city, whom he received, when infected with the disease, into his house, relinquishing to him his own apartment. Brown had the melancholy satisfaction of performing the last sad offices of affection to his dying friend. He himself soon became affected with the same disorder; and it was not till after a severe illness that he so far recovered as to be able to transfer his residence to Perth Amboy, the abode of Mr. Dunlap, where a pure and invigorating atmosphere, aided by the kind attentions of his host, gradually restored him to a sufficient degree of health and spirits for the prosecution of his literary labours.

The spectacle he had witnessed made too deep an impression on him to be readily effaced, and he resolved to transfer his own conceptions of it, while yet fresh, to the page of fiction, or, as it might rather be called, of history, for the purpose, as he intimates in his preface, of imparting to others some of the fruits of the melancholy lesson he had himself experienced. Such was the origin of his next novel, *Arthur Mervyn; or, Memoirs of the Year* 1793. This was the fatal year of the yellow fever in Philadelphia. The action of the story is chiefly confined to that city, but seems to be prepared with little contrivance, on no regular or systematic plan, consisting simply of a succession of incidents, having little cohesion except in reference to the hero, but affording situations of great interest, and frightful fidelity of colouring. The pestilence wasting a thriving and populous city has furnished a topic for more than one great master. It will be remembered as the terror of every schoolboy in the pages of Thucydides; it forms the gloomy portal to the light and airy fictions of Boccaccio; and it has furnished a subject for the graphic pencil of the English novelist De Foe, the only one of the three who never witnessed the horrors which he paints, but whose fictions wear an aspect of reality which history can rarely reach.

Brown has succeeded in giving the same terrible distinctness to his impressions by means of individual portraiture. He has, however, not confined himself to this, but, by a var'ety of touches, lays open to our view the whole interior of the city of the plague. Instead of expatiating on the loathsome symptoms and physical ravages of the disease, he selects the most striking moral circumstances which

4   C*

attend it; he dwells on the withering sensation that falls so heavily on the heart in the streets of the once busy and crowded city, now deserted and silent, save only where the wheels of the melancholy hearse are heard to rumble along the pavement. Our author not unfrequently succeeds in conveying more to the heart by the skilful selection of a single circumstance than would have flowed from a multitude of petty details. It is the art of the great masters of poetry and painting.

The same year in which Brown produced the first part of "Arthur Mervyn," he entered on the publication of a periodical entitled *The Monthly Magazine and American Review*, a work that, during its brief existence, which terminated in the following year, afforded abundant evidence of its editor's versatility of talent and the ample range of his literary acquisitions. Our hero was now fairly in the traces of authorship. He looked to it as his permanent vocation; and the indefatigable diligence with which he devoted himself to it may at least serve to show that he did not shrink from his professional engagements from any lack of industry or enterprise.

The publication of "Arthur Mervyn" was succeeded not long after by that of *Edgar Huntly ; or, the Adventures of a Sleepwalker*, a romance presenting a greater variety of wild and picturesque adventure, with more copious delineations of natural scenery, than is to be found in his other fictions; circumstances, no doubt, possessing more attractions for the mass of readers than the peculiarities of his other novels. Indeed, the author has succeeded perfectly in constantly stimulating the curiosity by a succession of as original incidents, perils, and hair-breadth escapes as ever flitted across a poet's fancy. It is no small triumph of the art to be able to maintain the curiosity of the reader unflagging through a succession of incidents, which, far from being sustained by one predominant passion, and forming parts of one whole, rely each for its interest on its own independent merits.

The story is laid in the western part of Pennsylvania, where the author has diversified his descriptions of a simple and almost primitive state of society with uncommonly animated sketches of rural scenery. It is worth observing how the sombre complexion of Brown's imagination, which so deeply tinges his moral portraiture, sheds its gloom over his pictures of material nature, raising the landscape into all the severe and savage sublimity of a Salvator Rosa. The somnambulism of this novel, which, like the ventriloquism of "Wieland," is the moving principle of all the machinery, has this advantage over the latter, that it does not necessarily impair the effect by perpetually suggesting a solution of mysteries, and thus dispelling the illusion on whose existence the effect of the whole story mainly depends. The adventures, indeed, built upon it are not the most probable in the world; but, waving this—we shall be well rewarded for such concession—there is no farther difficulty.

The extract already cited by us from the first of our author's novels has furnished the reader with an illustration of his power in displaying the conflict of passion under high moral excitement. We will now venture another quotation from the work before us, in order to exhibit more fully his talent for the description of external objects.

Edgar Huntly, the hero of the story, is represented in one of the wild mountain fastnesses of Norwalk, a district in the western part of Pennsylvania. He is on the brink of a ravine, from which the only avenue lies over the body of a tree thrown across the chasm, through whose dark depths below a rushing torrent is heard to pour its waters.

" While occupied with these reflections, my eyes were fixed upon the opposite steeps. The tops of the trees, waving to and fro in the wildest commotion, and their trunks occasionally bending to the blast, which, in these lofty regions, blew with a violence unknown in the tracts below, exhibited an awful spectacle. At length my attention was attracted by the trunk which lay across the gulf, and which I had converted into a bridge. I perceived that it had already swerved somewhat from its original position; that every blast broke or loosened some of the fibres by which its roots were connected with the opposite bank; and that, if the storm did not speedily abate, there was imminent danger of its being torn from the rock and precipitated into the chasm. Thus my retreat would be cut off, and

the evils from which I was endeavouring to rescue
another would be experienced by myself.

"I believed my destiny to hang upon the expedition with which I should recross this gulf. The
moments that were spent in these deliberations
were critical, and I shuddered to observe that the
trunk was held in its place by one or two fibres,
which were already stretched almost to breaking.

"To pass along the trunk, rendered slippery by
the wet, and unsteadfast by the wind, was eminently dangerous. To maintain my hold in passing, in
defiance of the whirlwind, required the most vigorous exertions. For this end, it was necessary to
discommode myself of my cloak, and of the volume
which I carried in the pocket of my coat.

"Just as I had disposed of these encumbrances,
and had risen from my seat, my attention was again
called to the opposite steep by the most unwelcome
object that at this time could possibly occur. Something was perceived moving among the bushes and
rocks, which, for a time, I hoped was nothing more
than a racoon or opossum, but which presently
appeared to be a panther. His gray coat, extended
claws, fiery eyes, and a cry which he at that moment uttered, and which, by its resemblance to the
human voice, is peculiarly terrific, denoted him to
be the most ferocious and untameable of that de-
tested race. The industry of our hunters has nearly
banished animals of prey from these precincts.
The fastnesses of Norwalk, however, could not but
afford refuge to some of them. Of late I had met

E

them so rarely that my fears were seldom alive,
and I trod without caution the ruggedest and most
solitary haunts. Still, however, I had seldom been
unfurnished in my rambles with the means of defence.

" The unfrequency with which I had lately encountered this foe, and the encumbrance of provis-
ion, made me neglect, on this occasion, to bring
with me my usual arms. The beast that was now
before me, when stimulated by hunger, was accustomed to assail whatever could provide him with a
banquet of blood. He would set upon the man and
the deer with equal and irresistible ferocity. His
sagacity was equal to his strength, and he seemed
able to discover when his antagonist was armed
and prepared for defence.

" My past experience enabled me to estimate the
full extent of my danger. He sat on the brow of
the steep, eyeing the bridge, and apparently delib-
erating whether he should cross it. It was probable that he had scented my footsteps thus far, and,
should he pass over, his vigilance could scarcely fail
of detecting my asylum.

" Should he retain his present station, my danger
was scarcely lessened. To pass over in the face
of a famished tiger was only to rush upon my fate.
The falling of the trunk, which had lately been so
anxiously deprecated, was now, with no less solicitude, desired. Every new gust, I hoped, would tear
asunder its remaining bands, and, by cutting off all
communication between the opposite steeps, place

me in security. My hopes, however, were destined
to be frustrated. The fibres of the prostrate tree
were obstinately tenacious of their hold, and presently the animal scrambled down the rock and proceeded to cross it.

"Of all kinds of death, that which now menaced
me was the most abhorred. To die by disease, or
by the hand of a fellow-creature, was propitious
and lenient in comparison with being rent to pieces
by the fangs of this savage. To perish in this obscure retreat by means so impervious to the anxious
curiosity of my friends, to lose my portion of existence by so untoward and ignoble a destiny, was
insupportable. I bitterly deplored my rashness in
coming hither unprovided for an encounter like
this.

"The evil of my present circumstances consisted
chiefly in suspense. My death was unavoidable,
but my imagination had leisure to torment itself by
anticipations. One foot of the savage was slowly
and cautiously moved after the other. He struck
his claws so deeply into the bark that they were
with difficulty withdrawn. At length he leaped
upon the ground. We were now separated by an
interval of scarcely eight feet. To leave the spot
where I crouched was impossible. Behind and beside me the cliff rose perpendicularly, and before me
was this grim and terrible visage. I shrunk still
closer to the ground, and closed my eyes.

"From this pause of horror I was aroused by the
noise occasioned by a second spring of the animal.

He leaped into the pit, in which I had so deeply regretted that I had not taken refuge, and disappeared. My rescue was so sudden, and so much beyond my belief or my hope, that I doubted for a moment whether my senses did not deceive me. This opportunity of escape was not to be neglected. I left my place and scrambled over the trunk with a precipitation which had like to have proved fatal. The tree groaned and shook under me, the wind blew with unexampled violence, and I had scarcely reached the opposite steep when the roots were severed from the rock, and the whole fell thundering to the bottom of the chasm.

"My trepidations were not speedily quieted. I looked back with wonder on my hair-breadth escape, and on that singular concurrence of events which had placed me in so short a period in absolute security. Had the trunk fallen a moment earlier, I should have been imprisoned on the hill or thrown headlong. Had its fall been delayed another moment, I should have been pursued; for the beast now issued from his den, and testified his surprise and disappointment by tokens the sight of which made my blood run cold.

"He saw me, and hastened to the verge of the chasm. He squatted on his hind legs, and assumed the attitude of one preparing to leap. My consternation was excited afresh by these appearances. It seemed at first as if the rift was too wide for any power of muscles to carry him in safety over; but I knew the unparalleled agility of this animal, and that his experience had made him a better judge of the practicability of this exploit than I was.

"Still there was hope that he would relinquish this design as desperate. This hope was quickly at an end. He sprung, and his fore legs touched the verge of the rock on which I stood. In spite of vehement exertions, however, the surface was too smooth and too hard to allow him to make good his hold. He fell, and a piercing cry uttered below showed that nothing had obstructed his descent to the bottom."

The subsequent narrative leads the hero through a variety of romantic adventures, especially with the savages, with whom he has several desperate rencounters and critical escapes. The track of adventure, indeed, strikes into the same wild solitudes of the forest that have since been so frequently travelled over by our ingenious countryman Cooper The light in which the character of the North American Indian has been exhibited by the two writers has little resemblance. Brown's sketches, it is true, are few and faint. As far as they go, however, they are confined to such views as are most conformable to the popular conceptions, bringing into full relief the rude and uncouth lineaments of the Indian character, its cunning, cruelty, and unmitigated ferocity, with no intimations of a more generous nature. Cooper, on the other hand, discards all the coarser elements of savage life, reserving those only of a picturesque and romantic cast, and elevating the souls of his warriors by such sentiments of courtesy, high-toned gallantry, and passionate tenderness as belong to the riper period of civilization. Thus idealized, the portrait, if not strictly that of the fierce and untamed son of the forest, is at least sufficiently true for poetical purposes. Cooper is indeed a poet. His descriptions of inanimate nature, no less than of savage man, are instinct with the breath of poetry. Witness his infinitely various pictures of the ocean; or still more, of the beautiful spirit that rides upon its bosom, the gallant ship, which under his touches becomes an animated thing, inspired by a living soul; reminding us of the beautiful superstition of the simple-hearted natives, who fancied the bark of Columbus some celestial visitant, descending on his broad pinions from the skies.

Brown is far less of a colourist. He deals less in external nature, but searches the depths of the soul. He may be rather called a philosophical than a poetical writer; for, though he has that intensity of feeling which constitutes one of the distinguishing attributes of the latter, yet in his most tumultuous bursts of passion we frequently find him pausing to analyze and coolly speculate on the elements which have raised it. This intrusion, indeed, of reason, *la raison froide*, into scenes of the greatest interest and emotion, has sometimes the unhappy effect of chilling them altogether.

In 1800 Brown published the second part of his *Arthur Mervyn*, whose occasional displays of energy and pathos by no means compensate the violent dislocations and general improbabilities cf the narrative. Our author was led into these defects by the unpardonable precipitancy of his composition. Three of his romances were thrown off in the course of one year. These were written with the printer's devil literally at his elbow, one being begun before another was completed, and all of them before a regular, well-digested plan was devised for their execution.

The consequences of this curious style of doing business are such as might have been predicted. The incidents are strung together with about as little connexion as the rhymes in "the House that Jack built;" and the whole reminds us of some bizarre, antiquated edifice, exhibiting a dozen styles of architecture, according to the caprice or convenience of its successive owners.

The reader is ever at a loss for a clew to guide him through the labyrinth of strange, incongruous incident. It would seem as if the great object of the author was to keep alive the state of suspense, on the player's principle, in the "Rehearsal," that "on the stage it is best to keep the audience in suspense; for to guess presently at the plot or the sense tires them at the end of the first act. Now here every line surprises you, and brings in new matter!" Perhaps, however, all this proceeds less from calculation than from the embarrassment which the novelist feels in attempting a solution of his own riddles, and which leads him to put off the reader, by multiplying incident after incident, unti' at length, entangled in the complicated snarl of his own intrigue, he is finally obliged, when the fatal hour arrives, to cut the knot which he cannot unravel. There is no other way by which we can account for the forced and violent *dénouemens* which bring up so many of Brown's fictions. Voltaire has remarked, somewhere in his Commentaries on Corneille, that "an author may write with the rapidity of genius, but should correct with scrupulous deliberation." Our author seems to have thought it sufficient to comply with the first half of the maxim.

In 1801 Brown published his novel of *Clara Howard,* and in 1804 closed the series with *Jane Talbot,* first printed in England. They are composed in a more subdued tone, discarding those startling preternatural incidents of which he had made such free use in his former fictions. In the preface to his first romance, " Wieland," he remarks, in allusion to the mystery on which the story is made to depend, that "it is a sufficient vindication of the writer if history furnishes one parallel fact." But the French critic, who tells us *le vrai peut quelquefois n'être pas vraisemblable,* has, with more judgment, condemned this vicious recurrence to extravagant and improbable incident. Truth cannot always be pleaded in vindication of the author of a fiction any more than of a libel. Brown seems to have subsequently come into the same opinion; for, in a letter addressed to his brother James, after the publication of "Edgar Huntly," he observes, "Your remarks upon the gloominess and out-of-nature incidents of 'Huntly,' if they be not just in their full extent, are doubtless such as most readers will make, which alone is a sufficient reason for dropping the doleful tone and assuming a cheerful one, or, at least, substituting moral causes and daily incidents in place of the prodigious or the singular. I shall not fall hereafter into that strain." The two last novels of our author, however, although purified from the more glaring defects of the preceding, were so inferior in their general power and originality of conception, that they never rose to the same level in public favour.

In the year 1801 Brown returned to his native city, Philadelphia, where he established his residence in the family of his brother. Here he continued, steadily pursuing his literary avocations; and in 1803 undertook the conduct of a periodical, entitled *The Literary Magazine and American Register*. A great change had taken place in his opinions on more than one important topic connected with human life and happiness, and, indeed, in his general tone of thinking, since abandoning his professional career. Brighter prospects, no doubt, suggested to him more cheerful considerations. Instead of a mere dreamer in the world of fancy, he had now become a practical man: larger experience and deeper meditation had shown him the emptiness of his Utopian theories; and, though his sensibilities were as ardent, and as easily enlisted as ever in the cause of humanity, his schemes of amelioration were built upon, not against the exist-

4   D *

ing institutions of society. The enunciation of the principles on which the periodical above alluded to was to be conducted, is so honourable every way to his heart and his understanding that we cannot refrain from making a brief extract from it.

"In an age like this, when the foundations of religion and morality have been so boldly attacked, it seems necessary, in announcing a work of this nature, to be particularly explicit as to the path which the editor means to pursue. He therefore avows himself to be, without equivocation or reserve, the ardent friend and the willing champion of the Christian religion. Christian piety he reveres as the highest excellence of human beings; and the amplest reward he can seek for his labour is the consciousness of having, in some degree, however inconsiderable, contributed to recommend the practice of religious duties. As in the conduct of this work a supreme regard will be paid to the interests of religion and morality, he will scrupulously guard against all that dishonours and impairs that principle. Everything that savours of indelicacy or licentiousness will be rigorously proscribed. His poetical pieces may be dull, but they shall at least be free from voluptuousness or sensuality; and his prose, whether seconded or not by genius and knowledge, shall scrupulously aim at the promotion of public and private virtue."

During his abode in New-York our author had formed an attachment to an amiable and accomplished young lady, Miss Elizabeth Linn, daughter of the excellent and highly-gifted Presbyterian divine, Dr. William Linn, of that city. Their mutual attachment, in which the impulses of the heart were sanctioned by the understanding, was followed by their marriage in November, 1804, after which he never again removed his residence from Philadelphia.

With the additional responsibilities of his new station, he pursued his literary labours with increased diligence. He projected the plan of an *Annual Register*, the first work of the kind in the country, and in 1806 edited the first volume of the publication, which was undertaken at the risk of an eminent bookseller of Philadelphia, Mr. Conrad, who had engaged his editorial labours in the conduct of the former Magazine, begun in 1803. When it is considered that both these periodicals were placed under the superintendence of one individual, and that he bestowed such indefatigable attention on them that they were not only prepared, but a large portion actually executed by his own hands, we shall form no mean opinion of the extent and variety of his stores of information and his facility in applying them. Both works are replete with evidences of the taste and erudition of their editor, embracing a wide range of miscellaneous articles, essays, literary criticism, and scientific researches. The historical portion of " The Register" in particular, comprehending, in addition to the political annals of the principal states of Europe and of our own country, an elaborate inquiry into the origin and organization of our domestic institutions, displays a discrimination in the selection of incidents, and a good faith and candour in the mode of discussing them, that entitle it to great authority as a record of contemporary transactions. Eight volumes were published of the first-mentioned periodical, and the latter was continued under his direction till the end of the fifth volume, 1809.

In addition to these regular, and, as they may be called, professional labours, he indulged his prolific pen in various speculations, both of a literary and political character, many of which appeared in the pages of the "Portfolio." Among other occasional productions, we may notice a beautiful biographical sketch of his wife's brother, Dr. J. B. Linn, pastor of the Presbyterian church in Philadelphia, whose lamented death occurred·in the year succeeding Brown's marriage. We must not leave out of the account three elaborate and extended pamphlets, published between 1803 and 1809, on political topics of deep interest to the community at that time. The first of these, on the cession of Louisiana to the French, soon went into a second edition. They all excited general attention at the time of their appearance by the novelty of their arguments, the variety and copiousness of their information, the liberality of their views, the independence, so rare at that day, of foreign prejudices; the exemption, still rarer, from the bitterness of party spirit; and, lastly, the tone of loyal and heartfelt patriotism—a patriotism without cant—with which the author dwells on the expanding glory and prosperity of his country in a strain of prophecy that it is our boast has now become history.

Thus occupied, Brown's situation seemed now to afford him all the means for happiness attainable in this life. His own labours secured to him an honourable independence and a high reputation, which, to a mind devoted to professional or other intellectual pursuits, is usually of far higher estimation than gain. Round his own fireside he found ample scope for the exercise of his affectionate sensibilities, while the tranquil pleasures of domestic life proved the best possible relaxation for a mind wearied by severe intellectual effort. His grateful heart was deeply sensible to the extent of his blessings; and in more than one letter he indulges in a vein of reflection which shows that his only solicitude was from the fear of their instability. His own health furnished too well-grounded cause for such apprehensions.

We have already noticed that he set out in life with a feeble constitution. His sedentary habits and intense application had not, as it may well be believed, contributed to repair the defects of Nature. He had for some time shown a disposition to pulmonary complaints, and had raised blood more than once, which he in vain endeavoured to persuade himself did not proceed from the lungs. As the real character of the disease disclosed itself in a manner not to be mistaken, his anxious friends would have persuaded him to cross the water in the hope of re-establishing his health by a seasonable change of climate. But Brown could not endure the thoughts of so long a separation from his beloved family, and he trusted to the effect of a temporary abstinence from business, and of one of those excursions into the country by which he had so often recruited his health and spirits.

In the summer of 1809 he made a tour into New-Jersey and New-York. A letter addressed to one of his family from the banks of the Hudson, during this journey, exhibits in melancholy colours how large a portion of his life had been clouded by disease, which now, indeed, was too oppressive to admit of any other alleviation than what he could find in the bosom of his own family.

" My dearest Mary—Instead of wandering about, and viewing more nearly a place that affords very pleasing landscapes, here am I, hovering over the images of wife, children, and sisters. I want to write to you and home; and though unable to procure paper enough to form a letter, I cannot help saying something even on this scrap.

"I am mortified to think how incurious and inactive a mind has fallen to my lot. I left home with reluctance. If I had not brought a beloved part of my home along with me, I should probably have not left it at all. At a distance from home, my enjoyments, my affections are beside you. If swayed by mere inclination, I should not be out of your company a quarter of an hour between my parting and returning hour; but I have some mercy on you and Susan, and a due conviction of my want of power to beguile your vacant hour with amusement, or improve it by instruction. Even if I were ever so well, and if my spirits did not continually hover on the brink of dejection, my talk could only make you yawn; as things are, my company can only tend to create a gap indeed.

"When have I known that lightness and vivacity of mind which the divine flow of health, even in calamity, produces in some men, and would produce in me, no doubt—at least, when not soured by misfortune? Never; scarcely ever; not longer than half an hour at a time since I have called myself man, and not a moment since I left you."

Finding these brief excursions productive of no salutary change in his health, he at length complied with the entreaties of his friends, and determined to try the effect of a voyage to Europe in the following spring. That spring he was doomed never to behold. About the middle of November he was taken with a violent pain in his left side, for which he was bled. From that time forward he was confined to his chamber. His malady was not attended with the exemption from actual pain with which Nature seems sometimes willing to compensate the sufferer for the length of its duration. His sufferings were incessant and acute; and they were supported, not only without a murmur, but with an appearance of cheerfulness, to which the hearts of his friends could but ill respond. He met the ap-

proach of Death in the true spirit of Christian philosophy. No other dread but that of separation
from those dear to him on earth had power to disturb his tranquillity for a moment. But the temper of his mind in his last hours is best disclosed
in a communication from that faithful partner who
contributed more than any other to support him
through them. "He always felt for others more
than for himself; and the evidences of sorrow in
those around him, which could not at all times be
suppressed, appeared to affect him more than his
own sufferings. Whenever he spoke of the probability of a fatal termination to his disease, it was in
an indirect and covert manner, as, 'you must do so
and so when I am absent,' or 'when I am asleep.'
He surrendered not up one faculty of his soul but
with his last breath. He saw death in every step
of his approach, and viewed him as a messenger
that brought with him no terrors. He frequently
expressed his resignation; but his resignation was
not produced by apathy or pain; for while he bowed
with submission to the Divine will, he felt with the
keenest sensibility his separation from those who
made this world but too dear to him. Towards
the last he spoke of death without disguise, and
appeared to wish to prepare his friends for the
event, which he felt to be approaching. A few
days previous to his change, as sitting up in the
bed, he fixed his eyes on the sky, and desired not
to be spoken to until he first spoke. In this position, and with a serene countenance, he continued

for some minutes, and then said to his wife, ' When I desired you not to speak to me, I had the most transporting and sublime feelings I have ever experienced ; I wanted to enjoy them, and know how long they would last;' concluding with requesting her to remember the circumstance."

A visible change took place in him on the morning of the 19th of February, 1810, and he caused his family to be assembled around his bed, when he took leave of each one of them in the most tender and impressive manner. He lingered, however, a few days longer, remaining in the full possession of his faculties to the 22d of the month, when he expired without a struggle. He had reached the thirty-ninth year of his age the month preceding his death. The family which he left consisted of a wife and four children.

There was nothing striking in Brown's personal appearance. His manners, however, were distinguished by a gentleness and unaffected simplicity which rendered them extremely agreeable. He possessed colloquial powers which do not always fall to the lot of the practised and ready writer. His rich and various acquisitions supplied an unfailing fund for the edification of his hearers. They did not lead him, however, to affect an air of superiority, or to assume too prominent a part in the dialogue, especially in large or mixed company, where he was rather disposed to be silent, reserving the display of his powers for the unrestrained intercourse of friendship. He was a stranger not only

4   E

to base and malignant passions, but to the paltry jealousies which sometimes sour the intercourse of men of letters. On the contrary, he was ever prompt to do ample justice to the merits of others. His heart was warm with the feeling of universal benevolence. Too sanguine and romantic views had exposed him to some miscalculations and consequent disappointments in youth, from which, however, he was subsequently retrieved by the strength of his understanding, which, combining with what may be called his natural elevation of soul, enabled him to settle the soundest principles for the regulation of his opinions and conduct in after life. His reading was careless and desultory, but his appetite was voracious; and the great amount of miscellaneous information which he thus amassed was all demanded to supply the outpourings of his mind in a thousand channels of entertainment and instruction. His unwearied application is attested by the large amount of his works, large even for the present day, when mind seems to have caught the accelerated movement so generally given to the operations of machinery. The whole number of Brown's printed works, comprehending his editorial as well as original productions, to the former of which his own pen contributed a very disproportionate share, is not less than four-and-twenty printed volumes, not to mention various pamphlets, anonymous contributions to divers periodicals, as well as more than one compilation of laborious research which he left unfinished at his death.

Of this vast amount of matter, produced within the brief compass of little more than ten years, that portion on which his fame as an author must permanently rest is his novels. We have already entered too minutely into the merits of these productions to require anything farther than a few general observations. They may probably claim to be regarded as having first opened the way to the successful cultivation of romantic fiction in this country. Great doubts were long entertained of our capabilities for immediate success in this department. We had none of the buoyant, stirring associations of a romantic age; none of the chivalrous pageantry, the feudal and border story, or Robin Hood adventure; none of the dim, shadowy superstitions, and the traditional legends, which had gathered like moss round every stone, hill, and valley of the olden countries. Everything here wore a spick-and-span new aspect, and lay in the broad, garish sunshine of everyday life. We had none of the picturesque varieties of situation or costume; everything lay on the same dull, prosaic level; in short, we had none of the most obvious elements of poetry: at least so it appeared to the vulgar eye. It required the eye of genius to detect the rich stores of romantic and poetic interest that lay beneath the crust of society. Brown was aware of the capabilities of our country, and the poverty of the results he was less inclined to impute to the soil than to the cultivation of it; at least this would appear from some remarks dropped in his correspondence in

1794, several years before he broke ground in this field himself. "It used to be a favourite maxim with me, that the genius of a poet should be sacred to the glory of his country. How far this rule can be reduced to practice by an American bard, how far he can prudently observe it, and what success has crowned the efforts of those who, in their compositions, have shown that they have not been unmindful of it, is perhaps not worth the inquiry.

"Does it not appear to you that, to give poetry a popular currency and universal reputation, a particular cast of manners and state of civilization is necessary? I have sometimes thought so, but perhaps it is an error; and the want of popular poems argues only the demerit of those who have already written, or some defect in their works, which unfits them for every taste or understanding."

The success of our author's experiment, which was entirely devoted to American subjects, fully established the soundness of his opinions, which have been abundantly confirmed by the prolific pens of Irving, Cooper, Sedgwick, and other accomplished writers, who, in their diversified sketches of national character and scenery, have shown the full capacity of our country for all the purposes of fiction. Brown does not direct himself, like them, to the illustration of social life and character. He is little occupied with the exterior forms of society. He works in the depths of the heart, dwelling less on human action than the sources of it. He has been said to have formed himself on Godwin. Indeed, he openly avowed his admiration of that eminent writer, and has certainly, in some respects, adopted his mode of operation, studying character with a philosophic rather than a poetic eye. But there is no servile imitation in all this. He has borrowed the same torch, indeed, to read the page of human nature, but the lesson he derives from it is totally different. His great object seems to be to exhibit the soul in scenes of extraordinary interest. For this purpose, striking and perilous situations are devised, or circumstances of strong moral excitement, a troubled conscience, partial gleams of insanity, or bodings of imaginary evil, which haunt the soul, and force it into all the agonies of terror. In the midst of the fearful strife, we are coolly invited to investigate its causes and all the various phenomena which attend it; every contingency, probability, nay, possibility, however remote, is discussed and nicely balanced. The heat of the reader is seen to evaporate in this cold-blooded dissection, in which our author seems to rival Butler's hero, who,

> "Profoundly skilled in analytic,
> Could distinguish and divide
> A hair 'twixt south and southwest side."

We are constantly struck with the strange contrast of over-passion and over-reasoning. But perhaps, after all, these defects could not be pruned away from Brown's composition without detriment to his peculiar excellences. *Si non errâsset, fecerat ille minus.* If so, we may willingly pardon the one for the sake of the other.

We cannot close without adverting to our au-

4   E*

thor's style. He bestowed great pains on the formation of it; but, in our opinion, without great success, at least in his novels. It has an elaborate, factitious air, contrasting singularly with the general simplicity of his taste and the careless rapidity of his composition. We are aware, indeed, that works of imagination may bear a higher flush of colour, a poetical varnish, in short, that must be refused to graver and more studied narrative. No writer has been so felicitous in reaching the exact point of good taste in this particular as Scott, who, on a groundwork of prose, may be said to have enabled his readers to breathe an atmosphere of poetry. More than one author, on the other hand, as Florian, in French, for example, and Lady Morgan, in English, in their attempts to reach this middle region, are eternally fluttering on the wing of sentiment, equally removed from good prose and good poetry.

Brown, perhaps willing to avoid this extreme, has fallen into the opposite one, forcing his style into unnatural vigour and condensation. Unusual and pedantic epithets, and elliptical forms of expression, in perpetual violation of idiom, are resorted to at the expense of simplicity and nature. He seems averse to telling simple things in a simple way. Thus, for example, we have such expressions as these: "I was *fraught with the persuasion* that my life was endangered." "The outer door was ajar. I shut it with trembling eagerness, and drew every bolt that *appended* to it." "His brain seemed to swell beyond its *continent*." "I waited till their slow and hoarser *inspirations* showed them to be both asleep. Just then, on changing my position, my head struck against some things which *depended* from the ceiling of the closet." "It was still dark, but my sleep was at an end, and by a common apparatus (tinder-box?) that lay beside my bed, I could instantly produce a light." "On recovering from *deliquium*, you found it where it had been dropped." It is unnecessary to multiply examples, which we should not have adverted to at all had not our opinions in this matter been at variance with those of more than one respectable critic. This sort of language is no doubt in very bad taste. It cannot be denied, however, that, although these defects are sufficiently general to give a colouring to the whole of his composition, yet his works afford many passages of undeniable eloquence and rhetorical beauty. It must be remembered, too, that his novels were his first productions, thrown off with careless profusion, and exhibiting many of the defects of an immature mind, which longer experience and practice might have corrected. Indeed, his later writings are recommended by a more correct and natural phraseology, although it must be allowed that the graver topics to which they are devoted, if they did not authorize, would at least render less conspicuous any studied formality and artifice of expression.

These verbal blemishes, combined with defects already alluded to in the development of his plots, but which all relate to the form rather than the *fond* of his subject, have made our author less ex-

tensively popular than his extraordinary powers
would have entitled him to be. His peculiar merits, indeed, appeal to a higher order of criticism
than is to be found in ordinary and superficial readers. Like the productions of Coleridge or Wordsworth, they seem to rely on deeper sensibilities than
most men possess, and tax the reasoning powers
more severely than is agreeable to readers who resort to works of fiction only as an epicurean indulgence. The number of their admirers is therefore
necessarily more limited than that of writers of less
talent, who have shown more tact in accommodating themselves to the tone of popular feeling or
prejudice.

But we are unwilling to part, with anything like
a tone of disparagement lingering on our lips, with
the amiable author to whom our rising literature is
under such large and various obligations; who first
opened a view into the boundless fields of fiction,
which subsequent adventurers have successfully explored; who has furnished so much for our instruction in the several departments of history and criticism, and has rendered still more effectual service
by kindling in the bosom of the youthful scholar
the same generous love of letters which glowed in
his own; whose writings, in fine, have uniformly
inculcated the pure and elevated morality exemplified in his life. The only thing we can regret
is, that a life so useful should have been so short,
if, indeed, that can be considered short which has
done so much towards attaining life's great end.

ASYLUM FOR THE BLIND.*

JULY, 1830.

THERE is nothing in which the moderns surpass the ancients more conspicuously than in their noble provisions for the relief of indigence and distress. The public policy of the ancients seems to have embraced only whatever might promote the aggrandizement or the direct prosperity of the state, and to have cared little for those unfortunate beings who, from disease or incapacity of any kind, were disqualified from contributing to this. But the beneficent influence of Christianity, combined with the general tendency of our social institutions, has led to the recognition of rights in the individual as sacred as those of the community, and has suggested manifold provisions for personal comfort and happiness.

The spirit of benevolence, thus widely, and oftentimes judiciously exerted, continued, until a very recent period, however, strangely insensible to the claims of a large class of objects, to whom nature, and no misconduct or imprudence of their own, as is too often the case with the subjects of public char'ty, had denied some of the most estimable faculties of man. No suitable institutions, until the close of the last century, have been provided for the nurture of the deaf and dumb, or the blind. Immu-

---

* An Act to Incorporate the New-England Asylum for the Blind. Approved March 2d, 1829.

H

red within hospitals and almshouses, like so many lunatics and incurables, they have been delivered over, if they escaped the physical, to all the moral contagion too frequently incident to such abodes, and have thus been involved in a mental darkness far more deplorable than their bodily one.

This injudicious treatment has resulted from the erroneous principle of viewing these unfortunate beings as an absolute burden on the public, utterly incapable of contributing to their own subsistence, or of ministering in any degree to their own intellectual wants. Instead, however, of being degraded by such unworthy views, they should have been regarded as, what in truth they are, possessed of corporeal and mental capacities perfectly competent, under proper management, to the production of the most useful results. If wisdom from one entrance was quite shut out, other avenues for its admission still remained to be opened.

In order to give effective aid to persons in this predicament, it is necessary to place ourselves as far as possible in their peculiar situation, to consider to what faculties this insulated condition is, on the whole, most favourable, and in what direction they can be exercised with the best chance of success. Without such foresight, all our endeavours to aid them will only put them upon efforts above their strength, and result in serious mortification.

The blind, from the cheerful ways of men cut off, are necessarily excluded from the busy theatre of human action. Their infirmity, however, which consigns them to darkness, and often to solitude, would seem favourable to contemplative habits, and to the pursuits of abstract science and pure specu- lation. Undisturbed by external objects, the mind necessarily turns within, and concentrates its ideas on any point of investigation with greater intensity and perseverance. It is no uncommon thing, there- fore, to find persons setting apart the silent hours of the evening for the purpose of composition or other purely intellectual exercise. Malebranche, when he wished to think intensely, used to close his shutters in the daytime, excluding every ray of light; and hence Democritus is said to have put out his eyes in order that he might philosophize the better—-a story, the veracity of which Cicero, who relates it, is prudent enough not to vouch for.

Blindness must also be exceedingly favourable to the discipline of the memory. Whoever has had the misfortune, from any derangement of the organ, to be compelled to derive his knowledge of books less from the eye than the ear, will feel the truth of this. The difficulty of recalling what has once es- caped, of reverting to, or dwelling on the passages read aloud by another, compels the hearer to give undivided attention to the subject, and to impress it more forcibly on his own mind by subsequent and methodical reflection. Instances of the cultivation of this faculty to an extraordinary extent have been witnessed among the blind, and it has been most ad- vantageously applied to the pursuit of abstract sci- ence, especially mathematics.

One of the most eminent illustrations of these remarks is the well-known history of Saunderson, who, though deprived in his infancy not only of sight, but of the organ itself, contrived to become so well acquainted with the Greek tongue as to read the works of the ancient mathematicians in the original. He made such advances in the higher departments of the science, that he was appointed, "though not matriculated at the University," to fill the chair which a short time previous had been occupied by Sir Isaac Newton at Cambridge. The lectures of this blind professor on the most abstruse points of the Newtonian philosophy, and especially on optics, naturally filled his audience with admiration; and the perspicuity with which he communicated his ideas is said to have been unequalled. He was enabled, by the force of his memory, to perform many long operations in arithmetic, and to carry in his mind the most complex geometrical figures. As, however, it became necessary to supply the want of vision by some symbols which might be sensible to the touch, he contrived a table in which pins, whose value was determined principally by their relative position to each other, served him instead of figures, while for his diagrams he employed pegs, inserted at the requisite angles to each other, representing the lines by threads drawn around them. He was so expert in his use of these materials, that, when performing his calculations, he would change the position of the pins with nearly the same facility that another person would indite figures, and when disturbed in an operation would afterward resume it again, ascertaining the posture in which he had left it by passing his hand carefully over the table. To such shifts and inventions does human ingenuity resort when stimulated by the thirst of knowledge; as the plant, when thrown into shade on one side, sends forth its branches eagerly in that direction where the light is permitted to fall upon it.

In like manner, the celebrated mathematician, Euler, continued, for many years after he became blind, to indite and publish the results of his scientific labours, and at the time of his decease left nearly a hundred memoirs ready for the press, most of which have since been given to the world. An example of diligence equally indefatigable, though turned in a different channel, occurs in our contemporary Huber, who has contributed one of the most delightful volumes within the compass of natural history, and who, if he employed the eyes of another, guided them in their investigation to the right results by the light of his own mind.

Blindness would seem to be propitious, also, to the exercise of the inventive powers. Hence poetry, from the time of Thamyris and the blind Mæonides down to the Welsh harper and the ballad-grinder of our day, has been assigned as the peculiar province of those bereft of vision,

" As the wakeful bird
Sings darkling, and, in shadiest covert hid,
Tunes her nocturnal note."

The greatest epic poem of antiquity was probably,

4 F

as that of the moderns was certainly, composed in darkness. It is easy to understand how the man who has once seen can recall and body forth in his conceptions new combinations of material beauty ; but it would seem scarcely possible that one born blind, excluded from all acquaintance with " coloured nature," as Condillac finely styles it, should excel in descriptive poetry. Yet there are eminent examples of this ; among others, that of Blacklock, whose verses abound in the most agreeable and picturesque images. Yet he could have formed no other idea of colours than was conveyed by their moral associations, the source, indeed, of most of the pleasures we derive from descriptive poetry. It was thus that he studied the variegated aspect of nature, and read in it the successive revolutions of the seasons, their freshness, their prime, and decay.

Mons. Guillié, in an interesting essay on the instruction of the blind, to which we shall have occasion repeatedly to refer, quotes an example of the association of ideas in regard to colours, which occurred in one of his own pupils, who, in reciting the well-known passage in Horace, " *rubente dexterâ sacras jaculatus arces*," translated the first two words by " fiery" or " burning right hand." On being requested to render it literally, he called it " red right hand," and gave as the reason for his former version, that he could form no positive conception of a red colour; but that, as fire was said to be red, he connected the idea of heat with this colour, and had therefore interpreted the wrath of Jupiter, demolishing town and tower, by the epithet "fiery or burning;" for "when people are angry," he added, "they are hot, and when they are hot, they must of course be red." He certainly seems to have formed a much more accurate notion of red than Locke's blind man.

But while a gift for poetry belongs only to the inspired few, and while many have neither taste nor talent for mathematical or speculative science, it is a consolation to reflect that the humblest individual who is destitute of sight may so far supply this deficiency by the perfection of the other senses as by their aid to attain a considerable degree of intellectual culture, as well as a familiarity with some of the most useful mechanic arts. It will be easier to conceive to what extent the perceptions of touch and hearing may be refined if we reflect how far that of sight is sharpened by exclusive reliance on it in certain situations. Thus the mariner descries objects at night, and at a distance upon the ocean, altogether imperceptible to the unpractised eye of a landsman. And the North American Indian steers his course undeviatingly through the trackless wilderness, guided only by such signs as escape the eye of the most inquisitive white man.

In like manner, the senses of hearing and feeling are capable of attaining such a degree of perfection in a blind person, that by them alone he can distinguish his various acquaintances, and even the presence of persons whom he has but rarely met before, the size of the apartment, and the general lo-

cality of the spots in which he may happen to be,
and guide himself safely across the most solitary
districts and amid the throng of towns. Dr. Bew,
in a paper in the Manchester Collection of Memoirs, gives an account of a blind man of his acquaintance in Derbyshire, who was much used as a
guide for travellers in the night over certain intri-
cate roads, and particularly when the tracks were
covered with snow. This same man was afterward
employed as a projector and surveyor of roads in
that county. We well remember a blind man in
the neighbouring town of Salem, who officiated
some twenty years since as the town crier, when
that functionary performed many of the advertising
duties now usurped by the newspaper, making his
diurnal round, and stopping with great precision at
every corner, trivium or quodrivium, to chime his
"melodious twang." Yet this feat, the familiarity
of which prevented it from occasioning any surprise, could have resulted only from the nicest observation of the undulations of the ground, or by an
attention to the currents of air, or the different sound
of the voice or other noises in these openings, signs
altogether lost upon the man of eyes.

Mons. Guillié mentions several apparently well-
attested anecdotes of blind persons who had the
power of discriminating colours by the touch. One
of the individuals noticed by him, a Dutchman, was
so expert in this way that he was sure to come off
conqueror at the card-table by the knowledge which
he thus obtained of his adversary's hand, whenever

it came to his turn to deal. This power of discrimination of colours, which seems to be a gift only of a very few of the finer-fingered gentry, must be founded on the different consistency or smoothness of the ingredients used in the various dyes. A more certain method of ascertaining these colours, that of tasting or touching them with the tongue, is frequently resorted to by the blind, who by this means often distinguish between those analogous colours, as black and dark blue, red and pink, which, having the greatest apparent affinity, not unfrequently deceive the eye.

Diderot, in an ingenious letter on the blind, à *l'usage de ceux qui voient*, has given a circumstantial narration of his visit to a blind man at Puisseaux, the son of a professor in the University of Paris, and well known in his day from the various accomplishments and manual dexterity which he exhibited, remarkable in a person in his situation. Being asked what notion he had formed of an eye, he replied, " I conceive it to be an organ on which the air produces the same effect as this staff on my hand. If, when you are looking at an object, I should interpose anything between your eyes and that object, it would prevent you from seeing it. And I am in the same predicament when I seek one thing with my staff and come across another." An explanation, says Diderot, as lucid as any which could be given by Descartes, who, it is singular, attempts, in his Dioptrics, to explain the analogy between the senses of feeling and seeing by figures of men blindfolded, groping their way with staffs in their hands. This same intelligent personage became so familiar with the properties of touch that he seems to have accounted them almost equally valuable with those of vision. On being interrogated if he felt a great desire to have eyes, he answered, " Were it not for the mere gratification of curiosity, I think I should do as well to wish for long arms. It seems to me that my hands would inform me better of what is going on in the moon than your eyes and telescopes ; and then the eyes lose the power of vision more readily than the hands that of feeling. It would be better to perfect the organ which I have than to bestow on me that which I have not."

Indeed, the "geometric sense" of touch, as Buffon terms it, as far as it reaches, is more faithful, and conveys oftentimes a more satisfactory idea of external forms than the eye itself. The great defect is that its range is necessarily so limited. It is told of Saunderson that on one occasion he detected by his finger a counterfeit coin which had deceived the eye of a connoisseur. We are hardly aware how much of our dexterity in the use of the eye arises from incessant practice. Those who have been relieved from blindness at an advanced, or even early period of life, have been found frequently to recur to the old and more familiar sense of touch, in preference to the sight. The celebrated English anatomist, Cheselden, mentions several illustrations of this fact in an account given by him of a blind boy whom he had successfully couched for cataracts, at the age of fourteen. It was long before the youth could discriminate by his eye between his old companions, the family cat and dog, dissimilar as such animals appear to us in colour and conformation. Being ashamed to ask the oft-repeated question, he was observed one day to pass his hand carefully over the cat, and then, looking at her steadfastly, to exclaim, " So, puss, I shall know you another time." It is more natural that he should have been deceived by the illusory art of painting, and it was long before he could comprehend that the objects depicted did not possess the same relief on the canvass as in nature. He inquired, " Which is the lying sense here, the sight or the touch ?"

The faculty of hearing would seem susceptible of a similar refinement with that of seeing. To prove this without going into farther detail, it is only necessary to observe that much the larger proportion of blind persons are, more or less, proficients in music, and that in some of the institutions for their education, as that in Paris, for instance, *all* the pupils are instructed in this delightful art. The gift of a natural ear for melody, therefore, deemed comparatively rare with the *clairvoyans*, would seem to exist so far in every individual as to be capable, by a suitable cultivation, of affording a high degree of relish, at least to himself.

As, in order to a successful education of the blind, it becomes necessary to understand what are the faculties, intellectual and corporeal, to the development and exercise of which their peculiar condition is best adapted, so it is equally necessary to understand how far, and in what manner, their moral constitution is likely to be affected by the insulated position in which they are placed. The blind man, shut up within the precincts of his own microcosm, is subjected to influences of a very different complexion from the bulk of mankind, inasmuch as each of the senses is best fitted to the introduction of a certain class of ideas into the mind, and he is deprived of that one through which the rest of his species receive by far the greatest number of theirs. Thus it will be readily understood that his notions of modesty and delicacy may a good deal differ from those of the world at large. The blind man of Puisseaux confessed that he could not comprehend why it should be reckoned improper to expose one part of the person rather than another. Indeed, the conventional rules, so necessarily adopted in society in this relation, might seem, in a great degree, superfluous in a blind community.

The blind man would seem, also, to be less likely to be endowed with the degree of sensibility usual with those who enjoy the blessing of sight. It is difficult to say how much of our early education depends on the looks, the frowns, the smiles, the tears, the example, in fact, of those placed over and around us. From all this the blind child is necessarily excluded. These, however, are the great sources of sympathy. We feel little for the joys or the sorrows which we do not witness. " Out of sight, out of

ASYLUM FOR THE BLIND.

mind," says the old proverb. Hence people are so
ready to turn away from distress which they cannot,
or their avarice will not suffer them to relieve.
Hence, too, persons whose compassionate hearts
would bleed at the infliction of an act of cruelty on
so large an animal as a horse or a dog, for example,
will crush without concern a wilderness of insects,
whose delicate organization, and whose bodily agonies are imperceptible to the naked eye. The
slightest injury occurring in our own presence affects us infinitely more than the tidings of the most
murderous battle, or the sack of the most populous
and flourishing city at the extremity of the globe.
Yet such, without much exaggeration, is the relative
position of the blind, removed by their infirmity at a
distance from the world, from the daily exhibition
of those mingled scenes of grief and gladness, which
have their most important uses, perhaps, in calling
forth our sympathies for our fellow-creatures.

It has been affirmed that the situation of the blind
is unpropitious to religious sentiment. They are necessarily insensible to the grandeur of the spectacle
which forces itself upon our senses every day of our
existence. The magnificent map of the heavens, with

> " Every star
> Which the clear concave of a winter's night
> Pours on the eye,"

is not unrolled for them. The revolutions of the
seasons, with all their beautiful varieties of form and
colour, and whatever glories of the creation lift the
soul in wonder and gratitude to the Creator, are not
for them. Their world is circumscribed by the little

circle which they can span with their own arms.
All beyond has for them no real existence. This
seems to have passed within the mind of the mathematician Saunderson, whose notions of a Deity
would seem to have been, to the last, exceedingly
vague and unsettled. The clergyman who visited
him in his latter hours endeavoured to impress upon
him the evidence of a God as afforded by the astonishing mechanism of the universe. "Alas!" said
the dying philosopher, "I have been condemned to
pass my life in darkness, and you speak to me of
prodigies which I cannot comprehend, and which
can only be felt by you, and those who see like you!"
When reminded of the faith of Newton, Leibnitz,
and Clarke, minds from whom he had drunk so
deeply of instruction, and for whom he entertained
the profoundest veneration, he remarked, "The testimony of Newton is not so strong for me as that of
Nature was for him; Newton believed on the Word
of God himself, while I am reduced to believe on that
of Newton." He expired with this ejaculation on
his lips, "God of Newton, have mercy on me!"

These, however, may be considered as the peevish ebullitions of a naturally skeptical and somewhat disappointed spirit, impatient of an infirmity
which obstructed, as he conceived, his advancement
in the career of science to which he had so zealously
devoted himself. It was in allusion to this, undoubtedly, that he depicted his life as having been "one
long desire and continued privation."

It is far more reasonable to believe that there are

certain peculiarities in the condition of the blind which more than counterbalance the unpropitious circumstances above described, and which have a decided tendency to awaken devotional sentiment in their minds. They are the subjects of a grievous calamity, which, as in all such cases, naturally disposes the heart to sober reflection, and, when permanent and irremediable, to passive resignation. Their situation necessarily excludes most of those temptations which so sorely beset us in the world—those tumultuous passions which, in the general rivalry, divide man from man, and imbitter the sweet cup of social life—those sordid appetites which degrade us to the level of the brutes. They are subjected, on the contrary, to the most healthful influences. Their occupations are of a tranquil, and oftentimes of a purely intellectual character. Their pleasures are derived from the endearments of domestic intercourse, and the attentions almost always conceded to persons in their dependant condition must necessarily beget a reciprocal kindliness of feeling in their own bosoms. In short, the uniform tenour of their lives is such as naturally to dispose them to resignation, serenity, and cheerfulness; and accordingly, as far as our own experience goes, these have usually been the characteristics of the blind.

Indeed, the cheerfulness almost universally incident to persons deprived of sight leads us to consider blindness as, on the whole, a less calamity than deafness. The deaf man is continually exposed to the sight of pleasures and to society in which he can take no part. He is the guest at a banquet of which he is not permitted to partake, the spectator at a theatre where he cannot comprehend a sylla-ble. If the blind man is excluded from sources of enjoyment equally important, he has, at least, the advantage of not perceiving, and not even compre-hending what he has lost. It may be added, that perhaps the greatest privation consequent on blind-ness is the inability to read, as that on deafness is the loss of the pleasures of society. Now the eyes of another may be made, in a great degree, to sup-ply this defect of the blind man, while no art can afford a corresponding substitute to the deaf for the privations to which he is doomed in social inter-course. He cannot hear with the ears of another. As, however, it is undeniable that blindness makes one more dependant than deafness, we may be con-tent with the conclusion that the former would be the most eligible for the rich, and the latter for the poor. Our remarks will be understood as applying to those only who are wholly destitute of the facul-ties of sight and hearing. A person afflicted only with a partial derangement or infirmity of vision is placed in the same tantalizing predicament above described of the deaf, and is, consequently, found to be usually of a far more impatient and irritable tem-perament, and, consequently, less happy than the totally blind. With all this, we doubt whether there be one of our readers, even should he assent to the general truth of our remarks, who would not infinitely prefer to incur partial to total blindness, and deafness to either. Such is the prejudice in favour of eyes!

Patience, perseverance, habits of industry, and, above all, a craving appetite for knowledge, are sufficiently common to be considered as characteristics of the blind, and have tended greatly to facilitate their education, which must otherwise prove somewhat tedious, and, indeed, doubtful as to its results, considering the formidable character of the obstacles to be encountered. A curious instance of perseverance in overcoming such obstacles occurred at Paris, when the institutions for the deaf and dumb and for the blind were assembled under the same roof in the convent of the Celestines. The pupils of the two seminaries, notwithstanding the apparently insurmountable barrier interposed between them by their respective infirmities, contrived to open a communication with each other, which they carried on with the greatest vivacity.

It was probably the consideration of those moral qualities, as well as of the capacity for improvement which we have described as belonging to the blind, which induced the benevolent Haüy, in conjunction with the Philanthropic Society of Paris, to open there, in 1784, the first regular seminary for their education ever attempted. This institution underwent several modifications, not for the better, during the revolutionary period which followed; until, in 1816, it was placed on the respectable basis on which it now exists, under the direction of

4   G

Dr. Guillié, whose untiring exertions have been blessed with the most beneficial results.

We shall give a brief view of the course of education pursued under his direction, as exhibited by him in the valuable treatise to which we have already referred, occasionally glancing at the method adopted in the corresponding institution at Edinburgh.

The fundamental object proposed in every scheme of education for the blind is, to direct the attention of the pupil to those studies and mechanic arts which he will be able afterward to pursue by means of his own exertions and resources, without any external aid. The sense of touch is the one, therefore, almost exclusively relied on. The fingers are the eyes of the blind. They are taught to read in Paris by feeling the surface of metallic types, and in Edinburgh by means of letters raised on a blank leaf of paper. If they are previously acquainted with spelling, which may be easily taught them before entering the institution, they learn to discriminate the several letters with great facility. Their perceptions become so fine by practice, that they can discern even the finest print, and when the fingers fail them, readily distinguish it by applying the tongue. A similar method is employed for instructing them in figures; the notation table, invented by Saunderson, and once used in the Paris seminary, having been abandoned as less simple and obvious, although his symbols for the representation of geometrical diagrams are still retained.

As it would be labour lost to learn the art of reading without having books to read, various attempts have been made to supply this desideratum. The first hint of the form now adopted for the impression of these books was suggested by the appearance exhibited on the reverse side of a copy as removed fresh from the printing-press. In imitation of this, a leaf of paper of a firm texture is forcibly impressed with types unstained by ink, and larger than the ordinary size, until a sufficiently bold relief has been obtained to enable the blind person to distinguish the characters by the touch. The French have adopted the Italian hand, or one very like it, for the fashion of the letters, while the Scotch have invented one more angular and rectilinear, which, besides the advantage of greater compactness, is found better suited to accurate discrimination by the touch than smooth and extended curves and circles.

Several important works have been already printed on this plan, viz., a portion of the Scriptures, catechisms, and offices for daily prayer; grammars in the Greek, Latin, French, English, Italian, and Spanish languages; a Latin *selecta*, a geography, a course of general history, a selection from English poets and prose-writers, a course of literature, with a compilation of the choicest specimens of French eloquence. With all this, the art of printing for the blind is still in its infancy. The characters are so unwieldy, and the leaves (which cannot be printed on the reverse side, as this would flatten the letters upon the other) are necessarily so numerous as to make the volume exceedingly bulky, and of course expensive. The Gospel of St. John, for example, expands into three large octavo volumes. Some farther improvement must occur, therefore, before the invention can become extensively useful. There can be no reason to doubt of such a result eventually, for it is only by long and repeated experiment that the art of printing in the usual way, and every other art, indeed, has been brought to its present perfection. Perhaps some mode may be adopted like that of stenography, which, although encumbering the learner with some additional difficulties at first, may abundantly compensate him in the condensed forms, and consequently cheaper and more numerous publications which could be afforded by it. Perhaps ink, or some other material of greater consistency than that ordinarily used in printing may be devised, which, when communicated by the type to the paper, will leave a character sufficiently raised to be distinguished by the touch. We have known a blind person able to decipher the characters in a piece of music to which the ink had been imparted more liberally than usual. In the mean time, what has been already done has conferred a service on the blind which we, who become insensible from the very prodigality of our blessings, cannot rightly estimate. The glimmering of the taper, which is lost in the blaze of day, is sufficient to guide the steps of the wanderer in darkness. The unsealed volume of Scripture will furnish him with the best sources of consolation under every privation; the various grammars are so many keys with which to unlock the stores of knowledge to enrich his after life, and the selections from the most beautiful portions of elegant literature will afford him a permanent source of recreation and delight.

One method used for instruction in writing is, to direct the pencil, or stylus, in a groove cut in the fashion of the different letters. Other modes, however, too complex for description here, are resorted to, by which the blind person is enabled not only to write, but to read what he has thus traced. A portable writing-case for this purpose has also been invented by one of the blind, who, it is observed, are the most ingenious in supplying, as they are best acquainted with, their own wants. A very simple method of epistolary correspondence, by means of a string-alphabet, as it is called, consisting of a cord or riband in which knots of various dimensions represent certain classes of letters, has been devised by two blind men at Edinburgh. This contrivance, which is so simple that it can be acquired in an hour's time by the most ordinary capacity, is asserted to have the power of conveying ideas with equal precision with the pen. A blind lady of our acquaintance, however, whose fine understanding and temper have enabled her to surmount many of the difficulties of her situation, after a trial of this invention, gives the preference to the mode usually adopted by her of pricking the letters on the paper with a pin—an operation which she performs with astonishing rapidity, and which, in addition to the

4   G *

advantage possessed by the string-alphabet of being legible by the touch, answers more completely the purposes of epistolary correspondence, since it may be readily interpreted by any one on being held up to the light.

The scheme of instruction at the institution for the blind in Paris comprehends geography, history, the Greek and Latin, together with the French, Italian, and English languages, arithmetic, and the higher branches of mathematics, music, and some of the most useful mechanic arts. For mathematics, the pupils appear to discover a natural aptitude, many of them attaining such proficiency as not only to profit by the public lectures of the most eminent professors in the sciences, but to carry away the highest prizes in the lyceums in a competition with those who possess the advantages of sight. In music, as we have before remarked, they all make greater or less proficiency. They are especially instructed in the organ, which, from its frequency in the churches, affords one of the most obvious means of obtaining a livelihood.

The method of tuition adopted is that of mutual instruction. The blind are ascertained to learn most easily and expeditiously from those in the same condition with themselves. Two male teachers, with one female, are in this way found adequate to the superintendence of eighty scholars, which, considering the obstacles to be encountered, must be admitted to be a small apparatus for the production of such extensive results.

In teaching them the mechanic arts, two principles appear to be kept in view, namely, to select such for each individual respectively as may be best adapted to his future residence and destination; the trades, for example, most suitable for a seaport being those least so for the country, and *vice versa.* Secondly, to confine their attention to such occupations as from their nature are most accessible to, and which can be most perfectly attained by, persons in their situation. It is absurd to multiply obstacles from the mere vanity of conquering them.

Printing is an art for which the blind show particular talent, going through all the processes of composing, serving the press, and distributing the types with the same accuracy with those who can see. Indeed, much of this mechanical occupation with the *clairvoyans* (we are in want of some such compendious phrase in our language) appears to be the result rather of habit than any exercise of the eye. The blind print all the books for their own use. They are taught also to spin, to knit, in which last operation they are extremely ready, knitting very finely, with open work, &c., and are much employed by the Parisian hosiers in the manufacture of elastic vests, shirts, and petticoats. They make purses, delicately embroidered with figures of animals and flowers, whose various tints are selected with perfect propriety. The fingers of the females are observed to be particularly adapted to this nicer sort of work, from their superior delicacy, ordinarily, to those of men. They are employed also in manufacturing girths, in netting in all its branches, in making shoes of list, plush, cloth, coloured skin, and list carpets, of which a vast number is annually disposed of. Weaving is particularly adapted to the blind, who perform all the requisite manipulation without any other assistance but that of setting up the warp. They manufacture whips, straw bottoms for chairs, coarse straw hats, rope, cord, packthread, baskets, straw, rush, and plush mats, which are very saleable in France.

The articles manufactured in the Asylum for the Blind in Scotland are somewhat different; and as they show for what an extensive variety of occupations they may be qualified in despite of their infirmity, we will take the liberty, at the hazard of being somewhat tedious, of quoting the catalogue of them exhibited in one of their advertisements. The articles offered for sale consist of cotton and linen cloths, ticked and striped Hollands, towelling and diapers, worsted net for fruit-trees; hair cloth, hair mats, and hair ropes; basket-work of every description; hair, India hemp, and straw door-mats; saddle girths; rope and twines of all kinds; netting for sheep-pens; garden and onion twine nets; fishing nets, beehives, mattresses, and cushions; feather beds, bolsters, and pillows; mattresses and beds of every description cleaned and repaired. The labours in this department are performed by the boys. The girls are employed in sewing, knitting stockings, spinning, making fine banker's twine, and various works besides, usually executed by well-educated females

Such is the emulation of the blind, according to Dr. Guillié, in the institution of Paris, that hitherto there has been no necessity of stimulating their exertions by the usual motives of reward or punishment. Delighted with their sensible progress in vanquishing the difficulties incident to their condition, they are content if they can but place themselves on a level with the more fortunate of their fellow-creatures. And it is observed that many, who in the solitude of their own homes have failed in their attempts to learn some of the arts taught in this institution, have acquired a knowledge of them with great alacrity when cheered by the sympathy of individuals involved in the same calamity with themselves, and with whom, of course, they could compete with equal probability of success.

The example of Paris has been followed in the principal cities in most of the other countries of Europe: in England, Scotland, Russia, Prussia, Austria, Switzerland, Holland, and Denmark. These establishments, which are conducted on the same general principles, have adopted a plan of education more or less comprehensive, some of them, like those of Paris and Edinburgh, involving the higher branches of intellectual education, and others, as in London and Liverpool, confining themselves chiefly to practical arts. The results, however, have been in the highest degree cheering to the philanthropist in the light thus poured in upon minds to which all the usual avenues were sealed up—in the opportunity afforded them of developing those latent pow

L

ers which had been hitherto wasted in inaction, and in the happiness thus imparted to an unfortunate class of beings, who now, for the first time, were permitted to assume their proper station in society, and instead of encumbering, to contribute, by their own exertions, to the general prosperity.

We rejoice that the inhabitants of our own city have been the first to give an example of such beneficent institutions in the New World. And it is principally with the view of directing the attention of the public towards it that we have gone into a review of what has been effected in this way in Europe. The credit of having first suggested the undertaking here is due to our townsman, Dr. John D. Fisher, through whose exertions, aided by those of several other benevolent individuals, the subject was brought before the Legislature of this state, and an act of incorporation was granted to the petitioners, bearing date March 2d, 1829, authorizing them, under the title of the "New-England Asylum for the Blind," to hold property, receive donations and bequests, and to exercise the other functions usually appertaining to similar corporations.

A resolution was subsequently passed, during the same session, requiring the selectmen of the several towns throughout the commonwealth to make returns of the number of blind inhabitants, with their ages, periods of blindness, personal condition, &c. By far the larger proportion of these functionaries, however, with a degree of apathy which does them very little credit, paid no attention whatever to this requisition. By the aid of such as did comply with it, and by means of circulars addressed to the clergymen of the various parishes, advices have been received from one hundred and forty-one towns, comprising somewhat less than half of the whole number within the state. From this imperfect estimate it would appear that the number of blind persons in these towns amounts to two hundred and forty-three, of whom more than one fifth are under thirty years of age, which period is assigned as the limit within which they cannot fail of receiving all the benefit to be derived from the system of instruction pursued in the institutions for the blind.

The proportion of the blind to our whole population, as founded on the above estimate, is somewhat higher than that established by Zeune for the corresponding latitudes in Europe, where blindness decreases in advancing from the equator to the poles, it being computed in Egypt at the rate of one to one hundred, and in Norway of one to one thousand, which last is conformable to ours.

Assuming the preceding estimate as the basis, it will appear that there are about five hundred blind persons in the State of Massachusetts at the present moment; and, adopting the census of 1820, there could not at that time, according to the same rate, be less than sixteen hundred and fifty in all New-England, one fifth being under thirty years of age; a number which, as the blind are usually retired from public observation, far exceeds what might be conceived on a cursory inspection.

From the returns it would appear that a large proportion of the blind in Massachusetts are in humble circumstances, and a still larger proportion of those in years indigent or paupers. This is imputable to their having learned no trade or profession in their youth, so that, when deprived of their natural guardians, they have necessarily become a charge upon the public.

Since the year 1825 an appropriation has been continued by the Legislature for the purpose of maintaining a certain number of pupils at the Asylum for the Deaf and Dumb at Hartford. A resolution was obtained during the last session of the General Court authorizing the governor to pay over to the Asylum for the Blind whatever balance of the sum thus appropriated might remain in the treasury unexpended at the end of the current year, and the same with every subsequent year to which the grant extended, unless otherwise advised. Seven hundred dollars only have been received as the balance of the past year, a sum obviously inadequate to the production of any important result, and far inferior to what had been anticipated by the friends of the measure. On the whole, we are inclined to doubt whether this will be found the most suitable mode of creating resources for the asylum. Although, in fact, it disposes only of the superfluity, it has the appearance of subtracting from the positive revenues of the Deaf and Dumb, an institution of equal merit and claims with any other whatever The Asylum for the Blind is an establishment of

too much importance to be left thus dependant on
a precarious contingent, and is worthy, were it only
in an economical point of view, of being placed by
the state on some more secure and ample basis.

As it is, the want of funds opposes a sensible ob-
struction to its progress. The pressure of the times
has made the present moment exceedingly unfavourable to personal solicitation, although so much has
been effected in this way, through the liberality of
a few individuals, that, as we understand, preparations are now making for procuring the requisite
instructers and apparatus on a moderate and somewhat reduced scale.

As to the comprehensiveness of the scheme of
education to be pursued at the the asylum, whether
it shall embrace intellectual culture, or be confined
simply to the mechanic arts, this must, of course, be
ultimately determined by the extent of its resources.
We trust, however, it will be enabled to adopt the
former arrangement, at least so far as to afford the
pupils an acquaintance with the elements of the
more popular sciences. There is such a diffusion
of liberal knowledge among all classes in this country, that if the blind are suffered to go without any
tincture of it from the institution, they will always,
whatever be the skill acquired by them in mechanical occupations, continue to feel a sense of their
own mental inferiority. The connexion of these
higher with the more direct objects of the institution will serve, moreover, to give it greater dignity
and importance. And while it will open sources

4   H

of knowledge from which many may be in a situation to derive permanent consolation, it will instruct the humblest individual in what may be of essential utility to him, as writing and arithmetic, for example, in his intercourse with the world.

To what extent it is desirable that the asylum be placed on a charitable foundation is another subject of consideration. This, we believe, is the character of most of the establishments in Europe. That in Scotland, for instance, contains about a hundred subjects, who, with their families included, amount to two hundred and fifty souls, all supported from the labours of the blind, conjointly with the funds of the institution. This is undoubtedly one of the noblest and most discriminating charities in the world. It seems probable, however, that this is not the plan best adapted to our exigencies. We want not to maintain the blind, but to put them in the way of contributing to their own maintenance. By placing the expenses of tuition and board as low as possible, the means of effecting this will be brought within the reach of a large class of them; and for the rest, it will be obvious economy in the state to provide them with the means of acquiring an education at once that may enable them to contribute permanently towards their own support, which, in some shape or other, is now chargeable on the public. Perhaps, however, some scheme may be devised for combining both these objects, if this be deemed preferable to the adoption of either exclusively.

We are convinced that, as far as the institution is to rely for its success on public patronage, it will not be disappointed. If once successfully in operation, and brought before the public eye, it cannot fail of exciting a very general sympathy, which, in this country, has never been refused to the calls of humanity. No one, we think, who has visited the similar endowments in Paris or in Edinburgh will easily forget the sensations which he experienced on witnessing so large a class of his unfortunate fellow-creatures thus restored from intellectual darkness to the blessings, if we may so speak, of light and liberty. There is no higher evidence of the worth of the human mind than its capacity of drawing consolation from its own resources under so heavy a privation; so that it not only can exhibit resignation and cheerfulness, but energy to burst the fetters with which it is encumbered. Who could refuse his sympathy to the success of these efforts, or withhold from the subject of them the means of attaining his natural level and usefulness in society, from which circumstances, less favourable to him than to ourselves, have hitherto excluded him?

IRVING'S CONQUEST OF GRANADA.*

OCTOBER, 1829.

ALMOST as many qualifications may be demanded
for a perfect historian, indeed the Abbé Mably has
enumerated as many, as Cicero stipulates for a perfect orator. He must be strictly impartial; a lover
of truth under all circumstances, and ready to declare it at all hazards: he must be deeply conver-
sant with whatever may bring into relief the character of the people he is depicting, not merely with
their laws, constitution, general resources, and all
the other more visible parts of the machinery of
government, but with the nicer moral and social relations, the informing spirit which gives life to the
whole, but escapes the eye of a vulgar observer. If
he has to do with other ages and nations, he must
transport himself into them, expatriating himself, as
it were, from his own, in order to get the very form
and pressure of the times he is delineating. He
must be conscientious in his attention to geography, chronology, &c., an inaccuracy in which has
been fatal to more than one good philosophical history; and, mixed up with all these drier details, he
must display the various powers of a novelist or
dramatist, throwing his characters into suitable lights
and shades, disposing his scenes so as to awaken

* "A Chronicle of the Conquest of Granada. By Fray Antonia Agapida." 1829 : 2 vols., 12mo. Philadelphia : Carey, Lea, and Carey.

and maintain an unflagging interest, and diffusing over the whole that finished style, without which his work will only become a magazine of materials for the more elegant edifices of subsequent writers. He must be—in short, there is no end to what a perfect historian must be and do. It is hardly necessary to add that such a monster never did and never will exist.

But, although we cannot attain to perfect excellence in this or any other science in this world, considerable approaches have been made to it, and different individuals have arisen at different periods, possessed, in an eminent degree, of some of the principal qualities which go to make up the aggregate of the character we have been describing. The peculiar character of these qualities will generally be determined in the writer by that of the age in which he lives. Thus, the earlier historians of Greece and Rome sought less to instruct than to amuse. They filled their pictures with dazzling and seductive images. In their researches into antiquity, they were not startled by the marvellous, like the more prudish critics of our day, but welcomed it as likely to stir the imaginations of their readers. They seldom interrupted the story by impertinent reflection. They bestowed infinite pains on the costume, the style of their history, and, in fine, made everything subordinate to the main purpose of conveying an elegant and interesting *narrative*. Such was Herodotus, such Livy, and such, too, the earlier chroniclers of modern Europe, whose

4   H *

pages glow with the picturesque and brilliant pageants of an age of chivalry. These last, as well as Herodotus, may be said to have written in the infancy of their nations, when the imagination is more willingly addressed than the understanding. Livy, who wrote in a riper age, lived, nevertheless, in a court and a period where tranquillity and opulence disposed the minds of men to elegant recreation rather than to severe discipline and exertion.

As, however, the nation advanced in years, or became oppressed with calamity, history also assumed a graver complexion. Fancy gave way to reflection. The mind, no longer invited to rove abroad in quest of elegant and alluring pictures, was driven back upon itself, speculated more deeply, and sought for support under the external evils of life in moral and philosophical truth. Description was abandoned for the study of character; men took the place of events; and the romance was converted into the drama. Thus it was with Tacitus, who lived under those imperial monsters who turned Rome into a charnel-house, and his compact narratives are filled with moral and political axioms sufficiently numerous to make a volume; and, indeed, Brotier has made one of them in his edition of the historian. The same philosophical spirit animates the page of Thucydides, himself one of the principal actors in the long, disastrous struggle that terminated in the ruin of his nation.

But, notwithstanding the deeper and more comprehensive thought of these later writers, there was

still a wide difference between the complexion giv-
en to history under their hands and that which it
has assumed in our time. We would not be understood as determining, but simply as discriminating their relative merits. The Greeks and Romans lived when the world, at least when the mind
was in its comparative infancy—when fancy and
feeling were most easily, and loved most to be excited. They possessed a finer sense of beauty than
the moderns. They were infinitely more solicitous
about the external dress, the finish, and all that
makes up the poetry of a composition. Poetry, indeed, mingled in their daily pursuits as well as pleasures; it determined their gravest deliberations. The
command of their armies was given, not to the best
general, but ofttimes to the most eloquent orator.
Poetry entered into their religion, and created those
beautiful monuments of architecture and sculpture
which the breath of time has not tarnished. It entered into their philosophy; and no one confessed its
influence more deeply than he who would have banished it from his republic. It informed the souls of
their orators, and prompted those magnificent rhapsodies which fall lifeless enough from the stammering tongue of the schoolboy, but which once awaked
to ecstasy the living populace of Athens. It entered deeply even into their latest history. It was first
exhibited in the national chronicles of Homer. It
lost little of its colouring, though it conformed to
the general laws of prosaic composition, under Herodotus. And it shed a pleasing grace over the so-

ber pages of Thucydides and Xenophon. The muse, indeed, was stripped of her wings. She no longer made her airy excursions into the fairy regions of romance ; but, as she moved along the earth, the sweetest wild-flowers seemed to spring up unbidden at her feet. We would not be understood as implying that Grecian history was ambitious of florid or meretricious ornament. Nothing could be more simple than its general plan and execution ; far too simple, we fear, for imitation in our day. Thus Thucydides, for example, distributes his events most inartificially, according to the regular revolutions of the seasons ; and the rear of every section is brought up with the same eternal repetion of ἔτος τῷ πολέμῳ ἐτέλευτα τῷδε, ὃν Θουκυδίδης ξυνέγραψε. But in the fictitious speeches with which he has illumined his narrative, he has left the choicest specimens of Attic eloquence ; and he elaborated his general diction into so high a finish, that Demosthenes, as is well known, in the hope of catching some of his rhetorical graces, thought him worthy of being thrice transcribed with his own hand.

Far different has been the general conception, as well as execution, of history by the moderns. In this, however, it was accommodated to the exigencies of their situation, and, as with the ancients, still reflected the spirit of the age. If the Greeks lived in the infancy of civilization, the contemporaries of our day may be said to have reached its prime. The same revolution has taken place as in the growth of an individual. The vivacity of the imagination has been blunted, but reason is matured. The credulity of youth has given way to habits of cautious inquiry, and sometimes to a phlegmatic skepticism. The productions, indeed, which first appeared in the doubtful twilight of morning exhibited the love of the marvellous, the light and fanciful spirit of a green and tender age. But a new order of things commenced as the stores of classical learning were unrolled to the eye of the scholar. The mind seemed at once to enter upon the rich inheritance which the sages of antiquity had been ages in accumulating, and to start, as it were, from the very point where they had terminated their career. Thus raised by learning and experience, it was enabled to take a wider view of its proper destiny—to understand that truth is the greatest good, and to discern the surest method of arriving at it. The Christian doctrine, too, inculcated that the end of being was best answered by a life of active usefulness, and not by one of abstract contemplation, or selfish indulgence, or passive fortitude, as variously taught by the various sects of antiquity. Hence a new standard of moral excellence was formed. Pursuits were estimated by their practical results, and the useful was preferred to the ornamental. Poetry, confined to her own sphere, was no longer permitted to mingle in the councils of philosophy. Intellectual and physical science, instead of floating on vague speculation, as with the ancients, was established on careful induction and experiment. The orator, in stead of adorning himself with the pomp and garniture of verse, sought only to acquire greater dexterity in the management of the true weapons of debate. The passions were less frequently assailed, the reason more. A wider field was open to the historian. He was no longer to concoct his narrative, if the scene lay in a remote period, from the superficial rumours of oral tradition. Libraries were to be ransacked; medals and monuments to be studied; obsolete manuscripts to be deciphered. Every assertion was to be fortified by an authority; and the opinions of others, instead of being admitted on easy faith, were to be carefully collated, and the balance of probability struck between them. With these qualifications of antiquarian and critic, the modern historian was to combine that of the philosopher, deducing from his mass of facts general theorems, and giving to them their most extended application.

By all this process, poetry lost much, but philosophy gained more. The elegant arts sensibly declined, but the most important and recondite secrets of nature were laid open. All those sciences which have for their object the happiness and improvement of the species, the science of government, of political economy, of education—natural and experimental science—were carried far beyond the boundaries which they could possibly have reached under the ancient systems.

The peculiar forms of historic writing, as it ex-

ists with the moderns, were not fully developed until the last century. It may be well to notice the intermediate shape which it assumed before it reached this period in Spain and Italy, but especially this
latter country, in the sixteenth century. The Italian historians of that age seemed to have combined
the generalizing and reflecting spirit characteristic
of the moderns, with the simple and graceful forms
of composition which have descended to us from
the ancients. Machiavelli, in particular, may remind us of some recent statue which exhibits all
the lineaments and proportions of a contemporary,
but to which the sculptor has given a sort of antique dignity by enveloping it in the folds of the
Roman toga. No one of the Spanish historians is
to be named with him. Mariana, who enjoys among
them the greatest celebrity, has, it is true, given to
his style, both in the Latin and Castilian, the elegant transparency of an ancient classic, but the mass
of detail is not quickened by a single spark of philosophy or original reflection. Mariana was a monk,
one of a community who have formed the most copious, but, in many respects, the most incompetent
chroniclers in the world, cut off, as they are, from
all sympathy with any portion of the species save
their own order, and predisposed by education to
admit as truth the grossest forgeries of fanaticism.
What can their narratives be worth, distorted thus
by prejudice and credulity? The Aragonese writers, and Zurita in particular, though far inferior as
to the literary execution of their works, exhibit a

pregnant thought and a manly independence of expression far superior to the Jesuit Mariana.

The Italian historians of the sixteenth century, moreover, had the good fortune not only to have been eyewitnesses, but to have played prominent parts in the events which they commemorated. And this gives a vitality to their touches which is in vain to be expected from those of a closet politician. This rare union of public and private excellence is delicately intimated in the inscription on Guicciardini's monument, "*Cujus negotium, an otium, gloriosius incertum.*"

The personage by whom the present laws of historic composition may be said to have been first arranged into a regular system was Voltaire. This extraordinary genius, whose works have been productive of so much mingled good and evil, discovers in them many traces of a humane and beneficent disposition. Nowhere is his invective more keenly directed than against acts of cruelty and oppression—above all, of religious oppression. He lived in an age of crying abuses both in Church and government. Unfortunately, he employed a weapon against them whose influence is not to be controlled by the most expert hand. The envenomed shaft of irony not only wounds the member at which it is aimed, but diffuses its poison to the healthiest and remotest regions of the body.

The free and volatile temper of Voltaire forms a singular contrast with his resolute pertinacity of purpose. Bard, philosopher, historian, this literary

Proteus animated every shape with the same mischievous spirit of philosophy. It never deserted him, even in the most sportive sallies of his fancy. It seasons his romances equally with his gravest pieces in the encyclopedia; his familiar letters and most licentious doggerel no less than his histories. The leading object of this philosophy may be defined by the single cant phrase, "the abolition of prejudices." But in Voltaire prejudices were too often confounded with principles.

In his histories, he seems ever intent on exhibiting, in the most glaring colours, the manifold inconsistencies of the human race; in showing the contradiction between profession and practice; in contrasting the magnificence of the apparatus with the impotence of the results. The enormous abuses of Christianity are brought into juxtaposition with the most meritorious features in other religions, and thus all are reduced to nearly the same level. The credulity of one half of mankind is set in opposition to the cunning of the other. The most momentous events are traced to the most insignificant causes, and the ripest schemes of wisdom are shown to have been baffled by the intervention of the most trivial accidents. Thus the conduct of the world seems to be regulated by chance; the springs of human action are resolved into selfishness; and religion, of whatever denomination, is only a different form of superstition. It is true that his satire is directed not so much against any particular system as the vices of that system; but the result left upon

I

the mind is not a whit less pernicious. His philosophical romance of " Candide" affords a good exemplification of his manner. The thesis of perfect optimism in this world, at which he levels this *jeu d'esprit*, is manifestly indefensible. But then he supports his position with such an array of gross and hyperbolical atrocities, without the intervention of a single palliative circumstance, and, withal, in such a tone of keen derision, that, if any serious impression be left on the mind, it can be no other than that of a baleful, withering skepticism. The historian rarely so far forgets his philosophy as to kindle into high and generous emotion the glow of patriotism, or moral and religious enthusiasm. And hence, too, his style, though always graceful, and often seasoned with the sallies of a piquant wit, never rises into eloquence or sublimity.

Voltaire has been frequently reproached for want of historical accuracy. But if we make due allowance for the sweeping tenour of his reflections, and for the infinite variety of his topics, we shall be slow in giving credit to this charge.* He was, indeed, oftentimes misled by his inveterate Pyrrhonism; a defect, when carried to the excess in which he indulged it, almost equally fatal to the historian with credulity or superstition. His researches frequently led him into dark, untravelled regions; but the aliment which he imported thence served only

---

* Indeed, Hallam and Warton—the one as diligent a labourer in the field of civil history as the other has been in literary—both bear testimony to his genera' veracity.

too often to minister to his pernicious philosophy
He resembled the allegorical agents of Milton, pa-
ving a way across the gulf of Chaos for the spirits
of mischief to enter more easily upon the earth.

Voltaire effected a no less sensible revolution in
the structure than in the spirit of history. Thus,
instead of following the natural consecutive order
of events, the work was distributed, on the principle of a *Catalogue raisonné*, into sections arranged
according to their subjects, and copious dissertations were introduced into the body of the narrative. Thus, in his *Essai sur les Mœurs*, &c., one
chapter is devoted to letters, another to religion, a
third to manners, and so on.   And in the same way,
in his "Age of Louis the Fourteenth," he has thrown
his various illustrations of the policy of government,
and of the social habits of the court, into a detached portion at the close of the book.

This would seem to be deviating from the natural course of things as they occur in the world,
where the multifarious pursuits of pleasure and business, the lights and shadows, as it were, of life
are daily intermingled in the motley panorama of
human existence.   But, however artificial this division, it enabled the reader to arrive more expeditiously at the results, for which alone history is valuable, while, at the same time, it put it in the power
of the writer to convey with more certainty and facility his own impressions.

This system was subsequently so much refined
upon, that Montesquieu, in his "Grandeur et Déca-

dence des Romains," laid no farther stress on historical facts than as they furnished him with illustrations of his particular theorems. Indeed, so little did his work rest upon the veracity of such facts, that, although the industry of Niebuhr, or, rather, of Beaufort, has knocked away almost all the foundations of early Rome, Montesquieu's treatise remains as essentially unimpaired in credit as before. Thus the materials which anciently formed the body of history now served only as ingredients from which its spirit was to be extracted. But this was not always the spirit of truth. And the arbitrary selection as well as disposition of incidents which this new method allowed, and the colouring which they were to receive from the author, made it easy to pervert them to the construction of the wildest hypotheses.

The progress of philosophical history is particularly observable in Great Britain, where it seems to have been admirably suited to the grave, reflecting temper of the people. In the graces of *narrative* they have ever been unequal to their French neighbours. Their ancient chronicles are inferior in spirit and execution to those either of France or Spain; and their more elaborate histories, down to the middle of the eighteenth century, could not in any way compete with the illustrious models of Italy. But soon after this period several writers appeared, exhibiting a combination of qualities, erudition, critical penetration, powers of generalization, and a political sagacity unrivalled in any other age or country.

The influence of the new forms of historical composition, however, was here, as elsewhere, made too frequently subservient to party and sectarian prejudices. Tory histories and Whig histories, Protestant and Catholic histories, successively appeared, and seemed to neutralize each other. The most venerable traditions were exploded as nursery tales. The statues decreed by antiquity were cast down, and the characters of miscreants whom the general suffrage of mankind had damned to infamy—of a Dionysius, a Borgia, or a Richard the Third—were now retraced by what Jovius distinguishes as "the golden pen" of the historian, until the reader, bewildered in the maze of uncertainty, is almost ready to join in the exclamation of Lord Orford to his son, "Oh quote me not history, for that I know to be false!" It is remarkable, indeed, that the last-mentioned monarch, Richard the Third, whose name has become a byword of atrocity, the burden of the ballad and the moral of the drama, should have been the subject of elaborate vindication by two eminent writers of the most opposite characters, the pragmatical Horace Walpole, and the circumspect and conscientious Sharon Turner. The apology of the latter exhibits a technical precision, a severe scrutiny into the authenticity of records, and a nice balancing of contradictory testimony, that give it all the air of a legal investigation. Thus history seems to be conducted on the principles of a judicial process, in which the writer, assuming the functions of an advocate, studiously suppresses whatever may make against his

4   I*

own side, supports himself by the strongest array of evidence which he can muster, discredits, as far as possible, that of the opposite party, and, by dexterous interpretation and ingenious inference, makes out the most plausible argument for his client that the case will admit.

But these, after all, are only the abuses of philosophical history, and the unseasonable length of remark into which we have been unwarily led in respect to them may give us the appearance of laying on them greater emphasis than they actually deserve. There are few writers in any country whose judgment has not been sometimes warped by personal prejudices. But it is to the credit of the principal British historians that, however they may have been occasionally under the influence of such human infirmity, they have conducted their researches, in the main, with equal integrity and impartiality. And while they have enriched their writings with the stores of a various erudition, they have digested from these details results of the most enlarged and practical application. History in their hands, although it may have lost much of the simplicity and graphic vivacity which it maintained with the ancients, has gained much more in the amount of useful knowledge and the lessons of sound philosophy which it inculcates.

There is no writer who exhibits more distinctly the full development of the principles of modern history, with all its virtues and defects, than Gibbon. His learning was fully equal to his vast subject. This, commencing with expiring civilization 'n ancient Rome, continues on until the period of its final and perfect resurrection in Italy in the fifteenth century, and thus may be said to furnish the lights which are to guide us through the long interval of darkness which divides the Old from the Modern world. The range of his subject was fully equal to its duration. Goths, Huns, Tartars, and all the rude tribes of the North, are brought upon the stage, together with the more cultivated natives of the South, the Greeks, Italians, and the intellectual Arab; and, as the scene shifts from one country to another, we behold its population depicted with that peculiarity of physiognomy and studied propriety of costume which belong to dramatic exhibition; for Gibbon was a more vivacious draughtsman than most writers of his school. He was, moreover, deeply versed in geography, chronology, antiquities, verbal criticism—in short, in all the sciences in any way subsidiary to his art. The extent of his subject permitted him to indulge in those elaborate disquisitions so congenial to the spirit of modern history on the most momentous and interesting topics, while his early studies enabled him to embellish the drier details of his narrative with the charms of a liberal and elegant scholarship.

What, then, was wanting to this accomplished writer? Good faith. His defects were precisely of the class of which we have before been speaking, and his most elaborate efforts exhibit too often the perversion of learning and ingenuity to the vindication of preconceived hypotheses. He cannot indeed, be convicted of ignorance or literal inaccuracy, as he has triumphantly proved in his discomfiture of the unfortunate Davis. But his disingenuous mode of conducting the argument leads precisely to the same unfair result. Thus, in his celebrated chapters on the "Progress of Christianity," which he tells us were "reduced by three successive revisals from a bulky volume to their present size," he has often slurred over in the text such particulars as might reflect most credit on the character of the religion, or shuffled them into a note at the bottom of the page, while all that admits of a doubtful complexion in its early propagation is ostentatiously blazoned, and set in contrast to the most amiable features of paganism. At the same time, by a style of innuendo that conveys "more than meets the ear," he has contrived, with Iago-like duplicity, to breathe a taint of suspicion on the purity which he dares not openly assail. It would be easy to furnish examples of all this were this the place for them; but the charges have no novelty, and have been abundantly substantiated by others.

It is a consequence of this skepticism in Gibbon, as with Voltaire, that his writings are nowhere warmed with a generous moral sentiment. The most sublime of all spectacles, that of the martyr who suffers for conscience sake, and this equally whether his creed be founded in truth or error, is contemplated by the historian with the smile, or, rather, sneer of philosophic indifference. This is not only bad taste, as he is addressing a Christian audience, but he thus voluntarily relinquishes one of the most powerful engines for the movement of human passion, which is never so easily excited as by deeds of suffering, self-devoted heroism.

But, although Gibbon was wholly defective in moral enthusiasm, his style is vivified by a certain exhilarating glow that kindles a corresponding warmth in the bosom of his reader. This may, perhaps, be traced to his egotism, or, to speak more liberally, to an ardent attachment to his professional pursuits, and to his inextinguishable love of letters. This enthusiasm appears in almost every page of his great work, and enabled him to triumph over all its difficulties. It is particularly conspicuous whenever he touches upon Rome, the *alma mater* of science, whose adopted son he may be said to have been from his earliest boyhood. Whenever he contemplates her fallen fortunes, he mourns over her with the fond solicitude that might become an ancient Roman; and when he depicts her pristine glories, dimly seen through the mist of so many centuries, he does it with such vivid accuracy of conception, that the reader, like the traveller who wanders through the excavations of Pompeii, seems to be gazing on the original forms and brilliant colours of antiquity.

To Gibbon's egotism—in its most literal sense, to his personal vanity—may be traced some of the peculiar defects for which his style is conspicuous. The "historian of the Decline and Fall" too rarely

O

forgets his own importance in that of his subject. The consequence which he attaches to his personal labours is shown in a bloated dignity of expression, and an ostentation of ornament that contrast whimsically enough with the trifling topics and commonplace thoughts on which, in the course of his long work, they are occasionally employed. He nowhere moves along with the easy freedom of nature, but seems to leap, as it were, from triad to triad by a succession of strained, convulsive efforts. He affected, as he tells us, the light, festive raillery of Voltaire; but his cumbrous imitation of the mercurial Frenchman may remind one, to make use of a homely simile, of the ass in Æsop's fable, who frisked upon his master in imitation of the sportive gambols of the spaniel. The first two octavo volumes of Gibbon's history were written in a comparatively modest and unaffected manner, for he was then uncertain of the public favour; and, indeed, his style was exceedingly commended by the most competent critics of that day, as Hume, Joseph Warton, and others, as is abundantly shown in their correspondence; but when he had tasted the sweets of popular applause, and had been crowned as the historian of the day, his increased consequence becomes at once visible in the assumed stateliness and magnificence of his bearing. But even after this period, whenever the subject is suited to his style, and when his phlegmatic temper is warmed by those generous emotions, of which, as we have said, it was sometimes susceptible, he exhibits his ideas in the most splendid and imposing forms of which the English language is capable.

The most eminent illustrations of the system of historical writing, which we have been discussing, that have appeared in England in the present century, are the works of Mr. Hallam, in which the author, discarding most of the circumstances that go to make up mere narrative, endeavours to fix the attention of the reader on the more important features of constitutional polity, employing his wide range of materials in strict subordination to this purpose.

But while history has thus been conducted on nearly the same principles in England for the last century, a new path has been struck out in France, or, rather, an attempt has lately been made there to retrace the old one. M. de Barante, no less estimable as a literary critic than as a historian, in the preliminary remarks to his "Histoire des Ducs de Bourgogne," considers the draughts of modern compilers as altogether wanting in the vivacity and freshness of their originals. They tell the reader how he should feel, instead of making him do so. They give him their own results, instead of enabling him, by a fair delineation of incidents, to form his own. And while the early chroniclers, in spite of their unformed and obsolete idiom, are still read with delight, the narratives of the former are too often dry, languid, and uninteresting. He proposes, therefore, by a close adherence to his originals, to extract, as it were, the spirit of their works, without any affectation, however, of their antiquated phraseology, and to exhibit as vivid and veracious a portraiture as possible of the times he is delineating, unbroken by any discussions or reflections of his own. The result has been a work in eleven octavo volumes, which, notwithstanding its bulk, has already passed into four editions.

The two last productions of our countryman, Mr. Irving, undoubtedly fall within the class of narrative history. To this he seems peculiarly suited by his genius, his fine perception of moral and natural beauty, his power of discriminating the most delicate shades of character, and of unfolding a series of events so as to maintain a lively interest in the reader, and a *lactea ubertas* of expression which can impart a living eloquence even to the most commonplace sentiments. Had the "Life of Columbus" been written by a historian of the other school of which we have been speaking, he would have enlarged with greater circumstantiality on the system adopted by Ferdinand and Isabella for the administration of their colonies, and for the regulation of trade; nor would he have neglected to descant on a topic, worn somewhat threadbare, it must be owned, so momentous as the moral and political consequences of the discovery of America; neither would such a writer, in an account of the conquest of Granada, have omitted to collect such particulars as might throw light on the genius, social institutions, and civil polity of the Spanish Arabs. But all these particulars, however pertinent to a philosophical history, would have been entirely out of keeping in Mr. Irving's, and might have produced a disagreeable discordance in the general harmony of his plan.

Mr. Irving has seldom selected a subject better suited to his peculiar powers than the conquest of Granada. Indeed, it would hardly have been possible for one of his warm sensibilities to linger so long among the remains of Moorish magnificence with which Spain is covered, without being interested in the fortunes of a people whose memory has almost passed into oblivion, but who once preserved the "sacred flame" when it had become extinct in every corner of Christendom, and whose influence is still visible on the intellectual culture of Modern Europe. It has been found no easy matter, however, to compile a satisfactory and authentic account of the Arabians, notwithstanding that the number of their historians, cited by D'Herbelot and Casiri, would appear to exceed that of any European nation. The despotic governments of the East have never been found propitious to that independence of opinion so essential to historical composition: "ubi sentire quæ velis, et quæ sentias dicere licet." And their copious compilations, prolific in frivolous and barren detail, are too often wholly destitute of the sap and vitality of history.

The social and moral institutions of Arabian Spain experienced a considerable modification from her long intercourse with the Europeans, and she offers a nobler field of research for the chronicler

4   K

than is to be found in any other country of the
Moslem. Notwithstanding this, the Castilian scholars, until of late, have done little towards elucidating
the national antiquities of their Saracen brethren;
and our most copious notices of their political history, until the recent posthumous publication of
Conde, have been drawn from the extracts which
M. Cardonne translated from the Arabic Manuscripts in the Royal Library at Paris.*

The most interesting periods of the Saracen do-
minion in Spain are that embraced by the empire
of the Omeyades of Cordova, between the years
755 and 1030, and that of the kingdom of Granada,
extending from the middle of the thirteenth to the
close of the fifteenth century. The intervening period of their existence in the Peninsula offers only a
spectacle of inextricable anarchy. The first of those
periods was that in which the Arabs attained their
meridian of opulence and power, and in which their
general illumination affords a striking contrast with
the deep barbarism of the rest of Europe; but it
was that, too, in which their character, having been
but little affected by contact with the Spaniards, retained most of its original Asiatic peculiarities. This
has never been regarded, therefore, by European
scholars, as a period of greatest interest in their his-

---

* [Since this article was written, the deficiency noticed in the text has
been supplied by the translation into English of Al-Makkarf's "Mohammedan Dynasties," with copious notes and illustrations by Don Pascual
de Gayangos, a scholar whose acute criticism has enabled him to rectify
many of the errors of his laborious predecessors, and whose profound
Oriental learning sheds a flood of light on both the civil and literary history of the Spanish Arabs.]

tory, nor has it ever, so far as we are aware, been selected for the purposes of romantic fiction. But when their territories became reduced within the limits of Granada, the Moors had insensibly submitted to the superior influences of their Christian neighbours. Their story, at this time, abounds in passages of uncommon beauty and interest. Their wars were marked by feats of personal prowess and romantic adventure, while the intervals of peace were abandoned to all the license of luxurious revelry. Their character, therefore, blending the various peculiarities of Oriental and European civilization, offers a rich study for the poet and the novelist. As such, it has been liberally employed by the Spaniards, and has not been altogether neglected by the writers of other nations. Thus Florian, whose sentiments, as well as his style, seem to be always floundering midway between the regions of prose and poetry, has made out of the story of this people his popular romance of "Gonsalvo of Cordova." It also forms the burden of an Italian epic, entitled "Il Conquista di Granata," by Girolamo Gratiani, a Florentine—much lauded by his countrymen. The ground, however, before the appearance of Mr. Irving, had not been occupied by any writer of eminence in the English language for the purposes either of romance or history.

The conquest of Granada, to which Mr. Irving has confined himself, so disastrous to the Moors, was one of the most brilliant achievements in the most brilliant period of Spanish history. Nothing is more usual than overweening commendations of antiquity; the "good old times," whose harsher features, like those of a rugged landscape, lose all their asperity in the distance. But the period of which we are speaking, embracing the reigns of Ferdinand and Isabella, at the close of the fifteenth and beginning of the sixteenth centuries, was undoubtedly that in which the Spanish nation displayed the fulness of its moral and physical energies, when, escaping from the license of a youthful age, it seems to have reached the prime of manhood and the perfect development of those faculties, whose overstrained exertions were soon to be followed by exhaustion and premature decrepitude.

The remnant of Spaniards, who, retreating to the mountains of the north, escaped the overwhelming inundation of the Saracens at the beginning of the eighth century, continued to cherish the free institutions of their Gothic ancestors. The "Fuero Juzgo," the ancient Visi-Gothic code, was still retained by the people of Castile and Leon, and may be said to form the basis of all their subsequent legislation, while in Aragon the dissolution of the primitive monarchy opened the way for even more liberal and equitable forms of government. The independence of character thus fostered by the peculiar constitutions of these petty states, was still farther promoted by the circumstances of their situation. Their uninterrupted wars with the infidel— the necessity of winning back from him, inch by inch, as it were, the conquered soil—required the active co-operation of every class of the community, and gave to the mass of the people an intrepidity, a personal consequence, and an extent of immunities, such as were not enjoyed by them in any other country of Europe. The free cities acquired considerable tracts of the reconquered territory, with rights of jurisdiction over them, and sent their representatives to Cortes, near a century before a similar privilege was conceded to them in England. Even the peasantry, so degraded, at this period, throughout the rest of Europe, assumed under this state of things a conscious dignity and importance, which are visible in their manners at this day ; and it was in this class, during the late French invasions, that the fire of ancient patriotism revived with greatest force, when it seemed almost extinct in the breasts of the degenerate nobles.

The religious feeling which mingled in their wars with the infidels, gave to their characters a tinge of lofty enthusiasm ; and the irregular nature of this warfare suggested abundant topics for that popular minstrelsy which acts so powerfully on the passions of a people. The "Poem of the Cid," which appeared, according to Sanchez, before the middle of the twelfth century, contributed, in no slight degree, by calling up the most inspiring national recollections, to keep alive the generous glow of patriotism. This influence is not imaginary. Heeren pronounces the "poems of Homer to have been the principal bond which united the Grecian states ;" and every one knows the influence exercised over the

Scottish peasantry by the Border minstrelsy. Many anecdotes might be quoted to show the veneration universally entertained by the Spaniards, broken, as they were, into as many discordant states as ever swarmed over Greece, for their favourite hero of ro mance and history. Among others, Mariana relates one of a king of Navarre, who, making an incursion into Castile about a century after the warrior's death, was carrying off a rich booty, when he was met by an abbot of a neighbouring convent, with his monks, bearing aloft the standard of the Cid, who implored him to restore the plunder to the inhabitants from whom he had ravished it. And the monarch, moved by the sight of the sacred relic, after complying with his request, escorted back the banner in solemn procession with his whole army to the place of its deposite.

But, while all these circumstances conspired to give an uncommon elevation to the character of the ancient Spaniard, even of the humblest rank, and while the prerogative of the monarch was more precisely as well as narrowly defined, than in most of the other nations of Christendom, the aristocracy of the country was insensibly extending its privileges, and laying the foundation of a power that eventually overshadowed the throne, and wellnigh subverted the liberties of the state. In addition to the usual enormous immunities claimed by this order in feudal governments (although there is no reason to believe that the system of feudal tenure obtained in Castile, as it certainly did in Aragon), they enjoyed a constitutional privilege of withdrawing their allegiance from their sovereign on sending him a forma notice of such renunciation, and the sovereign, on his part, was obliged to provide for the security of their estates and families so long as they might choose to continue in such overt rebellion. These anarchical provisions in their Constitution did not remain a dead letter, and repeated examples of their pernicious application are enumerated both by the historians of Aragon and Castile. The long minorities with which the latter country was afflicted, moreover, contributed still farther to swell the overgrown power of the privileged orders; and the violent revolution which, in 1368, placed the house of Trastamarre upon the throne, by impairing the revenues, and consequently the authority of the crown, opened the way for the wild uproar which reigned throughout the kingdom during the succeeding century. Alonso de Palencia, a contemporary chronicler, dwells with melancholy minuteness on the calamities of this unhappy period, when the whole country was split into factions of the nobles, the monarch openly contemned, the commons trodden in the dust, the court become a brothel, the treasury bankrupt, public faith a jest, and private morals too loose and audacious to court even the veil of hypocrisy.

The wise administration of Ferdinand and Isabella could alone have saved the state in this hour of peril. It effected, indeed, a change on the face of things as magical as that produced by the wand of an enchanter in some Eastern tale. Their reign wears a more glorious aspect from its contrast with the turbulent period which preceded it, as the landscape glows with redoubled brilliancy when the sunshine has scattered the tempest. We shall briefly notice some of the features of the policy by which they effected this change.

They obtained from the Cortes an act for the resumption of the improvident grants made by their predecessor, by which means an immense accession of revenue, which had been squandered upon unworthy favourites, was brought back to the royal treasury. They compelled many of the nobility to resign, in favour of the crown, such of its possessions as they had acquired by force, fraud, or intrigue, during the late season of anarchy. The son of that gallant Marquis Duke of Cadiz, for instance, with whom the reader has become so familiar in Mr. Irving's Chronicle, was stripped of his patrimony of Cadiz, and compelled to exchange it for the humbler territory of Arcos, from whence the family henceforth derived their title. By all these expedients, the revenues of the state, at the demise of Isabella, were increased twelvefold beyond what they had been at the time of her accession. They reorganized the ancient institution of the " Hermandad"—a very different association, under their hands, from the " Holy Brotherhood" which we meet with in Gil Blas. Every hundred householders were obliged to equip and maintain a horseman at their joint expense; and this corps furnished a vigilant police in civil emergencies, and an effectual aid in war. It was found, moreover, of especial service in suppressing the insurrections and disorders of the nobility. They were particularly solicitous to abolish the right and usage of private war, claimed by this haughty order, compelling them, on all occasions, to refer their disputes to the constituted tribunals of justice. But it was a capital feature in the policy of the Catholic sovereigns to counterbalance the authority of the aristocracy by exalting, as far as prudent, that of the commons. In the various convocations of the national Legislature, or Cortes, in this reign, no instance occurs of any city having lost its prescriptive right of furnishing representatives, as had frequently happened under preceding monarchs, who, from negligence or policy, had omitted to summon them.

But it would be tedious to go into all the details of the system employed by Ferdinand and Isabella for the regeneration of the decayed fabric of government; of their wholesome regulations for the encouragement of industry; of their organization of a national militia and an efficient marine; of the severe decorum which they introduced within the corrupt precincts of the court; of the temporary economy by which they controlled the public expenditures, and of the munificent patronage which they, or, rather, their almoner on this occasion, that most enlightened of bigots, Cardinal Ximenes, dispensed to science and letters. In short, their sagacious provisions were not merely remedial of former abuses, but were intended to call forth all the latent energies of the Spanish character, and, with these excellent materials, to erect a constitution of government which should secure to the nation tranquillity at home, and enable it to go forward in its ambitious career of discovery and conquest.

The results were certainly equal to the wisdom of the preparations. The first of the series of brilliant enterprises was the conquest of the Moorish kingdom of Granada—those rich and lovely regions of the Peninsula, the last retreat of the infidel, and which he had held for nearly eight centuries. This, together with the subsequent occupation of Navarre by the crafty Ferdinand, consolidated the various principalities of Spain into one monarchy, and, by extending its boundaries in the Peninsula to their present dimensions, raised it from a subordinate situation to the first class of European powers. The Italian wars, under the conduct of the "Great Captain," secured to Spain the more specious, but less useful acquisition of Naples, and formed that invincible infantry which enabled Charles the Fifth to dictate laws to Europe for nearly half a century. And, lastly, as if the Old World could not afford a theatre sufficiently vast for their ambition, Columbus gave a New World to Castile and Leon.

Such was the attitude assumed by the nation under the Catholic kings, as they were called. It was the season of hope and youthful enterprise, when the nation seemed to be renewing its ancient energies, and to prepare like a giant to run its course.

The modern Spaniard who casts his eye over the long interval that has since elapsed, during the first half of which the nation seemed to waste itself on schemes of mad ambition or fierce fanaticism, and, in the latter half to sink into a state of paralytic torpor—the Spaniard, we say, who casts a melancholy glance over this dreary interval, will turn with satisfaction to the close of the fifteenth century as the most glorious epoch in the annals of his country. This is the period to which Mr. Irving has introduced us in his late work. And if his portraiture of the Castilian of that day wears somewhat of a romantic, and, it may be, incredible aspect to those who contrast it with the present, they must remember that he is only reviving the tints which had faded on the canvass of history. But it is time that we should return from this long digression, into which we have been led by the desire of exhibiting in stronger relief some peculiarities in the situation and spirit of the nation at the period from which Mr. Irving has selected the materials of his last, indeed, his last two publications.

Our author, in his "Chronicle of Granada," has been but slightly indebted to Arabic authorities. Neither Conde nor Cardonne has expended more than fifty or sixty pages on this humiliating topic, but ample amends have been offered in the copious prolixity of the Castilian writers. The Spaniards can boast a succession of chronicles from the period of the great Saracen invasion. Those of a more early date, compiled in rude Latin, are sufficiently

meager and unsatisfactory; but from the middle of
the thirteenth century the stream of history runs full
and clear, and their chronicles, composed in the
vernacular, exhibit a richness and picturesque variety of incident that gave them inestimable value as
a body of genuine historical documents. The reigns
of Ferdinand and Isabella were particularly fruitful
in these sources of information. History then, like
most of the other departments of literature, seemed
to be in a state of transition, when the fashions of
its more antiquated costume began to mingle insensibly with the peculiarities of the modern; when, in
short, the garrulous graces of narration were beginning to be tempered by the tone of grave and philosophical reflection.

We will briefly notice a few of the eminent sources from which Mr. Irving has drawn his account of
the "Conquest of Granada." The first of these is
the Epistles of Peter Martyr, an Italian *savant*, who,
having passed over with the Spanish ambassador
into Spain, and being introduced into the court of
Isabella, was employed by her in some important
embassies. He was personally present at several
campaigns of this war. In his " Letters" he occasionally smiles at the caprice which had led him to
exchange the pen for the sword, while his speculations on the events passing before him, being those
of a scholar rather than of a soldier, afford in their
moral complexion a pleasing contrast to the dreary
details of blood and battle. Another authority is
the Chronicle of Bernaldez, a worthy ecclesiastic of

that period, whose bulky manuscript, like that of many a better writer, lies still ingulfed in the dust of some Spanish library, having never been admitted to the honours of the press. Copies of it, however, are freely circulated. It is one of those good-natured, gossiping memorials of an antique age, abounding equally in curious and commonplace incident, told in a way sufficiently prolix, but not without considerable interest. The testimony of this writer is of particular value, moreover, on this occasion, from the proximity of his residence in Andalusia to those scenes which were the seat of the war. His style overflows with that religious loyalty with which Mr. Irving has liberally seasoned the effusions of Fra Antonio Agapida. Hernando del Pulgar, another contemporary historian, was the secretary and counsellor of their Catholic majesties, and appointed by them to the post of national chronicler, an office familiar both to the courts of Castile and Aragon, in which latter country, especially, it has been occupied by some of its most distinguished historians. Pulgar's long residence at court, his practical acquaintance with affairs, and, above all, the access which he obtained, by means of his official station, to the best sources of information, have enabled him to make his work a rich repository of facts relating to the general resources of government, the policy of its administration, and, more particularly, the conduct of the military operations in the closing war of Granada, of which he was himself an eyewitness. In addition to these writers, this period

4   L

has been illumined by the labours of the most celebrated historians of Castile and Aragon, Mariana
and Zurita, both of whom conclude their narratives
with it, the last expanding the biography of Ferdinand alone into two volumes folio.   Besides these,
Mr. Irving has derived collateral lights from many
sources of inferior celebrity, but not less unsuspicious
credit.   So that, in conclusion, notwithstanding a
certain dramatic colouring which Fra Agapida's
" Chronicle" occasionally wears, and notwithstanding the romantic forms of a style which, to borrow
the language of Cicero, seems " to flow, as it were,
from the very lips of the Muses," we may honestly
recommend it as substantially an authentic record
of one of the most interesting, and, as far as English
scholars are concerned, one of the most untravelled
portions of Spanish history

CERVANTES.*

July, 1837.

The publication, in this country, of an important Spanish classic in the original, with a valuable commentary, is an event of some moment in our literary annals, and indicates a familiarity, rapidly increasing, with the beautiful literature to which it belongs. It may be received as an omen favourable to the cause of modern literature in general, the study of which, in all its varieties, may be urged on substantially the same grounds. The growing importance attached to this branch of education is visible in other countries quite as much as in our own. It is the natural, or, rather, necessary result of the changes which have taken place in the social relations of man in this revolutionary age. Formerly, a nation, pent up within its own barriers, knew less of its neighbours than we now know of what is going on in Siam or Japan. A river, a chain of mountains, an imaginary line, even, parted them as far asunder as if oceans had rolled between. To speak correctly, it was their imperfect civilization, their

* "*El Ingenioso Hidalgo Don Quijote de la Mancha*, compuesto por Miguel de Cervantes Saavedra. Nueva Edicion Clásica, illustrada con Notas Históricas, Grammaticales y Críticas, por la Academia Española, sus Individuos de Número Pellicer, Arrieta, y Clemencin. Emmendada y corregida por Francisco Sales, A.M., Instructor de Frances y Español en la Universidad de Harvard, en Cambrigia, Estado de Massachusetts, Norte América," 2 vols. 12mo, Boston, 1836.

ignorance of the means and the subjects of communication, which thus kept them asunder. Now, on the contrary, a change in the domestic institutions of one country can hardly be effected without a corresponding agitation in those of its neighbours. A treaty of alliance can scarcely be adjusted without the intervention of a general Congress. The sword cannot be unsheathed in one part of Christendom without thousands leaping from their scabbards in every other. The whole system is bound together by as nice sympathies as if animated by a common pulse, and the remotest countries of Europe are brought into contiguity as intimate as were in ancient times the provinces of a single monarchy.

This intimate association has been prodigiously increased of late years by the unprecedented discoveries which science has made for facilitating intercommunication. The inhabitant of Great Britain, that "ultima Thule" of the ancients, can now run down to the extremity of Italy in less time than it took Horace to go from Rome to Brundusium. A steamboat of fashionable tourists will touch at all the places of note in the Iliad and Odyssey in fewer weeks than it would have cost years to an ancient Argonaut, or a crusader of the Middle Ages. Every one, of course, travels, and almost every capital and noted watering-place on the Continent swarms with its thousands, and Paris with its tens of thousands of itinerant Cockneys, many of whom, perhaps, have not wandered beyond the sound of Bow bells in their own little island.

Few of these adventurers are so dull as not to be quickened into something like curiosity respecting the language and institutions of the strange people among whom they are thrown, while the better sort and more intelligent are led to study more carefully the new forms, whether in arts or letters, under which human genius is unveiled to them.

The effect of all this is especially visible in the reforms introduced into the modern systems of education. In both the universities recently established in London, the apparatus for instruction, instead of being limited to the ancient tongues, is extended to the whole circle of modern literature ; and the editorial labours of many of the professors show that they do not sleep on their posts. Periodicals, under the management of the ablest writers, furnish valuable contributions of foreign criticism and intelligence; and regular histories of the various Continental literatures, a department in which the English are singularly barren, are understood to be now in actual preparation.

But, although barren of literary, the English have made important contributions to the political history of the Continental nations. That of Spain has employed some of their best writers, who, it must be admitted, however, have confined themselves so far to the foreign relations of the country as to have left the domestic in comparative obscurity. Thus Robertson's great work is quite as much the history of Europe as of Spain under Charles the Fifth ; and Watson's " Reign of Philip the Second" might with equal propriety be styled " The War of the Netherlands," which is its principal burden.

A few works recently published in the United States have shed far more light on the interior organization and intellectual culture of the Spanish nation. Such, for example, are the writings of Irving, whose gorgeous colouring reflects so clearly the chivalrous splendours of the fifteenth century, and the travels of Lieutenant Slidell, presenting sketches equally animated of the social aspect of that most picturesque of all lands in the present century. In Mr. Cushing's "Reminiscences of Spain" we find, mingled with much characteristic fiction, some very laborious inquiries into curious and recondite points of history. In the purely literary department, Mr. Ticknor's beautiful lectures before the classes of Harvard University, still in manuscript, embrace a far more extensive range of criticism than is to be found in any Spanish work, and display, at the same time, a degree of thoroughness and research which the comparative paucity of materials will compel us to look for in vain in Bouterwek or Sismondi. Mr. Ticknor's successor, Professor Longfellow, favourably known by other compositions, has enriched our language with a noble version of the ' Coplas de Manrique," the finest gem, beyond all comparison, in the Castilian verse of the fifteenth century. We have also read with pleasure a clever translation of Quevedo's " Visions," no very easy achievement, by Mr. Elliot, of Philadelphia, though the translator is wrong in supposing his the first Eng-

lish version. The first is as old as Queen Anne's
time, and was made by the famous Sir Roger
L'Estrange. To close the account, Mr. Sales, the
venerable instructer in Harvard College, has now
given, for the first time in the New World, an elaborate edition of the prince of Castilian classics, in a
form which may claim, to a certain extent, the merit
of originality.

We shall postpone the few remarks we have to
make on this edition to the close of our article; and,
in the mean time, we propose, not to give the life of
Cervantes, but to notice such points as are least familiar in his literary history, and especially in regard
to the composition and publication of his great work,
the Don Quixote; a work which, from its wide and
long-established popularity, may be said to constitute part of the literature, not merely of Spain, but
of every country in Europe.

The age of Cervantes was that of Philip the Second, when the Spanish monarchy, declining somewhat from its palmy state, was still making extraordinary efforts to maintain, and even to extend its already overgrown empire. Its navies were on every
sea, and its armies in every quarter of the Old World
and in the New. Arms was the only profession
worthy of a gentleman; and there was scarcely a
writer of any eminence—certainly no bard—of the
age, who, if he were not in orders, had not borne
arms, at some period, in the service of his country.
Cervantes, who, though poor, was born of an ancient family (it must go hard with a Castilian who

cannot make out a pedigree for himself), had a full measure of this chivalrous spirit, and, during the first half of his life, we find him in the midst of all the stormy and disastrous scenes of the iron trade of war. His love of the military profession, even after the loss of his hand, or of the use of it, for it is uncertain which, is sufficient proof of his adventurous spirit. In the course of his checkered career he visited the principal countries in the Mediterranean, and passed five years in melancholy captivity at Algiers. The time was not lost, however, which furnished his keen eye with those glowing pictures of Moslem luxury and magnificence with which he has enriched his pages. After a life of unprecedented hardship, he returned to his own country, covered with laurels and scars, with very little money in his pocket, but with plenty of that experience which, regarding him as a novelist, might be considered his stock in trade.

The poet may draw from the depths of his own fancy; the scholar from his library; but the proper study of the dramatic writer, whether in verse or in prose, is man—man, as he exists in society. He who would faithfully depict human character cannot study it too nearly and variously. He must sit down, like Scott, by the fireside of the peasant, and listen to the "auld wife's" tale; he must preside, with Fielding, at a petty justice Sessions, or share with some Squire Western in the glorious hazards of a foxhunt; he must, like Smollett and Cooper, study the mysteries of the deep, and mingle on the stormy element itself with the singular beings whose destinies he is to describe ; or, like Cervantes, he must wander among other races and in other climes before his pencil can give those chameleon touches which reflect the shifting, many-coloured hues of actual life. He may, indeed, like Rousseau, if it were possible to imagine another Rousseau, turn his thoughts inward, and draw from the depths of his own soul ; but he would see there only his own individual passions and prejudices, and the portraits he might sketch, however various in subordinate details, would be, in their characteristic features, only the reproduction of himself. He might, in short, be a poet, a philosopher, but not a painter of life and manners.

Cervantes had ample means for pursuing the study of human character, after his return to Spain, in the active life which engaged him in various parts of the country. In Andalusia he might have found the models of the sprightly wit and delicate irony with which he has seasoned his fictions; in Seville, in particular, he was brought in contact with the fry of small sharpers and pickpockets, who make so respectable a figure in his *picaresco* novels; and in La Mancha he not only found the geography of his Don Quixote, but that whimsical contrast of pride and poverty in the natives, which has furnished the outlines of many a broad caricature to the comic writers of Spain.

During all this while he had made himself known only by his pastoral fiction, the "Galatea," a beau-

R

tiful specimen of an insipid class, which, with all its literary merits, afforded no scope for the power of depicting human character, which he possessed, perhaps, unknown to himself. He wrote, also, a good number of plays, all of which, except two, and these recovered only at the close of the last century, have perished. One of these, " The Siege of Numantia," displays that truth of drawing and strength of colour which mark the consummate artist. It was not until he had reached his fifty-seventh year that he completed the First Part of his great work, the Don Quixote. The most celebrated novels, unlike most works of imagination, seem to have been the production of the later period of life. Fielding was between forty and fifty when he wrote " Tom Jones." Richardson was sixty, or very near it, when he wrote " Clarissa ;" and Scott was some years over forty when he began the series of the Waverley novels. The world, the school of the novelist, cannot be run through like the terms of a university, and the knowledge of its manifold varieties must be the result of long and diligent training.

The First Part of the Quixote was begun, as the author tells us, in a prison, to which he had been brought, not by crime or debt, but by some offence, probably, to the worthy people of La Mancha. It is not the only work of genius which has struggled into being in such unfavourable quarters. The "Pilgrim's Progress," the most popular, probably, of English fictions, was composed under similar circumstances. But we doubt if such brilliant fancies and such flashes of humour ever lighted up the walls of the prison-house before the time of Cervantes.

The First Part of the Don Quixote was given to the public in 1605. Cervantes, when the time arrived for launching his satire against the old, deep-rooted prejudices of his countrymen, probably regarded it, as well he might, as little less rash than his own hero's tilt against the windmills. He sought, accordingly, to shield himself under the cover of a powerful name, and asked leave to dedicate the book to a Castilian grandee, the Duke de Bejar. The duke, it is said, whether ignorant of the design, or doubting the success of the work, would have declined, but Cervantes urged him first to peruse a single chapter. The audience summoned to sit in judgment were so delighted with the first pages, that they would not abandon the novel till they had heard the whole of it. The duke, of course, without farther hesitation, condescended to allow his name to be inserted in this passport to immortality.

There is nothing very improbable in the story. It reminds one of a similar experiment by St. Pierre, who submitted his manuscript of " Paul and Virginia" to a circle of French *littérateurs*, Monsieur and Madame Necker, the Abbé Galiani, Thomas, Buffon, and some others, all wits of the first water in the metropolis. Hear the result, in the words of his biographer, or, rather, his agreeable translator: " At first the author was heard in silence; by degrees the attention grew languid; they began to whisper, to gape, and listened no longer. M. de

Buffon looked at his watch, and called for his horses; those near the door slipped out; Thomas went to sleep; M. Necker laughed to see the ladies weep; and the ladies, ashamed of their tears, did not dare to confess that they had been interested. The reading being finished, nothing was praised. Madame Necker alone criticised the conversation of Paul and the old man. This *moral* appeared to her tedious and commonplace; it broke the action, chilled the reader, and was a sort of *glass of iced water*. M. de St. Pierre retired in a state of indescribable depression. He regarded what had passed as his sentence of death. The effect of his work on an audience like that to which he had read it left him no hope for the future." Yet this work was "Paul and Virginia," one of the most popular books in the French language. So much for criticism!

The truth seems to be, that the judgment of no private circle, however well qualified by taste and talent, can afford a sure prognostic of that of the great public. If the manuscript to be criticised is our friend's, of course the verdict is made up before perusal. If some great man modestly sues for our approbation, our self-complacency has been too much flattered for us to withhold it. If it be a little man (and St. Pierre was but a little man at that time), our prejudices—the prejudices of poor human nature—will be very apt to take an opposite direction. Be the cause what it may, whoever rests his hopes of public favour on the smiles of a *coterie* runs the risk of finding himself very unpleasantly deceived. Many a trim bark which has flaunted gayly in a summer lake has gone to pieces amid the billows and breakers of the rude ocean.

The prognostic, in the case of Cervantes, however, proved more correct. His work produced an instantaneous effect on the community. He had struck a note which found an echo in every bosom. Four editions were published in the course of the first year; two in Madrid, one in Valencia, and another at Lisbon.

This success, almost unexampled in any age, was still more extraordinary in one in which the reading public was comparatively limited. That the book found its way speedily into the very highest circles in the kingdom is evident from the well-known explanation of Philip the Third, when he saw a student laughing immoderately over some volume: " The man must be either out of his wits, or reading Don Quixote." Notwithstanding this, its author felt none of that sunshine of royal favour which would have been so grateful in his necessities.

The period was that of the golden prime of Castilian literature. But the monarch on the throne, one of the ill-starred dynasty of Austria, would have been better suited to the darkest of the Middle Ages. His hours, divided between his devotions and his debaucheries, left nothing to spare for letters ; and his minister, the arrogant Duke of Lerma, was too much absorbed by his own selfish, though shallow schemes of policy, to trouble himself with romance

4   M

writers, or their satirist. Cervantes, however, had entered on a career which, as he intimates in some of his verses, might lead to fame, but not to fortune. Happily, he did not compromise his fame by precipitating the execution of his works from motives of temporary profit. It was not till several years after the publication of the Don Quixote that he gave to the world his Exemplary Novels, as he called them; fictions which, differing from anything before known, not only in the Castilian, but, in some respects, in any other literature, gave ample scope to his dramatic talent, in the contrivance of situations, and the nice delineation of character. These works, whose diction was uncommonly rich and attractive, were popular from the first.

One cannot but be led to inquire why, with such success as an author, he continued to be so straitened in his circumstances, as he plainly intimates was the case more than once in his writings. From the Don Quixote, notwithstanding its great run, he probably received little, since he had parted with the entire copyright before publication, when the work was regarded as an experiment, the result of which was quite doubtful. It is not so easy to explain the difficulty, when his success as an author had been so completely established. Cervantes intimates his dissatisfaction, in more than one place in his writings, with the booksellers themselves. " What, sir !" replies an author introduced into his Don Quixote, " would you have me sell the profit of my labour to a bookseller for three maravedis a sheet? for that is the most they will bid, nay, and expect, too, I should thank them for the offer." This burden of lamentation, the alleged illiberality of the publisher towards the poor author, is as old as the art of book-making itself. But the public receive the account from the party aggrieved only. If the bookseller reported his own case, we should, no doubt, have a different version. If Cervantes was in the right, the trade in Castile showed a degree of dexterity in their proceedings which richly entitled them to the pillory. In one of his tales, we find a certain licentiate complaining of "the tricks and deceptions they put upon an author when they buy a copyright from him; and still more, the manner in which they cheat him if he prints the book at his own charges; since nothing is more common than for them to agree for fifteen hundred, and have privily, perhaps, as many as three thousand thrown off, one half, at the least, of which they sell, not for his profit, but their own.

The writings of Cervantes appear to have gained him, however, two substantial friends in Cabra, the Count of Lemos, and the Archbishop of Toledo, of the ancient family of Rojas; and the patronage of these illustrious individuals has been nobly recompensed by having their names forever associated with the imperishable productions of genius.

There was still one kind of patronage wanting in this early age, that of a great, enlightened community—the only patronage which can be received without some sense of degradation by a generous mind. There was, indeed, one golden channel of public favour, and that was the theatre. The drama has usually flourished most at the period when a nation is beginning to taste the sweets of literary culture. Such was the early part of the seventeenth century in Europe; the age of Shakspeare, Jonson, and Fletcher in England; of Ariosto, Machiavelli, and the wits who first successfully wooed the comic muse of Italy; of the great Corneille, some years later, in France; and of that miracle, or, rather, "monster of nature," as Cervantes styled him, Lope de Vega in Spain. Theatrical exhibitions are a combination of the material with the intellectual, at which the ordinary spectator derives less pleasure, probably, from the beautiful creations of the poet than from the scenic decorations, music, and other accessories which address themselves to the senses The fondness for *spectacle* is characteristic of an early period of society, and the theatre is the most brilliant of pageants. With the progress of education and refinement, men become less open to, or, at least, less dependant on the pleasures of sense, and seek their enjoyment in more elevated and purer sources. Thus it is that, instead of

> "Sweating in the crowded theatre, squeezed
> And bored with elbow-points through both our sides,"

as the sad minstrel of nature sings, we sit quietly at home, enjoying the pleasures of fiction around our own firesides, and the poem or the novel takes the place of the acted drama. The decline of dramatic writing may justly be lamented as that of one of the most beautiful varieties in the garden of literature. But it must be admitted to be both a symptom and a necessary consequence of the advance of civilization.

The popularity of the stage, at the period of which we are speaking, in Spain, was greatly augmented by the personal influence and reputation of Lope de Vega, the idol of his countrymen, who threw off the various inventions of his genius with a rapidity and profusion that almost staggers credibility. It is impossible to state the results of his labours in any form that will not powerfully strike the imagination. Thus, he has left 21,300,000 verses in print, besides a mass of manuscript. He furnished the theatre, according to the statement of his intimate friend, Montalvan, with 1800 regular plays, and 400 *autos* or religious dramas—all acted. He composed, according to his own statement, more than 100 comedies in the almost incredible space of twenty-four hours each, and a comedy averaged between two and three thousand verses, great part of them rhymed and interspersed with sonnets and other more difficult forms of versification. He lived seventy-two years; and supposing him to have employed fifty of that period in composition, although he filled a variety of engrossing vocations during that time, he must have averaged a play a week, to say nothing of twenty-one volumes quarto of miscellaneous works, including five epics, written in his leisure moments, and all now in print!

4   M*

The only achievements we can recall in literary history bearing any resemblance to, though falling far short of this, are those of our illustrious contemporary, Sir Walter Scott. The complete edition of his works, recently advertised by Murray, with the addition of two volumes, of which Murray has not the copyright, probably contains ninety volumes small octavo. To these should farther be added a large supply of matter for the Edinburgh Annual Register, as well as other anonymous contributions. Of these, forty-eight volumes of novels and twenty-one of history and biography were produced between 1814 and 1831, or in seventeen years. These would give an average of four volumes a year, or one for every three months during the whole of that period, to which must be added twenty-one volumes of poetry and prose previously published. The mere mechanical execution of so much work, both in his case and Lope de Vega's, would seem to be scarce possible in the limits assigned. Scott, too, was as variously occupied in other ways as his Spanish rival, and probably, from the social hospitality of his life, spent a much larger portion of his time in no literary occupation at all.

Notwithstanding we have amused ourselves, at the expense of the reader's patience perhaps, with these calculations, this certainly is not the standard by which we should recommend to estimate works of genius. Wit is not to be measured, like broadcloth, by the yard. Easy writing, as the adage says, and as we all know, is apt to be very hard reading.

This brings to our recollection a conversation, in the presence of Captain Basil Hall, in which some allusion having been made to the astonishing amount of Scott's daily composition, the literary argonaut remarked, "There was nothing astonishing in all that, and that he did as much himself nearly every day before breakfast." Some one of the company unkindly asked "whether he thought the *quality* was the same." It is the quality, undoubtedly, which makes the difference. And in this view Lope de Vega's miracles lose much of their effect. Of all his multitudinous dramas, one or two only retain possession of the stage, and few, very few are now even read. His facility of composition was like that of an Italian improvisatore, whose fertile fancy easily clothes itself in verse, in a language the vowel terminations of which afford such a plenitude of rhymes. The Castilian presents even greater facilities for this than the Italian. Lope de Vega was an improvisatore.

With all his negligences and defects, however, Lope's interesting intrigues, easy, sprightly dialogue, infinite variety of inventions, and the breathless rapidity with which they followed one another, so dazzled and bewildered the imagination, that he completely controlled the public, and became, in the words of Cervantes, "sole monarch of the stage." The public repaid him with such substantial gratitude as has never been shown, probably, to any other of its favourites. His fortune at one time, although he was careless of his expenses, amounted to one hundred thousand ducats, equal, probably, to between seven and eight hundred thousand dollars of the present day. In the same street in which dwelt this spoiled child of fortune, who, amid the caresses of the great, and the lavish smiles of the public, could complain that his merits were neglected, lived Cervantes, struggling under adversity, or at least earning a painful subsistence by the labours of his immortal pen. What a contrast do these pictures present to the imagination! If the suffrages of a *coterie*, as we have said, afford no warrant for those of the public, the example before us proves that the award of one's contemporaries is quite as likely to be set aside by posterity. Lope de Vega, who gave his name to his age, has now fallen into neglect even among his countrymen, while the fame of Cervantes, gathering strength with time, has become the pride of his own nation, as his works still continue to be the delight of the whole civilized world.

However stinted may have been the recompense of his deserts at home, it is gratifying to observe how widely his fame was diffused in his own lifetime, and that in foreign countries, at least, he enjoyed the full consideration to which he was entitled. An interesting anecdote illustrating this is recorded, which, as we have never seen it in English, we will lay before the reader. On occasion of a visit made by the Archbishop of Toledo to the French ambassador, resident at Madrid, the prelate's suite fell into conversation with the attendants of the minister, in the course of which Cervantes was mentioned. The

French gentlemen expressed their unqualified admiration of his writings, specifying the Galatea, Don Quixote, and the Novels, which, they said, were read in all the countries round, and in France particularly, where there were some who might be said to know them actually by heart. They intimated their desire to become personally acquainted with so eminent a man, and asked many questions respecting his present occupations, his circumstances, and way of life. To all this the Castilians could only reply that he had borne arms in the service of his country, and was now old and poor. "What!" exclaimed one of the strangers, "is Señor Cervantes not in good circumstances? Why is he not maintained, then, out of the public treasury?" "Heaven forbid," rejoined another, "that his necessities should be ever relieved, if it is these which make him write, since it is his poverty that makes the world rich."

There are other evidences, though not of so pleasing a character, of the eminence which he had reached at home in the jealousy and ill will of his brother poets. The Castilian poets of that day seem to have possessed a full measure of that irritability which has been laid at the door of all their tribe since the days of Horace; and the freedom of Cervantes's literary criticisms, in his Don Quixote and other writings, though never personal in their character, brought down on his head a storm of arrows, some of which, if not sent with much force, were, at least, well steeped in venom. Lope de Vega is even said to have appeared among the assailants, and a sonnet, still preserved, is currently imputed to him, in which, after much eulogy on himself, he predicts that the works of his rival will find their way into the kennel. But the author of this bad prophecy and worse poetry could never have been the great Lope, who showed, on all occasions, a generous spirit, and whose literary success must have made such an assault unnecessary, and in the highest degree unmanly. On the contrary, we have evidence of a very different feeling, in the homage which he renders to the merits of his illustrious contemporary, in more than one passage of his acknowledged works, especially in his "Laurel de Apolo," in which he concludes his poetical panegyric with the following touching conceit :

> "Porque se diga que una mano herida,
> Pudo dar á su dueño eterna vida."

This poem was published by Lope in 1630, fourteen years after the death of his rival ; notwithstanding, Mr. Lockhart informs his readers, in his biographical preface to the Don Quixote, that "as Lope de Vega was dead (1615), there was no one to divide with Cervantes the literary empire of his country."

In the dedication of his ill-fated comedies, 1615 (for Cervantes, like most other celebrated novelists, found it difficult to concentrate his expansive vein within the compass of dramatic rules), the public was informed that "Don Quixote was already booted," and preparing for another sally. It may seem strange that the author, considering the great popu larity of his hero, had not sent him on his adventures before. But he had probably regarded them as already terminated; and he had good reason to do so, since every incident in the First Part, as it has been styled only since the publication of the Second, is complete in itself, and the Don, although not actually killed on the stage, is noticed as dead, and his epitaph transcribed for the reader. However this may be, the immediate execution of his purpose, so long delayed, was precipitated by an event equally unwelcome and unexpected. This was the continuation of his work by another hand.

The author's name, his *nom de guerre*, was Avellaneda, a native of Tordesillas. Adopting the original idea of Cervantes, he goes forward with the same characters, through similar scenes of comic extravagance, in the course of which he perpetrates sundry plagiarisms from the First Part, and has some incidents so much resembling those in the Second Part, already written by Cervantes, that it has been supposed he must have had access to his manuscript. It is more probable, as the resemblance is but general, that he obtained his knowledge through hints, which may have fallen in conversation, from Cervantes, in the progress of his own work. The spurious continuation had some little merit, and attracted, probably, some interest, as any work conducted under so popular a name could not have failed to do. It was, however, on the whole, a vulgar performance, thickly sprinkled with such gross scurrility and indecency, as was too strong even for the palate of that not very fastidious age. The public feeling may be gathered from the fact that the author did not dare to depart from his incognito, and claim the honours of a triumph. The most diligent inquiries have established nothing farther than that he was an Aragonese, judging from his diction, and from the complexion of certain passages in the work probably an ecclesiastic, and one of the swarm of small dramatists, who felt themselves rudely handled by the criticism of Cervantes. The work was subsequently translated, or rather paraphrased, by Le Sage, who has more than once given a substantial value to gems of little price in Castilian literature by the brilliancy of his setting. The original work of Avellaneda, always deriving an interest from the circumstances of its production, has been reprinted in the present century, and is not difficult to be met with. To have thus coolly invaded an author's own property, to have filched from him the splendid, though unfinished creations of his genius, before his own face, and while, as was publicly known, he was in the very process of completing them, must be admitted to be an act of unblushing effrontery, not surpassed in the annals of literature.

Cervantes was much annoyed, it appears, by the circumstance. The continuation of Avellaneda reached him, probably, when on the fifty-ninth chapter of the Second Part. At least, from that time he begins to discharge his gall on the head of the offender, who, it should be added, had consummated his impudence by sneering, in his introduction, at the qualifications of Cervantes. The best retort of the latter, however, was the publication of his own book, which followed at the close of 1615.

The English novelist, Richardson, experienced a treatment not unlike that of the Castilian. His popular story of Pamela was continued by another and very inferior hand, under the title of "Pamela in High Life." The circumstance prompted Richardson to undertake the continuation himself; and it turned out, like most others, a decided failure. Indeed, a skilful continuation seems to be the most difficult work of art. The first effort of the author breaks, as it were, unexpectedly on the public, taking their judgments by surprise, and by its very success creating a standard by which the author himself is subsequently to be tried. Before, he was compared with others; he is now to be compared with himself. The public expectation has been raised. A degree of excellence, which might have found favour at first, will now scarcely be tolerated. It will not even suffice for him to maintain his own level. He must rise above himself. The reader, in the mean while, has naturally filled up the blank, and insensibly conducted the characters and the story to a termination in his own way. As the reality seldom keeps pace with the ideal, the author's execution will hardly come up to the imagination of his readers; at any rate, it will differ from them, and so far be displeasing. We experience something of this disappointment in the dramas borrowed from popular novels, where the development of the char-

4   N

acters by the dramatic author, and the new direction given to the original story in his hands, rarely fail to offend the taste and preconceived ideas of the spectator. To feel the force of this, it is only necessary to see the Guy Mannering, Rob Roy and other plays dramatized from the Waverley novels.

Some part of the failure of such continuations is no doubt, fairly chargeable, in most instances, on the author himself, who goes to his new task with little of his primitive buoyancy and vigour. He no longer feels the same interest in his own labours, which, losing their freshness, have become as familiar to his imagination as a thrice-told tale. The new composition has, of course, a different complexion from the former, cold, stiff, and disjointed, like a bronze statue, whose parts have been separately put together, instead of being cast in one mould when the whole metal was in a state of fusion.

The continuation of Cervantes forms a splendid exception to the general rule. The popularity of his First Part had drawn forth abundance of criticism, and he availed himself of it to correct some material blemishes in the design of the Second, while an assiduous culture of the Castilian enabled him to enrich his style with greater variety and beauty.

He had now reached the zenith of his fame, and the profits of his continuation may have relieved the pecuniary embarrassments under which he had struggled. But he was not long to enjoy his

triumph. Before his death, which took place in
the following year, he completed his romance of
" Persiles and Sigismunda," the dedication to which,
written a few days before his death, is strongly characteristic of its writer. It is addressed to his old
patron, the Conde de Lemos, then absent from the
country. After saying, in the words of the old
Spanish proverb, that he had "*one foot in the stir-
rup*," in allusion to the distant journey on which he
was soon to set out, he adds, " Yesterday I received
the extreme unction ; but, now that the shadows of
death are closing around me, I still cling to life,
from the love of it, as well as from the desire to behold you again. But if it is decreed otherwise (and
the will of Heaven be done), your excellency will
at least feel assured there was one person whose
wish to serve you was greater than the love of life
itself." After these reminiscences of his benefactor
he expresses his own purpose, should life be spared,
to complete several works he had already begun.
Such were the last words of this illustrious man ;
breathing the same generous sensibility, the same
ardent love of letters, and beautiful serenity of temper which distinguished him through life. He died
a few days after, on the 23d of April, 1616. His
remains were laid, without funeral pomp, in the monastery of the Holy Trinity at Madrid. No memorial points out the spot to the eye of the traveller,
nor is it known at this day. And, while many a
costly construction has been piled on the ashes of
the little great, to the shame of Spain be it spoken,

no monument has yet been erected in honour of the greatest genius she has produced. He has built, however, a monument for himself more durable than brass or sculptured marble.

Don Quixote is too familiar to the reader to require any analysis; but we will enlarge on a few circumstances attending its composition but little known to the English scholar, which may enable him to form a better judgment for himself. The age of chivalry, as depicted in romances, could never, of course, have had any real existence; but the sentiments which are described as animating that age have been found more or less operative in different countries and different periods of society. In Spain, especially, this influence is to be discerned from a very early date. Its inhabitants may be said to have lived in a romantic atmosphere, in which all the extravagances of chivalry were nourished by their peculiar situation. Their hostile relations with the Moslem kept alive the full glow of religious and patriotic feeling. Their history is one interminable crusade. An enemy always on the borders, invited perpetual displays of personal daring and adventure. The refinement and magnificence of the Spanish Arabs throw a lustre over these contests, such as could not be reflected from the rude skirmishes with their Christian neighbours. Lofty sentiments, embellished by the softer refinements of courtesy, were blended in the martial bosom of the Spaniard, and Spain became emphatically the land of romantic chivalry.

The very laws themselves, conceived in this spirit, contributed greatly to foster it. The ancient code of Alfonso the Tenth, in the thirteenth century, after many minute regulations for the deportment of the good knight, enjoins on him to "invoke the name of his mistress in the fight, that it may infuse new ardour into his soul, and preserve him from the commission of unknightly actions." Such laws were not a dead letter. The history of Spain shows that the sentiment of romantic gallantry penetrated the nation more deeply, and continued longer than in any other quarter of Christendom.

Foreign chroniclers, as well as domestic, of the fifteenth and sixteenth centuries, notice the frequent appearance of Spanish knights in different courts of Europe, whither they had travelled, in the language of an old writer, "to seek honour and reverence" by their feats of arms. In the Paston Letters, written in the time of Henry the Sixth of England, we find a notice of a Castilian knight who presented himself before the court, and, with his mistress's favour around his arm, challenged the English cavaliers "to run a course of sharp spears with him for his sovereign lady's sake." Pulgar, a Spanish chronicler of the close of the sixteenth century, speaks of this roving knight-errantry as a thing of familiar occurrence among the young cavaliers of his day; and Oviedo, who lived somewhat later, notices the necessity under which every true knight found himself, of being in love, or *feigning to be so*, in order to give a suitable lustre and incentive to his achievements. But the most singular proof of the extravagant pitch to which these romantic feelings were carried in Spain occurs in the account of the jousts appended to the fine old chronicle of Alvaro de Luna, published by the Academy in 1784. The principal champion was named Sueño de Quenones, who, with nine companions in arms, defended a pass at Orbigo, not far from the shrine of Compostella, against all comers, in the presence of King John the Second and his court. The object of this passage of arms, as it was called, was to release the knight from the obligation imposed on him by his mistress, of publicly wearing an iron collar round his neck every Thursday. The jousts continued for thirty days, and the doughty champions fought without shield or target, with weapons bearing points of Milan steel. Six hundred and twenty-seven encounters took place, and one hundred and sixty-six lances were broken, when the emprise was declared to be fairly achieved. The whole affair is narrated, with becoming gravity, by an eyewitness, and the reader may fancy himself perusing the adventures of a Launcelot or an Amadis. The particulars of this tourney are detailed at length in Mills's Chivalry (vol. ii., chap. v.), where, however, the author has defrauded the successful champions of their full honours by incorrectly reporting the number of lances broken as only sixty-six.

The taste for these romantic extravagances naturally fostered a corresponding taste for the perusal of tales of chivalry. Indeed, they acted reciprocally on each other. These chimerical legends had once, also, beguiled the long evenings of our Norman ancestors; but, in the progress of civilization, had gradually given way to other and more natural forms of composition. They still maintained their ground in Italy, whither they had passed later, and where they were consecrated by the hand of genius. But Italy was not the true soil of chivalry, and the inim itable fictions of Bojardo, Pulci, and Ariosto were composed with that lurking smile of half-suppressed mirth which, far from a serious tone, could raise only a corresponding smile of incredulity in the reader.

In Spain, however, the marvels of romance were all taken in perfect good faith. Not that they were received as literally true; but the reader surrendered himself up to the illusion, and was moved to admiration by the recital of deeds which, viewed in any other light than as a wild frolic of imagination, would be supremely ridiculous; for these tales had not the merit of a seductive style and melodious versification to relieve them. They were, for the most part, an ill-digested mass of incongruities, in which there was as little keeping and probability in the characters as in the incidents, while the whole was told in that stilted "Hercles' vein," and with that licentiousness of allusion and imagery which could not fail to debauch both the taste and the morals of the youthful reader. The mind, familiarized with these monstrous, over-coloured pictures, lost all relish for the chaste and sober productions of art. The love of the gigantic and the marvellous indisposed the reader for the simple delineations of truth in real history. The feelings expressed by a sensible Spaniard of the sixteenth century, the anonymous author of the " Dialogo de las Lenguas," probably represent those of many of his contemporaries. " Ten of the best years of my life," says he, " were spent no more profitably than in devouring these lies, which I did even while eating my meals; and the consequence of this depraved appetite was, that if I took in hand any true book of history, or one that passed for such, I was unable to wade through it."

The influence of this meretricious taste was nearly as fatal on the historian himself as on his readers, since he felt compelled to minister to the public appetite such a mixture of the marvellous in all his narrations as materially discredited the veracity of his writings. Every hero became a demigod, who put the labours of Hercules to shame ; and every monk or old hermit was converted into a saint, who wrought more miracles, before and after death, than would have sufficed to canonize a monastery. The fabulous ages of Greece are scarcely more fabulous than the close of the Middle Ages in Spanish history, which compares very discreditably, in this particular, with similar periods in most European countries. The confusion of fact and fiction continues to a very late age ; and as one gropes his way through the twilight of tradition, he is at a loss whether the dim objects are men or shadows. The most splendid names in Castilian annals—names incorporated with the glorious achievements of the land, and embalmed alike in the page of the chronicler and the song of the minstrel—names associated with the most stirring, patriotic recollections—are now found to have been the mere coinage of fancy. There seems to be no more reason for believing in the real existence of Bernardo del Carpio, of whom so much has been said and sung, than in that of Charlemagne's paladins, or of the Knights of the Round Table. Even the Cid, the national hero of Spain, is contended, by some of the shrewdest native critics of our own times, to be an imaginary being; and it is certain that the splendid fabric of his exploits, familiar as household words to every Spaniard, has crumbled to pieces under the rude touch of modern criticism. These heroes, it is true, flourished before the introduction of romances of chivalry; but the legends of their prowess have been multiplied beyond bounds, in consequence of the taste created by these romances, and an easy faith accorded to them at the same time, such as would never have been conceded in any other civilized nation. In short, the elements of truth and falsehood became so blended, that history was converted into romance, and romance received the credit due only to history.

These mischievous consequences drew down the animadversions of thinking men, and at length provoked the interference of government itself. In 1543, Charles the Fifth, by an edict, prohibited books of chivalry from being imported into his Ameri-

U

can colonies, or being printed, or even read there. The legislation for America proceeded from the crown alone, which had always regarded the New World as its own exclusive property. In 1555, however, the Cortes of the kingdom presented a *petition* (which requires only the royal signature to become at once the law), setting forth the manifold evils resulting from these romances. There is an air at once both of simplicity and solemnity in the language of this instrument which may amuse the reader: "Moreover, we say that it is very notorious what mischief has been done to young men and maidens, and other persons, by the perusal of books full of lies and vanities, like Amadis, and works of that description, since young people especially, from their natural idleness, resort to this kind of reading, and, becoming enamoured of passages of love or arms, or other nonsense which they find set forth therein, when situations at all analogous offer, are led to act much more extravagantly than they otherwise would have done. And many times the daughter, when her mother has locked her up safely at home, amuses herself with reading these books, which do her more hurt than she would have received from going abroad. All which redounds, not only to the dishonour of individuals, but to the great detriment of conscience, by diverting the affections from holy, true, and Christian doctrine, to those wicked vanities with which the wits, as we have intimated, are completely bewildered. To remedy this, we entreat your majesty that no book treating of such matters be henceforth permitted to be read, that those now printed be collected and burned, and that none be published hereafter without special license; by which measures your majesty will render great service to God as well as to these kingdoms," &c., &c.

Notwithstanding this emphatic expression of public disapprobation, these enticing works maintained their popularity. The Emperor Charles, unmindful of his own interdict, took great satisfaction in their perusal. The royal *fêtes* frequently commemorated the fabulous exploits of chivalry, and Philip the Second, then a young man, appeared in these spectacles in the character of an adventurous knight-errant. Moratin enumerates more than seventy bulky romances, all produced in the sixteenth century, some of which passed through several editions, while many more works of the kind have, doubtless, escaped his researches. The last on his catalogue was printed in 1602, and was composed by one of the nobles at the court. Such was the state of things when Cervantes gave to the world the First Part of his Don Quixote; and it was against prejudices which had so long bade defiance to public opinion and the law itself that he now aimed the delicate shafts of his irony. It was a perilous emprise.

To effect his end, he did not produce a mere humorous travesty, like several of the Italian poets, who, having selected some well-known character in romance, make him fall into such low dialogue and such gross buffoonery as contrast most ridiculously

with his assumed name; for this, though a very good
jest in its way, was but a jest, and Cervantes wanted the biting edge of satire. He was, besides, too
much of a poet—was too deeply penetrated with
the true spirit of chivalry not to respect the noble
·qualities which were the basis of it. He shows this
in the *auto da fé* of the Don's library, where he spares
the Amadis de Gaula and some others, the best of
their kind. He had once himself, as he tells us, actually commenced a serious tale of chivalry.

Cervantes brought forward a personage, therefore,
in whom were imbodied all those generous virtues
which belong to chivalry : disinterestedness, contempt of danger, unblemished honour, knightly courtesy, and those aspirations after ideal excellence
which, if empty dreams, are the dreams of a magnanimous spirit. They are, indeed, represented by
Cervantes as too ethereal for this world, and are
successively dispelled as they come in contact with
the coarse realities of life. It is this view of the
subject which has led Sismondi, among other critics, to consider that the principal end of the author
was "the ridicule of enthusiasm—the contrast of the
heroic with the vulgar," and he sees something profoundly sad in the conclusions to which it leads.
This sort of criticism appears to be over-refined. It
resembles the efforts of some commentators to alle-
gorize the great epics of Homer and Virgil, throwing a disagreeable mistiness over the story by converting mere shadows into substances, and substances into shadows.

The great purpose of Cervantes was, doubtless, that expressly avowed by himself, namely, to correct the popular taste for romances of chivalry. It is unnecessary to look for any other in so plain a tale, although, it is true, the conduct of the story produces impressions on the reader, to a certain extent, like those suggested by Sismondi. The melancholy tendency, however, is, in a great degree, counteracted by the exquisitely ludicrous character of the incidents. Perhaps, after all, if we are to hunt for a moral as the key of the fiction, we may, with more reason, pronounce it to be the necessity of proportioning our undertakings to our capacities.

The mind of the hero, Don Quixote, is an ideal world, into which Cervantes has poured all the rich stores of his own imagination, the poet's golden dreams, high romantic exploit, and the sweet visions of pastoral happiness; the gorgeous chimeras of the fancied age of chivalry, which had so long entranced the world; splendid illusions, which, floating before us like the airy bubbles which the child throws off from his pipe, reflect, in a thousand variegated tints, the rude objects around, until, brought into collision with these, they are dashed in pieces, and melt into air. These splendid images derive tenfold beauty from the rich, antique colouring of the author's language, skilfully imitated from the old romances, but which necessarily escapes in the translation into a foreign tongue. Don Quixote's insanity operates both in mistaking the ideal for the real, and the real for the ideal. Whatever he has found

4   O

in romances, he believes to exist in the world; and he converts all he meets with in the world into the visions of his romances. It is difficult to say which of the two produces the most ludicrous results.

For the better exposure of these mad fancies, Cervantes has not only put them into action in real life, but contrasted them with another character which may be said to form the reverse side of his hero's. Honest Sancho represents the material principle as perfectly as his master does the intellectual or ideal. He is of the earth, earthy. Sly, selfish, sensual, his dreams are not of glory, but of good feeding. His only concern is for his carcass. His notions of honour appear to be much the same with those of his jovial contemporary, Falstaff, as conveyed in his memorable soliloquy. In the sublime night-piece which ends with the fulling-mills—truly sublime until we reach the *dénouement*—Sancho asks his master, "Why need you go about this adventure? It is main dark, and there is never a living soul sees us; we have nothing to do but to sheer off and get out of harm's way. Who is there to take notice of our flinching?" Can anything be imagined more exquisitely opposed to the true spirit of chivalry? The whole compass of fiction nowhere displays the power of contrast so forcibly as in these two characters: perfectly opposed to each other, not only in their minds and general habits, but in the minutest details of personal appearance.

It was a great effort of art for Cervantes to maintain the dignity of his hero's character in the midst of the whimsical and ridiculous distresses in which he has perpetually involved him. His infirmity leads us to distinguish between his character and his conduct, and to absolve him from all responsibility for the latter. The author's art is no less shown in regard to the other principal figure in the piece, Sancho Panza, who, with the most contemptible qualities, contrives to keep a strong hold on our interest by the kindness of his nature and his shrewd understanding. He is far too shrewd a person, indeed, to make it natural for him to have followed so crack-brained a master unless bribed by the promise of a substantial recompense. He is a personification, as it were, of the popular wisdom—a "bundle of proverbs," as his master somewhere styles him; and proverbs are the most compact form in which the wisdom of a people is digested. They have been collected into several distinct works in Spain, where they exceed in number those of any other, if not every other, country in Europe. As many of them are of great antiquity, they are of inestimable price with the Castilian purists, as affording rich samples of obsolete idioms and the various mutations of the language.

The subordinate portraits in the romance, though not wrought with the same care, are admirable studies of national character. In this view, the Don Quixote may be said to form an epoch in the history of letters, as the original of that kind of composition, the Novel of Character, which is one of the distinguishing peculiarities of modern literature.

When well executed, this sort of writing rises to the dignity of history itself, and may be said to perform no insignificant part of the functions of the latter. History describes men less as they are than as they appear, as they are playing a part on the great political theatre — men in masquerade. It rests on state documents, which too often cloak real purposes under an artful veil of policy, or on the accounts of contemporaries blinded by passion or interest. Even without these deductions, the revolutions of states, their wars, and their intrigues do not present the only aspect, nor, perhaps, the most interesting under which human nature can be studied. It is man in his domestic relations, around his own fireside, where alone his real character can be truly disclosed; in his ordinary occupations in society, whether for purposes of profit or of pleasure; in his every-day manner of living, his tastes and opinions, as drawn out in social intercourse; it is, in short, under all those forms which make up the interior of society that man is to be studied, if we would get the true form and pressure of the age—if, in short, we would obtain clear and correct ideas of the actual progress of civilization.

But these topics do not fall within the scope of the historian. He cannot find authentic materials for them. They belong to the novelist, who, indeed, contrives his incidents and creates his characters, but who, if true to his art, animates them with the same tastes, sentiments, and motives of action which belong to the period of his fiction. His portrait is not the less true because no individual has sat for it. He has seized the physiognomy of the times. Who is there that does not derive a more distinct idea of the state of society and manners in Scotland from the Waverley novels than from the best of its historians? of the condition of the Middle Ages, from the single romance of Ivanhoe, than from the volumes of Hume or Hallam? In like manner, the pencil of Cervantes has given a far more distinct and a richer portraiture of life in Spain in the sixteenth century than can be gathered from a library of monkish chronicles.

Spain, which furnished the first good model of this kind of writing, seems to have possessed more ample materials for it than any other country except England. This is perhaps owing, in a great degree, to the freedom and originality of the popular character. It is the country where the lower classes make the nearest approach, in their conversation, to what is called humour. Many of the national proverbs are seasoned with it, as well as the *picaresco* tales, the indigenous growth of the soil, where, however, the humour runs rather too much to mere practical jokes. The free expansion of the popular characteristics may be traced, in part, to the freedom of the political institutions of the country before the iron hand of the Austrian dynasty was laid on it. The long wars with the Moslem invaders called every peasant into the field, and gave him a degree of personal consideration. In some of the provinces, as Catalonia, the Democratic spirit frequently rose to an uncontrollable height. In this free atmosphere the rich and peculiar traits of national character were unfolded. The territorial divisions which marked the Peninsula, broken up anciently into a number of petty and independent states, gave, moreover, great variety to the national portraiture. The rude Asturian, the haughty and indolent Castilian, the industrious Aragonese, the independent Catalan, the jealous and wily Andalusian, the effeminate Valencian, and magnificent Granadine, furnished an infinite variety of character and costume for the study of the artist. The intermixture of Asiatic races, to an extent unknown in any other European land, was favourable to the same result. The Jews and the Moors were settled in too great numbers, and for too many centuries, in the land, not to have left traces of their Oriental civilization. The best blood of the country has flowed from what the modern Spaniard—the Spaniard of the Inquisition—regards as impure sources; and a work, popular in the Peninsula, under the name of *Tizon de España*, or "Brand of Spain," maliciously traces back the pedigrees of the noblest houses in the kingdom to a Jewish or Morisco origin. All these circumstances have conspired to give a highly poetic interest to the character of the Spaniards; to make them, in fact, the most picturesque of European nations, affording richer and far more various subjects for the novelist than other nations whose peculiarities have been kept down by the weight of a despotic government, or the artificial and levelling laws of fashion.

There is one other point of view in which the Don Quixote presents itself, that of its didactic import. It is not merely moral in its general tendency, though this was a rare virtue in the age in which it was written, but is replete with admonition and criticism, oftentimes requiring great boldness, as well as originality, in the author. Such, for instance, are the derision of witchcraft, and other superstitions common to the Spaniards; the ridicule of torture, which, though not used in the ordinary courts, was familiar to the Inquisition; the frequent strictures on various departments and productions of literature. The literary criticism scattered throughout the work shows a profound acquaintance with the true principles of taste far before his time, and which has left his judgments of the writings of his countrymen still of paramount authority. In truth, the great scope of his work was didactic, for it was a satire against the false taste of his age. And never was there a satire so completely successful. The last romance of chivalry, before the appearance of the Don Quixote, came out in 1602. It was the last that was ever published in Spain. So completely was this kind of writing, which had bade defiance to every serious effort, now extinguished by the breath of ridicule,

"That soft and summer breath, whose subtile power
Passes the strength of storms in their most desolate hour."

It was impossible for any new author to gain an audience. The public had seen how the thunder was fabricated. The spectator had been behind the scenes, and witnessed of what cheap materials kings and queens were made. It was impossible for him by any stretch of imagination, to convert the tinsel and painted bawbles which he had seen there into diadems and sceptres. The illusion had fled forever.

Satire seldom survives the local or temporary interests against which it is directed. It loses its life with its sting. The satire of Cervantes is an exception. The objects at which it was aimed have long since ceased to interest. The modern reader is attracted to the book simply by its execution as a work of art, and, from want of previous knowledge, comprehends few of the allusions which gave such infinite zest to the perusal in its own day. Yet, under all these disadvantages, it not only maintains its popularity, but is far more widely extended, and enjoys far higher consideration, than in the life of its author. Such are the triumphs of genius!

Cervantes correctly appreciated his own work. He more than once predicted its popularity. "I will lay a wager," says Sancho, "that before long there will not be a chophouse, tavern, or barber's stall but will have a painting of our achievements." The honest squire's prediction was verified in his own day; and the author might have seen paintings of his work on wood and on canvass, as well as copper-plate engravings of it. Besides several editions of it at home, it was printed, in his own time, in Portugal, Flanders, and Italy. Since that period it has passed into numberless editions both in Spain and other countries. It has been translated into nearly every European tongue over and over again; into English ten times, into French eight, and others less frequently. We will close the present notice with a brief view of some of the principal editions, together with that at the head of our article.

The currency of the romance among all classes frequently invited its publication by incompetent hands; and the consequence was a plentiful crop of errors, until the original text was nearly despoiled of its beauty, while some passages were omitted, and foreign ones still more shamefully interpolated. The first attempt to retrieve the original from these harpies, who thus foully violated it, singularly enough, was made in England. Queen Caroline, the wife of George the Second, had formed a collection of books of romance, which she playfully named the "library of the sage Merlin." The romance of Cervantes alone was wanting; and a nobleman, Lord Carteret, undertook to provide her with a suitable copy at his own expense. This was the origin of the celebrated edition published by Tonson, in London, 1738, 4 tom. 4to. It contained the Life of the Author, written for it by the learned Mayans y Siscar. It was the first biography (which merits the name) of Cervantes; and it shows into what oblivion his personal history had already fallen, that no less than seven towns claimed each the honour of giving him birth. The fate of Cervantes resembled that of Homer.

The example thus set by foreigners excited an honourable emulation at home; and at length, in

1780, a magnificent edition, from the far-famed press of Ibarra, was published at Madrid, in 4 tom. 4to, under the auspices of the Royal Spanish Academy; which, unlike many other literary bodies of sounding name, has contributed most essentially to the advancement of letters, not merely by original memoirs, but by learned and very beautiful editions of ancient writers. Its Don Quixote exhibits a most careful revision of the text, collated from the several copies printed in the author's lifetime, and supposed to have received his own emendations. There is too good reason to believe that these corrections were made with a careless hand; at all events, there is a plentiful harvest of typographical blunders in these primitive editions.

Prefixed to the publication of the Academy is the Life of Cervantes, by Rios, written with uncommon elegance, and containing nearly all that is of much interest in his personal history. A copious analysis of the romance follows, in which a parallel is closely elaborated between it and the poems of Homer. But the romantic and the classical differ too widely from each other to admit of such an approximation; and the method of proceeding necessarily involves its author in infinite absurdities, which show an entire ignorance of the true principles of philosophical criticism, and which he would scarcely have fallen into had he given heed to the maxims of Cervantes himself.

In the following year, 1781, there appeared another edition in England deserving of particular notice. It was prepared by the Rev. Mr. Bowle, a clergyman at Idemestone, who was so enamoured of the romance of Cervantes, that, after collecting a library of such works as could any way illustrate his author, he spent fourteen years in preparing a suitable commentary on him. There was ample scope for such a commentary. Many of the satirical allusions of the romance were misunderstood, as we have said, owing to ignorance of the books of chivalry at which they were aimed. Many incidents and usages, familiar to the age of Cervantes, had long since fallen into oblivion; and much of the idiomatic phraseology had grown to be obsolete, and required explanation. Cervantes himself had fallen into some egregious blunders, which in his subsequent revision of the work he had neglected to set right. The reader will readily call to mind the confusion as to Sancho's Dapple, who appears and disappears, most unaccountably, on the scene, according as the author happens to remember or forget that he was stolen. He afterward corrected this in two or three instances, but left three or four others unheeded. To the same account must be charged numberless gross anachronisms. Indeed, the whole Second Part is an anachronism, since the author introduces his hero criticising his First Part, in which his own epitaph is recorded.

Cervantes seems to have had a great distaste for the work of revision. Some of his blunders he laid at the printer's door, and others he dismissed with the remark, more ingenious than true, that they were like moles, which, though blemishes in themselves, add to the beauty of the countenance. He little dreamed that his lapses were to be watched so narrowly, that a catalogue was actually to be set down of all his repetitions and inconsistencies, and that each of his hero's sallies was to be adjusted by an accurate chronological table like any real history. He would have been still slower to believe that in the middle of the eighteenth century a learned society, the Academy of Literature and Fine Arts at Troyes, in Champagne, should have chosen a deputation of their body to visit Spain and examine the library of the Escurial, in order to obtain, if possible, the original MS. of that Arabian sage from whom Cervantes professed to have translated his romance. This was to be more mad than Don Quixote himself; yet this actually happened.

Bowle's edition was printed in six volumes quarto; the two last contained notes, illustrations, and index, *all, as well as the text, in Castilian.* Watt, in his laborious "Bibliotheca Britannica," remarks, that the book did not come up to the public expectation. If so, the public must have been very unreasonable. It was a marvellous achievement for a foreigner. It was the first attempt at a commentary on the Quixote, and, although doubtless exhibiting inaccuracies which a native might have escaped, has been a rich mine of illustration, from which native critics have helped themselves most liberally, and sometimes with scanty acknowledgment.

The example of the English critic led to similar

labours in Spain, among the most successful of which
may be mentioned the edition by Pellicer, which has
commended itself to every scholar by its very learned disquisitions on many topics both of history and
criticism. It also contains a valuable memoir of
Cervantes, whose life has since been written in a
manner which leaves nothing farther to be desired
by Navarrete, well known by his laborious publication of documents relative to the early Spanish discoveries. His biography of the novelist comprehends all the information, direct and subsidiary,
which can now be brought together for the eluci-
dation of his personal or literary history. If Cervantes, like his great contemporary, Shakspeare, has
left few authentic details of his existence, the deficiency has been diligently supplied in both cases by
speculation and conjecture.

There was still wanting a classical commentary
on the Quixote devoted to the literary execution of
the work. Such a commentary has at length appeared from the pen of Clemencin, the accomplished secretary of the Spanish Academy of History,
who had acquired a high reputation for himself by
the publication of the sixth volume of its memoirs,
the exclusive work of his own hand. In his edition
of the romance, besides illuminating with rare learning many of the obscure points in the narrative, he
has accompanied the text with a severe but enlightened criticism, which, while it boldly exposes occasional offences against taste or grammar, directs the
eye to those latent beauties which might escape a

4   P

rapid or an ordinary reader. We much doubt if any Castilian classic has been so ably illustrated. Unfortunately, the First Part only was completed by the commentator, who died very recently. It will not be easy to find a critic equally qualified by his taste and erudition for the completion of the work.

The English, as we have noticed, have evinced their relish for Cervantes, not only by their critical labours, but by repeated translations. Some of these are executed with much skill, considering the difficulty of correctly rendering the idiomatic phraseology of humorous dialogue. The most popular versions are those of Motteux, Jarvis, and Smollett. Perhaps the first is the best of all. It was by a Frenchman, who came over to England in the time of James the Second. It betrays nothing of its foreign parentage, however, while its rich and racy diction and its quaint turns of expression are admirably suited to convey a lively and very faithful image of the original. The slight tinge of antiquity which belongs to the time is not displeasing, and comports well with the tone of knightly dignity which distinguishes the hero. Lockhart's notes and poetical versions of old Castilian ballads, appended to the recent edition of Motteux, have rendered it by far the most desirable translation. It is singular that the first classical edition of Don Quixote, the first commentary, and probably the best foreign translation, should have been all produced in England; and farther, that the English commentator should have written in Spanish, and the English translation have been by a Frenchman.

We now come to Mr. Sales's recent edition of the original, the first, probably, which has appeared in the New World, of the one half of which the Spanish is the spoken language. There was great need of some uniform edition to meet the wants of our University, where much inconvenience has been long experienced from the discrepancies of the copies used. The only ones to be procured in this country are contemptible both in regard to printing and paper, and are defaced by the grossest errors. They are the careless manufacture of ill-informed Spanish booksellers, made to sell, and dear to boot.

Mr. Sales has adopted a right plan for remedying these several evils. He has carefully formed his text on that of the last and most correct edition of the Academy, and as he has stereotyped the work, any verbal errors may be easily rectified. The Academy has substituted the modern orthography for that of Cervantes, who, independently of the change which has gradually taken place in the language, seems to have had no uniform system himself. Mr. Sales has conformed to the rules prescribed by this high authority for regulating his orthography, accent, and punctuation. In some instances, only, he has adopted the ancient usage in beginning words with *f* instead of *h*, and retaining obsolete terminations of verbs, as *hablades* for *hablais*, *hablabades* for *hablabais*, *amades* for *amais*, *amabades* for *amabais*, &c., no doubt as better suited to the lofty tone of the good knight's discourses, who himself affected a reverence for the antique in his conversation to which his translators have not always sufficiently attended.

In one respect the present editor has made some alterations not before attempted, we believe, in the text of his original. We have already noticed the inaccuracies of the early copies of the Don Quixote, partly imputable to Cervantes himself, and in a greater degree, doubtless, to his printers. There is no way of rectifying such errors by collation with the author's manuscript, which has long since disappeared. All that can now be done, therefore, is to point out the purer reading in a note, as Clemencin, Arrieta, and other commentators have done, or, as Mr. Sales has preferred, to introduce it into the body of the text. We will give one or two specimens of these alterations:

"Poco mas ó menos."—Tom. i., p. 141.

The reading in the old editions is "poco mas á menos," a phrase as unintelligible in Spanish now as its literal translation would be in English, although in use, it would seem from other authorities, in the age of Cervantes.

"Por tales os juzgué y tuve."—Tom. i., p. 104.

The old editions add "siempre," which clearly is incorrect, since Don Quixote is speaking of the present occasion.

"Don Quijote quedó admirado."—Tom. i., p. 143.

Other editions read "El cual quedó," &c. The use

of the relative leaves the reader in doubt who is intended, and Mr. Sales, in conformity to Clemencin's suggestion, has made the sentence clear by substituting the name of the knight.

" Donde les *sucedieron* cosas," &c.—Tom. ii., p. 44.

In other editions, "*sucedió*;" bad grammar, since it agrees with a plural noun.

" En tan poco espacio de tiempo como ha que *estuvo* allá," &c. (tom. ii., p. 132), instead of "*está* allá," clearly the wrong tense, since the verb refers to past time.

It is unnecessary to multiply examples, a sufficient number of which have been cited to show on what principles the emendations have been made. They have been confined to the correction of such violations of grammar, or such inaccuracies of expression, as obscure or distort the meaning. They have been made with great circumspection, and in obedience to the suggestion of the highest authorities in the language. For the critical scholar, who would naturally prefer the primitive text with all its impurities, they were not designed. But they are of infinite value to the general reader and the student, who may now read this beautiful classic purified from those verbal blemishes which, however obvious to a native, could not fail to mislead a foreigner.

Besides these emendations, Mr. Sales has illustrated the work by prefixing to it the admirable preliminary discourse of Clemencin, and by a considerable body of notes, selected and abridged from the most approved commentators; and as the object has been

4

P*

to explain the text to the reader, not to involve him in antiquarian or critical disquisitions, when his authorities have failed to do this, the editor has supplied notes of his own, throwing much light on matters least familiar to a foreigner. In this part of his work we think he might have derived considerable aid from Bowle, whom he does not appear to have consulted. The Castilian commentator, Arrieta, whom he liberally uses, is largely indebted to the English critic, who, as a foreigner, moreover, has been led into many seasonable explanations that would be superfluous to a Spaniard.

We may notice another peculiarity in the present edition, that of breaking up the text into reasonable paragraphs, in imitation of the English translations; a great relief to the spirits of the reader, which are seriously damped, in the ancient copies, by the interminable waste of page upon page, without these convenient halting-places.

But our readers, we fear, will think we are running into an interminable waste of discussion. We will only remark, therefore, in conclusion, that the mechanical execution of the book is highly creditable to our press. It is, moreover, adorned with etchings by our American Cruikshank, Johnston— some of them original, but mostly copies from the late English edition of Smollett's translations. They are designed and executed with much spirit, and, no doubt, would have fully satisfied honest Sancho, who predicted this kind of immortality for himself and his master.

We congratulate the public on the possession of an edition of the pride of Castilian literature, from our own press, in so neat a form, and executed with so much correctness and judgment; and we trust that the ambition of its respectable editor will be gratified by its becoming, as it well deserves to be, the manual of the student in every seminary throughout the country where the noble Castilian language is taught.

SIR WALTER SCOTT.*

APRIL, 1838.

THERE is no kind of writing, which has truth and instruction for its main object, so interesting and popular, on the whole, as biography. History, in its larger sense, has to deal with masses, which, while they divide the attention by the dazzling variety of objects, from their very generality are scarcely capable of touching the heart. The great objects on which it is employed have little relation to the daily occupations with which the reader is most intimate. A nation, like a corporation, seems to have no soul, and its checkered vicissitudes may be contemplated rather with curiosity for the lessons they convey than with personal sympathy. How different are the feelings excited by the fortunes of an individual —one of the mighty mass, who in the page of history is swept along the current unnoticed and unknown! Instead of a mere abstraction, at once we see a being like ourselves, " fed with the same food, hurt with the same weapons, subject to the same diseases, healed by the same means, warmed and cooled by the same winter and summer" as we are. We place ourselves in his position, and see the passing current of events with the same eyes. We

---

* 1. "Memoirs of the Life of Sir Walter Scott, Bart., by J. G. Lockhart. Five vols. 12mo. Boston: Otis, Broaders, & Co., 1837."

2. "Recollections of Sir Walter Scott, Bart., 16mo. London: James Fraser, 1837."

become a party to all his little schemes, share in his triumphs, or mourn with him in the disappointment of defeat. His friends become our friends. We learn to take an interest in their characters from their relation to him. As they pass away from the stage one after another, and as the clouds of misfortune, perhaps, or of disease, settle around the evening of his own day, we feel the same sadness that steals over us on a retrospect of earlier and happier hours. And when at last we have followed him to the tomb, we close the volume, and feel that we have turned over another chapter in the history of life.

On the same principles, probably, we are more moved by the exhibition of those characters whose days have been passed in the ordinary routine of domestic and social life than by those most intimately connected with the great public events of their age. What, indeed, is the history of such men but that of the times? The life of Wellington or of Bonaparte is the story of the wars and revolutions of Europe. But that of Cowper, gliding away in the seclusion of rural solitude, reflects all those domestic joys, and, alas! more than the sorrows, which gather around every man's fireside and his heart. In this way the story of the humblest individual, faithfully recorded, becomes an object of lively interest. How much is that interest increased in the case of a man like Scott, who, from his own fireside, has sent forth a voice to cheer and delight millions of his fellow-men; whose life was

Z

passed within the narrow circle of his own village as it were, but who, nevertheless, has called up more shapes and fantasies within that magic circle, acted more extraordinary parts, and afforded more marvels for the imagination to feed on, than can be furnished by the most nimble-footed, nimble-tongued traveller, from Marco Polo down to Mrs. Trollope, and that literary Sinbad, Captain Hall.

Fortunate as Sir Walter Scott was in his life, it is not the least of his good fortunes that he left the task of recording it to one so competent as Mr. Lockhart, who, to a familiarity with the person and habits of his illustrious subject, unites such entire sympathy with his pursuits, and such fine tact and discrimination in arranging the materials for their illustration. We have seen it objected that the biographer has somewhat transcended his lawful limits in occasionally exposing what a nice tenderness for the reputation of Scott should have led him to conceal ; but, on reflection, we are not inclined to adopt these views. It is difficult to prescribe any precise rule by which the biographer should be guided in exhibiting the peculiarities, and, still more, the defects of his subject. He should, doubtless, be slow to draw from obscurity those matters which are of a strictly personal and private nature, particularly when they have no material bearing on the character of the individual. But whatever the latter has done, said, or written to others can rarely be made to come within this rule. A swell of panegyric, where everything is in broad sunshine, without the relief of a shadow to contrast it, is out of nature, and must bring discredit on the whole. Nor is it much better when a sort of twilight mystification is spread over a man's actions, until, as in the case of all biographies of Cowper previous to that of Southey, we are completely bewildered respecting the real motives of conduct. If ever there was a character above the necessity of any management of this sort, it was Scott's; and we cannot but think that the frank exposition of the minor blemishes which sully it, by securing the confidence of the reader in the general fidelity of the portraiture, and thus disposing him to receive, without distrust, those favourable statements in his history which might seem incredible, as they certainly are unprecedented, is, on the whole, advantageous to his reputation. As regards the moral effect on the reader, we may apply Scott's own argument for not always recompensing suffering virtue, at the close of his fictions, with temporal prosperity—that such an arrangement would convey no moral to the heart whatever, since a glance at the great picture of life would show that virtue is not always thus rewarded.

In regard to the literary execution of Mr. Lockhart's work, the public voice has long since pronounced on it. A prying criticism may discern a few of those contraband epithets and slipshod sentences, more excusable in *young* "Peter's Letters to his Kinsfolk," where, indeed, they are thickly sown, than in the production of a grave Aristarch of

British criticism. But this is small game, where every reader of the least taste and sensibility must find so much to applaud. It is enough to say, that in passing from the letters of Scott, with which the work is enriched, to the text of the biographer, we find none of those chilling transitions which occur on the like occasions in more bungling productions; as, for example, in that recent one in which the unfortunate Hannah More is done to death by her friend Roberts. On the contrary, we are sensible only to a new variety of beauty in the style of composition. The correspondence is illumined by all that is needed to make it intelligible to a stranger, and selected with such discernment as to produce the clearest impression of the character of its author. The mass of interesting details is conveyed in language, richly coloured with poetic sentiment, and, at the same time, without a tinge of that mysticism which, as Scott himself truly remarked, " will never do for a writer of fiction, no, nor of history, nor moral essays, nor sermons ;" but which, nevertheless, finds more or less favour in our own community, at the present day, in each and all of these.

The second work which we have placed at the head of this article, and from which the last remark of Sir Walter's was borrowed, is a series of notices originally published in " Fraser's Magazine," but now collected, with considerable additions, into a separate volume. Its author, Mr. Robert Pierce Gillies, is a gentleman of the Scotch bar, favourably known by translations from the German. The work conveys a lively report of several scenes and events, which, before the appearance of Lockhart's book, were of more interest and importance than they can now be, lost, as they are, in the flood of light which is poured on us from that source. In the absence of the sixth and last volume, however, Mr. Gillies may help us to a few particulars respecting the closing years of Sir Walter's life, that may have some novelty—we know not how much to be relied on—for the reader. In the present notice of a work so familiar to most persons, we shall confine ourselves to some of those circumstances which contribute to form, or have an obvious connexion with, his literary character.

Walter Scott was born at Edinburgh, August 15th, 1771. The character of his father, a respectable member of that class of attorneys who in Scotland are called Writers to the Signet, is best conveyed to the reader by saying that he sat for the portrait of Mr. Saunders Fairford in "Redgauntlet." His mother was a woman of taste and imagination, and had an obvious influence in guiding those of her son. His ancestors, by both father's and mother's side, were of "gentle blood," a position which, placed between the highest and the lower ranks in society, was extremely favourable, as affording facilities for communication with both. A lameness in his infancy—a most fortunate lameness for the world, if, as Scott says, it spoiled a soldier—and a delicate constitution, made it expedient to try the efficacy of country air and diet, and he was placed

4 Q

under the roof of his paternal grandfather at Sandy-Knowe, a few miles distant from the capital. Here his days were passed in the open fields, " with no other fellowship," as he says, " than that of the sheep and lambs ;" and here, in the lap of Nature,

" Meet nurse for a poetic child,"

his infant vision was greeted with those rude, romantic scenes which his own verses have since hallowed for the pilgrims from every clime. In the long evenings, his imagination, as he grew older, was warmed by traditionary legends of border heroism and adventure, repeated by the aged relative, who had herself witnessed the last gleams of border chivalry. His memory was one of the first powers of his mind which exhibited an extraordinary development. One of the longest of these old ballads, in particular, stuck so close to it, and he repeated it with such stentorian vociferation, as to draw from the minister of a neighbouring kirk the testy exclamation, " One may as well speak in the mouth of a cannon as where that child is."

On his removal to Edinburgh, in his eighth year, he was subjected to different influences. His worthy father was a severe martinet in all the forms of his profession, and, it may be added, of his religion, which he contrived to make somewhat burdensome to his more volatile son. The tutor was still more strict in his religious sentiments, and the lightest literary diversion in which either of them indulged was such as could be gleaned from the time-honoured folios of Archbishop Spottiswoode or worthy

Robert Wodrow. Even here, however, Scott's young mind contrived to gather materials and impulses for future action. In his long arguments with Master Mitchell, he became steeped in the history of the Covenanters and the persecuted Church of Scotland, while he was still more rooted in his own Jacobite notions, early instilled into his mind by the tales of his relatives of Sandy-Knowe, whose own family had been out in the "affair of forty-five." Amid the professional and polemical worthies of his father's library, Scott detected a copy of Shakspeare, and he relates with what *goût* he used to creep out of his bed, where he had been safely deposited for the night, and, by the light of the fire, *in puris naturalibus*, pore over the pages of the great magician, and study those mighty spells by which he gave to airy fantasies the forms and substance of humanity. Scott distinctly recollected the time and the spot where he first opened a volume of Percy's "Reliques of English Poetry;" a work which may have suggested to him the plan and the purpose of the "Border Minstrelsy." Every day's experience shows how much more actively the business of education goes on out of school than in it; and Scott's history shows equally that genius, whatever obstacles may be thrown in its way in one direction, will find room for its expansion in another, as the young tree sends forth its shoots most prolific in that quarter where the sunshine is permitted to fall on it.

At the High School, in which he was placed by his father at an early period, he seems not to have been particularly distinguished in the regular course of studies. His voracious appetite for books, however, of a certain cast, as romances, chivalrous tales, and worm-eaten chronicles scarcely less chivalrous, and his wonderful memory for such reading as struck his fancy, soon made him regarded by his fellows as a phenomenon of black-letter scholarship, which, in process of time, achieved for him the cognomen of that redoubtable schoolman, Duns Scotus. He now also gave evidence of his powers of creation as well as of acquisition. He became noted for his own stories, generally bordering on the marvellous, with a plentiful seasoning of knight-errantry, which suited his bold and chivalrous temper. " Slink over beside me, Jamie," he would whisper to his schoolfellow Ballantyne, "and I'll tell you a story." Jamie was, indeed, destined to sit beside him during the greater part of his life.

The same tastes and talents continued to display themselves more strongly with increasing years. Having beaten pretty thoroughly the ground of romantic and legendary lore, at least so far as the English libraries to which he had access would permit, he next endeavoured, while at the University, to which he had been transferred from the High School, to pursue the same subject in the Continental languages. Many were the strolls which he took in the neighbourhood, especially to Arthur's Seat and Salisbury Crags, where, perched on some almost inaccessible eyry, he might be seen conning over his Ariosto or Cervantes, or some other bard of romance, with some favourite companion of his studies, or pouring into the ears of the latter his own boyish legends, glowing with

> "achievements high,
> And circumstance of chivalry."

A critical knowledge of these languages he seems not to have obtained, and even in the French made but an indifferent figure in conversation. An accurate acquaintance with the pronunciation and prosody of a foreign tongue is undoubtedly a desirable accomplishment; but it is, after all, a mere accomplishment subordinate to the great purposes for which a language is to be learned. Scott did not, as is too often the case, mistake the shell for the kernel. He looked on language only as the key to unlock the foreign stores of wisdom, the pearls of inestimable price, wherever found, with which to enrich his native literature.

After a brief residence at the University, he was regularly indented as an apprentice to his father in 1786. One can hardly imagine a situation less congenial with the ardent, effervescing spirit of a poetic fancy, fettered down to a daily routine of drudgery scarcely above that of a mere scrivener. It proved, however, a useful school of discipline to him. It formed early habits of method, punctuality, and laborious industry; business habits, in short, most adverse to the poetic temperament, but indispensable to the accomplishment of the gigantic tasks which he afterward assumed. He has himself borne testimony to his general diligence in his new vocation, and

4   Q *

tells us that on one occasion he transcribed no less than a hundred and twenty folio pages at a sitting.

In the midst of these mechanical duties, he did not lose sight of the favourite objects of his study and meditation. He made frequent excursions into the Lowland as well as Highland districts in search of traditionary relics. These pilgrimages he frequently performed on foot. His constitution, now become hardy by severe training, made him careless of exposure, and his frank and warm-hearted manners—eminently favourable to his purposes, by thawing at once any feelings of frosty reserve which might have encountered a stranger — made him equally welcome at the staid and decorous manse, and at the rough but hospitable board of the peasant. Here was, indeed, the study of the future novelist; the very school in which to meditate those models of character and situation which he was afterward, long afterward, to transfer, in such living colours, to the canvass. "He was makin' himsell a' the time," says one of his companions, "but he didna ken, maybe, what he was about till years had passed. At first he thought o' little, I dare say, but the queerness and the fun." The honest writer to the signet does not seem to have thought it either so funny or so profitable; for on his son's return from one of these *raids*, as he styled them, the old gentleman peevishly inquired how he had been living so long. "Pretty much like the young ravens," answered Walter; "I only wished I had been as good a player on the flute as poor George Primrose in the Vicar of Wakefield. If I had his art, I should like nothing better than to tramp like him from cottage to cottage over the world." "I doubt," said the grave clerk to the signet, "I greatly doubt, sir, you were born for nae better than a *gangrel scrape-gut!*" Perhaps even the revelation, could it have been made to him, of his son's future literary glory, would scarcely have satisfied the worthy father, who, probably, would have regarded a seat on the bench of the Court of Sessions as much higher glory. At all events, this was not far from the judgment of Dominie Mitchell, who, in his notice of his illustrious pupil, "sincerely regrets that Sir Walter's precious time was devoted to the *dulce* rather than the *utile* of composition, and that his great talents should have been wasted on such subjects!"

It is impossible to glance at Scott's early life without perceiving how powerfully all its circumstances, whether accidental or contrived, conspired to train him for the peculiar position he was destined to occupy in the world of letters. There never was a character in whose infant germ the mature and fully-developed lineaments might be more distinctly traced. What he was in his riper age, so he was in his boyhood. We discern the same tastes, the same peculiar talents, the same social temper and affections, and, in a great degree, the same habits—in their embryo state, of course, but distinctly marked—and his biographer has shown no little skill in enabling us to trace their gradual, progressive expansion, from the hour of his birth up to the full prime and maturity of manhood.

In 1792, Scott, whose original destination of a writer had been changed to that of an advocate—from his father's conviction, as it would seem, of the superiority of his talents to the former station—was admitted to the Scottish bar. Here he continued in assiduous attendance during the regular terms, but more noted for his stories in the Outer House than his arguments in court. It may appear singular, that a person so gifted, both as a writer and as a *raconteur*, should have had no greater success in his profession. But the case is not uncommon Indeed, experience shows that the most eminent writers have not made the most successful speakers. It is not more strange than that a good writer of novels should not excel as a dramatic author. Perhaps a consideration of the subject would lead us to refer the phenomena in both cases to the same principle. At all events, Scott was an exemplification of both, and we leave the solution to those who have more leisure and ingenuity to unravel the mystery.

Scott's leisure, in the mean time, was well employed in storing his mind with German romance, with whose wild fictions, intrenching on the grotesque, he found at that time more sympathy than in later life. In 1796 he first appeared before the public as a translator of Bürger's well-known ballads, thrown off by him at a heat, and which found favour with the few into whose hands they passed. He subsequently adventured in Monk Lewis's crazy bark, " Tales of Wonder," which soon went to pieces, leaving, however, among its surviving fragments the scattered contributions of Scott.

At last, in 1802, he gave to the world his first two volumes of the "Border Minstrelsy," printed by his old schoolfellow Ballantyne, and which, by the beauty of the typography, as well as literary execution, made an epoch in Scottish literary history. There was no work of Scott's after life which showed the result of so much preliminary labour. Before ten years old, he had collected several volumes of ballads and traditions, and we have seen how diligently he pursued the same vocation in later years. The publication was admitted to be far more faithful, as well as skilfully collated, than its prototype, the "Reliques" of Bishop Percy; while his notes contained a mass of antiquarian information relative to border life, conveyed in a style of beauty unprecedented in topics of this kind, and enlivenod with a higher interest than poetic fiction. Percy's "Reliques" had prepared the way for the kind reception of the "Minstrelsy," by the general relish—notwithstanding Dr. Johnson's protest—it had created for the simple pictures of a pastoral and heroic time. Burns had since familiarized the English ear with the Doric melodies of his native land; and now a greater than Burns appeared, whose first production, by a singular chance, came into the world in the very year in which the Ayrshire minstrel was withdrawn from it, as if Nature had intended that the chain of poetic inspiration should not be broken. The delight of the public was farther augmented on the appearance of the third volume of the " Minstrelsy," containing various imitations of the old ballad, which displayed the rich fashion of the antique, purified from the mould and rust by which the beauties of such weather-beaten trophies are defaced.

The first edition of the " Minstrelsy," consisting of eight hundred copies, went off, as Lockhart tells us, in less than a year ; and the poet, on the publication of a second, received five hundred pounds sterling from Longman—an enormous price for such a commodity, but the best bargain, probably, that the bookseller ever made, as the subsequent sale has since extended to twenty thousand copies.

Scott was not in great haste to follow up his success. It was three years later before he took the field as an independent author, in a poem which at once placed him among the great original writers of his country. The "Lay of the Last Minstrel," a complete expansion of the ancient ballad into an epic form, was published in 1805. It was opening a new creation in the realm of fancy. It seemed as if the author had transfused into his page the strong delineations of the Homeric pencil, the rude, but generous gallantry of a primitive period, softened by the more airy and magical inventions of Italian romance,* and conveyed in tones of natural melody, such as had not been heard since the strains of

---

* " Mettendo lo Turpin, lo metto anch' io,"
says Ariosto, playfully, when he tells a particularly tough story.
" I cannot tell how the truth may be,
I say the tale as 'twas said to me,"
says the author of the " Lay" on a similar occasion. The resemblance

Burns. The book speedily found that unprecedented circulation which all his subsequent compositions attained. Other writers had addressed themselves to a more peculiar and limited feeling; to a narrower, and, generally, a more select audience. But Scott was found to combine all the qualities of interest for every order. He drew from the pure springs which gush forth in every heart. His narrative chained every reader's attention by the stirring variety of its incidents, while the fine touches of sentiment with which it abounded, like wild flowers, springing up spontaneously around, were full of freshness and beauty, that made one wonder others should not have stooped to gather them before.

The success of the " Lay" determined the course of its author's future life. Notwithstanding his punctual attention to his profession, his utmost profits for any one year of the ten he had been in practice had not exceeded two hundred and thirty pounds; and of late they had sensibly declined. Latterly, indeed, he had coqueted somewhat too openly with the Muse for his professional reputation. Themis has always been found a stern and jealous mistress, chary of dispensing her golden favours to those who are seduced into a flirtation with her more volatile sister.

Scott, however, soon found himself in a situation that made him independent of her favours. His in-

might be traced much farther than mere forms of expression, to the Italian, who, like

" *the Ariosto of the North,*
Sung ladye-love, and war, romance, and knightly worth."

come from the two offices to which he was promoted, of Sheriff of Selkirk, and Clerk of the Court
of Sessions, was so ample, combined with what fell
to him by inheritance and marriage, that he was
left at liberty freely to consult his own tastes. Amid
the seductions of poetry, however, he never shrunk
from his burdensome professional duties; and he
submitted to all their drudgery with unflinching con-
stancy, when the labours of his pen made the emolu-
ments almost beneath consideration. He never relished the idea of being divorced from active life by
the solitary occupations of a recluse. And his official functions, however severely they taxed his time,
may be said to have, in some degree, compensated
him by the new scenes of life which they were constantly disclosing—the very materials of those fictions on which his fame and his fortune were to be
built.

Scott's situation was eminently propitious to literary pursuits. He was married, and passed the
better portion of the year in the country, where the
quiet pleasures of his fireside circle, and a keen relish for rural sports, relieved his mind, and invigorated
both health and spirits. In early life, it seems, he
had been crossed in love; and, like Dante and Byron,
to whom, in this respect, he is often compared, he
had more than once, according to his biographer,
shadowed forth in his verses the object of his unfortunate passion. He does not appear to have taken
it very seriously, however, nor to have shown the
morbid sensibility in relation to it discovered by both

Byron and Dante, whose stern and solitary natures were cast in a very different mould from the social temper of Scott.

His next great poem was his "Marmion," transcending, in the judgment of many, all his other epics, and containing, in the judgment of all, passages of poetic fire which he never equalled, but which, nevertheless, was greeted on its entrance into the world by a critique, in the leading journal of the day, of the most caustic and unfriendly temper. The journal was the Edinburgh, to which he had been a frequent contributor, and the reviewer was his intimate friend, Jeffrey. The unkindest cut in the article was the imputation of a neglect of Scottish character and feeling. "There is scarcely one trait of true Scottish nationality or patriotism introduced into the whole poem; and Mr. Scott's only expression of admiration for the beautiful country to which he belongs is put, if we rightly remember, into the mouth of one of his Southern favourites." This of Walter Scott!

Scott was not slow, after this, in finding the political principles of the Edinburgh so repugnant to his own (and they certainly were as opposite as the poles), that he first dropped the journal, and next laboured with unwearied diligence to organize another, whose main purpose should be to counteract the heresies of the former. This was the origin of the London Quarterly, more imputable to Scott's exertions than to those of any, indeed all other persons. The result has been, doubtless, highly ser-

4   R

viceable to the interests of both morals and letters.
Not that the new Review was conducted with more
fairness, or, in this sense, *principle*, than its antagonist. A remark of Scott's own, in a letter to Ellis,
shows with how much principle. "I have run up
an attempt on ' The Curse of Kehama' for the
Quarterly. It affords cruel openings to the quiz-
zers, and I suppose will get it roundly in the Edinburgh Review. I would have made a very different hand of it, indeed, had the order of the day been
pour déchirer." But, although the fate of the individual was thus, to a certain extent, a matter of caprice, or, rather, prejudgment in the critic, yet the
great abstract questions in morals, politics, and literature, by being discussed on both sides, were presented in a fuller, and, of course, fairer light to the
public. Another beneficial result to letters was—
and we shall gain credit, at least, for candour in
confessing it—that it broke down somewhat of that
divinity which hedged in the despotic *we* of the reviewer, so long as no rival arose to contest the scep-
tre. The claims to infallibility, so long and slavish-
ly acquiesced in, fell to the ground when thus stoutly asserted by conflicting parties. It was pretty
clear that the same thing could not be all black and
all white at the same time. In short, it was the old
story of pope and anti-pope ; and the public began
to find out that there might be hopes for the salva-
tion of an author, though damned by the literary
popedom. Time, by reversing many of its decisions,
must at ength have shown the same thing.

But to return. Scott showed how nearly he had been touched to the quick by two other acts not so discreet. These were, the establishment of an Annual Register, and of the great publishing house of the Ballantynes, in which he became a silent partner. The last step involved him in grievous embarrassments, and stimulated him to exertions which required "a frame of adamant and soul of fire." At the same time, we find him overwhelmed with poetical, biographical, historical, and critical compositions, together with editorial labours of appalling magnitude. In this multiplication of himself in a thousand forms, we see him always the same, vigorous and effective. "Poetry," he says in one of his letters, "is a scourging crop, and ought not to be hastily repeated. Editing, therefore, may be considered as a green crop of turnips or pease, extremely useful to those whose circumstances do not admit of giving their farm a summer fallow." It might be regretted, however, that he should have wasted powers fitted for so much higher culture on the coarse products of a kitchen garden, which might have been safely trusted to inferior hands.

In 1811, Scott gave to the world his exquisite poem, "The Lady of the Lake." One of his fair friends had remonstrated with him on thus risking again the laurel he had already won. He replied, with characteristic, and, indeed, prophetic spirit, "If I fail, *I will write prose all my life.* But if I succeed,

> ' Up wi' the bonnie blue bonnet,
> The dirk and the feather an a' !' "

In his eulogy on Byron, Scott remarks, "There has been no reposing under the shade of his laurels, no living upon the resource of past reputation ; none of that *coddling* and petty precaution which little authors call 'taking care of their fame.' Byron let his fame take care of itself." Scott could not have more accurately described his own character.

The "Lady of the Lake" was welcomed with an enthusiasm surpassing that which attended any other of his poems. It seemed like the sweet breathings of his native pibroch, stealing over glen and mountain, and calling up all the delicious associations of rural solitude, which beautifully contrasted with the din of battle and the shrill cry of the war-trumpet, that stirred the soul in every page of his "Marmion." The publication of this work carried his fame as a poet to its most brilliant height. The post-horse duty rose to an extraordinary degree in Scotland, from the eagerness of travellers to visit the localities of the poem. A more substantial evidence was afforded in its amazing circulation, and, consequently, its profits. The press could scarcely keep pace with the public demand, and no less than fifty thousand copies of it have been sold since the date of its appearance. The successful author received more than two thousand guineas from his production. Milton received ten pounds for the two editions which he lived to see of his "Paradise Lost." The Ayrshire bard had sighed for "a lass wi' a tocher." Scott had now found one where it was hardly to be expected, in the Muse.

While the poetical fame of Scott was thus at its zenith, a new star rose above the horizon, whose eccentric course and dazzling radiance completely bewildered the spectator. In 1812, " Childe Harold" appeared, and the attention seemed to be now called, for the first time, from the outward form of man and visible nature, to the secret depths of the soul. The darkest recesses of human passion were laid open, and the note of sorrow was prolonged in tones of agonized sensibility, the more touching as coming from one who was placed on those dazzling heights of rank and fashion which, to the vulgar eye at least, seem to lie in unclouded sunshine. Those of the present generation who have heard only the same key thrummed *ad nauseam* by the feeble imitators of his lordship, can form no idea of the effect produced when the chords were first swept by the master's fingers. It was found impossible for the ear, once attuned to strains of such compass and ravishing harmony, to return with the same relish to purer, it might be, but tamer melody ; and the sweet voice of the Scottish minstrel lost much of its power to charm, let him charm never so wisely. While "Rokeby" was in preparation, bets were laid on the rival candidates by the wits of the day. The sale of this poem, though great, showed a sensible decline in the popularity of its author. This became still more evident on the publication of " The Lord of the Isles ;" and Scott admitted the conviction with his characteristic spirit and good-nature. "' Well, James' (he said to his printer), ' I have giv-

4   R *

en you a week—what are people saying about the Lord of the Isles?' I hesitated a little, after the fashion of Gil Blas, but he speedily brought the matter to a point. 'Come,' he said, 'speak out, my good fellow; what has put it into your head to be on so much ceremony *with me* all of a sudden? But I see how it is; the result is given in one word— *Disappointment.*' My silence admitted his inference to the fullest extent. His countenance certainly did look rather blank for a few seconds; in truth, he had been wholly unprepared for the event. At length he said, with perfect cheerfulness, 'Well, well, James, so be it; but you know we must not droop, for we can't afford to give over. Since one line has failed, we must stick to something else.'" This *something else* was a mine he had already hit upon, of invention and substantial wealth, such as Thomas the Rhymer, or Michael Scott, or any other adept in the black art had never dreamed of.

Everybody knows the story of the composition of "Waverley"—the most interesting story in the annals of letters—and how, some ten years after its commencement, it was fished out of some old lumber in an attic, and completed in a few weeks for the press in 1814. Its appearance marks a more distinct epoch in English literature than that of the poetry of its author. All previous attempts in the same school of fiction—a school of English growth —had been cramped by the limited information or talent of the writers. Smollett had produced his spirited sea-pieces, and Fielding his warm sketches

of country life, both of them mixed up witn so much
Billingsgate as required a strong flavour of wit to
make them tolerable. Richardson had covered
acres of canvass with his faithful family pictures.
Mrs. Radcliffe had dipped up to the elbows in horrors ; while Miss Burney's fashionable gossip, and
Miss Edgeworth's Hogarth drawings of the prose—
not the poetry—of life and character, had each and
all found favour in their respective ways. But a
work now appeared in which the author swept over
the whole range of character with entire freedom as
well as fidelity, ennobling the whole by high historic
associations, and in a style varying with his theme,
but whose pure and classic flow was tinctured with
just so much of poetic colouring as suited the purposes of romance. It was Shakspeare in prose.

The work was published, as we know, anony-
mously. Mr. Gillies states, however, that, while in
the press, fragments of it were communicated to
' Mr. Mackenzie, Dr. Brown, Mrs. Hamilton, and
other *savans* or *savantes,* whose dicta on the merits
of a new novel were considered unimpeachable.''
By their approbation " a strong body of friends was
formed, and the curiosity of the public prepared the
way for its reception.'' This may explain the rapidity with which the anonymous publication rose
into a degree of favour, which, though not less surely, perhaps, it might have been more slow in achieving. The author jealously preserved his incognito,
and, in order to heighten the mystification, flung off,
almost simultaneously, a variety of works, in prose

and poetry, any one of which might have been the labour of months. The public for a moment was at fault. There seemed to be six Richmonds in the field. The world, therefore, was reduced to the dilemma of either supposing that half a dozen different hands could work in precisely the same style, or that one could do the work of half a dozen. With time, however, the veil wore thinner and thinner, until at length, and long before the ingenious argument of Mr. Adolphus, there was scarcely a critic so purblind as not to discern behind it the features of the mighty minstrel.

Constable had offered seven hundred pounds for the new novel. "It was," says Mr. Lockhart, "ten times as much as Miss Edgeworth ever realized from any of her popular Irish tales." Scott declined the offer, which had been a good one for the bookseller had he made it as many thousand. But it passed the art of necromancy to divine this.

Scott, once entered on this new career, followed it up with an energy unrivalled in the history of literature. The public mind was not suffered to cool for a moment, before its attention was called to another miracle of creation from the same hand. Even illness, that would have broken the spirits of most men, as it prostrated the physical energies of Scott, opposed no impediment to the march of composition. When he could no longer write he could dictate, and in this way, amid the agonies of a racking disease, he composed "The Bride of Lammermoor," the "Legend of Montrose," and a great part of "Ivanhoe." The first, indeed, is darkened with those deep shadows that might seem thrown over it by the sombre condition of its author. But what shall we say of the imperturbable dry humour of the gallant Captain Dugald Dalgetty of Drumthwacket, or of the gorgeous revelries of Ivanhoe—

> "Such sights as youthful poets dream,
> On summer eves by haunted stream"—

what shall we say of such brilliant day-dreams for a bed of torture? Never before had the spirit triumphed over such agonies of the flesh. "The best way," said Scott, in one of his talks with Gillies, "is, *if possible*, to triumph over disease by setting it at defiance; somewhat on the same principle as one avoids being stung by boldly grasping a nettle."

The prose fictions were addressed to a much larger audience than the poems could be. They had attractions for every age and every class. The profits, of course, were commensurate. Arithmetic has never been so severely taxed as in the computation of Scott's productions and the proceeds resulting from them. In one year he received (or, more properly, was credited with, for it is somewhat doubtful how much he actually received) fifteen thousand pounds for his novels, comprehending the first edition and the copyright. The discovery of this rich mine furnished its fortunate proprietor with the means of gratifying the fondest and even most chimerical desires. He had always coveted the situation of a lord of acres—a Scottish laird—where his passion for planting might find scope in the creation

C c

of whole forests—for everything with him was on a magnificent scale—and where he might indulge the kindly feelings of his nature in his benevolent offices to a numerous and dependant tenantry. The few acres of the original purchase now swelled into hundreds, and, for aught we know, thousands; for one tract alone we find incidentally noticed as costing thirty thousand pounds. "It rounds off the property so handsomely," he says, in one of his letters. There was always a corner to "round off." The mansion, in the mean time, from a simple cottage *ornée*, was amplified into the dimensions almost, as well as the bizarre proportions, of some old feudal castle. The furniture and decorations were of the costliest kind : the wainscots of oak and cedar; the floors tesselated with marbles, or woods of different dyes; the ceilings fretted and carved with the delicate tracery of a Gothic abbey; the storied windows blazoned with the richly-coloured insignia of heraldry, the walls garnished with time-honoured trophies, or curious specimens of art, or volumes sumptuously bound—in short, with all that luxury could demand or ingenuity devise; while a copious reservoir of gas supplied every corner of the mansion with such fountains of light as must have puzzled the genius of the *lamp* to provide for the less fortunate Aladdin.

Scott's exchequer must have been seriously taxed in another form by the crowds of visiters whom he entertained under his hospitable roof. There was scarcely a person of note, or, to say truth, not of note, who visited that country without paying his respects to the Lion of Scotland. Lockhart reckons up a full sixth of the British peerage, who had been there within his recollection; and Captain Hall, in his amusing Notes, remarks, that it was not unusual for a dozen or more coach loads to find their way into his grounds in the course of the day, most of whom found or forced an entrance into the mansion. Such was the heavy tax paid by his celebrity, and, we may add, his good-nature; for, if the one had been a whit less than the other, he could never have tolerated such a nuisance.

The cost of his correspondence gives one no light idea of the demands made on his time, as well as purse, in another form. His postage for letters, independently of franks, by which a large portion of it was covered, amounted to a hundred and fifty pounds, it seems, in the course of the year. In this, indeed, should be included ten pounds for a pair of unfortunate *Cherokee Lovers*, sent all the way from our own happy land in order to be god-fathered by Sir Walter on the London boards. Perhaps the smart-money he had to pay on this interesting occasion had its influence in mixing up rather more acid than was natural to him in his judgments of our countrymen. At all events, the Yankees find little favour on the few occasions on which he has glanced at them in his correspondence. " I am not at all surprised," he says, in a letter to Miss Edgeworth, "I am not at all surprised at what you say of the Yankees. They are a people possessed of very considerable energy.

quickened and brought into eager action by an honourable love of their country and pride in their institutions; but they are as yet rude in their ideas of social intercourse, and totally ignorant, speaking generally, of all the art of good-breeding, which consists chiefly in a postponement of one's own petty wishes or comforts to those of others. By rude questions and observations, an absolute disrespect to other people's feelings, and a ready indulgence of their own, they make one feverish in their company, though perhaps you may be ashamed to confess the reason. But this will wear off, and is already wearing away. Men, when they have once got benches, will soon fall into the use of cushions. They are advancing in the lists of our literature, and they will not be long deficient in the *petite morale*, especially as they have, like ourselves, the rage for travelling." On another occasion, he does, indeed, admit having met with, in the course of his life, "four or five well-lettered Americans, ardent in pursuit of knowledge, and free from the ignorance and forward presumption which distinguish many of their countrymen." This seems hard measure, but perhaps we should find it difficult, among the many who have visited this country, to recollect as great a number of Englishmen—and Scotchmen to boot—entitled to a higher degree of commendation. It can hardly be that the well-informed and well-bred men of both countries make a point of staying at home; so we suppose we must look for the solution of the matter in the existence of some disagreeable ingredient, common to the characters of both nations, sprouting, as they do, from a common stock, which remains latent at home, and is never fully disclosed till they get into a foreign climate. But as this problem seems pregnant with philosophical, physiological, and, for aught we know, psychological matter, we have not courage for it here, but recommend the solution to Miss Martineau, to whom it will afford a very good title for a new chapter in her next edition. The strictures we have quoted, however, to speak more seriously, are worth attending to, coming as they do from a shrewd observer, and one whose judgments, though here somewhat coloured, no doubt, by political prejudice, are, in the main, distinguished by a sound and liberal philanthropy. But were he ten times an enemy, we would say, "Fas est ab hoste doceri."

With the splendid picture of the baronial residence at Abbotsford, Mr. Lockhart closes all that at this present writing we have received of his delightful work in this country; and in the last sentence the melancholy sound of "the muffled drum" gives ominous warning of what we are to expect in the sixth and concluding volume. In the dearth of more authentic information, we will piece out our sketch with a few facts gleaned from the somewhat meager bill of fare—meager by comparison with the rich banquet of the true Amphitryon—afforded by the "Recollections" of Mr. Robert Pierce Gillies.

The unbounded popularity of the Waverley Novels led to still more extravagant anticipations on the part both of the publishers and author. Some hints

4   S

of a falling off, though but slightly, in the public favour, were unheeded by both parties, though, to say
truth, the exact state of things was never disclosed
to Scott, it being Ballantyne's notion that it would
prove a damper, and that the true course was "to
press on more sail as the wind lulled." In these
sanguine calculations, not only enormous sums, or,
to speak correctly, *bills*, were given for what had been
written, but the author's draughts, to the amount of
many thousand pounds, were accepted by Constable
in favour of works, the very embryos of which lay,
not only unformed, but unimagined in the womb of
time. In return for this singular accommodation,
Scott was induced to endorse the draughts of his
publisher, and in this way an amount of liabilities
was incurred, which, considering the character of the
house and its transactions, it is altogether inexplicable that a person in the independent position of
Sir Walter Scott should have subjected himself to
for a moment. He seems to have had entire confidence in the stability of the firm, a confidence to
which it seems, from Mr. Gillies's account, not to
have been entitled from the first moment of his connexion with it. The great reputation of the house,
however, the success and magnitude of some of its
transactions, especially the publication of these novels, gave it a large credit, which enabled it to go
forward with a great show of prosperity in ordinary
times, and veiled its tottering state probably from
Constable's own eyes. It is but the tale of yesterday. The case of Constable and Co. is, unhappily,

a very familiar one to us. But when the hurricane of 1825 came on, it swept away all those buildings that were not founded on a rock, and those of Messrs. Constable, among others, soon became literally mere *castles in the air*—in plain English, the firm stopped payment. The assets were very trifling in comparison with the debts; and Sir Walter Scott was found on their paper to the frightful amount of one hundred thousand pounds!

His conduct on the occasion was precisely what was to have been anticipated from one who had declared on a similar, though much less appalling conjuncture, "I am always ready to make any sacrifices to do justice to my engagements, and would rather sell anything, or everything, than be less than a true man to the world." He put up his house and furniture in town at auction, delivered over his personal effects at Abbotsford, his plate, books, furniture, &c., to be held in trust for his creditors (the estate itself had been recently secured to his son on occasion of his marriage), and bound himself to discharge a certain amount annually of the liabilities of the insolvent firm. He then, with his characteristic energy, set about the performance of his Herculean task. He took lodgings in a third-rate house in St. David's-street, saw but little company, abridged the hours usually devoted to his meals and his family, gave up his ordinary exercise, and, in short, adopted the severe habits of a regular Grub-street stipendiary.

"For many years," he said to Mr. Gillies, "I have

been accustomed to hard work, because I found it a pleasure; now, with all due respect for Falstaff's principle, 'nothing on compulsion,' I certainly will not shrink from work because it has become necessary."

One of his first tasks was his "Life of Bonaparte," achieved in the space of thirteen months. For this he received fourteen thousand pounds, about eleven hundred per month—not a bad bargain either, as it proved, for the publishers. The first two volumes of the nine which make up the English edition were a *rifacimento* of what he had before compiled for the "Annual Register." With every allowance for the inaccuracies, and the excessive expansion incident to such a flashing rapidity of execution, the work, taking into view the broad range of its topics, its shrewd and sagacious reflections, and the free, bold, and picturesque colouring of its narration, and, above all, considering *the brief time in which it was written*, is indisputably one of the most remarkable monuments of genius and industry—perhaps the most remarkable ever recorded.

Scott's celebrity made everything that fell from him, however trifling—the dewdrops from the lion's mane—of value. But none of the many adventures he embarked in, or, rather, set afloat, proved so profitable as the republication of his novels, with his notes and illustrations. As he felt his own strength in the increasing success of his labours, he appears to have relaxed somewhat from them, and to have again resumed somewhat of his ancient habits, and, in a mitigated degree, his ancient hospitality. But still his exertions were too severe, and pressed heavily on the springs of his health, already deprived by age of their former elasticity and vigour. At length, in 1831, he was overtaken by one of those terrible shocks of paralysis which seem to have been constitutional in his family, but which, with more precaution, and under happier auspices, might, doubtless, have been postponed, if not wholly averted. At this time he had, in the short space of little more than five years, by his sacrifices and efforts, discharged about two thirds of the debt for which he was responsible: an astonishing result, wholly unparalleled in the history of letters! There is something inexpressibly painful in this spectacle of a generous heart thus courageously contending with fortune, bearing up against the tide with unconquerable spirit, and finally overwhelmed by it just within reach of shore.

The rest of his story is one of humiliation and sorrow. He was induced to take a voyage to the Continent to try the effect of a more genial climate. Under the sunny sky of Italy, he seemed to gather new strength for a while; but his eye fell with indifference on the venerable monuments which, in better days, would have kindled all his enthusiasm. The invalid sighed for his own home at Abbotsford. The heat of the weather and the fatigue of rapid travel brought on another shock, which reduced him to a state of deplorable imbecility. In this condition he returned to his own halls, where the sight of early

4   S*

friends, and of the beautiful scenery, the creation, as it were, of his own hands, seemed to impart a gleam of melancholy satisfaction, which soon, however, sunk into insensibility. To his present situation might well be applied the exquisite verses which he indited on another melancholy occasion:

> " Yet not the landscape to mine eye
>   Bears those bright hues that once it bore;
> Though Evening, with her richest dye,
>   Flames o'er the hills of Ettrick's shore.
>
> " With listless look along the plain
>   I see Tweed's silver current glide,
> And coldly mark the holy fane
>   Of Melrose rise in ruined pride.
>
> " The quiet lake, the balmy air,
>   The hill, the stream, the tower, the tree,
> Are they still such as once they were,
>   Or is the dreary change in me ?"

Providence, in its mercy, did not suffer the shattered frame long to outlive the glorious spirit which had informed it. He breathed his last on the 21st of September, 1832. His remains were deposited, as he had always desired, in the hoary abbey of Dryburgh, and the pilgrim from many a distant clime shall repair to the consecrated spot so long as the reverence for exalted genius and worth shall survive in the human heart.

This sketch, brief as we could make it, of the literary history of Sir Walter Scott, has extended so far as to leave but little space for—what Lockhart's volumes afford ample materials for—his personal character. Take it for all and all, it is not too much to say that this character is probably the most remark-

able on record. There is no man of historical celebrity that we now recall, who combined, in so eminent a degree, the highest qualities of the moral,
the intellectual, and the physical. He united in his
own character what hitherto had been found incompatible. Though a poet, and living in an ideal
world, he was an exact, methodical man of business; though achieving with the most wonderful facility of genius, he was patient and laborious; a
mousing antiquarian, yet with the most active interest in the present, and whatever was going on
around him; with a strong turn for a roving life
and military adventure, he was yet chained to his
desk more hours, at some periods of his life, than a
monkish recluse; a man with a heart as capacious
as his head; a Tory, brim full of Jacobitism, yet
full of sympathy and unaffected familiarity with all
classes, even the humblest; a successful author, without pedantry and without conceit; one, indeed, at
the head of the republic of letters, and yet with a
lower estimate of letters, as compared with other intellectual pursuits, than was ever hazarded before.

The first quality of his character, or, rather, that
which forms the basis of it, as of all great characters,
was his energy. We see it, in his early youth, triumphing over the impediments of nature, and, in
spite of lameness, making him conspicuous in every
sort of athletic exercise—clambering up dizzy pre-
cipices, wading through treacherous fords, and performing feats of pedestrianism that make one's joints
ache to read of. As he advanced in life, we see the

same force of purpose turned to higher objects. A striking example occurs in his organization of the journals and the publishing house in opposition to Constable. In what Herculean drudgery did not this latter business, in which he undertook to supply matter for the nimble press of Ballantyne, involve him! while, in addition to his own concerns, he had to drag along by his solitary momentum a score of heavier undertakings, that led Lockhart to compare him to a steam-engine, with a train of coal wagons hitched to it. "Yes," said Scott, laughing, and making a crashing cut with his axe (for they were felling larches), "and there was a cursed lot of dung carts too."

We see the same powerful energies triumphing over disease at a later period, when nothing but a resolution to get the better of it enabled him to do so. "Be assured," he remarked to Mr. Gillies, "that if pain could have prevented my application to literary labour, not a page of Ivanhoe would have been written. Now if I had given way to mere feelings, and ceased to work, it is a question whether the disorder might not have taken a deeper root, and become incurable." But the most extraordinary instance of this trait is the readiness with which he assumed and the spirit with which he carried through, till his mental strength broke down under it, the gigantic task imposed on him by the failure of Constable It mattered little what the nature of the task was whether it were organizing an opposition to a political faction, or a troop of cavalry to resist invasion

or a medley of wild Highlanders or Edinburgh cockneys to make up a royal puppet-show—a loyal cel-
ebration—for "His Most Sacred Majesty"—he was
the master-spirit that gave the cue to the whole
dramatis personæ. This potent impulse showed itself in the thoroughness with which he prescribed,
not merely the general orders, but the execution of
the minutest details, in his own person. Thus all
around him was the creation, as it were, of his individual exertion. His lands waved with forests
planted with his own hands, and, in process of time,
cleared by his own hands. He did not lay the stones
in mortar, exactly, for his whimsical castle, but he
seems to have superintended the operation from the
foundation to the battlements. The antique relics, the
curious works of art, the hangings and furniture, even,
with which his halls were decorated, were specially
contrived or selected by him; and, to read his letters
at this time to his friend Terry, one might fancy
himself perusing the correspondence of an upholsterer, so exact and technical is he in his instructions
We say this not in disparagement of his great qualities. It is only the more extraordinary; for, while
he stooped to such trifles, he was equally thorough
in matters of the highest moment. It was a trait of
character.

Another quality, which, like the last, seems to have
given the tone to his character, was his social or benevolent feelings. His heart was an unfailing fountain, which not merely the distresses, but the joys of
his fellow-creatures made to flow like water. In

early life, and possibly sometimes in ater, high spirits and a vigorous constitution led him occasionally to carry his social propensities into convivial excess: but he never was in danger of the habitual excess to which a vulgar mind—and sometimes, alas! one more finely tuned—abandons itself. With all his conviviality, it was not the sensual relish, but the social, which acted on him. He was neither *gourmé* nor *gourmand;* but his social meetings were endeared to him by the free interchange of kindly feelings with his friends. La Bruyère says (and it is odd he should have found it out in Louis the Fourteenth's court), "the heart has more to do than the head with the pleasures, or, rather, promoting the pleasures of society ;" "Un homme est d'un meilleur commerce dans la société par le cœur que par l'esprit." If report—the report of travellers—be true, we Americans, at least the New-Englanders, are too much perplexed with the cares and crosses of life to afford many genuine specimens of this *bonhommie* However this may be, we all, doubtless, know some such character, whose shining face, the index of a cordial heart, radiant with beneficent pleasure, diffuses its own exhilarating glow wherever it appears. Rarely, indeed, is this precious quality found united with the most exalted intellect. Whether it be that Nature, chary of her gifts, does not care to shower too many of them on one head ; or that the public admiration has led the man of intellect to set too high a value on himself, or at least his own pursuits, to take an interest in the inferior concerns of others;

or that the fear of compromising his dignity puts him " on points" with those who approach him ; or whether, in truth, the very magnitude of his own reputation throws a freezing shadow over us little people in his neighbourhood—whatever be the cause, it is too true that the highest powers of mind are very often deficient in the only one which can make the rest of much worth in society—the power of pleasing.

Scott was not one of these little great. His was not one of those dark-lantern visages which concentrate all their light on their own path, and are black as midnight to all about them. He had a ready sympathy, a word of contagious kindness, or cordial greeting, for all. His manners, too, were of a kind to dispel the icy reserve and awe which his great name was calculated to inspire. His frank address was a sort of *open sesame* to every heart. He did not deal in sneers, the poisoned weapons which come not from the head, as the man who launches them is apt to think, but from an acid heart, or, perhaps, an acid stomach, a very common laboratory of such small artillery. Neither did Scott amuse the company with parliamentary harangues or metaphysical disquisitions. His conversation was of the narrative kind, not formal, but as casually suggested by some passing circumstance or topic, and thrown in by way of illustration. He did not repeat himself, however, but continued to give his anecdotes such variations, by rigging them out in a new "cocked hat and walking-cane," as he called it, that they never tired like the thrice-told tale of a chronic *raconteur*. He allowed others, too, to take their turn, and thought with the Dean of St. Patrick's:

> " Carve to all, but just enough,
> Let them neither starve nor stuff:
> And, that you may have your due,
> Let your neighbours carve for you."

He relished a good joke, from whatever quarter it came, and was not over-dainty in his manner of testifying his satisfaction. "In the full tide of mirth, he did indeed laugh the heart's laugh," says Mr. Adolphus. "Give me an honest laugher," said Scott himself, on another occasion, when a buckram man of fashion had been paying him a visit at Abbotsford. His manners, free from affectation or artifice of any sort, exhibited the spontaneous movements of a kind disposition, subject to those rules of good breeding which Nature herself might have dictated. In this way he answered his own purpose admirably as a painter of character, by putting every man in good humour with himself, in the same manner as a cunning portrait-painter amuses his sitters with such store of fun and anecdote as may throw them off their guard, and call out the happiest expressions of their countenances.

Scott, in his wide range of friends and companions, does not seem to have been over-fastidious. In the instance of John Ballantyne, it has exposed him to some censure. In truth, a more worthless fellow never hung on the skirts of a great man; for he did not take the trouble to throw a decent veil over the grossest excesses. But then he had been the schoolboy friend of Scott; had grown up with him in a sort of dependance—a relation which begets a kindly feeling in the party that confers the benefits, at least. How strong it was in him may be inferred from his remark at his funeral. "I feel," said Scott, mournfully, as the solemnity was concluded, "I feel as if there would be less sunshine for me from this day forth." It must be admitted, however, that his intimacy with little Rigdumfunnidos, whatever apology it may find in Scott's heart, was not very creditable to his taste.

But the benevolent principle showed itself not merely in words, but in the more substantial form of actions. How many are the cases recorded of indigent merit, which he drew from obscurity, and almost warmed into life by his own generous and most delicate patronage! Such were the cases, among others, of Leyden, Weber, Hogg. How often and how cheerfully did he supply such literary contributions as were solicited by his friends— and they taxed him pretty liberally—amid all the pressure of business, and at the height of his fame, when his hours were golden hours to him! In the more vulgar and easier forms of charity, he did not stint his hand, though, instead of direct assistance, he preferred to enable others to assist themselves; in this way fortifying their good habits, and relieving them from the sense of personal degradation.

But the place where his benevolent impulses found their proper theatre for expansion was his

4   T

own home; surrounded by a happy family, and dispensing all the hospitalities of a great feudal proprietor. "There are many good things in life," he says, in one of his letters, "whatever satirists and misanthropes may say to the contrary; but probably the best of all, next to a conscience void of offence (without which, by-the-by, they can hardly exist), are the quiet exercise and enjoyment of the social feelings, in which we are at once happy ourselves, and the cause of happiness to them who are dearest to us." Every page of the work, almost, shows us how intimately he blended himself with the pleasures and the pursuits of his own family, watched over the education of his children, shared in their rides, their rambles, and sports, losing no opportunity of kindling in their young minds a love of virtue, and honourable principles of action. He delighted, too, to collect his tenantry around him, multiplying holydays, when young and old might come together under his roof-tree, when the jolly punch was liberally dispensed by himself and his wife among the elder people, and the *Hogmanay* cakes and pennies were distributed among the young ones; while his own children mingled in the endless reels and hornpipes on the earthen floor, and the *laird* himself, mixing in the groups of merry faces, had " his private joke for every old wife or 'gausie carle,' his arch compliment for the ear of every bonny lass, and his hand and his blessing for the head of every little *Eppie Daidle* from Abbotstown or Broomylees." " Sir Walter," said one of his old retainers, " speaks

to every man as if he were his blood relation." No
wonder that they should have returned this feeling
with something warmer than blood relations usually
do. Mr. Gillies tells an anecdote of the Ettrick
Shepherd, showing how deep a root such feelings,
notwithstanding his rather odd way of expressing
them, sometimes, had taken in his honest nature.
"Mr. James Ballantyne, walking home with him
one evening from Scott's, where, by-the-by, Hogg
had gone uninvited, happened to observe, 'I do not
at all like this illness of Scott's. I have often seen
him look jaded of late, and am afraid it is serious.'
'Haud your tongue, or I'll gar you measure your
length on the pavement!' replied Hogg. 'You
fause, down-hearted loon that you are; ye daur to
speak as if Scott were on his death-bed! It cannot
be—it *must* not be! I will not suffer you to speak
that gait.' The sentiment was like that of Uncle
Toby at the bedside of Le Fevre; and, at these
words, the Shepherd's voice became suppressed with
emotion."

But Scott's sympathies were not confined to his
species, and if he treated them like blood relations,
he treated his brute followers like personal friends.
Every one remembers old Maida and faithful Camp,
the "dear old friend," whose loss cost him a dinner.
Mr. Gillies tells us that he went into his study on
one occasion, when he was winding off his "Vision
of Don Roderick." "'Look here,' said the poet, 'I
have just begun to copy over the rhymes that you
heard to-day and applauded so much. Return to

supper if you can; only don't be late, as you perceive we keep early hours, and Wallace will not suffer me to rest after six in the morning. Come, good
dog, and help the poet.' At this hint, Wallace seated himself upright on a chair next his master, who
offered him a newspaper, which he directly seized,
looking very wise, and holding it firmly and content-
edly in his mouth. Scott looked at him with great
satisfaction, for he was excessively fond of dogs.
'Very well,' said he; '*now* we shall get on.' And so
I left them abruptly, knowing that my 'absence
would be the best company.'" This fellowship extended much farther than to his canine followers, of
which, including hounds, terriers, mastiffs, and mon-
grels, he had certainly a goodly assortment. We
find, also, Grimalkin installed in a responsible post in
the library, and out of doors pet hens, pet donkeys,
and—tell it not in Judæa—a pet pig!

Scott's sensibilities, though easily moved and
widely diffused, were warm and sincere. None
shared more cordially in the troubles of his friends;
but on all such occasions, with a true manly feeling,
he thought less of mere sympathy than of the most
effectual way for mitigating their sorrows. After a
touching allusion in one of his epistles to his dear
friend Erskine's death, he concludes, " I must turn
to and see what can be done about getting some pension for his daughters." In another passage, which
may remind one of some of the exquisite touches in
Jeremy Taylor, he indulges in the following beautiful strain of philosophy : " The last three or four

years have swept away more than half the friends
with whom I lived in habits of great intimacy. So
it must be with us

          ' When ance life's day draws near the gloamin','

and yet we proceed with our plantations and plans
as if any tree but the sad cypress would accompany
us to the grave, where our friends have gone before
us. It is the way of the world, however, and must
be so; otherwise life would be spent in unavailing
mourning for those whom we have lost. It is better
to enjoy the society of those who remain to us."
His well-disciplined heart seems to have confessed
the influence of this philosophy in his most ordinary
relations. " I can't help it," was a favourite maxim
of his, " and therefore will not think about it; for
that, at least, I *can* help."

Among his admirable qualities must not be omitted a certain worldly sagacity or shrewdness, which
is expressed as strongly as any individual trait can
be in some of his portraits, especially in the excellent
one of him by Leslie. Indeed, his countenance
would seem to exhibit, ordinarily, much more of
Dandie Dinmont's benevolent shrewdness than of
the eye glancing from earth to heaven, which in
fancy we assign to the poet, and which, in some
moods, must have been his. This trait may be
readily discerned in his business transactions, which
he managed with perfect knowledge of character as
well as of his own rights. No one knew better than
he the market value of an article; and, though he

4   T *

underrated his literary wares as to their mere literary rank, he set as high a money value on them, and made as sharp a bargain as any of the *trade* could have done. In his business concerns, indeed, he managed rather too much, or, to speak more correctly, was too fond of mixing up mystery in his transactions, which, like most mysteries, proved of little service to their author. Scott's correspondence, especially with his son, affords obvious examples of shrewdness, in the advice he gives as to his deportment in the novel situations and society into which the young cornet was thrown. Occasionally, in the cautious hints about etiquette and social observances, we may be reminded of that ancient ' arbiter elegantiarum," Lord Chesterfield, though it must be confessed there is throughout a high moral tone, which the noble lord did not very scrupulously affect.

Another feature in Scott's character was his loyalty, which some people would extend into a more general deference to rank not royal. We do certainly meet with a tone of deference, occasionally, to the privileged orders (or, rather, privileged persons, as the king, or his own chief, for to the mass of stars and garters he showed no such respect), which falls rather unpleasantly on the ear of a Republican. But, independently of the feelings which rightfully belonged to him as the subject of a monarchy, and without which he must have been a false-hearted subject, his own were heightened by a poetical colouring, that mingled in his mind even with much more vulgar relations of life. At the opening of the regalia in Holyrood House, when the honest burgomaster deposited the crown on the head of one of the young ladies present, the good man probably saw nothing more in the dingy diadem than we should have seen—a headpiece for a set of men no better than himself, and, if the old adage of a "dead lion" holds true, not quite so good. But to Scott's imagination other views were unfolded. "A thousand years their cloudy wings expanded" around him, and, in the dim visions of distant times, he beheld the venerable line of monarchs who had swayed the councils of his country in peace and led her armies in battle. The "golden round" became in his eye the symbol of his nation's glory; and as he heaved a heavy oath from his heart, he left the room in agitation, from which he did not speedily recover. There was not a spice of affectation in this—for who ever accused Scott of affectation?—but there was a good deal of poetry, the poetry of sentiment.

We have said that this feeling mingled in the more common concerns of his life. His cranium, indeed, to judge from his busts, must have exhibited a strong development of the organ of veneration. He regarded with reverence everything connected with antiquity. His establishment was on the feudal scale; his house was fashioned more after the feudal ages than his own; and even in the ultimate distribution of his fortune, although the circumstance of having made it himself relieved him from any legal necessity of contravening the suggestions of natural justice, he showed such attachment to the old aristocratic usage as to settle nearly the whole of it on his eldest son.

The influence of this poetic sentiment is discernible in his most trifling acts, in his tastes, his love of the arts, his social habits. His museum, house, and grounds were adorned with relics, curious not so much from their workmanship as their historic associations. It was the ancient fountain from Edinburgh, the Tolbooth lintels, the blunderbuss and spleughan of Rob Roy, the drinking-cup of Prince Charlie, or the like. It was the same in the arts. The tunes he loved were not the refined and complex melodies of Italy, but the simple notes of his native minstrelsy, from the bagpipe of John of Skye, or from the harp of his own lovely and accomplished daughter. So, also, in painting. It was not the masterly designs of the great Flemish and Italian schools that adorned his walls, but some portrait of Claverhouse, or of Queen Mary, or of "glorious old John." In architecture we see the same spirit in the singular " romance of stone and lime," which may be said to have been his own device, down to the minutest details of its finishing. We see it again in the joyous celebrations of his feudal tenantry, the good old festivals, the Hogmanay, the Kirn, &c., long fallen into desuetude, when the old Highland piper sounded the same wild pibroch that had so often summoned the clans together, for war or for wassail, among the fastnesses of the mountains. To the same source, in fine, may be traced the feelings of superstition which seemed to hover round Scott's mind like some "strange, mysterious dream," giving a romantic colouring to his conversation and his writings, but rarely, if ever, influencing his actions. It was a poetic sentiment.

Scott was a Tory to the backbone. Had he come into the world half a century sooner, he would, no doubt, have made a figure under the banner of the Pretender. He was at no great pains to disguise his political creed; witness his jolly drinking-song on the acquittal of Lord Melville. This was verse; but his prose is not much more qualified. "As for Whiggery in general," he says, in one of his letters, "I can only say that, as no man can be said to be utterly overset until his rump has been higher than his head, so I cannot read in history of any free state which has been brought to slavery until the rascal and uninstructed populace had had their short hour of anarchical government, which naturally leads to the stern repose of military despotism. . . . . With these convictions, I am very jealous of Whiggery under all modifications, and I must say my acquaintance with the total want of principle in some of its warmest professors does not tend to recommend it." With all this, however, his Toryism was not, practically, of that sort which blunts a man's sensibilities for those who are not of the same porcelain clay with himself. No man, Whig or Radical, ever had less of this pretension, or treated his inferiors with greater kindness, and even familiarity; a circumstance noticed by every visiter at his hospi-

F F

table mansion who saw him strolling round his grounds, taking his pinch of snuff out of the mull of some "gray-haired old hedger," or leaning on honest Tom Purdie's shoulder, and taking sweet counsel as to the right method of thinning a plantation. But, with all this familiarity, no man was better served by his domestics. It was the service of love, the only service that power cannot command and money cannot buy.

Akin to the feelings of which we have been speaking was the truly chivalrous sense of honour which stamped his whole conduct. We do not mean that Hotspur honour which is roused only by the drum and fife—though he says of himself, "I like the sound of a drum as well as Uncle Toby ever did"—but that honour which is deep-seated in the heart of every true gentleman, shrinking with sensitive delicacy from the least stain, or imputation of a stain, on his faith. "If we lose everything else," writes he, on a trying occasion to a friend who was not so nice in this particular, "we will at least keep our honour unblemished." It reminds one of the pithy epistle of a kindred chivalrous spirit, Francis the First, to his mother, from the unlucky field of Pavia : " Tout est perdu, fors l'honneur." Scott's latter years furnished a noble commentary on the sincerity of his manly principles.

Little is said directly of his religious sentiments in the biography. They seem to have harmonized well with his political. He was a member of the English Church, a stanch champion of established forms, and a sturdy enemy to everything that savoured of the sharp tang of Puritanism. On this ground, indeed, the youthful Samson used to wrestle manfully with worthy Dominie Mitchell, who, no doubt, furnished many a screed of doctrine for the Rev. Peter Pound-text, Master Nehemiah Holdenough, and other lights of the Covenant. Scott was no friend to cant under any form. But, whatever were his speculative opinions, in practice his heart overflowed with that charity which is the life-spring of our religion; and whenever he takes occasion to allude to the subject directly, he testifies a deep reverence for the truths of revelation, as well as for its Divine original.

Whatever estimate be formed of Scott's moral qualities, his intellectual were of a kind which well entitled him to the epithet conferred on Lope de Vega, " monstruo de naturaleza" (a miracle of nature). His mind scarcely seemed to be subjected to the same laws that control the rest of his species. His memory, as is usual, was the first of his powers fully developed. While an urchin at school, he could repeat whole cantos, he says, of Ossian and of Spenser. In riper years we are constantly meeting with similar feats of his achievement. Thus, on one occasion, he repeated the whole of a poem in some penny magazine, incidentally alluded to, which he had not seen since he was a schoolboy. On another, when the Ettrick Shepherd was trying ineffectually to fish up from his own recollections some scraps of a ballad he had himself manufactured years before, Scott called to him, "Take your pencil,

Jemmy, and I will tell it to you, word for word;" and he accordingly did so. But it is needless to multiply examples of feats so startling as to look almost like the tricks of a conjuror.

What is most extraordinary is, that while he acquired with such facility, that the bare perusal, or the repetition of a thing once to him, was sufficient, he yet retained it with the greatest pertinacity. Other men's memories are so much jostled in the rough and tumble of life, that most of the facts get sifted out nearly as fast as they are put in; so that we are in the same dilemma with those unlucky daughters of Danaus, of schoolboy memory, obliged to spend the greater part of the time in replenishing. But Scott's memory seemed to be hermetically sealed, suffering nothing once fairly in to leak out again. This was of immense service to him when he took up the business of authorship, as his whole multifarious stock of facts, whether from books or observation, became, in truth, his stock in trade, ready furnished to his hands. This may explain in part—though it is not less marvellous—the cause of his rapid execution of works, often replete with rare and curious information. The labour, the preparation, had been already completed. His whole life had been a business of preparation. When he ventured, as in the case of "Rokeby" and of "Quentin Durward," on ground with which he had not been familiar, we see how industriously he set about new acquisitions.

In most of the prodigies of memory which we

have ever known, the overgrowth of that faculty seems to have been attained at the expense of all the others; but in Scott, the directly opposite power of the imagination, the inventive power, was equally strongly developed, and at the same early age; for we find him renowned for story-craft while at school. How many a delightful fiction, warm with the flush of ingenuous youth, did he not throw away on the ears of thoughtless childhood, which, had they been duly registered, might now have amused children of a larger growth! We have seen Scott's genius in its prime and its decay. The frolic graces of childhood are alone wanting.

The facility with which he threw his ideas into language was also remarked very early. One of his first ballads, and a long one, was dashed off at the dinner-table. His "Lay" was written at the rate of a canto a week. "Waverley," or, rather, the last two volumes of it, cost the evenings of a summer month. Who that has ever read the account can forget the movements of that mysterious hand, as described by the two students from the window of a neighbouring attic, throwing off sheet after sheet, with untiring rapidity, of the pages destined to immortality? Scott speaks pleasantly enough of this marvellous facility in a letter to his friend Morritt: "When once I set my pen to the paper, it will walk fast enough. I am sometimes tempted to leave it alone, and see whether it will not write as well without the assistance of my head as with it. A hopeful prospect for the reader."

4   U

As to the time and place of composition, he appears to have been nearly indifferent. He possessed entire power of abstraction, and it mattered little whether he were nailed to his clerk's desk, under the drowsy eloquence of some long-winded barrister, or dashing his horse into the surf on Portobello sands, or rattling in a post-chaise, or amid the hum of guests in his overflowing halls at Abbotsford—it mattered not; the same well-adjusted little packet, " nicely corded and sealed," was sure to be ready, at the regular time, for the Edinburgh mail. His own account of his composition to a friend, who asked when he found time for it, is striking enough. " Oh," said Scott, " I lie *simmering* over things for an hour or so before I get up, and there's the time I am dressing to overhaul my half sleeping, half waking *projet de chapitre ;* and when I get the paper before me, it commonly runs off pretty easily. Besides, I often take a doze in the plantations, and while Tom marks out a dike or a drain as I have directed, one's fancy may be running its ain riggs in some other world." Never did this sort of simmering produce such a splendid bill of fare.

The quality of the material, under such circumstances, is, in truth, the great miracle of the whole. The execution of so much work, as a mere feat of penmanship, would undoubtedly be very extraordinary, but as a mere scrivener's miracle, would be hardly worth recording. It is a sort of miracle that is every day performing under our own eyes, as it were, by Messrs James, Bulwer, & Co., who, in all the various staples of "comedy, history, pastoral-comical, historical-pastoral," &c., supply their own market, and ours too, with all that can be wanted. In Spain, and in Italy also, we may find abundance of *improvvisatori* and *improvvisatrici*, who perform miracles of the same sort, in verse, too, in languages whose vowel terminations make it very easy for the thoughts to tumble into rhyme, without any malice prepense. Sir Stamford Raffles, in his account of Java, tells us of a splendid avenue of trees before his house, which in the course of a year shot up to the height of forty feet. But who shall compare the brief, transitory splendours of a fungus vegetation with the mighty monarch of the forest, sending his roots deep into the heart of the earth, and his branches, amid storm and sunshine, to the heavens? And is not the latter the true emblem of Scott? For who can doubt that his prose creations, at least, will gather strength with time, living on through succeeding generations, even when the language in which they are written, like those of Greece and Rome, shall cease to be a living language?

The only writer deserving, in these respects, to be named with Scott, is Lope de Vega, who in his own day held as high a rank in the republic of letters as our great contemporary. The beautiful dramas which he threw off for the entertainment of the capital, and whose success drove Cervantes from the stage, outstripped the abilities of an amanuensis to copy. His intimate friend, Montalvan, one of the most popular and prolific authors of the time, tells us that he undertook with Lope once to supply the theatre with a comedy—in verse, and in three acts, as the Spanish dramas usually were—at a very short notice. In order to get through his half as soon as his partner, he rose by two in the morning, and at eleven had completed it; an extraordinary feat, certainly, since a play extended to between thirty and forty pages, of a hundred lines each. Walking into the garden, he found his brother poet pruning an orange-tree. "Well, how do you get on?" said Montalvan. "Very well," answered Lope. "I rose betimes—at five; and after I had got through, eat my breakfast; since which I have written a letter of fifty triplets, and watered the whole of the garden, which has tired me a good deal."

But a little arithmetic will best show the comparative fertility of Scott and Lope de Vega. It is so german to the present matter, that we shall make no apology for transcribing here some computations from our last July number; and as few of our readers, we suspect, have the air-tight memory of Sir Walter, we doubt not that enough of it has escaped them by this time to excuse us from equipping it with one of those "cocked hats and walking-sticks" with which he furbished up an old story.

"It is impossible to state the results of Lope de Vega's labours in any form that will not powerfully strike the imagination. Thus, he has left twenty-one million three hundred thousand verses in print, besides a mass of manuscript. He furnished the theatre, according to the statement of his intimate

friend, Montalvan, with eighteen hundred regular
plays, and four hundred *autos* or religious dramas—
all acted He composed, according to his own statement, more than one hundred comedies in the almost incredible space of twenty-four hours each;
and a comedy averaged between two and three thousand verses, great part of them rhymed, and interspersed with sonnets, and other more difficult forms
of versification. He lived seventy-two years; and
supposing him to have employed fifty of that period
in composition, although he filled a variety of engrossing vocations during that time, he must have
averaged a play a week, to say nothing of twenty-
one volumes, quarto, of miscellaneous works, including five epics, written in his leisure moments, and
all now in print!

"The only achievements we can recall in literary history bearing any resemblance to, though falling far short of this, are those of our illustrious contemporary, Sir Walter Scott. The complete edition
of his works, recently advertised by Murray, with
the edition of two volumes of which Murray has
not the copyright, probably contains ninety volumes,
small octavo. [To these should farther be added a
large supply of matter for the Edinburgh Annual
Register, as well as other anonymous contributions.]
Of these, forty-eight volumes of novels, and twenty-
one of history and biography, were produced between 1814 and 1831, or in seventeen years. These
would give an average of four volumes a year, or
one for every three months during the whole of that

period; to which must be added twenty-one volumes of poetry and prose, previously published. The mere mechanical execution of so much work, both in his case and Lope de Vega's, would seem to be scarce possible in the limits assigned. Scott, too, was as variously occupied in other ways as his Spanish rival; and probably, from the social hospitality of his life, spent a much larger portion of his time in no literary occupation at all."

Of all the wonderful dramatic creations of Lope de Vega's genius, what now remains? Two or three plays only keep possession of the stage, and few, very few, are still read with pleasure in the closet. They have never been collected into a uniform edition, and are now met with in scattered sheets only on the shelves of some mousing bookseller, or collected in miscellaneous parcels in the libraries of the curious.

Scott, with all his facility of execution, had none of that pitiable affectation sometimes found in men of genius, who think that the possession of this quality may dispense with regular, methodical habits of study. He was most economical of time. He did not, like Voltaire, speak of it as " a terrible thing that so much time should be wasted in talking." He was too little of a pedant, and far too benevolent, not to feel that there are other objects worth living for than mere literary fame; but he grudged the waste of time on merely frivolous and heartless objects. " As for dressing when we are quite alone," he remarked one day to Mr. Gillies, whom he had taken home with him to a family dinner, "it is out of the question. Life is not long enough for such fiddle-faddle." In the early part of his life he worked late at night, but, subsequently, from a conviction of the superior healthiness of early rising, as well as the desire to secure, at all hazards, a portion of the day for literary labour, he rose at five the year round; no small effort, as any one will admit who has seen the pain and difficulty which a regular bird of night finds in reconciling his eyes to daylight. He was scrupulously exact, moreover, in the distribution of his hours. In one of his letters to his friend Terry, the player, replete, as usual, with advice that seems to flow equally from the head and the heart, he says, in reference to the practice of *dawdling* away one's time, "A habit of the mind it is which is very apt to beset men of intellect and talent, especially when their time is not regularly filled up, but left to their own arrangement. But it is like the ivy round the oak, and ends by limiting, if it does not destroy, the power of manly and necessary exertion. I must love a man so well, to whom I offer such a word of advice, that I will not apologize for it, but expect to hear you are become *as regular as a Dutch clock—hours, quarters, minutes, all marked and appropriated.*" With the same emphasis he inculcates the like habits on his son. If any man might dispense with them, it was surely Scott. But he knew that without them the greatest powers of mind will run to waste, and water but the desert.

Some of the literary opinions of Scott are singular, considering, too, the position he occupied in the world of letters. "I promise you," he says, in an epistle to an old friend, "my oaks will outlast my laurels; and I pique myself more on my compositions for manure than on any other compositions to which I was ever accessary." This may seem *badinage*; but he repeatedly, both in writing and conversation, places literature, as a profession, below other intellectual professions, and especially the military. The Duke of Wellington, the representative of the last, seems to have drawn from him a very extraordinary degree of deference, which we cannot but think smacks a little of that strong relish for gunpowder which he avows in himself.

It is not very easy to see on what this low estimate of literature rested. As a profession, it has too little in common with more active ones, to afford much ground for running a parallel. The soldier has to do with externals; and his contests and triumphs are over matter in its various forms, whether of man or material nature. The poet deals with the bodiless forms of air, of fancy lighter than air. His business is contemplative, the other's is active, and depends for its success on strong moral energy and presence of mind. He must, indeed, have genius of the highest order to effect his own combinations, anticipate the movements of his enemy, and dart with eagle eye on his vulnerable point. But who shall say that this practical genius, if we may so term it, is to rank higher in the scale than the creative power of the poet, the spark from the mind of divinity itself?

The orator might seem to afford better ground for comparison, since, though his theatre of action is abroad, he may be said to work with much the same tools as the writer. Yet how much of his success depends on qualities other than intellectual! "Action," said the father of eloquence, "action, action are the three most essential things to an orator." How much depends on the look, the gesture, the magical tones of voice, modulated to the passions he has stirred; and how much on the contagious sympathies of the audience itself, which drown everything like criticism in the overwhelming tide of emotion! If any one would know how much, let him, after patiently standing

> "till his feet throb,
> And his head thumps, to feed upon the breath
> Of patriots bursting with heroic rage,"

read the same speech in the columns of a morning newspaper, or in the well-concocted report of the orator himself. The productions of the writer are subjected to a fiercer ordeal. He has no excited sympathies of numbers to hurry his readers along over his blunders. He is scanned in the calm silence of the closet. Every flower of fancy seems here to wither under the rude breath of criticism; every link in the chain of argument is subjected to the touch of prying scrutiny, and if there be the least flaw in it, it is sure to be detected. There is no tribunal so stern as the secret tribunal of a man's own closet, far removed from all the sympathetic impulses of humanity. Surely there is no form in which *intellect* can be exhibited to the world so completely stripped of all adventitious aids as the form of written composition. But, says the practical man, let us estimate things by their utility. "You talk of the poems of Homer," said a mathematician, "but, after all, what do they *prove?*" A question which involves an answer somewhat too voluminous for the tail of an article. But if the poems of Homer were, as Heeren asserts, the principal bond which held the Grecian states together, and gave them a national feeling, they "prove" more than all the arithmeticians of Greece—and there were many cunning ones in it—ever proved. The results of military skill are indeed obvious. The soldier, by a single victory, enlarges the limits of an empire; he may do more—he may achieve the liberties of a nation, or roll back the tide of barbarism ready to overwhelm them. Wellington was placed in such a position, and nobly did he do his work; or, rather, he was placed at the head of such a gigantic moral and physical apparatus as enabled him to do it. With his own unassisted strength, of course, he could have done nothing. But it is on his own solitary resources that the great writer is to rely. And yet, who shall say that the triumphs of Wellington have been greater than those of Scott, whose works are familiar as household words to every fireside in his own land, from the castle to the cottage; have crossed oceans and deserts, and, with healing on their wings, found their way to the remotest regions; have helped to form the character, until his own mind may be said to be incorporated into those of hundreds of thousands of his fellow-men? Who is there that has not, at some time or other, felt the heaviness of his heart lightened, his pains mitigated, and his bright moments of life made still brighter by the magical touches of his genius? And shall we speak of his victories as less real, less serviceable to humanity, less truly glorious than those of the greatest captain of his day? The triumphs of the warrior are bounded by the narrow theatre of his own age; but those of a Scott or a Shakspeare will be renewed with greater and greater lustre in ages yet unborn, when the victorious chieftain shall be forgotten, or shall live only in the song of the minstrel and the page of the chronicler.

But, after all, this sort of parallel is not very gracious nor very philosophical, and, to say truth, is somewhat foolish. We have been drawn into it by the not random, but very deliberate, and, in our poor judgment, very disparaging estimate by Scott of his own vocation; and, as we have taken the trouble to write it, our readers will excuse us from blotting it out. There is too little ground for the respective parties to stand on for a parallel. As to the pedantic *cui bono* standard, it is impossible to tell the final issues of a single act; how can we then hope to those of a course of action? As for the *honour* of different vocations, there never was a truer sentence than the stale one of Pope—stale now, because it is so true—

"Act well your part—there all the honour lies."

And it is the just boast of our own country, that in no civilized nation is the force of this philanthropic maxim so nobly illustrated as in ours—thanks to our glorious institutions.

A great cause, probably, of Scott's low estimate of letters was the facility with which he wrote. What costs us little we are apt to prize little. If diamonds were as common as pebbles, and gold-dust as any other, who would stoop to gather them? It was the prostitution of his muse, by-the-by, for this same gold-dust, which brought a sharp rebuke on the poet from Lord Byron, in his " English Bards :"

"For this we spurn Apollo's venal son ;"

a coarse cut, and the imputation about as true as most satire, that is, not true at all. This was indited in his lordship's earlier days, when he most chivalrously disclaimed all purpose of bartering his rhymes for gold. He lived long enough, however, to weigh his literary wares in the same money-balance used by more vulgar manufacturers; and, in truth, it would be ridiculous if the produce of the brain should not bring its price in this form as well as any other. There is little danger, we imagine, of finding too much gold in the bowels of Parnassus.

Scott took a more sensible view of things. In a letter to Ellis, written soon after the publication of " The Minstrelsy," he observes, " People may say this and that of the pleasure of fame, or of profit, as a motive of writing, I think the only pleasure is in

the actual exertion and research, and I would no
more write upon any other terms than I would hunt
merely to dine upon hare soup. At the same time,
if credit and profit came unlooked for, I would no
more quarrel with them than with the soup." Even
this declaration was somewhat more magnanimous
than was warranted by his subsequent conduct.
The truth is, he soon found out, especially after the
Waverley vein had opened, that he had hit on a
gold-mine. The prodigious returns he got gave the
whole thing the aspect of a speculation. Every new
work was an adventure, and the proceeds naturally
suggested the indulgence of the most extravagant
schemes of expense, which, in their turn, stimulated
him to fresh efforts. In this way the "profits" became, whatever they might have been once, a principal incentive to, as they were the recompense of,
exertion. His productions were cash articles, and
were estimated by him more on the Hudibrastic rule
of "the real worth of a thing" than by any fanciful
standard of fame. He bowed with deference to the
judgment of the booksellers, and trimmed his sails
dexterously as the "aura popularis" shifted. "If it
is na weil bobbit," he writes to his printer, on turn
ing out a less lucky novel, "we'll bobbit again."
His muse was of that school who seek the greatest
happiness of the greatest number. We can hardly
imagine him invoking her like Milton:

" Still govern thou my song,
Urania, and fit audience find, though few."

Still less can we imagine him, like the blind old

4   V

bard, feeding his soul with visions of posthumous glory, and spinning out epics for five pounds apiece.

It is singular that Scott, although he set as high a money value on his productions as the most enthusiastic of the "trade" could have done, in a literary view should have held them so cheap. "Whatever others may be," he said, " I have never been a partisan of my own poetry; as John Wilkes declared, that, 'in the height of his success, he had himself never been a Wilkite.' " Considering the poet's popularity, this was but an indifferent compliment to the taste of his age. With all this disparagement of his own productions, however, Scott was not insensible to criticism. He says somewhere that, "if he had been conscious of a single vulnerable point in himself, he would not have taken up the business of writing;" but, on another occasion, he writes, "I make it a rule never to read the attacks made upon me;" and Captain Hall remarks, " He never reads the criticisms on his books; this I know, from the most unquestionable authority. Praise, he says, gives him no pleasure, and censure annoys him." Madame de Graffigny says, also, of Voltaire, " that he was altogether indifferent to praise, but the least word from his enemies dròve him crazy." Yet both these authors banqueted on the sweets of panegyric as much as any who ever lived. They were in the condition of an epicure whose palate has lost its relish for the dainty fare in which it has been so long revelling, without becoming less sensible to the annoyances of sharper and coarser flavours. It may afford some consolation to humble mediocrity, to the less fortunate votaries of the muse, that those who have reached the summit of Parnassus are not much more contented with their condition than those who are scrambling among the bushes at the bottom of the mountain. The fact seems to be, as Scott himself intimates more than once, that the joy is in the chase, whether in the prose or the poetry of life.

But it is high time to terminate our lucubrations, which, however imperfect and unsatisfactory, have already run to a length that must trespass on the patience of the reader. We rise from the perusal of these delightful volumes with the same sort of melancholy feeling with which we wake from a pleasant dream. The concluding volume, of which such ominous presage is given in the last sentence of the fifth, has not yet reached us; but we know enough to anticipate the sad catastrophe it is to unfold of the drama. In those which we have seen, we have beheld a succession of interesting characters come upon the scene and pass away to their long home. "Bright eyes now closed in dust, gay voices forever silenced," seem to haunt us, too, as we write. The imagination reverts to Abbotsford —the romantic and once brilliant Abbotsford—the magical creation of *his* hands. We see its halls radiant with the hospitality of *his* benevolent heart; thronged with pilgrims from every land, assembled to pay homage at the shrine of genius; echoing to the blithe music of those festal holydays when young and old met to renew the usages of the good old times.

"These were its charms, but all these charms are fled."

Its courts are desolate, or trodden only by the foot of the stranger. The stranger sits under the shadows of the trees which his hand planted. The spell of the enchanter is dissolved; his wand is broken; and the mighty minstrel himself now sleeps in the bosom of the peaceful scenes embellished by his taste, and which his genius has made immortal.

CHATEAUBRIAND'S ENGLISH LITERATURE.*

OCTOBER, 1839.

THERE are few topics of greater attraction, or, when properly treated, of higher importance, than literary history.   For what is it but a faithful register of the successive steps by which a nation has advanced in the career of civilization?   Civil history records the crimes and the follies, the enterprises, discoveries, and triumphs, it may be, of humanity.   But to what do all these tend, or of what moment are they in the eye of the philosopher, except as they accelerate or retard the march of civilization?   The history of literature is the history of the human mind.   It is, as compared with other histories, the intellectual as distinguished from the material—the informing spirit, as compared with the outward and visible.

When such a view of the mental progress of a people is combined with individual biography, we have all the materials for the deepest and most varied interest.   The life of the man of letters is not always circumscribed by the walls of a cloister; and was not, even in those days when the cloister was the familiar abode of science.   The history of Dante and of Petrarch is the best commentary on that of their age.   In later times, the man of letters has

---

* "Sketches of English Literature; with considerations on the Spirit of the Times, Men, and Revolutions.   By the Viscount de CHATEAUBRIAND" 2 vols, 8vo. London, 1836.

4   V*

taken part in all the principal concerns of public and social life. But, even when the story is to derive its interest from personal character, what a store of entertainment is supplied by the eccentricities of genius—the joys and sorrows, not visible to vulgar eyes, but which agitate his finer sensibilities as powerfully as the greatest shocks of worldly fortune would a hardier and less visionary temper! What deeper interest can romance afford than is to be gathered from the melancholy story of Petrarch, Tasso, Alfieri, Rousseau, Byron, Burns, and a crowd of familiar names, whose genius seems to have been given them only to sharpen their sensibility to suffering? What matter if their sufferings were, for the most part, of the imagination? They were not the less real to *them*. They lived in a world of imagination, and, by the gift of genius, unfortunate to its proprietor, have known how, in the language of one of the most unfortunate, " to make madness beautiful" in the eyes of others.

But, notwithstanding the interest and importance of literary history, it has hitherto received but little attention from English writers. No complete survey of the treasures of our native tongue has been yet produced, or even attempted. The earlier periods of the poetical development of the nation have been well illustrated by various antiquaries. Warton has brought the history of poetry down to the season of its first vigorous expansion—the age of Elizabeth. But he did not penetrate beyond the magnificent vestibule of the temple. Dr. Johnson's "Lives of the Poets" have done much to supply the deficiency in this department. But much more remains to be done to afford the student anything like a complete view of the progress of poetry in England. Johnson's work, as every one knows, is conducted on the most capricious and irregular plan. The biographies were dictated by the choice of the bookseller. Some of the most memorable names in British literature are omitted to make way for a host of minor luminaries, whose dim radiance, unassisted by the critic's magnifying lens, would never have penetrated to posterity. The same irregularity is visible in the proportion he has assigned to each of his subjects ; the principal figures, or what should have been such, being often thrown into the background, to make room for some subordinate person whose story was thought to have more interest.

Besides these defects of plan, the critic was certainly deficient in sensibility to the more delicate, the minor beauties of poetic sentiment. He analyzes verse in the cold-blooded spirit of a chemist, until all the aroma, which constituted its principal charm, escapes in the decomposition. By this kind of process, some of the finest fancies of the Muse, the lofty dithyrambics of Gray, the ethereal effusions of Collins, and of Milton too, are rendered sufficiently vapid. In this sort of criticism, all the effect that relies on *impressions* goes for nothing. Ideas are alone taken into the account, and all is weighed in the same hard, matter-of-fact scales of common sense, like so much solid prose. What a sorry figure would Byron's Muse make subjected to such an ordeal! The doctor's taste in composition, to judge from his own style, was not of the highest order. It was a style, indeed, of extraordinary power, suited to the expression of his original thinking, bold, vigorous, and glowing with all the lustre of pointed antithesis. But the brilliancy is cold, and the ornaments are much too florid and overcharged for a graceful effect. When to these minor blemishes we add the graver one of an obliquity of judgment, produced by inveterate political and religious prejudice, which has thrown a shadow over some of the brightest characters subjected to his pencil, we have summed up a fair amount of critical deficiencies. With all this, there is no one of the works of this great and good man in which he has displayed more of the strength of his mighty intellect, shown a more pure and masculine morality, more sound principles of criticism in the abstract, more acute delineation of character, and more gorgeous splendour of diction. His defects, however, such as they are, must prevent his maintaining with posterity that undisputed dictatorship in criticism which was conceded to him in his own day. We must do justice to his errors as well as to his excellences, in order that we may do justice to the characters which have come under his censure. And we must admit that his work, however admirable as a gallery of splendid portraits, is inadequate to convey anything like a complete or impartial view of English poetry.

The English have made but slender contributions

to the history of foreign literatures. The most important, probably, are Roscoë's works, in which literary criticism, though but a subordinate feature, is the most valuable part of the composition. As to anything like a general survey of this department, they are wholly deficient. The deficiency, indeed, is likely to be supplied, to a certain extent, by the work of Mr. Hallam, now in progress of publication; the first volume of which—the only one which has yet issued from the press—gives evidence of the same curious erudition, acuteness, honest impartiality, and energy of diction which distinguish the other writings of this eminent scholar. But the extent of his work, limited to four volumes, precludes anything more than a survey of the most prominent features of the vast subject he has undertaken.

The Continental nations, under serious discouragements, too, have been much more active than the British in this field. The Spaniards can boast a general history of letters, extending to more than twenty volumes in length, and compiled with sufficient impartiality. The Italians have several such. Yet these are the lands of the Inquisition, where reason is hoodwinked, and the honest utterance of opinion has been recompensed by persecution, exile, and the stake. How can such a people estimate the character of compositions which, produced under happier institutions, are instinct with the spirit of freedom? How can they make allowance for the manifold eccentricities of a literature where thought

I I

is allowed to expatiate in all the independence of individual caprice ? How can they possibly, trained to pay such nice deference to outward finish and mere verbal elegance, have any sympathy with the rough and homely beauties which emanate from the people and are addressed to the people ?

The French, nurtured under freer forms of government, have contrived to come under a system of literary laws scarcely less severe. Their first great dramatic production gave rise to a scheme of critical legislation, which has continued ever since to press on the genius of the nation in all the higher walks of poetic art. Amid all the mutations of state, the tone of criticism has remained essentially the same to the present century, when, indeed, the boiling passions and higher excitements of a revolutionary age have made the classic models on which their literature was cast appear somewhat too frigid, and a warmer colouring has been sought by an infusion of English sentiment. But this mixture, or, rather, confusion of styles, neither French nor English, seems to rest on no settled principles, and is, probably, too alien to the genius of the people to continue permanent.

The French, forming themselves early on a foreign and antique model, were necessarily driven to rules, as a substitute for those natural promptings which have directed the course of other modern nations in the career of letters. Such rules, of course, while assimilating them to antiquity, drew them aside from sympathy with their own contemporaries. How can they, thus formed on an artificial system, enter into the spirit of other literatures so uncongenial with their own ?

That the French continued subject to such a system, with little change to the present age, is evinced by the example of Voltaire, a writer whose lawless ridicule

> " like the wind,
> Blew where it listed, laying all things prone,"

but whose revolutionary spirit made no serious changes in the principles of the national criticism. Indeed, his commentaries on Corneille furnish evidence of a willingness to contract still closer the range of the poet, and to define more accurately the laws by which his movements were to be controlled. Voltaire's history affords an evidence of the truth of the Horatian maxim, " *naturam expellas,*" &c. In his younger days he passed some time, as is well known, in England, and contracted there a certain relish for the strange models which came under his observation. On his return he made many attempts to introduce the foreign school with which he had become acquainted to his own countrymen. His vanity was gratified by detecting the latent beauties of his barbarian neighbours, and by being the first to point them out to his countrymen. It associated him with names venerated on the other side of the Channel, and at home transferred a part of their glory to himself. Indeed, he was not backward in transferring as much as he could of it, by borrowing on his own account, where he could venture. *mani-*

bus plenis, and with very little acknowledgment.
The French at length became so far reconciled to
the monstrosities of their neighbours, that a regular
translation of Shakspeare, the lord of the British
Pandemonium, was executed by Letourneur, a scholar of no great merit; but the work was well received. Voltaire, the veteran, in his solitude of Ferney,
was roused, by the applause bestowed on the English poet in his Parisian costume, to a sense of his
own imprudence. He saw, in imagination, the altars which had been raised to him, as well as to the
other master-spirits of the national drama, in a fair
way to be overturned, in order to make room for an
idol of his own importation. " Have you seen," he
writes, speaking of Letourneur's version, " his abominable trash ? Will you endure the affront put upon
France by it ? There are no epithets bad enough,
nor fool's-caps, nor pillories enough in all France
for such a scoundrel. The blood tingles in my old
veins in speaking of him. What is the most dread-
ful part of the affair is, the monster has his party in
France ; and, to add to my shame and consternation, it was I who first sounded the praises of *this
Shakspeare ;* I who first showed the pearls, picked
here and there, from his overgrown dungheap. Little did I anticipate that I was helping to trample
under foot, at some future day, the laurels of Racine
and Corneille to adorn the brows of a barbarous
player—this drunkard of a Shakspeare." Not content with this expectoration of his bile, the old poet
transmitted a formal letter of remonstrance to D'Alem-

bert, which was read publicly, as designed, at a regular *séance* of the Academy. The document, after expatiating at length on the blunders, vulgarities, and indecencies of the English bard, concludes with this appeal to the critical body he was addressing : " Paint to yourselves, gentlemen, Louis the Fourteenth in his gallery at Versailles, surrounded by his brilliant court: a tatterdemalian advances, covered with rags, and proposes to the assembly to abandon the tragedies of Racine for a mountebank, full of grimaces, with nothing but a lucky hit, now and then, to redeem them."

At a later period, Ducis, the successor of Voltaire, if we remember right, in the Academy, a writer of far superior merit to Letourneur, did the British bard into much better French than his predecessor ; though Ducis, as he takes care to acquaint us, " did his best to efface those startling impressions of horror which would have damned his author in the polished theatres of Paris !" Voltaire need not have taken the affair so much to heart. Shakspeare, reduced within the compass, as much as possible, of the rules, with all his eccentricities and peculiarities—all that made him English, in fact— smoothed away, may be tolerated, and to a certain extent countenanced, in the " polished theatres of Paris." But this is not

" Shakspeare, *Nature's* child,
Warbling his native wood-notes wild."

The Germans are just the antipodes of their French neighbours. Coming late on the arena of

4   W

modern literature, they would seem to be particularly qualified for excelling in criticism by the variety
of styles and models for their study supplied by
other nations. They have, accordingly, done wonders in this department, and have extended their
critical wand over the remotest regions, dispelling
the mists of old prejudice, and throwing the light of
learning on what before was dark and inexplicable.
They certainly are entitled to the credit of a singularly cosmopolitan power of divesting themselves of
local and national prejudice. No nation has done
so much to lay the foundations of that reconciling
spirit of criticism, which, instead of condemning a
difference of taste in different nations as a departure
from it, seeks to explain such discrepancies by the
peculiar circumstances of the nation, and thus from
the elements of discord, as it were, to build up a
universal and harmonious system. The exclusive
and unfavourable views entertained by some of their
later critics respecting the French literature, indeed,
into which they have been urged, no doubt, by a desire to counteract the servile deference shown to that
literature by their countrymen of the preceding age,
forms an important exception to their usual candour.

As general critics, however, the Germans are open
to grave objections. The very circumstances of
their situation, so favourable, as we have said, to the
formation of a liberal criticism, have encouraged the
taste for theories and for system-building, always unpropitious to truth. Whoever broaches a theory has
a hard battle to fight with conscience. If the theo-

ry cannot conform to the facts, so much the worse for the facts, as some wag has said; they must, at all events, conform to the theory. The Germans have put together hypotheses with the facility with which children construct card-houses, and many of them bid fair to last as long. They show more industry in accumulating materials than taste or discretion in their arrangement. They carry their fantastic imagination beyond the legitimate province of the muse into the sober fields of criticism. Their philosophical systems, curiously and elaborately de vised, with much ancient lore and solemn imaginings, may remind one of some of those venerable English Cathedrals where the magnificent and mysterious Gothic is blended with the clumsy Saxon. The effect, on the whole, is grand, but grotesque withal.

The Germans are too often sadly wanting in discretion, or, in vulgar parlance, taste. They are perpetually overleaping the modesty of nature. They are possessed by a cold-blooded enthusiasm, if we may say so—since it seems to come rather from the head than the heart—which spurs them on over the plainest barriers of common sense, until even the right becomes the wrong. A striking example of these defects is furnished by the dramatic critic, Schlegel, whose "Lectures" are, or may be, familiar to every reader, since they have been reprinted in the English version in this country. No critic, not even a native, has thrown such a flood of light on the characteristics of the sweet bard of Avon. He has

made himself so intimately acquainted with the peculiar circumstances of the poet's age and country,
that he has been enabled to speculate on his productions as those of a contemporary. In this way he
has furnished a key to the mysteries of his composition, has reduced what seemed anomalous to system,
and has supplied Shakspeare's own countrymen with
new arguments for vindicating the spontaneous suggestions of feeling on strictly philosophical principles. Not content with this important service, he,
as usual, pushes his argument to extremes, vindicates
obvious blemishes as necessary parts of a system, and
calls on us to admire, in contradiction to the most
ordinary principles of taste and common sense.
Thus, for example, speaking of Shakspeare's notorious blunders in geography and chronology, he
coolly tells us, "I undertake to prove that Shakspeare's anachronisms are, for the most part, committed purposely, and after great consideration." In
the same vein, speaking of the poet's villanous puns
and quibbles, which, to his shame, or, rather, that of
his age, so often bespangle with tawdry brilliancy the
majestic robe of the Muse, he assures us that "the
poet here probably, as everywhere else, has followed principles which will bear a strict examination."
But the intrepidity of criticism never went farther
than in the conclusion of this same analysis, where
he unhesitatingly assigns several apocryphal plays to
Shakspeare, gravely informing us that the last three,
"Sir John Oldcastle," "A Yorkshire Tragedy," and
"Thomas Lord Cromwell," of which the English

critics speak with unreserved contempt, "are not only unquestionably Shakspeare's, but, in his judgment, rank among the best and ripest of his works!" The old bard, could he raise his head from the tomb, where none might disturb his bones, would exclaim, we imagine, " *Non tali auxilio !*"

It shows a tolerable degree of assurance in a critic thus to dogmatize on nice questions of verbal resemblance which have so long baffled the natives of the country, who, on such questions, obviously can be the only competent judges. It furnishes a striking example of the want of discretion noticeable in so many of the German scholars. With all these defects, however, it cannot be denied that they have widely extended the limits of rational criticism, and, by their copious stores of erudition, furnished the student with facilities for attaining the best points of view for a comprehensive survey of both ancient and modern literature.

The English have had advantages, on the whole, greater than those of any other people, for perfecting the science of general criticism. They have had no academies to bind the wing of genius to the earth by their thousand wire-drawn subtleties. No Inquisition has placed its burning seal upon the lip, and thrown its dark shadow over the recesses of the soul. They have enjoyed the inestimable privilege of thinking what they pleased, and of uttering what they thought. Their minds, trained to independence, have had no occasion to shrink from encountering any topic, and have acquired a masculine con-

4   W *

fidence, indispensable to a calm appreciation of the mighty and widely-diversified productions of genius, as unfolded under the influences of as widely-diversified institutions and national character. Their own literature, with chameleon-like delicacy, has reflected all the various aspects of the nation in the successive stages of its history. The rough, romantic beauties and gorgeous pageantry of the Elizabethan age, the stern, sublime enthusiasm of the Commonwealth, the cold brilliancy of Queen Anne, and the tumultuous movements and ardent sensibilities of the present generation, all have been reflected as in a mirror, in the current of English literature, as it has flowed down through the lapse of ages. It is easy to understand what advantages this cultivation of all these different styles of composition at home must give the critic in divesting himself of narrow and local prejudice, and in appreciating the genius of foreign literatures, in each of which some one or other of these different styles has found favour. To this must be added the advantages derived from the structure of the English language itself, which, compounded of the Teutonic and the Latin, offers facilities for a comprehension of other literatures not afforded by those languages, as the German and the Italian, for instance, almost exclusively derived from but one of them.

With all this, the English, as we have remarked, have made fewer direct contributions to general literary criticism than the Continental nations, unless, indeed, we take into the account the periodical criticism, which has covered the whole field with a light skirmishing, very unlike any systematic plan of operations. The good effect of this *guerilla* warfare may well be doubted. Most of these critics for the nonce (and we certainly are competent judges on this point) come to their work with little previous preparation. Their attention has been habitually called, for the most part, in other directions, and they throw off an accidental essay in the brief intervals of other occupation. Hence their views are necessarily often superficial, and sometimes contradictory, as may be seen from turning over the leaves of any journal where literary topics are widely discussed; for, whatever consistency may be demanded in politics or religion, very free scope is offered, even in the same journal, to literary speculation. Even when the article may have been the fruit of a mind ripened by study and meditation on congenial topics, it too often exhibits only the partial view suggested by the particular and limited direction of the author's thoughts in this instance. Truth is not much served by this irregular process; and the general illumination, indispensable to a full and fair survey of the whole ground, can never be supplied from such scattered and capricious gleams, thrown over it at random.

Another obstacle to a right result is founded in the very constitution of review-writing. Miscellaneous in its range of topics, and addressed to a miscellaneous class of readers, its chief reliance for success in competition with the thousand novelties of the day, is in the temporary interest it can excite Instead of a conscientious discussion and cautious examination of the matter in hand, we too often find an attempt to stimulate the popular appetite by piquant sallies of wit, by caustic sarcasm, or by a pert, dashing confidence, that cuts the knot it cannot readily unloose. Then, again, the spirit of periodical criticism would seem to be little favourable to perfect impartiality. The critic, shrouded in his secret tribunal, too often demeans himself like a stern inquisitor, whose business is rather to convict than to examine. Criticism is directed to scent out blemishes instead of beauties. "*Judex damnatur cùm nocens absolvitur*" is the bloody motto of a well-known British periodical, which, under this piratical flag, has sent a broadside into many a gallant bark that deserved better at its hands.

When we combine with all this the spirit of patriotism, or, what passes for such with nine tenths of the world, the spirit of national vanity, we shall find abundant motives for a deviation from a just, impartial estimate of foreign literatures. And if we turn over the pages of the best-conducted English journals, we shall probably find ample evidence of the various causes we have enumerated. We shall find, amid abundance of shrewd and sarcastic observation, smart skirmish of wit, and clever antithesis, a very small infusion of sober, dispassionate criticism; the criticism founded on patient study and on strictly philosophical principles; the criticism on which one can safely rely as the criterion of good

taste, and which, however tame it may appear to
the jaded appetite of the literary lounger, is the only
one that will attract the eye of posterity.

The work named at the head of our article will,
we suspect, notwithstanding the author's brilliant
reputation, never meet this same eye of posterity.
Though purporting to be, in its main design, an Essay on English Literature, it is, in fact, a multifarious
compound of as many ingredients as entered into
the witches' caldron, to say nothing of a gallery of
portraits of dead and living, among the latter of
whom M. de Chateaubriand himself is not the least
conspicuous. "I have treated of everything," he
says, truly enough, in his preface, "the Present, the
Past, the Future." The parts are put together in
the most grotesque and disorderly manner, with
some striking coincidences, occasionally, of characters and situations, and some facts not familiar to
every reader. The most unpleasant feature in the
book is the doleful lamentation of the author over
the evil times on which he has fallen. He has, indeed, lived somewhat beyond his time, which was
that of Charles the Tenth, of pious memory—the
good old time of apostolicals and absolutists, which
will not be likely to revisit France again very soon.
Indeed, our unfortunate author reminds one of some
weather-beaten hulk which the tide has left high
and dry on the strand, and whose signals of distress
are little heeded by the rest of the convoy, which
have trimmed their sails more dexterously, and sweep
merrily on before the breeze. The present work

affords glimpses, occasionally, of the author's happier style, which has so often fascinated us in his earlier productions. On the whole, however, it will add little to his reputation, nor, probably, much subtract from it. When a man has sent forth a score or two of octavos into the world, and as good as some of M. de Chateaubriand's, he can bear up under a poor one now and then. This is not the first indifferent work laid at his door, and, as he promises to keep the field for some time longer, it will probably not be the last.

We pass over the first half of the first volume to come to the Reformation, the point of departure, as it were, for modern civilization. Our author's views in relation to it, as we might anticipate, are not precisely those we should entertain.

"In a religious point of view," he says, " the Reformation is leading insensibly to indifference, or the complete absence of faith ; the reason is, that the independence of the mind terminates in two gulfs, doubt and incredulity.

"By a very natural reaction, the Reformation, at its birth, rekindled the dying flame of Catholic fanaticism. It may thus be regarded as the indirect cause of the massacre of St. Bartholomew, the disturbances of the League, the assassination of Henry the Fourth, the murders in Ireland, and of the revocation of the Edict of Nantes, and the *dragonnades !*" —Vol i., p. 193.

As to the tendency of the Reformation towards doubt and incredulity, we know that free inquiry, continually presenting new views as the sphere of observation is enlarged, may unsettle old principles without establishing any fixed ones in their place, or, in other words, lead to skepticism; but we doubt if this happens more frequently than under the opposite system, inculcated by the Romish Church, which, by precluding examination, excludes the only ground of rational belief. At all events, skepticism, in the former case, is much more remediable than in the latter; since the subject of it, by pursuing his inquiries, will, it is to be hoped, as truth is mighty, arrive at last at a right result; while the Romanist, inhibited from such inquiry, has no remedy. The ingenious author of " Doblado's Letters from Spain" has painted in the most affecting colours the state of such a mind, which, declining to take its creed at the bidding of another, is lost in a labyrinth of doubt without a clew to guide it. As to charging on the Reformation the various enormities with which the above extract concludes, the idea is certainly new. It is, in fact, making the Protestants guilty of their own persecution, and Henry the Fourth of his own assassination; quite an original view of the subject, which, as far as we know, has hitherto escaped the attention of historians.

A few pages farther, and we find the following information respecting the state of Catholicism in our own country:

" Maryland, a Catholic and very populous state, made common cause with the others, and *now most of the Western States are Catholic.* The progress of this communion in the United States of America exceeds belief. There it has been invigorated in its evangelical aliment, popular liberty, *while other communions decline in profound indifference."*—Vol. i., p. 201.

We were not aware of this state of things. We did indeed know that the Roman Church had increased much of late years, especially in the Valley of the Mississippi: but so have other communions, as the Methodist and Baptist, for example, the latter of which comprehends five times as many disciples as the Roman Catholic. As to the population of the latter in the West, the whole number of Catholics in the Union does not amount, probably, to three fourths of the number of inhabitants in the single western State of Ohio. The truth is, that, in a country where there is no established or favoured sect, and where the clergy depend on voluntary contribution for their support, there must be constant efforts at proselytism, and a mutation of religious opinion, according to the convictions, or fancied convictions of the converts. What one denomination gains another loses, till roused, in its turn, by its rival, new efforts are made to retrieve its position, and the equilibrium is restored. In the mean time, the population of the whole country goes forward with giant strides, and each sect boasts, and boasts with truth, of the hourly augmentation of its numbers. Those of the Roman Catholics are swelled, moreover, by a considerable addition from emigration, many of the poor foreigners, especially the Irish, being of that persuasion. But this is no ground of triumph, as it infers no increase to the sum of Catholicism, since what is thus gained in the New World is lost in the Old.

Our author pronounces the Reformation hostile to the arts, poetry, eloquence, elegant literature, and even the spirit of military heroism. But hear his own words:

"The Reformation, imbued with the spirit of its founder, declared itself hostile to the arts. It sacked tombs, churches, and monuments, and made in France and England heaps of ruins.". . . .

"The beautiful in literature will be found to exist in a greater or less degree, in proportion as writers have approximated to the genius of the Roman Church.". . . .

"If the Reformation restricted genius in poetry, eloquence, and the arts, it also checked heroism in war, for heroism is imagination in the military order."—Vol. i., p. 194–207.

This is a sweeping denunciation; and, as far as the arts of design are intended, may probably be defended. The Romish worship, its stately ritual and gorgeous ceremonies, the throng of numbers assisting, in one form or another, at the service, all required spacious and magnificent edifices, with the rich accessories of sculpture and painting, and music also, to give full effect to the spectacle. Never was there a religion which addressed itself more directly to the senses. And, fortunately for it, the immense power and revenues of its ministers enabled

4   X

them to meet its exorbitant demands. On so splendid a theatre, and under such patronage, the arts were called into life in modern Europe, and most of all in that spot which represented the capital of Christendom. It was there, amid the pomp and luxury of religion, that those beautiful structures rose, with those exquisite creations of the chisel and the pencil, which imbodied in themselves all the elements of ideal beauty.

But, independently of these external circumstances, the spirit of Catholicism was eminently favourable to the artist. Shut out from free inquiry—from the Scriptures themselves—and compelled to receive the dogmas of his teachers upon trust, the road to conviction lay less through the understanding than the heart. The heart was to be moved, the affections and sympathies to be stirred, as well as the senses to be dazzled. This was the machinery by which alone could an effectual devotion to the faith be maintained in an ignorant people. It was not, therefore, Christ as a teacher delivering lessons of practical wisdom and morality that was brought before the eye, but Christ filling the offices of human sympathy, ministering to the poor and sorrowing, giving eyes to the blind, health to the sick, and life to the dead. It was Christ suffering under persecution, crowned with thorns, lacerated with stripes, dying on the cross. These sorrows and sufferings were understood by the dullest soul, and told more than a thousand homilies. So with the Virgin. It was not that sainted mother of the

Saviour whom Protestants venerate, but do not worship; it was the Mother of God, and entitled, like him, to adoration. It was a woman, and, as such, the object of those romantic feelings which would profane the service of the Deity, but which are not the less touching as being in accordance with human sympathies. The respect for the Virgin, indeed, partook of that which a Catholic might feel for his tutelar saint and his mistress combined. Orders of chivalry were dedicated to her service; and her shrine was piled with more offerings and frequented by more pilgrimages than the altars of the Deity himself. Thus, feelings of love, adoration, and romantic honour, strangely blended, threw a halo of poetic glory around their object, making it the most exalted theme for the study of the artist. What wonder that this subject should have called forth the noblest inspirations of his genius? What wonder that an artist like Raphael should have found in the simple portraiture of a woman and a child the materials for immortality?

It was something like a kindred state of feeling which called into being the arts of ancient Greece, when her mythology was comparatively fresh, and faith was easy; when the legends of the past, familiar as Scripture story at a later day, gave a real existence to the beings of fancy, and the artist, imbodying these in forms of visible beauty, but finished the work which the poet had begun.

The Reformation brought other trains of ideas, and with them other influences on the arts, than those

of Catholicism. Its first movements were decidedly
hostile, since the works of art, with which the temples were adorned, being associated with the religion
itself, became odious as the symbols of idolatry. But
the spirit of the Reformation gave thought a new
direction even in the cultivation of art. It was no
longer sought to appeal to the senses by brilliant display, or to waken the sensibilities by those superficial
emotions which find relief in tears. A sterner, deeper feeling was roused. The mind was turned within,
as it were, to ponder on the import of existence and
its future destinies; for the chains were withdrawn
from the soul, and it was permitted to wander at
large in the regions of speculation. Reason took
the place of sentiment—the useful of the merely ornamental. Facts were substituted for forms, even
the ideal forms of beauty. There were to be no
more Michael Angelos and Raphaels; no glorious
Gothic temples which consumed generations in their
building. The sublime and the beautiful were not
the first objects proposed by the artist. He sought
truth—fidelity to nature. He studied the characters
of his species as well as the forms of imaginary perfection. He portrayed life as developed in its thousand peculiarities before his own eyes, and the ideal
gave way to the natural. In this way, new schools
of painting, like that of Hogarth, for example, arose,
which, however inferior in those great properties for
which we must admire the masterpieces of Italian
art, had a significance and philosophic depth which
furnished quite as much matter for study and meditation.

A similar tendency was observable in poetry, eloquence, and works of elegant literature. The influence of the Reformation here was undoubtedly favourable, whatever it may have been on the arts. How could it be otherwise on literature, the written expression of thought, in which no grace of visible forms and proportions, no skill of mechanical execution, can cheat the eye with the vain semblance of genius? But it was not until the warm breath of the Reformation had dissolved the icy fetters which had so long held the spirit of man in bondage that the genial current of the soul was permitted to flow, that the gates of reason were unbarred, and the mind was permitted to taste of the tree of knowledge, forbidden tree no longer. Where was the scope for eloquence when thought was stifled in the very sanctuary of the heart? for out of the fulness of the heart the mouth speaketh.

There might, indeed, be an elaborate attention to the outward forms of expression, an exquisite finish of verbal arrangement, the dress and garniture of thought. And, in fact, the Catholic nations have surpassed the Protestant in attention to verbal elegance and the soft music of numbers, to nice rhetorical artifice and brilliancy of composition. The poetry of Italy and the prose of France bear ample evidence how much time and talent have been expended on this beauty of outward form, the rich vehicle of thought. But where shall we find the powerful reasoning, various knowledge, and fearless energy of diction which stamp the oratory of Protestant Eng-

4   X*

land and America? In France, indeed, where prose has received a higher polish and classic elegance than in any other country, pulpit eloquence has reached an uncommon degree of excellence; for though much was excluded, the avenues to the heart, as with the painter and the sculptor, were still left open to the orator. If there has been a deficiency in this respect in the English Church, which all will not admit, it arises probably from the fact that the mind, unrestricted, has been occupied with reasoning rather than rhetoric, and sought to clear away old prejudices and establish new truths, instead of wakening a transient sensibility, or dazzling the imagination with poetic flights of eloquence. That it is the fault of the preacher, at all events, and not of Protestantism, is shown by a striking example under our own eyes, that of our distinguished countryman, Dr. Channing, whose style is irradiated with all the splendours of a glowing imagination, showing, as powerfully as any other example, probably, in English prose, of what melody and compass the language is capable under the touch of genius instinct with genuine enthusiasm. Not that we would recommend this style, grand and beautiful as it is, for imitation. We think we have seen the ill effects of this already in more than one instance. In fact, no style should be held up as a model for imitation. Dr. Johnson tells us, in one of those oracular passages somewhat threadbare now, that "whoever wishes to attain an English style, familiar but not coarse, and elegant but not ostentatious, must give his days and nights to the volumes of Addison." With all deference to the great critic, who, by the formal cut of the sentence just quoted, shows that he did not care to follow his own prescription, we think otherwise. Whoever would write a good English style, we should say, should acquaint himself with the mysteries of the language as revealed in the writings of the best masters, but should form his own style on nobody but himself. Every man, at least every man with a spark of originality in his composition, has his own peculiar way of thinking, and, to give it effect, it must find its way out in its own peculiar language. Indeed, it is impossible to separate language from thought in that delicate blending of both which is called style; at least, it is impossible to produce the same effect with the original by any copy, however literal. We may imitate the structure of a sentence, but the ideas which gave it its peculiar propriety we cannot imitate. The forms of expression that suit one man's train of thinking no more suit another's than one man's clothes will suit another. They will be sure to be either too large or too small, or, at all events, not to make what gentlemen of the needle call a *good fit*. If the party chances, as is generally the case, to be rather under size, and the model is over size, this will only expose his own littleness the more. There is no case more in point than that afforded by Dr. Johnson himself. His brilliant style has been the ambition of every schoolboy, and of some children of larger growth since the days of the Rambler. But the nearer they come to it the worse. The beautiful is turned into the fantastic, and the sublime into the ridiculous. The most curious example of this within our recollection is the case of Dr. Symmons, the English editor of Milton's prose writings, and the biographer of the poet. The little doctor has maintained throughout his ponderous volume a most exact imitation of the great doctor, his sesquipedalian words, and florid rotundity of period. With all this cumbrous load of brave finery on his back, swelled to twice his original dimensions, he looks, for all the world, as he is, like a mere bag of wind—a scarecrow, to admonish others of the folly of similar depredations.

But to return. The influence of the Reformation on elegant literature was never more visible than in the first great English school of poets, which came soon after it, at the close of the sixteenth century. The writers of that period displayed a courage, originality, and truth highly characteristic of the new revolution, which had been introduced by breaking down the old landmarks of opinion, and giving unbounded range to speculation and inquiry. The first great poet, Spenser, adopted the same vehicle of imagination with the Italian bards of chivalry, the romantic epic; but instead of making it, like them, a mere revel of fancy, with no farther object than to delight the reader by brilliant combinations, he moralized his song, and gave it a deeper and more solemn import by the mysteries of Allegory, which, however prejudicial to its effect as a work of art, showed a mind too intent on serious thoughts and inquiries itself to be content with the dazzling but impotent coruscations of genius, that serve no other end than that of amusement.

In the same manner, Shakspeare and the other dramatic writers of the time, instead of adopting the formal rules recognised afterward by the French writers, their long rhetorical flourishes, their exaggerated models of character, and ideal forms, went freely and fearlessly into all the varieties of human nature, the secret depths of the soul, touching on all the diversified interests of humanity—for he might touch on all without fear of persecution—and thus making his productions a storehouse of philosophy, of lessons of practical wisdom, deep, yet so clear that he who runs may read.

But the spirit of the Reformation did not descend in all its fulness on the Muse till the appearance of Milton. That great poet was in heart as thoroughly a Reformer, and in doctrine much more thoroughly so than Luther himself. Indignant at every effort to crush the spirit, and to cheat it, in his own words, "of that liberty which rarefies and enlightens it like the influence of heaven," he proclaimed the rights of man as a rational, immortal being, undismayed by menace and obloquy, amid a generation of servile and unprincipled sycophants. The blindness which excluded him from the things of earth opened to him more glorious and spiritualized conceptions of heaven, and aided him in exhibiting the full influence of those sublime truths which the privilege of free inquiry in religious matters had poured upon the

M m

mind. His Muse was as eminently the child of Protestantism as that of Dante, who resembled him in so many traits of character, was of Catholicism. The latter poet, coming first among the moderns, after the fountains of the great deep, which had so long overwhelmed the world, were broken up, displayed, in his wonderful composition, all the elements of modern institutions as distinguished from those of antiquity. He first showed the full and peculiar influence of Christianity on literature, but it was Christianity under the form of Catholicism. His subject, spiritual in its design, like Milton's, was sustained by all the auxiliaries of a visible and material existence. His passage through the infernal abyss is a series of tragic pictures of human wo, suggesting greater refinements of cruelty than were ever imagined by a heathen poet. Amid all the various forms of mortal anguish, we look in vain for the mind as a means of torture. In like manner, in ascending the scale of celestial being, we pass through a succession of brilliant *fêtes*, made up of light, music, and motion, increasing in splendour and velocity, till all are lost and confounded in the glories of the Deity. Even the pencil of the great master, dipped in these gorgeous tints of imagination, does not shrink from the attempt to portray the outlines of Deity itself. In this he aspired to what many of his countrymen in the sister arts of design have since attempted, and, like him, have failed; for who can hope to give form to the Infinite? In the same false style Dante personifies the spirits of evil, including Satan himself. Much was doubtless owing to the age, though much, also, must be referred to the genius of Catholicism, which, appealing to the senses, has a tendency to materialize the spiritual, as Protestantism, with deeper reflection, aims to spiritualize the material. Thus Milton, in treading similar ground, borrows his illustrations from intellectual sources, conveys the image of the Almighty by his attributes, and, in the frequent portraiture which he introduces of Satan, suggests only vague conceptions of form, the faint outlines of matter, as it were, stretching vast over many a rood, but towering sublime by the unconquerable energy of will—the fit representative of the principle of evil. Indeed, Milton has scarcely anything of what may be called scenic decorations to produce a certain stage effect. His actors are few, and his action nothing. It is only by their intellectual and moral relations—by giving full scope to the

"Cherub Contemplation—
He that soars on golden wing,
Guiding the fiery-wheeled throne"

that he has prepared for us visions of celestial beauty and grandeur which never fade from our souls.

In the dialogue with which the two poets have seasoned their poems, we see the action of the opposite influences we have described. Both give vent to metaphysical disquisition, of learned sound, and much greater length than the reader would desire; but in Milton it is the free discussion of a mind trained to wrestle boldly on abstrusest points of met-

aphysical theology, while Dante follows in the same
old barren footsteps which had been trodden by the
schoolmen. Both writers were singularly bold and
independent. Dante asserted that liberty which
should belong to the citizen of every free state; that
civil liberty which had been sacrificed in his own
country by the spirit of faction. But Milton claimed a higher freedom; a freedom of thinking and of
giving utterance to thought, uncontrolled by human
authority. He had fallen on evil times; but he had
a generous confidence that his voice would reach to
posterity, and would be a guide and a light to the
coming generations. And truly has it proved so;
for in his writings we find the germs of many of the
boasted discoveries of our own day in government
and education, so that he may be fairly considered
as the morning star of that higher civilization which
distinguishes our happier era.

Milton's poetical writings do not seem, however,
to have been held in that neglect by his contemporaries which is commonly supposed. He had attracted too much attention as a political controver-
sialist, was too much feared for his talents, as well
as hated for his principles, to allow anything which
fell from his pen to pass unnoticed. Although the
profits went to others, he lived to see a second edition of "Paradise Lost," and this was more than
was to have been fairly anticipated of a composition
of this nature, however well executed, falling on
such times. Indeed, its sale was no evidence that
its merits were comprehended, and may be referred

to the general reputation of its author; for we find so accomplished a critic as Sir William Temple, some years later, omitting the name of Milton in his roll of writers who have done honour to modern literature, a circumstance which may, perhaps, be imputed to that reverence for the ancients which blinded Sir William to the merits of their successors. How could Milton be understood in his own generation, in the grovelling, sensual court of Charles the Second? How could the dull eyes, so long fastened on the earth, endure the blaze of his inspired genius? It was not till time had removed him to a distance that he could be calmly gazed on and his merits fairly contemplated. Addison, as is well known, was the first to bring them into popular view, by a beautiful specimen of criticism that has permanently connected his name with that of his illustrious subject. More than half a century later, another great name in English criticism, perhaps the greatest in general reputation, Johnson, passed sentence of a very different kind on the pretensions of the poet. A production more discreditable to the author is not to be found in the whole of his voluminous works; equally discreditable, whether regarded in an historical light or as a sample of literary criticism. What shall we say of the biographer who, in allusion to that affecting passage where the blind old bard talks of himself as " in darkness, and with dangers compass'd round," can coolly remark that " this darkness, had his eyes been better employed, might undoubtedly have deserved compassion?" Or what of the critic who

4   Y

can say of the most exquisite effusion of Doric minstrelsy that our language boasts, "Surely no man
could have fancied that he read 'Lycidas' with
pleasure, had he not known the author;" and of
"Paradise Lost" itself, that "its perusal is a duty
rather than a pleasure?" Could a more exact measure be afforded than by this single line of the poetic
sensibility of the critic, and his unsuitableness for the
office he had here assumed? His "Life of Milton"
is a humiliating testimony of the power of political
and religious prejudices to warp a great and good
mind from the standard of truth, in the estimation,
not merely of contemporary excellence, but of the
great of other years, over whose frailties Time might
be supposed to have drawn his friendly mantle.

Another half century has elapsed, and ample justice has been rendered to the fame of the poet by
two elaborate criticisms: the one in the Edinburgh
Review, from the pen of Mr. Macaulay; the other by
Dr. Channing, in the "Christian Examiner," since
republished in his own works; remarkable performances, each in the manner highly characteristic of
its author, and which have contributed, doubtless, to
draw attention to the prose compositions of their
subject, as the criticism of Addison did to his poetry.
There is something gratifying in the circumstance
that this great advocate of intellectual liberty should
have found his most able and eloquent expositor
among us, whose position qualifies us, in a peculiar
manner, for profiting by the rich legacy of his genius.
It was but discharging a debt of gratitude.

Chateaubriand has much to say about Milton, for whose writings, both prose and poetry, notwithstanding the difference of their sentiments on almost all points of politics and religion, he appears to entertain the most sincere reverence. His criticisms are liberal and just; they show a thorough study of his author; but neither the historical facts nor the reflections will suggest much that is new on a subject now become trite to the English reader.

We may pass over a good deal of skimble-skamble stuff about men and things, which our author may have cut out of his commonplace-book, to come to his remarks on Sir Walter Scott, whom he does not rate so highly as most critics.

"The illustrious painter of Scotland," he says, "seems to me to have created a false class; he has, in my opinion, confounded history and romance. The novelist has set about writing historical romances, and the historian romantic histories."—Vol. ii., p. 306.

We should have said, on the contrary, that he had improved the character of both; that he had given new value to romance by building it on history, and new charms to history by embellishing it with the graces of romance.

To be more explicit. The principal historical work of Scott is the "Life of Napoleon." It has, unquestionably, many of the faults incident to a dashing style of composition, which precluded the possibility of compression and arrangement in the best form of which the subject was capable. This,

in the end, may be fatal to the perpetuity of the
work, for posterity will be much less patient than
our own age. He will have a much heavier load to
carry, inasmuch as he is to bear up under all of his
own time, and ours too. It is very certain, then,
some must go by the board; and nine sturdy volumes, which is the amount of Sir Walter's English
edition, will be somewhat alarming. Had he confined himself to half the quantity, there would have
been no ground for distrust. Every day, nay, hour,
we see, ay, and feel, the ill effects of this rapid style
of composition, so usual with the best writers of our
day. The immediate profits which such writers are
pretty sure to get, notwithstanding the example of
M. Chateaubriand, operate like the dressing improv-
idently laid on a naturally good soil, forcing out
noxious weeds in such luxuriance as to check, if not
absolutely to kill, the more healthful vegetation.
Quantities of trivial detail find their way into the
page, mixed up with graver matters. Instead of
that skilful preparation by which all the avenues
verge at last to one point, so as to leave a distinct
impression—an impression of unity—on the reader,
he is hurried along zigzag, in a thousand directions,
or round and round, but never, in the cant of the
times, "going ahead" an inch. He leaves off pretty
much where he set out, except that his memory may
be tolerably well stuffed with facts, which, from want
of some principle of cohesion, will soon drop out of
it. He will find himself like a traveller who has
been riding through a fine country, it may be, by

moonlight, getting glimpses of everything, but no complete, well-illuminated view of the whole ("*quale per incertam lunam*," &c.) ; or, rather, like the same traveller, whizzing along in a locomotive so rapidly as to get even a glimpse fairly of nothing, instead of making his tour in such a manner as would enable him to pause at what was worth his attention, to pass by night over the barren and uninteresting, and occasionally to rise to such elevations as would afford the best points of view for commanding the various prospect.

The romance writer labours under no such embarrassments. He may, undoubtedly, precipitate his work, so that it may lack proportion, and the nice arrangement required by the rules which, fifty years ago, would have condemned it as a work of art. But the criticism of the present day is not so squeamish, or, to say truth, pedantic. It is enough for the writer of fiction if he give pleasure ; and this, everybody knows, is not effected by the strict observance of artificial rules. It is of little consequence how the plot is entangled, or whether it be untied or cut, in order to extricate the *dramatis personæ.* At least, it is of little consequence compared with the true delineation of character. The story is serviceable only as it affords a means for the display of this ; and if the novelist but keep up the interest of his story and the truth of his characters, we easily forgive any dislocations which his light vehicle may encounter from too heedless motion. Indeed, rapidity of motion may in some sort favour him, keeping up the glow of his invention, and striking out, as he dashes along, sparks of wit and fancy, that give a brilliant illumination to his track. But in history there must be another kind of process—a process at once slow and laborious. Old parchments are to be ransacked, charters and musty records to be deciphered, and stupid, worm-eaten chroniclers, who had much more of passion, frequently, to blind, than good sense to guide them, must be sifted and compared. In short, a sort of Medea-like process is to be gone through, and many an old bone is to be boiled over in the caldron before it can come out again clothed in the elements of beauty. The dreams of the novelist—the poet of prose—on the other hand, are beyond the reach of art, and the magician calls up the most brilliant forms of fancy by a single stroke of his wand.

Scott, in his History, was relieved, in some degree, from this necessity of studious research, by borrowing his theme from contemporary events. It was his duty, indeed, to examine evidence carefully, and sift out contradictions and errors. This demanded shrewdness and caution, but not much previous preparation and study. It demanded, above all, candour; for it was his business, not to make out a case for a client, but to weigh both sides, like an impartial judge, before summing up the evidence, and delivering his conscientious opinion. We believe there is no good ground for charging Scott with having swerved from this part of his duty. Those who expected to see him deify his hero, and raise altars to his memory, were disappointed; and so were those, also, who demanded that the tail and cloven hoof should be made to peep out beneath the imperial robe. But this proves his impartiality. It would be unfair, however, to require the degree of impartiality which is to be expected from one removed to a distance from the theatre of strife, from those national interests and feelings which are so often the disturbing causes of historic fairness. An American, no doubt, would have been, in this respect, in a more favourable point of view for contemplating the European drama. The ocean, stretched between us and the Old World, has the effect of time, and extinguishes, or, at least, cools the hot and angry feelings, which find their way into every man's bosom within the atmosphere of the contest. Scott was a Briton, with all the peculiarities of one—at least of a North Briton; and the future historian, who gathers materials from his labours, will throw these national predilections into the scale in determining the probable accuracy of his statements. These are not greater than might occur to any man, and allowance will always be made for them, on the ground of a general presumption; so that a greater degree of impartiality, by leading to false conclusions in this respect, would scarcely have served the cause of truth better with posterity. An individual who felt his reputation compromised may have joined issue on this or that charge of inaccuracy, but no such charge has come from any of the leading journals in the country, which would not have been slow to expose it, and which would not, considering the great popularity, and, consequently, influence of the work, have omitted, as they did, to notice it at all, had it afforded any obvious ground of exception on this score. Where, then, is the romance which our author accuses Sir Walter of blending with history?

Scott was, in truth, master of the picturesque. He understood, better than any historian since the time of Livy, how to dispose his lights and shades so as to produce the most striking result. This property of romance he had a right to borrow. This talent is particularly observable in the animated parts of his story—in his battles, for example. No man ever painted those terrible scenes with greater effect. He had a natural relish for gunpowder; and his mettle roused, like that of the war-horse, at the sound of the trumpet. His acquaintance with military science enabled him to employ a technical phraseology, just technical enough to give a knowing air to his descriptions, without embarrassing the reader by a pedantic display of unintelligible jargon. This is a talent rare in a civilian. Nothing can be finer than many of his battle-pieces in his " Life of Bonaparte," unless, indeed, we except one or two in his " History of Scotland:" as the fight of Bannockburn, for example, in which Burns's " Scots, wha hae" seems to breathe in every line.

It is when treading on Scottish ground that he seems to feel all his strength. " I seem always to step more firmly," he said to some one, " when on my own native heather." His mind was steeped in Scottish lore, and his bosom warmed with a sympathetic glow for the age of chivalry. Accordingly, his delineations of this period, whether in history or romance, are unrivalled; as superior in effect to those of most compilers, as the richly-stained glass of the feudal ages is superior in beauty and brilliancy of tints to a modern imitation. If this be borrowing something from romance, it is, we repeat, no more than what is lawful for the historian, and explains the meaning of our assertion that he has improved history by the embellishments of fiction.

Yet, after all, how wide the difference between the province of history and of romance, under Scott's own hands, may be shown by comparing his account of Mary's reign in his "History of Scotland," with the same period in the novel of "The Abbot." The historian must keep the beaten track of events. The novelist launches into the illimitable regions of fiction, provided only that his historic portraits be true to their originals. By due attention to this, fiction is made to minister to history, and may, in point of fact, contain as much real truth—truth of character, though not of situation. "The difference between the historian and me," says Fielding, "is, that with him everything is false but the names and dates, while with me nothing is false but these." There is, at least, as much truth in this as in most witticisms.

It is the great glory of Scott, that, by nice attention to costume and character in his novels, he has raised them to historic importance, without impairing their interest as works of art. Who now would imagine that he could form a satisfactory notion of the golden days of Queen Bess, that had not read "Kenilworth?" or of Richard Cœur-de-Lion and his brave paladins, that had not read "Ivanhoe?" Why, then, it has been said, not at once incorporate into regular history all these traits which give such historical value to the novel? Because, in this way, the strict truth which history requires would be violated. This cannot be. The fact is, History and Romance are too near akin ever to be lawfully united. By mingling them together, a confusion is produced, like the mingling of day and night, mystifying and distorting every feature of the landscape. It is enough for the novelist if he be true to the spirit; the historian must be true, also, to the letter. He cannot coin pertinent remarks and anecdotes to illustrate the characters of his drama. He cannot even provide them with suitable costumes. He must take just what Father Time has given him, just what he finds in the records of the age, setting down neither more nor less. Now the dull chroniclers of the old time rarely thought of putting down the smart sayings of the great people they biographize, still less of entering into minute circumstances of personal interest. These were too familiar to contemporaries to require it, and, therefore, they waste their breath on more solemn matters of state, all important in their generation, but not worth a rush in the present. What would the historian not give, could he borrow those fine touches of nature with which the novelist illustrates the characters of his actors—natural touches, indeed, but, in truth, just as artificial as any other part—all coined in the imagination of the writer. There is the same difference between his occupation and that of the novelist that there is between the historical and the portrait painter. The former necessarily takes some great subject, with great personages, all strutting about in gorgeous state attire, and air of solemn tragedy, while his brother artist insinuates himself into the family groups, and picks out natural, familiar scenes and faces, laughing or weeping, but in the charming undress of nature. What wonder that novel-reading should be so much more amusing than history?

But we have already trespassed too freely on the patience of our readers, who will think the rambling spirit of our author contagious. Before dismissing him, however, we will give a taste of his quality by one or two extracts, not very germane to English literature, but about as much so as a great part of the work. The first is a poetical sally on Bonaparte's burial-place, quite in Monsieur Chateaubriand's peculiar vein.

"The solitude of Napoleon, in his exile and his tomb, has thrown another kind of spell over a brilliant memory. Alexander did not die in sight of Greece; he disappeared amid the pomp of distant Babylon. Bonaparte did not close his eyes in the presence of France; he passed away in the gorgeous horizon of the torrid zone. The man who had shown himself in such powerful reality, vanished like a dream; his life, which belonged to history, co-operated in the poetry of his death. He now sleeps forever, like a hermit or a paria, beneath a willow, in a narrow valley, surrounded by steep rocks, at the extremity of a lonely path. The depth of the silence which presses upon him can only be compared to the vastness of that tumult which had surrounded him. Nations are absent; their throng has retired. The bird of the tropics, harnessed to the car of the sun, as Buffon magnificently expresses it, speeding his flight downward from the planet of light, rests alone, for a moment, over the ashes, the weight of which has shaken the equilibrium of the globe.

"Bonaparte crossed the ocean to repair to his final exile, regardless of that beautiful sky which delighted Columbus, Vasco de Gama, and Camoëns. Stretched upon the ship's stern, he perceived not that unknown constellations were sparkling over his head. His powerful glance, for the first time, encountered their rays. What to him were stars which he had never seen from his bivouacs, and which had never shone over his empire? Nevertheless, not one of them has failed to fulfil its destiny: one half of the firmament spread its light over his cradle, the other half was reserved to illuminate his tomb."—Vol. ii., p. 185, 186.

The next extract relates to the British statesman, William Pitt:

"Pitt, tall and slender, had an air at once melancholy and sarcastic. His delivery was cold, his intonation monotonous, his action scarcely perceptible. At the same time, the lucidness and the fluency of his thoughts, the logic of his arguments, suddenly irradiated with flashes of eloquence, rendered his talent something above the ordinary line.

"I frequently saw Pitt walking across St. James's Park from his own house to the palace. On his part, George the Third arrived from Windsor, after drinking beer out of a pewter pot with the farmers of the neighbourhood; he drove through the mean courts of his mean habitation in a gray chariot, followed by a few of the horse-guards. This was the master of the kings of Europe, as five or six merchants of the city are the masters of India. Pitt, dressed in black, with a steel-hilted sword by his side, and his hat under his arm, ascended, taking two or three steps at a time. In his passage he only met with three or four emigrants, who had nothing to do. Casting on us a disdainful look, he turned up his nose and his pale face, and passed on.

"At home, this great financier kept no sort of order; he had no regular hours for his meals or for sleep. Over head and ears in debt, he paid nobody, and never could take the trouble to cast up a bill. A *valet de chambre* managed his house. Ill dressed, without pleasure, without passion, greedy of power, he despised honours, and would not be anything more than William Pitt.

"In the month of June, 1822, Lord Liverpool

4   Z

took me to dine at his country-house. As we crossed Putney Heath, he showed me the small house
where the son of Lord Chatham, the statesman who
had had Europe in his pay, and distributed with his
own hand all the treasures of the world, died in
poverty."—Vol. ii., p. 277, 278.

The following extracts show the changes that
have taken place in English manners and society,
and may afford the "whiskered pandour" of our own
day an opportunity of contrasting his style of dan-
dyism with that of the preceding generation:

"Separated from the Continent by a long war,
the English retained their manners and their national character till the end of the last century. All was
not yet machine in the working classes—folly in the
upper classes. On the same pavements where you
now meet squalid figures and men in frock coats,
you were passed by young girls with white tippets,
straw hats tied under the chin with a riband, with
a basket on the arm, in which was fruit or a book:
all kept their eyes cast down; all blushed when one
looked at them. Frock coats, without any other,
were so unusual in London in 1793, that a woman,
deploring with tears the death of Louis the Sixteenth, said to me, 'But, my dear sir, is it true that
the poor king was dressed in a frock coat when they
cut off his head?'

"The gentlemen-farmers had not yet sold their
patrimony to take up their residence in London;
they still formed, in the House of Commons, that
independent fraction which, transferring their sup-

port from the opposition to the ministerial side, up-
held the ideas of order and propriety. They hunted
the fox and shot pheasants in autumn, ate fat goose
at Michaelmas, greeted the sirloin with shouts of
'Roast beef forever!' complained of the present, extolled the past, cursed Pitt and the war, which doubled the price of port wine, and went to bed drunk,
to begin the same life again on the following day.
They felt quite sure that the glory of Great Britain
would not perish so long as 'God save the King' was
sung, the rotten boroughs maintained, the game-laws
enforced, and hares and partridges could be sold by
stealth at market, under the names of lions and os-
triches."—Vol. ii., p. 279, 280.

"In 1822, at the time of my embassy to London,
the fashionable was expected to exhibit, at the first
glance, an unhappy and unhealthy man; to have an
air of negligence about his person, long nails, a beard
neither entire nor shaven, but as if grown for a moment unawares, and forgotten during the preoccupa-
tions of wretchedness; hair in disorder; a sublime,
mild, wicked eye; lips compressed in disdain of human nature; a Byronian heart, overwhelmed with
weariness and disgust of life.

"The dandy of the present day must have a conquering, frivolous, insolent look. He must pay particular attention to his toilet, wear mustaches, or a
beard trimmed into a circle like Queen Elizabeth's
ruff, or like the radiant disc of the sun. He shows
the proud independence of his character by keeping
his hat upon his head, by lolling upon sofas, by

thrusting his boots into the faces of the ladies seated in admiration upon chairs before him. He rides with a cane, which he carries like a taper, regardless of the horse, which he bestrides, as it were, by accident. His health must be perfect, and he must always have five or six felicities upon his hands. Some radical dandies, who have advanced the farthest towards the future, have a pipe. But, no doubt, all this has changed, even during the time that I have taken to describe it."—Vol. ii., p. 303, 304.

The avowed purpose of the present work, singular as it may seem from the above extracts, is to serve as an introduction to a meditated translation of Milton into French, since wholly, or in part, completed by M. Chateaubriand, who thinks, truly enough, that Milton's " political ideas make him a man of our own epoch." When an exile in England, in his early life, during the troubles of the Revolution, our author earned an honourable subsistence by translating some of Milton's verses; and he now proposes to render the bard and himself the same kind office by his labours on a more extended scale. Thus he concludes: "I again seat myself at the table of my poet. He will have nourished me in my youth and my old age. It is nobler and safer to have recourse to glory than to power." Our author's situation is an indifferent commentary on the value of literary fame, at least on its pecuniary value. No man has had more of it in his day. No man has been more alert to make the most of it by frequent, reiterated appearance before the public—whether in full dress or dishabille, yet always before them; and now, in the decline of life, we find him obtaining a scanty support by "French translation and Italian song." We heartily hope that the bard of "Paradise Lost" will do better for his translator than he did for himself, and that M. de Chateaubriand will put more than five pounds in his pocket by his literary labour.

4

Z*

BANCROFT'S UNITED STATES.*

JANUARY, 1841.

THE celebrated line of Bishop Berkeley,

"Westward the *course* of empire takes its way,"

is too gratifying to national vanity not to be often quoted (though not always quoted right) ; and if we look on it in the nature of a prediction, the completion of it not being limited to any particular time, it will not be easy to disprove it. Had the bishop substituted " freedom" for " empire," it would be already fully justified by experience. It is curious to observe how steadily the progress of freedom, civil and religious—of the enjoyment of those rights, which may be called the natural rights of humanity—has gone on from east to west, and how precisely the more or less liberal character of the social institutions of a country may be determined by its geographical position, as falling within the limits of one of the three quarters of the globe occupied wholly or in part by members of the great Caucasian family.

Thus, in Asia we find only far-extended despotisms, in which but two relations are recognised, those of master and slave : a solitary master, and a nation of slaves. No Constitution exists there to limit his authority; no intermediate body to coun-

* " History of the United States from the Discovery of the American Continent. By George Bancroft." Vol. iii. Boston : Charles C Little and James Brown. 8vo, pp. 468.

terbalance, or, at least, shield the people from its
exercise. The people have no political existence.
The monarch is literally the state. The religion
of such countries is of the same complexion with
their government. The free spirit of Christianity,
quickening and elevating the soul by the consciousness of its glorious destiny, made few proselytes
there; but Mohammedanism, with its doctrines of
blind fatality, found ready favour with those who
had already surrendered their wills—their responsibility—to an earthly master. In such countries, of
course, there has been little progress in science.
Ornamental arts, and even the literature of imagination, have been cultivated with various success; but
little has been done in those pursuits which depend
on freedom of inquiry, and are connected with the
best interests of humanity. The few monuments
of an architectural kind that strike the traveller's
eye are the cold memorials of pomp and selfish vanity, not those of public spirit, directed to enlarge the
resources and civilization of an empire.

As we cross the boundaries into Europe, among
the people of the same primitive stock and under
the same parallels, we may imagine ourselves transplanted to another planet. Man no longer grovels
in the dust beneath a master's frown. He walks
erect, as lord of the creation, his eyes raised to that
heaven to which his destinies call him. He is a
free agent—thinks, speaks, acts for himself; enjoys
the fruits of his own industry; follows the career
suited to his own genius and taste; explores fear-

lessly the secrets of time and nature; lives under laws which he has assisted in framing; demands justice as his right when those laws are invaded. In his freedom of speculation and action he has devised various forms of government. In most of them the monarchical principle is recognised; but the power of the monarch is limited by written or customary rules. The people at large enter more or less into the exercise of government; and a numerous aristocracy, interposed between them and the crown, secures them from the oppression of Eastern tyranny, while this body itself is so far an improvement in the social organization, that the power, instead of being concentrated in a single person — plaintiff, judge, and executioner — is distributed among a large number of different individuals and interests. This is a great advance, in itself, towards popular freedom.

The tendency, almost universal, is to advance still farther. It is this war of opinion—this contest between light and darkness, now going forward in most of the countries of Europe—which furnishes the point of view from which their history is to be studied in the present, and, it may be, the following centuries; for revolutions in society, when founded on opinion—the only stable foundation, the only foundation at which the friend of humanity does not shudder—must be the slow work of time; and who would wish the good cause to be so precipitated that, in eradicating the old abuses which have interwoven themselves with every stone and pillar of the building, the noble building itself, which has so long afforded security to its inmates, should be laid in ruins? What is the best, what the worst form of government, in the abstract, may be matter of debate; but there can be no doubt that the best will become the worst to a people who blindly rush into it without the preliminary training for comprehending and conducting it. Such transitions must, at least, cost the sacrifice of generations; and the patriotism must be singularly pure and abstract which, at such cost, would purchase the possible, or even probable, good of a remote posterity. Various have been the efforts in the Old World at popular forms of government, but, from some cause or other, they have failed; and however time, a wider intercourse, a greater familiarity with the practical duties of representation, and, not least of all, our own auspicious example, may prepare the European mind for the possession of Republican freedom, it is very certain that, at the present moment, Europe is not the place for Republics.

The true soil for these is our own continent, the New World, the last of the three great geographical divisions of which we have spoken. This is the spot on which the beautiful theories of the European philosopher—who had risen to the full freedom of speculation, while action was controlled—have been reduced to practice. The atmosphere here seems as fatal to the arbitrary institutions of the Old World as that has been to the Democratic forms of our own. It seems scarcely possible that any other

P P

organization than these latter should exist here. In three centuries from the discovery of the country, the various races by which it is tenanted, some of them from the least liberal of the European monarchies, have, with few exceptions, come into the adoption of institutions of a Republican character. Toleration, civil and religious, has been proclaimed, and enjoyed to an extent unknown since the world began, throughout the wide borders of this vast continent. Alas! for those portions which have assumed the exercise of these rights without fully comprehending their import; who have been intoxicated with the fumes of freedom instead of drawing nourishment from its living principle.

It was a fortunate, or, to speak more properly, a providential thing, that the discovery of the New World was postponed to the precise period when it occurred. Had it taken place at an earlier time—during the flourishing period of the feudal ages, for example—the old institutions of Europe, with their hallowed abuses, might have been ingrafted on this new stock, and, instead of the fruit of the tree of life, we should have furnished only varieties of a kind already far exhausted and hastening to decay. But, happily, some important discoveries in science, and, above all, the glorious Reformation, gave an electric shock to the intellect, long benumbed under the influence of a tyrannical priesthood. It taught men to distrust authority, to trace effects back to their causes, to search for themselves, and to take no guide but the reason which God had given them. It taught

them to claim the right of free inquiry as their in-
alienable birthright, and, with free inquiry, freedom
of action. The sixteenth and seventeenth centuries
were the period of the mighty struggle between the
conflicting elements of religion, as the eighteenth
and nineteenth have been that of the great contest
for civil liberty.

It was in the midst of this universal ferment, and
in consequence of it, that these shores were first
peopled by our Puritan ancestors. Here they found
a world where they might verify the value of those
theories which had been derided as visionary or
denounced as dangerous in their own land. All
around was free—free as nature herself: the mighty
streams rolling on in their majesty, as they had continued to roll from the creation; the forests, which
no hand had violated, flourishing in primeval grandeur and beauty; their only tenants the wild animals, or the Indians nearly as wild, scarcely held
together by any tie of social polity. Nowhere was
the trace of civilized man or of his curious contrivances. Here was no Star Chamber nor Court of
High Commission; no racks, nor jails, nor gibbets;
no feudal tyrant to grind the poor man to the dust
on which he toiled; no Inquisition, to pierce into
the thought, and to make thought a crime. The
only eye that was upon them was the eye of Heaven.

True, indeed, in the first heats of suffering enthusiasm they did not extend that charity to others
which they claimed for themselves. It was a blot
on their characters, but one which they share in

common with most reformers. The zeal requisite for great revolutions, whether in church or state, is rarely attended by charity for difference of opinion. Those who are willing to do and to suffer bravely for their own doctrines, attach a value to them which makes them impatient of opposition from others. The martyr for conscience' sake cannot comprehend the necessity of leniency to those who denounce those truths for which he is prepared to lay down his own life. If he set so little value on his own life, is it natural he should set more on that of others? The Dominican, who dragged his victims to the fires of the Inquisition in Spain, freely gave up his ease and his life to the duties of a missionary among the heathen. The Jesuits, who suffered martyrdom among the American savages in the propagation of their faith, stimulated those very savages to their horrid massacres of the Protestant settlements of New-England. God has not often combined charity with enthusiasm. When he has done so, he has produced his noblest work—a More, or a Fenelon.

But if the first settlers were intolerant in practice, they brought with them the living principle of freedom, which would survive when their generation had passed away. They could not avoid it; for their coming here was in itself an assertion of that principle. They came for conscience' sake—to worship God in their own way. Freedom of political institutions they at once avowed. Every citizen took his part in the political scheme, and enjoyed all the consideration of an equal participation in civil privileges: and liberty in political matters gradually brought with it a corresponding liberty in religious concerns. In their subsequent contest with the mother country they learned a reason for their faith, and the best manner of defending it. Their liberties struck a deep root in the soil amid storms which shook, but could not prostrate them. It is this struggle with the mother country, this constant assertion of the right of self-government, this tendency—feeble in its beginning, increasing with increasing age —towards Republican institutions, which connects the Colonial history with that of the Union, and forms the true point of view from which it is to be regarded.

The history of this country naturally divides itself into three great periods: the Colonial, when the idea of independence was slowly and gradually ripening in the American mind; the Revolutionary, when this idea was maintained by arms; and that of the Union, when it was reduced to practice. The first two heads are now ready for the historian; the last is not yet ripe for him. Important contributions may be made to it in the form of local narratives, personal biographies, political discussions, subsidiary documents, and *mémoires pour servir*; but we are too near the strife, too much in the dust and mist of the parties, to have reached a point sufficiently distant and elevated to embrace the whole field of operations in one view, and paint it in its true colours and proportions for the eye of posterity. We are, besides, too new as an independent nation,

4   2 A

our existence has been too short, to satisfy the skepticism of those who distrust the perpetuity of our political institutions. They do not consider the problem, so important to humanity, as yet solved. Such
skeptics are found, not only abroad, but at home.
Not that the latter suppose the possibility of again
returning to those forms of arbitrary government
which belong to the Old World. It would not be
more chimerical to suspect the Emperor Nicholas,
or Prince Metternich, or the citizen-king Louis
Philippe, of being Republicans at heart, and sighing
for a democracy, than to suspect the people of this
country (above all, of New-England, the most thorough democracy in existence)—who have inherited
Republican principles and feelings from their ancestors, drawn them in with their mother's milk, breathed the atmosphere of them from their cradle, participated in their equal rights and glorious privileges—
of foregoing their birthright and falsifying their nature so far as to acquiesce in any other than a popular form of government. But there are some skeptics who, when they reflect on the fate of similar
institutions in other countries; when they see our
sister states of South America, after nobly winning
their independence, split into insignificant fractions;
when they see the abuses which from time to time
have crept into our own administration, and the violence offered, in manifold ways, to the Constitution;
when they see ambitious and able statesmen in one
section of the country proclaiming principles which
must palsy the arm of the Federal Government, and

urging the people of their own quarter to efforts for
securing their independence of every other quarter
—there are, we say, some wise and benevolent
minds among us, who, seeing all this, feel a natural
distrust as to the stability of the federal compact, and
consider the experiment as still in progress.

We, indeed, are not of that number, while we respect and feel the weight of their scruples.   We
sympathize fully in those feelings, those hopes, it
may be, which animate the great mass of our countrymen.   Hope is the attribute of republics : it
should be peculiarly so of ours.   Our fortune is all
in the advance.   We have no past, as compared
with the nations of the Old World.   Our existence
is but two centuries, dating from our embryo state ;
our real existence as an independent people little
more than half a century.   We are to look forward,
then, and go forward, not with vainglorious boasting, but with resolution and honest confidence.
Boasting, indecorous in all, is peculiarly so in those
who take credit for the great things they are going
to do, not those they have done.   The glorification
of an Englishman or a Frenchman, with a long line
of annals in his rear, may be offensive ; that of an
American is ridiculous.   But we may feel a just
confidence from the past that we shall be true to
ourselves for the future ; that, to borrow a cant
phrase of the day, we shall be true to our *mission*—
the most momentous ever intrusted to a nation ; that
there is sufficient intelligence and moral principle in
the people, if not always to choose the best rulers,

at least to right themselves by the ejection of bad
ones when they find they have been abused; that
they have intelligence enough to understand that
their only consideration, their security as a nation,
is in union; that separation into smaller communities is the creation of so many hostile states; that
a large extent of empire, instead of being an evil,
from embracing regions of irreconcilable local interests, is a benefit, since it affords the means of that
commercial reciprocity which makes the country,
by its own resources, independent of every other;
and that the representatives drawn from these "magnificent distances" will, on the whole, be apt to le-
gislate more independently, and on broader principles, than if occupied with the concerns of a petty
state, where each legislator is swayed by the paltry
factions of his own village. In all this we may honestly confide; but our confidence will not pass for
argument, will not be accepted as a solution of the
problem. Time only can solve it; and until the period has elapsed which shall have fairly tried the
strength of our institutions, through peace and through
war, through adversity and more trying prosperity,
the time will not have come to write the history of
the Union.*

* The preceding cheering remarks on the auspicious destinies of our
country were written more than four years ago; and it is not now as
many days since we have received the melancholy tidings that the pro-
ject for the *Annexation of Texas* has been sanctioned by Congress. The
remarks in the text on "the extent of empire" had reference only to that
legitimate extent which might grow out of the peaceful settlement and
civilization of a territory, sufficiently ample certainly, that already belongs to us. The craving for foreign acquisitions has ever been a most

But still, results have been obtained sufficiently glorious to give great consideration to the two preliminary narratives, namely, of the Colonies and the Revolution, which prepared the way for the Union. Indeed, without these results, they would both, however important in themselves, have lost much of their dignity and interest. Of these two narratives, the former, although less momentous than the latter, is most difficult to treat.

It is not that the historian is called on to pry into the dark recesses of antiquity, the twilight of civilization, mystifying and magnifying every object to the senses, nor to unravel some poetical mythology, hanging its metaphorical illusions around everything in nature, mingling fact with fiction, the material with the spiritual, until the honest inquirer after truth may fold his arms in despair before he can cry εὕρηκα; nor is he compelled to unroll musty, worm-eaten parchments, and dusty tomes in venerable black letter, of the good times of honest Caxton and Winken de Worde, nor to go about gleaning traditionary tales and ballads in some obsolete provin-

fatal symptom in the history of republics; but when these acquisitions are made, as in the present instance, in contempt of constitutional law, and in disregard of the great principles of international justice, the evil assumes a tenfold magnitude; for it flows not so much from the single act as from the principle on which it rests, and which may open the way to the indefinite perpetration of such acts. In glancing my eye over the text at this gloomy moment, and considering its general import, I was unwilling to let it go into the world with my name to it, without entering my protest, in common with so many better and wiser in our country, against a measure which every friend of freedom, both at home and abroad, may justly lament as the most serious shock yet given to the stability of our glorious institutions.

cial *patois*. The record is plain and legible, and he need never go behind it. The antiquity of his story goes but little more than two centuries back; a very modern antiquity. The commencement of it was not in the dark ages, but in a period of illumination; an age yet glowing with the imagination of Shakspeare and Spenser, the philosophy of Bacon, the learning of Coke and of Hooker. The early passages of his story—coeval with Hampden, and Milton, and Sidney—belong to the times in which the same struggle for the rights of conscience was going on in the land of our fathers as in our own. There was no danger that the light of the Pilgrim should be hid under a bushel, or that there should be any dearth of chronicler or bard—such as they were—to record his sacrifice. And fortunate for us that it was so, since in this way every part of this great enterprise, from its conception to its consummation, is brought into the light of day. We are put in possession, not merely of the action, but of the motives which led to it; and as to the character of the actors, are enabled to do justice to those who, if we pronounce from their actions only, would seem not always careful to do justice to themselves.

The embarrassment of the Colonial history arises from the difficulty of obtaining a central point of interest among so many petty states, each independent of the others, and all, at the same time, so dependant on a foreign one as to impair the historic dignity which attaches to great, powerful, and self-regulated communities. This embarrassment must be

overcome by the author's detecting, and skilfully
keeping before the reader, some great principle of
action, if such exist, that may give unity, and, at the
same time, importance to the theme. Such a principle did exist in that tendency to independence,
which, however feeble, till fanned by the breath of
persecution into a blaze, was nevertheless the vivifying principle, as before remarked, of our ante-rev-
olutionary annals.

Whoever has dipped much into historical reading
is aware how few have succeeded in weaving an
harmonious tissue from the motley and tangled skein
of general history. The most fortunate illustration
of this within our recollection is Sismondi's *Répub-
liques Italiennes*, a work in sixteen volumes, in which
the author has brought on the stage all the various
governments of Italy for a thousand years, and in
almost every variety of combination. Yet there is
a pervading principle in this great mass of apparently discordant interests. That principle was the rise
and decline of liberty. It is the key-note to every
revolution that occurs. It give an harmonious tone
to the many-coloured canvass, which would else
have offended by its glaring contrasts, and the startling violence of its transitions. The reader is interested in spite of the transitions, but knows not the
cause. This is the skill of the great artist. So true
is this, that the same author has been able to concentrate what may be called the essence of his
bulky history into a single volume, in which he con-
fines himself to the development of the animating

principle of his narrative, stripped of all the superfluous accessories, under the significant title of
"Rise, Progress, and Decline of Italian Freedom."

This embarrassment has not been easy to overcome by the writers of our Colonial annals. The
first volume of Marshall's "Life of Washington" has
great merit as a wise and comprehensive survey of
this early period, but the plan is too limited to afford room for anything like a satisfactory fulness of
detail. The most thorough work, and incompara-
bly the best on the subject, previous to the appearance of Mr. Bancroft's, is the well-known history by
Mr. Grahame, a truly valuable book, in which the
author, though a foreigner, has shown himself capable of appreciating the motives and comprehending
the institutions of our Puritan ancestors. He has
spared no pains in the investigation of such original
sources as were at his command, and has conducted his inquiries with much candour, manifesting
throughout the spirit of a scholar and a gentleman.
It is not very creditable to his countrymen that
they should have received his labours with the apathy which he tells us they have, amid the ocean of
contemptible trash with which their press is daily
deluged. But, in truth, the Colonial and Revolutionary story of this country is a theme too ungrateful to British ears for us to be astonished at any insensibility on this score.

Mr. Grahame's work, however, with all its merit,
is the work of a *foreigner*, and that word comprehends much that cannot be overcome by the best

writer. He may produce a beautiful composition, faultless in style, accurate in the delineation of prominent events, full of sound logic and most wise conclusions, but he cannot enter into the sympathies, comprehend all the minute feelings, prejudices, and peculiar ways of thinking which form the idiosyncrasy of the nation. What can he know of these who has never been warmed by the same sun, lingered among the same scenes, listened to the same tales in childhood, been pledged to the same interests in manhood by which these fancies are nourished—the loves, the hates, the hopes, the fears, that go to form national character? Write as he will, he is still an alien, speaking a tongue in which the nation will detect the foreign accent. He may produce a book without a blemish in the eyes of foreigners; it may even contain much for the instruction of the native that he would not be likely to find in his own literature; but it will afford evidence on every page of its exotic origin. Botta's "History of the War of the Revolution" is the best treatise yet compiled of that event. It is, as every one knows, a most classical and able work, doing justice to most of the great heroes and actions of the period; but, we will venture to say, no well-informed American ever turned over its leaves without feeling that the writer was not nourished among the men and the scenes he is painting. With all its great merits, it cannot be, at least for Americans, *the* history of the Revolution.

It is the same as in portrait painting. The artist

may catch the prominent lineaments, the complexion, the general air, the peculiar costume of his subject—all that a stranger's eye will demand; but he
must not hope, unless he has had much previous intimacy with the sitter, to transfer those fleeting shades
of expression, the almost imperceptible play of features, which are revealed to the eye of his own family.

Who would think of looking to a Frenchman for
a history of England? to an Englishman for the
best history of France? Ill fares it with the nation
that cannot find writers of genius to tell its own
story. What foreign hand could have painted, like
Herodotus and Thucydides, the achievements of the
Greeks? Who, like Livy and Tacitus, have portrayed the shifting character of the Roman, in his
rise, meridian, and decline? Had the Greeks trusted their story to these same Romans, what would
have been their fate with posterity? Let the Carthaginians tell. All that remains of this nation, the
proud rival of Rome, who once divided with her
the empire of the Mediterranean, and surpassed her
in commerce and civilization—nearly all that now
remains to indicate her character, is a poor proverb,
Punica fides, a brand of infamy given by the Roman
historian, and one which the Romans merited probably as richly as the Carthaginians. Yet America,
it is too true, must go to Italy for the best history of
the Revolution, and to Scotland for the best history
of the Colonies. Happily, the work before us bids
fair, when completed, to supply this deficiency; and
it is quite time we should turn to it.

Mr. Bancroft's first two volumes have been too long before the public to require anything to be now said of them. Indeed, the first has already been the subject of a particular notice in this Journal. These volumes are mainly occupied with the settlement of the country by the different colonies, and the institutions gradually established among them, with a more particular illustration of the remarkable features in their character or policy.

In the present volume the immediate point of view is somewhat changed. It was no longer necessary to treat each of the colonies separately, and a manifest advantage in respect to unity is gained by their being brought more under one aspect. A more prominent feature is gradually developed by the relations with the mother country. This is the mercantile system, as it is called by economical writers, which distinguishes the colonial policy of modern Europe from that of ancient. The great object of this system was to get as much profit from the colonies, with as little cost to the mother country as possible. The former, instead of being regarded as an integral part of the empire, were held as property, to be dealt with for the benefit of the proprietors. This was the great object of legislation, almost the sole one. The system, so different from anything known in antiquity, was introduced by the Spaniards and Portuguese, and by them carried to an extent which no other nation has cared to follow. By the most cruel and absurd system of prohibitory legislation, their colonies were cut off from intercourse with all but the parent country; and, as the latter was unable to supply their demands for even the necessaries of life, an extensive contraband trade was introduced, which, without satisfying the wants of the colonies, corrupted their morals. It is an old story, and the present generation has witnessed the results, in the ruin of those fine countries and the final assertion of their independence, which the degraded condition in which they have so long been held has wholly unfitted them to enjoy.

The English government was too wise and liberal to press thus heavily on its transatlantic subjects; but the policy was similar, consisting, as is well known, and is ably delineated in these volumes, of a long series of restrictive measures, tending to cramp their free trade, manufactures, and agriculture, and to secure the commercial monopoly of Great Britain. This is the point from which events in the present volume are to be more immediately contemplated, all subordinate, like those in the preceding, to that leading principle of a Republican tendency — the centre of attraction, controlling the movements of the numerous satellites in our colonial system.

The introductory chapter in the volume opens with a view of the English Revolution in 1688, which, though not popular, is rightly characterized as leading the way to popular liberty. Its great object was the security of property; and our author has traced its operation, in connexion with the gradual progress of commercial wealth, to give greater authority to the mercantile system. We select the following original sketch of the character of William the Third :

"The character of the new monarch of Great Britain could mould its policy, but not its Constitution. True to his purposes, he yet wins no sympathy. In political sagacity, in force of will, far superior to the English statesmen who environed him; more tolerant than his ministers or his Parliaments, the childless man seems like the unknown character in algebra, which is introduced to form the equation, and dismissed when the problem is solved. In his person thin and feeble, with eyes of a hectic lustre, of a temperament inclining to the melancholic, in conduct cautious, of a self-relying humour, with abiding impressions respecting men, he sought no favour, and relied for success on his own inflexibility, and the greatness and maturity of his designs. Too wise to be cajoled, too firm to be complaisant, no address could sway his resolve. In Holland he had not scrupled to derive an increased power from the crimes of rioters and assassins; in England, no filial respect diminished the energy of his ambition. His exterior was chilling; yet he had a passionate delight in horses and the chase. In conversation he was abrupt, speaking little and slowly, and with repulsive dryness; in the day of battle he was all activity, and the highest energy of life, without kindling his passions, animated his frame. His trust in Providence was so connected with faith in general laws, that in every action he sought the principle which should range it on an absolute decree. Thus unconscious to himself, he had sympathy with the people, who always have faith in Providence. 'Do you dread death in my company?' he cried to the anxious sailors, when the ice on the coast of Holland had almost crushed the boat that was bearing him to the shore. Courage and pride pervaded the reserve of the prince, who spurning an alliance with a bastard daughter of Louis XIV., had made himself the centre of a gigantic opposition to France. For England, for the English people, for English liberties, he had no affection, indifferently employing the Whigs, who found their pride in the Revolution, and the Tories, who had opposed his elevation, and who yet were the fittest instruments 'to carry the prerogative high.' One great passion had absorbed his breast—the independence of his native country. The harsh encroachments of Louis XIV., which in 1672 had made William of Orange a Revolutionary stadtholder, now assisted to constitute him a Revolutionary king, transforming the impassive champion of Dutch independence into the defender of the liberties of Europe."—Vol. iii., p. 2–4.

The chapter proceeds to examine the relations, not always of the most friendly aspect, between England and the colonies, in which Mr. Bancroft pays a well-merited tribute to the enlightened policy of Penn, and the tranquillity he secured to his settlement. At the close of the chapter is an account of that lamentable—farce, we should have called it, had it not so tragic a conclusion—the Salem witchcraft.

Our author has presented some very striking sketches of these deplorable scenes, in which poor human nature appears in as humiliating a plight as would be possible in a civilized country. The Inquisition, fierce as it was, and most unrelenting in its persecutions, had something in it respectable in comparison with this wretched and imbecile self-delusion. The historian does not shrink from distributing his censure, in full measure, to those to whom he thinks it belongs. The erudite divine, Cotton Mather, in particular, would feel little pleasure in the contemplation of the portrait sketched for him on this occasion. Vanity, according to Mr. Bancroft, was quite as active an incentive to his movements as religious zeal; and, if he began with the latter, there seems no reason to doubt that pride of opinion, an unwillingness to expose his error, so humiliating to the world, perhaps even to his own heart, were powerful stimulants to his continuing the course he had begun, though others faltered in it.

Mr. Bancroft has taken some pains to show that the prosecutions were conducted before magistrates not appointed by the people, but the crown; and that a stop was not put to them till after the meeting of the representatives of the people. This, in our view, is a distinction somewhat fanciful. The judges held their commissions from the governor; and if he was appointed by the crown, it was, as our author admits, at the suggestion of Increase Mather, a minister of the people. The accusers.

the witnesses, the jurors, were all taken from the people. And when a stop was put to farther proceedings by the seasonable delay interposed by the General Court, before the assembling of the "legal colonial" tribunal (thus giving time for the illusion to subside), it was, in part, from the apprehension that, in the rising tide of accusation, no man, however elevated might be his character or condition, would be safe.

In the following chapter, after a full exposition of the prominent features in the system of commercial monopoly which controlled the affairs of the colonies, we are introduced to the great discoveries in the northern and western regions of the continent, made by the Jesuit missionaries of France. Nothing is more extraordinary in the history of this remarkable order than their bold enterprise in spreading their faith over this boundless wilderness, in defiance of the most appalling obstacles which man and nature could present. Faith and zeal triumphed over all, and, combined with science and the spirit of adventure, laid open unknown regions in the heart of this vast continent, then roamed over by the buffalo and the savage, and now alive with the busy hum of an industrious and civilized population.

The historian has diligently traced the progress of the missionaries in their journeys into the western territory of Michigan, Wisconsin, Illinois, down the deep basin of the Mississippi to its mouth. He has identified the scenes of some striking events in the history of discovery, as, among others, the place where Marquette first met the Illinois tribe, at Iowa. No preceding writer has brought into view the results of these labours in a compass which may be embraced, as it were, in a single glance. The character of this order, and their fortune, form one of the most remarkable objects for contemplation in the history of man. Springing up, as it were, to prop the crumbling edifice of Catholicism when it was reeling under the first shock of the Reformation, it took up its residence, indifferently, within the precincts of palaces, or in the boundless plains and forests of the wilderness; held the consciences of civilized monarchs in its keeping, and directed their counsels, while, at the same time, it was gathering barbarian nations under its banners, and pouring the light of civilization into the farthest and darkest quarters of the globe.

" The establishment of 'the Society of Jesus,'" says Mr. Bancroft, "by Loyola had been contemporary with the Reformation, of which it was designed to arrest the progress, and its complete organization belongs to the period when the first full edition of Calvin's 'Institutes' saw the light. Its members were, by its rules, never to become prelates, and could gain power and distinction only by influence over mind. Their vows were poverty, chastity, absolute obedience, and a constant readiness to go on missions against heresy or heathenism. Their cloisters became the best schools in the world. Emancipated, in a great degree, from the forms of

4   2 B *

piety, separated from domestic ties, constituting a
community essentially intellectual as well as essentially plebeian, bound together by the most perfect
organization, and having for their end a control
over opinion among the scholars and courts of Europe, and throughout the habitable globe, the order
of the Jesuits held as its ruling maxims the widest diffusion of its influence, and the closest internal unity.
Immediately on its institution, their missionaries,
kindling with a heroism that defied every danger
and endured every toil, made their way to the ends
of the earth; they raised the emblem of man's sal-
vation on the Moluccas, in Japan, in India, in Thibet, in Cochin China, and in China; they penetrated Ethiopia, and reached the Abyssinians ; they
planted missions among the Caffres : in California,
on the banks of the Marañhon, in the plains of Par-
aguay, they invited the wildest of barbarians to the
civilization of Christianity."

"Religious enthusiasm," he adds, "colonized New-
England ; and religious enthusiasm founded Mont-
real, made a conquest of the wilderness on the upper
Lakes, and explored the Mississippi. Puritanism
gave New-England its worship and its schools ; the
Roman Church created for Canada its altars, its
hospitals, and its seminaries. The influence of
Calvin can be traced to every New-England village;
in Canada, the monuments of feudalism and the
Catholic Church stand side by side ; and the names
of Montmorenci and Bourbon, of Levi and Condé,
are mingled with memorials of St. Athanasius and

Augustin, of St. Francis of Assisi, and Ignatius Loyola."—*Ibid.*, p. 120, 121.

We hardly know which to select from the many brilliant and spirited sketches in which this part of the story abounds. None has more interest, on the whole, than the discovery of the Mississippi by Marquette and his companions, and the first voyage of the white men down its majestic waters.

"Behold, then, in 1673, on the tenth day of June, the meek, single-hearted, unpretending, illustrious Marquette, with Joliet for his associate, five Frenchmen as his companions, and two Algonquins as guides, lifting their two canoes on their backs, and walking across the narrow portage that divides the Fox River from the Wisconsin. They reach the water-shed; uttering a special prayer to the immaculate Virgin, they leave the streams that, flowing onward, could have borne their greetings to the Castle of Quebec; already they stand by the Wisconsin. 'The guides returned,' says the gentle Marquette, 'leaving us alone in this unknown land, in the hands of Providence.' France and Christianity stood in the Valley of the Mississippi. Embarking on the broad Wisconsin, the discoverers, as they sailed west, went solitarily down the stream, between alternate prairies and hill-sides, beholding neither man nor the wonted beasts of the forest: no sound broke the appalling silence but the ripple of their canoe and the lowing of the buffalo. In seven days 'they entered happily the Great River, with a joy that could not be expressed;' and the two birchbark 'canoes, raising their happy sails under new skies and to unknown breezes, floated gently down the calm magnificence of the ocean stream, over the broad, clear sandbars, the resort of innumerable water-fowl—gliding past islands that swelled from the bosom of the stream, with their tufts of massive thickets, and between the wide plains of Illinois and Iowa, all garlanded as they were with majestic forests, or checkered by island grove and the open vastness of the prairie.

"About sixty leagues below the mouth of the Wisconsin, the western bank of the Mississippi bore on its sands the trail of men; a little footpath was discerned leading into a beautiful prairie; and, leaving the canoes, Joliet and Marquette resolved alone to brave a meeting with the savages. After walking six miles, they beheld a village on the banks of a river, and two others on a slope, at a distance of a mile and a half from the first. The river was the Mou-in-gou-e-na, or Moingona, of which we have corrupted the name into Des Moines. Marquette and Joliet were the first white men who trod the soil of Iowa. Commending themselves to God, they uttered a loud cry. The Indians hear; four old men advance slowly to meet them, bearing the peace-pipe brilliant with many-coloured plumes. 'We are Illinois,' said they; that is, when translated, 'We are men;' and they offered the calumet. An aged chief received them at his cabin with upraised hands, exclaiming, 'How beautiful is the sun, Frenchmen, when thou comest to visit us! Our whole village awaits thee; thou shalt enter in peace into all our dwellings.' And the pilgrims were followed by the devouring gaze of an astonished crowd.

"At the great council, Marquette published to them the one true God, their creator. He spoke, also, of the great captain of the French, the Governor of Canada, who had chastised the Five Nations and commanded peace; and he questioned them respecting the Mississippi and the tribes that possessed its banks. For the messengers who announced the subjection of the Iroquois, a magnificent festival was prepared of hominy, and fish, and the choicest viands from the prairies.

"After six days' delay, and invitations to new visits, the chieftain of the tribe, with hundreds of warriors, attended the strangers to their canoes; and, selecting a peace-pipe embellished with the head and neck of brilliant birds, and all feathered over with plumage of various hues, they hung around Marquette the mysterious arbiter of peace and war, the sacred calumet, a safeguard among the nations.

The little group proceeded onward. 'I did not fear death,' says Marquette; 'I should have esteemed it the greatest happiness to have died for the glory of God.' They passed the perpendicular rocks, which wore the appearance of monsters; they heard at a distance the noise of the waters of the Missouri, known to them by the Algonquin name of Pekitanoni; and when they came to the most beautiful confluence of waters in the world—where the swifter Missouri rushes like a conqueror into the

S s

calmer Mississippi, dragging it, as it were, hastily to
the sea—the good Marquette resolved in his heart,
anticipating Lewis and Clarke, one day to ascend
the mighty river to its source; to cross the ridge
that divides the oceans, and, descending a westerly
flowing stream, to publish the Gospel to all the
people of this New World.

"In a little less than forty leagues, the canoes
floated past the Ohio, which was then, and long afterward, called the Wabash. Its banks were tenanted by numerous villages of the peaceful Shawnees,
who quailed under the incursions of the Iroquois.

"The thick canes begin to appear so close and
strong that the buffalo could not break through
them; the insects become intolerable; as a shelter
against the suns of July, the sails are folded into an
awning. The prairies vanish; thick forests of
whitewood, admirable for their vastness and height,
crowd even to the skirts of the pebbly shore. It is
also observed that, in the land of the Chickasas, the
Indians have guns.

"Near the latitude of thirty-three degrees, on the
western bank of the Mississippi, stood the village of
Mitchigamea, in a region that had not been visited
by Europeans since the days of De Soto. 'Now,'
thought Marquette, 'we must indeed ask the aid of
the Virgin.' Armed with bows and arrows, with
clubs, axes, and bucklers, amid continual whoops,
the natives, bent on war, embark in vast canoes
made out of the trunks of hollow trees; but, at the
sight of the mysterious peace-pipe held aloft, God

touched the hearts of the old men, who checked the impetuosity of the young, and, throwing their bows and quivers into the canoes as a token of peace, they prepared a hospitable welcome.

"The next day, a long wooden canoe, containing ten men, escorted the discoverers, for eight or ten leagues, to the village of Akansea, the limit of their voyage. They had left the region of the Algonquins, and, in the midst of the Sioux and Chicasas, could speak only by an interpreter. A half league above Akansea they were met by two boats, in one of which stood the commander, holding in his hand the peace-pipe, and singing as he drew near. After offering the pipe, he gave bread of maize. The wealth of his tribe consisted in buffalo-skins; their weapons were axes of steel—a proof of commerce with Europeans.

"Thus had our travellers descended below the entrance of the Arkansas, to the genial climes that have almost no winter but rains, beyond the bound of the Huron and Algonquin languages, to the vicinity of the Gulf of Mexico, and to tribes of Indians that had obtained European arms by traffic with Spaniards or with Virginia.

"So, having spoken of God and the mysteries of the Catholic faith; having become certain that the Father of Rivers went not to the ocean east of Florda, nor yet to the Gulf of California, Marquette and Joliet left Akansea and ascended the Mississippi.

"At the thirty-eighth degree of latitude they entered the River Illinois, and discovered a country

without its paragon for the fertility of its beautiful
prairies, covered with buffaloes and stags; for the
loveliness of its rivulets, and the prodigal abundance
of wild duck and swans, and of a species of parrots
and wild turkeys. The tribe of Illinois, that tenanted its banks, entreated Marquette to come and reside
among them. One of their chiefs, with their young
men, conducted the party, by way of Chicago, to
Lake Michigan; and, before the end of September,
all were safe in Green Bay.

"Joliet returned to Quebec to announce the discovery, of which the fame, through Talon, quickened the ambition of Colbert; the unaspiring Marquette remained to preach the Gospel to the Miamis,
who dwelt in the north of Illinois, round Chicago.
Two years afterward, sailing from Chicago to Mack-
inaw, he entered a little river in Michigan. Erect-
ing an altar, he said mass after the rites of the Catholic Church; then, begging the men who conducted
his canoe to leave him alone for half an hour

> 'in the darkling wood,
> Amid the cool and silence, he knelt down,
> And offered to the Mightiest solemn thanks
> And supplication.'

At the end of the half hour they went to seek him,
and he was no more. The good missionary, discoverer of a world, had fallen asleep on the margin of
the stream that bears his name. Near its mouth the
canoe-men dug his grave in the sand. Ever after,
the forest rangers, if in danger on Lake Michigan,
would invoke his name. The people of the West
will build his monument."—*Ibid.*, p. 157, 162.

The list of heroic adventurers in the path of discovery is closed by La Salle, the chivalrous Frenchman of whom we have made particular record in a previous number of this Journal,* and whose tremendous journey from the Illinois to the French settlements in Canada, a distance of fifteen hundred miles, is also noticed by Mr. Bancroft. His was the first European bark that emerged from the mouth of the Mississippi; and Mr. Bancroft, as he notices the event, and the feelings it gave rise to in the mind of the discoverer, gives utterance to his own in language truly sublime:

"As he raised the cross by the Arkansas—as he planted the arms of France near the Gulf of Mexico, he anticipated the future affluence of emigrants, and heard in the distance the footsteps of the advancing multitude that were coming to take possession of the valley."—*Ibid.*, p. 168.

This descent of the Great River our author places, without hesitation, in 1682, being a year earlier than the one assigned by us in the article referred to.† Mr. Bancroft is so familiar with the whole ground, and has studied the subject so carefully, that great weight is due to his opinions; but he has not explained the precise authority for his conclusions in this particular.

This leads us to enlarge on what we consider a defect in our author's present plan. His notes are discarded altogether, and his references transferred

* See "North American Review," vol. xlviii., p. 69, *et seq.*
† Ibid., p. 84, 85

from the bottom of the page to the side margin. This is very objectionable, not merely on account of the disagreeable effect produced on the eye, but from the more serious inconvenience of want of room for very frequent and accurate reference. Titles are necessarily much abridged, sometimes at the expense of perspicuity. The first reference in this volume is "Hallam, iv., 374;" the second is "Archdale." Now Hallam has written several works, published in various forms and editions. As to the second authority, we have no means of identifying the passage at all. This, however, is not the habit of Mr. Bancroft where the fact is of any great moment, and his references throughout are abundant. But the practice of references in the side margin, though warranted by high authority, is unfavourable, from want of room, for very frequent or very minute specification.

The omission of notes we consider a still greater evil. It is true, they lead to great abuses, are often the vehicle of matter which should have been incorporated in the text, more frequently of irrelevant matter which should not have been admitted anywhere, and thus exhaust the reader's patience, while they spoil the effect of the work by drawing the attention from the continuous flow of the narrative, checking the heat that is raised by it in the reader's mind, and not unfrequently jarring on his feelings by some misplaced witticism, or smart attempt at one. For these and the like reasons, many competent critics have pronounced against the use of notes,

considering that a writer who could not bring all he
had to say into the compass of his text was a bun-
gler. Gibbon, who practised the contrary, intimates
a regret in one of his letters that he had been over-
ruled so far as to allow his notes to be printed at
the bottom of the page instead of being removed to
the end of the volume.   But from all this we dissent,
especially in reference to a work of research like the
present History.   We are often desirous here to
have the assertion of the author, or the sentiment
quoted by him, if important, verified by the original
extract, especially when this is in a foreign language.
We want to see the grounds of his conclusions, the
scaffolding by which he has raised his structure; to
estimate the true value of his authorities; to know
something of their characters, positions in society,
and the probable influences to which they were exposed.   Where there is contradiction, we want to
see it stated; the *pros* and the *cons*, and the grounds
for rejecting this and admitting that.   We want to
have a reason for our faith, otherwise we are merely
led blindfold.   Our guide may be an excellent guide;
he may have travelled over the path till it has become a beaten track to him; but we like to use our
own eyesight too, to observe somewhat for ourselves,
and to know, if possible, why he has taken this particular road in preference to that which his predecessors have travelled.

The objections made to notes are founded rather
on the abuse than the proper use of them.   Gibbon
only wished to remove his own to the end of his

volume; though in this we think he erred, from
the difficulty and frequent disappointment which the
reader must have experienced in consulting them—
a disappointment of little moment when unattended
by difficulty. But Gibbon knew too well the worth
of this part of his labours to him to wish to discard
them altogether. He knew his reputation stood on
them as intimately as on his narrative. Indeed,
they supply a body of criticism, and well-selected,
well-digested learning, which of itself would make
the reputation of any scholar. Many accomplished
writers, however, and Mr. Bancroft among the number, have come to a different conclusion; and he
has formed his, probably, with deliberation, having
made the experiment in both forms.

It is true, the fulness of the extracts from original
sources with which his text is inlaid, giving such
life and presence to it, and the frequency of his references, supersede much of the necessity of notes.
We should have been very glad of one, however, of
the kind we are speaking of, at the close of his expedition of La Salle.

We have no room for the discussion of the topics
in the next chapter, relating to the hostilities for the
acquisition of colonial territory between France and
England, each of them pledged to the same system
of commercial monopoly, but must pass to the author's account of the Aborigines east of the Mississippi. In this division of his subject he brings into
view the geographical positions of the numerous
tribes, their languages, social institutions, religious

faith, and probable origin. All these copious topics are brought within the compass of a hundred pages ; arranged with great harmony, and exhibited with perspicuity and singular richness of expression. It is, on the whole, the most elaborate and finished portion of the volume.

His remarks on the localities of the tribes, instead of a barren muster-roll of names, are constantly enlivened by picturesque details connected with their situation. His strictures on their various languages are conceived in a philosophical spirit. The subject is one that has already employed the pens of the ablest philologists in this country, among whom it is only necessary to mention the names of Du Ponceau, Pickering, and Gallatin. Our author has evidently bestowed much labour and thought on the topic. He examines the peculiar structure of the languages, which, though radically different, bear a common resemblance in their compounded and synthetic organization. He has omitted to notice the singular exception to the polysynthetic formation of the Indian languages presented by the Otomie, which has afforded a Mexican philologist so ingenious a parallel, in its structure, with the Chinese. Mr. Bancroft concludes his review of them by admitting the copiousness of their combinations, and by inferring that this copiousness is no evidence of care and cultivation, but the elementary form of expression of a rude and uncivilized people ; in proof of which, he cites the example of the partially civilized Indian in accommodating his idiom gradually to the analytic structure of the European languages. May not this be explained by the circumstance that the influence under which he makes this, like his other changes, is itself European? But we pass to a more popular theme, the religious faith of the red man, whose fanciful superstitions are depicted by our author with highly poetical colouring.

"The red man, unaccustomed to generalization, obtained no conception of an absolute substance, of a self-existent being, but saw a divinity in every power. Wherever there was being, motion, or action, there to him was a spirit; and, in a special manner, wherever there appeared singular excellence among beasts, or birds, or in the creation, there to him was the presence of a divinity. When he feels his pulse throb or his heart beat, he knows that it is a spirit. A god resides in the flint, to give forth the kindling, cheering fire; a spirit resides in the mountain cliff; a spirit makes its abode in the cool recesses of the grottoes which nature has adorned; a god dwells in each 'little grass' that springs miraculously from the earth. 'The woods, the wilds, and the waters respond to savage intelligence; the stars and the mountains live; the river, and the lake, and the waves have a spirit.' Every hidden agency, every mysterious influence, is personified. A god dwells in the sun, and in the moon, and in the firmament; the spirit of the morning reddens in the eastern sky; a deity is present in the ocean and in the fire; the crag that overhangs the river has its genius; there is a spirit to the waterfall; a household god dwells in the Indian's wigwam, and consecrates his home; spirits climb upon the forehead to weigh down the eyelids in sleep. Not the heavenly bodies only, the sky is filled with spirits that minister to man. To the savage, divinity, broken, as it were, into an infinite number of fragments, fills all place and all being. The idea of unity in the creation may exist contemporaneously, but it existed only in the germ, or as a vague belief derived from the harmony of the universe. Yet faith in the Great Spirit, when once presented, was promptly seized and appropriated, and so infused itself into the heart of remotest tribes, that it came to be often considered as a portion of their original faith. Their shadowy aspirations and creeds assumed, through the reports of missionaries, a more complete development, and a religious system was elicited from the pregnant but rude materials."—*Ibid.*, p. 285, 286.

The following pictures of the fate of the Indian infant, and the shadowy pleasures of the land of spirits, have also much tenderness and beauty :

" The same motive prompted them to bury with the warrior his pipe and his manitou, his tomahawk, quiver, and bow ready bent for action, and his most splendid apparel; to place by his side his bowl, his maize, and his venison, for the long journey to the country of his ancestors. Festivals in honour of the dead were also frequent, when a part of the food was given to the flames, that so it might serve to nourish the departed. The traveller would find in the forests a dead body placed on a scaffo'd erected upon piles, carefully wrapped in bark for its shroud, and attired in warmest furs. If a mother lost her babe, she would cover it with bark, and envelop it anxiously in the softest beaver-skins; at the burial-place she would put by its side its cradle, its beads, and its rattles; and, as a last service of maternal love, would draw milk from her bosom in a cup of bark, and burn it in the fire, that her infant might still find nourishment on its solitary journey to the land of shades. Yet the newborn babe would be buried, not, as usual, on a scaffold, but by the wayside, that so its spirit might secretly steal into the bosom of some passing matron, and be born again under happier auspices. On burying her daughter, the Chippewa mother adds, not snow-shoes, and beads, and moccasins only, but (sad emblem of woman's lot in the wilderness!) the carrying-belt and the paddle. 'I know my daughter will be restored to me,' she once said, as she clipped a lock of hair as a memorial; 'by this lock of hair I shall discover her, for I shall take it with me;' alluding to the day when she too, with her carrying-belt and paddle, and the little relic of her child, should pass through the grave to the dwelling-place of her ancestors."

" The faith, as well as the sympathies of the savage, descended also to inferior things. Of each kind of animal they say there exists one, the source and origin of all, of a vast size, the type and original of the whole class. From the immense invisible beaver come all the beavers, by whatever run of water they are found; the same is true of the elk and buftalo, of the eagle and robin, of the meanest quadruped of the forest, of the smallest insect that buzzes in the air. There lives for each class of animals this invisible, vast type, or elder brother. Thus the savage established his right to be classed by philosophers in the rank of Realists, and his chief effort at generalization was a reverent exercise of the religious sentiment. Where these older brothers dwell they do not exactly know ; yet it may be that the giant manitous, which are brothers to beasts, are hid beneath the waters, and that those of the birds make their homes in the blue sky. But the Indian believes also, of each individual animal, that it possesses the mysterious, the indestructible principle of life ; there is not a breathing thing but has its shade, which never can perish. Regarding himself, in comparison with other animals, but as the first among co-ordinate existences, he respects the brute creation, and assigns to it, as to himself, a perpetuity of being. ' The ancients of these lands believed that the warrior, when released from life, renews the passions and activity of this world ; is seated once more among his friends ; shares again the joyous feast ; walks through shadowy forests, that are alive with the spirits of birds ; and there, in his paradise,

> " ' By midnight moons, o'er moistening dews,
>   In vestments for the chase arrayed,
>   The hunter still the deer pursues—
>   The hunter and the deer a shade.' "
>
> *Ibid.*, p. 295, 298.

At the close of this chapter the historian grapples with the much-vexed question respecting the origin of the Aborigines—that *pons asinorum* which has called forth so much sense and nonsense on both sides of the water, and will continue to do so as long as a new relic or unknown hieroglyphic shall turn up to irritate the nerves of the antiquary.

Mr. Bancroft passes briefly in review the several arguments adduced in favour of the connexion with Eastern Asia. He lays no stress on the affinity of languages, or of customs and religious notions, considering these as spontaneous expressions of similar ideas and wants in similar conditions of society. He attaches as little value to the resemblance established by Humboldt between the signs of the Mexican calendar and those of the signs of the zodiac in Thibet and Tartary; and as for the far-famed Dighton Rock, and the learned lucubrations thereon, he sets them down as so much moonshine, pronouncing the characters Algonquin. The *tumuli*—the great tumuli of the West—he regards as the work of no mortal hand, except so far as they have been excavated for a sepulchral purpose. He admits, however, vestiges of a migratory movement on our continent, from the northeast to the southwest; shows very satisfactorily, by estimating the distances of the intervening islands, the practicability of a passage in the most ordinary sea-boat from the Asiatic to the American shores in the high latitudes; and, by a comparison of the Indian and Mongolian sculls, comes to the conclusion that the two races are probably identical in origin. But the epoch of their divergence he places at so remote a period, that the peculiar habits, institutions, and culture of the Aborigines must be regarded as all their own—as indigenous. This is the outline of his theory.

By this hypothesis he extricates the question from the embarrassment caused by the ignorance which the Aborigines have manifested in the use of iron and milk, known to the Mongol hordes, but which he, of course, supposes were not known at the time of the migration. This is carrying the exodus back to a far period. But the real objection seems to be that, by thus rejecting all evidence of communication but that founded on anatomical resemblance, he has unnecessarily narrowed the basis on which it rests. The resemblance between a few specimens of Mongolian and American sculls is a narrow basis indeed, taken as the only one, for so momentous a theory.

In fact, this particular point of analogy does not strike us as by any means the most powerful of the arguments in favour of a communication with the East, when we consider the small number of the specimens on which it is founded, the great variety of formation in individuals of the same family—some of the specimens approaching even nearer to the Caucasian than the Mongolian—and the very uniform deviation from the latter in the prominence and the greater angularity of the features.

This connexion with the East derives, in our judgment, some support, feeble though it be, from affinities of language; but this is a field which remains to be much more fully explored. The analogy is much more striking of certain usages and institutions, particularly of a religious character, and, above all, the mythological traditions which those who have had occasion to look into the Aztec antiquities cannot fail to be struck with. This resemblance is oftentimes in matters so purely arbitrary, that it can hardly be regarded as founded in the constitution of man; so very exact that it can scarcely be considered as accidental. We give up the Dighton Rock, that rock of offence to so many antiquaries, who may read in it the hand-writing of the Phœnicians, Egyptians, or Scandinavians, quite as well as anything else. Indeed, the various *fac similes* of it, made for the benefit of the learned, are so different from one another, that, like Sir Hudibras, one may find in it

"A leash of languages at once."

We are agreed with our author that it is very good Algonquin. But the zodiac, the Tartar zodiac, which M. de Humboldt has so well shown to resemble, in its terms, those of the Aztec calendar, we cannot so easily surrender. The striking coincidence established by his investigations between the astronomical signs of the two nations — in a similar corresponding series, moreover, although applied to different uses—is, in our opinion, one of the most powerful arguments yet adduced for the affinity of the two races. Nor is Mr. Bancroft wholly right in supposing that the Asiatic hieroglyphics referred only to the zodiac. Like the Mexican, they also presided over the years, days, and even hours. The strength of evidence, founded on numerous analogies, cannot be shown without going into details, for which there is scarce room in the compass of a separate article, much less in the heel of one. Whichever way we turn, the subject is full of perplexity. It is the sphinx's riddle, and the Œdipus must be called from the grave who is to solve it.

In closing our remarks, we must express our satisfaction that the favourable notice we took of Mr. Bancroft's labours on his first appearance has been fully ratified by his countrymen, and that his Colonial History establishes his title to a place among the great historical writers of the age. The reader will find the pages of the present volume filled with matter not less interesting and important than the preceding. He will meet with the same brilliant and daring style, the same picturesque sketches of character and incident, the same acute reasoning and compass of erudition.

In the delineation of events Mr. Bancroft has been guided by the spirit of historic faith. Not that it would be difficult to discern the colour of his politics; nor, indeed, would it be possible for any one strongly pledged to any set of principles, whether in politics or religion, to disguise them in the discussion of abstract topics, without being false to himself, and giving a false tone to the picture; but, while he is true to himself, he has an equally imperative duty to perform—to be true to others, to those on whose characters and conduct he sits in judgment as a historian. No pet theory nor party predilections can justify him in swerving one hair's-breadth from truth in his delineation of the mighty dead, whose portraits he is exhibiting to us on the canvass of history.

Whenever religion is introduced, Mr. Bancroft has shown a commendable spirit of liberality. Catholics and Calvinists, Jesuits, Quakers, and Church-of-England men, are all judged according to their deeds, and not their speculative tenets; and even in the latter particular he generally contrives to find something deserving of admiration, some commendable doctrine or aspiration in most of them. And what Christian sect—we might add, what sect of any denomination—is there which has not some beauty of doctrine to admire? Religion is the homage of man to his Creator. The forms in which it is expressed are infinitely various; but they flow from the same source, are directed to the same end, and all claim from the historian the benefit of toleration.

What Mr. Bancroft has done for the Colonial history is, after all, but preparation for a richer theme, the history of the War of Independence; a subject which finds its origin in the remote past, its results in the infinite future; which finds a central point of unity in the ennobling principle of independence, that gives dignity and grandeur to the most petty details of the conflict, and which has its foreground occupied by a single character, to which all others converge as to a centre—the character of Washington, in war, in peace, and in private life the most sublime on historical record. Happy the writer who shall exhibit this theme worthily to the eyes of his countrymen!

The subject, it is understood, is to engage the attention, also, of Mr. Sparks, whose honourable labours have already associated-his name imperishably with our Revolutionary period. Let it not be feared that there is not compass enough in the subject for two minds so gifted. The field is too rich to be exhausted by a single crop, and will yield fresh laurels to the skilful hand that shall toil for them. The labours of Hume did not supersede those of Lingard, or Turner, or Mackintosh, or Hallam. The history of the English Revolution has called forth, in our own time, the admirable essays of Mackintosh and Guizot; and the palm of excellence, after the libraries that have been written on the French Revolution, has just been assigned to the dissimilar histories of Mignet and Thiers. The points of view under which a thing may be contemplated are as diversified as mind itself. The most honest inquirers after truth rarely come to precisely the same results, such is the influence of education, prejudice, principle. Truth, indeed, is single, but opinions are infinitely various, and it is only by comparing these opinions together that we can hope to ascertain what is truth.

MADAME CALDERON'S LIFE IN MEXICO.*

JANUARY, 1843.

IN the present age of high literary activity, travellers make not the least importunate demands on public attention, and their lucubrations, under whatever name—Rambles, Notices, Incidents, Pencillings—are nearly as important a staple for the "trade" as novels and romances. A book of travels, formerly, was a very serious affair. The traveller set out on his distant journey with many a solemn preparation, made his will, and bade adieu to his friends like one who might not again return. If he did return, the results were imbodied in a respectable folio, or at least quarto, well garnished with cuts, and done up in a solid form, which argued that it was no fugitive publication, but destined for posterity.

All this is changed. The voyager nowadays leaves home with as little ceremony and leave-taking as if it were for a morning's drive. He steps into the bark that is to carry him across thousands of miles of ocean with the moral certainty of returning in a fixed week, almost at a particular day. Parties of gentlemen and ladies go whizzing along in their steamships over the track which cost so many weary days to the Argonauts of old, and run over the choicest scenes of classic antiquity, scatter-

* "Life in Mexico, during a Residence of Two Years in that Country. By Madame C—— de la B——." Boston : Little and Brown. Two volumes, 12mo.

ed through Europe, Asia, and Africa, in less time
than it formerly took to go from one end of the British isles to the other. The Cape of Good Hope, so
long the great stumbling-block to the navigators of
Europe, is doubled, or the Red Sea coasted, in the
same way, by the fashionable tourist—who glides
along the shores of Arabia, Persia, Afghanistan, Bom-
bay, and Hindostan, farther than the farthest limits
of Alexander's conquests—before the last leaves of
the last new novel which he has taken by the way
are fairly cut. The facilities of communication
have, in fact, so abridged distances, that geography,
as we have hitherto studied it, may be said to be
entirely reformed. Instead of leagues, we now com-
pute by hours, and we find ourselves next-door
neighbours to those whom we had looked upon as
at the antipodes.

The consequence of these improvements in the
means of intercourse is, that all the world goes
abroad, or, at least, one half is turned upon the other. Nations are so mixed up by this process that
they are in some danger of losing their idiosyncrasy;
and the Egyptian and the Turk, though they still
cling to their religion, are becoming European in
their notions and habits more and more every day.

The taste for pilgrimage, however, it must be
owned, does not stop with the countries where it
can be carried on with such increased facility. It
has begotten a nobler spirit of adventure, something
akin to what existed in the fifteenth century, when
the world was new or newly discovering, and a

navigator who did not take in sail, like the cautious seamen of Knickerbocker, might run down some strange continent in the dark; for, in these times of dandy tourists and travel-mongers, the boldest achievements, that have hitherto defied the most adventurous spirits, have been performed: the Himmalaya Mountains have been scaled, the Niger ascended, the burning heart of Africa penetrated, the icy Arctic and Antarctic explored, and the mysterious monuments of the semi-civilized races of Central America have been thrown open to the public gaze. It is certain that this is a high-pressure age, and every department of science and letters, physical and mental, feels its stimulating influence.

No nation, on the whole, has contributed so largely to these itinerant expeditions as the English. Uneasy, it would seem, at being cooped up in their little isle, they sally forth in all directions, swarming over the cultivated and luxurious countries of the neighbouring continent, or sending out stragglers on other more distant and formidable missions. Whether it be that their soaring spirits are impatient of the narrow quarters which nature has assigned them, or that there exists a supernumerary class of idlers, who, wearied with the monotony of home, and the same dull round of dissipation, seek excitement in strange scenes and adventures; or whether they go abroad for the sunshine, of which they have heard so much but seen so little—whatever be the cause, they furnish a far greater number of tourists than all the world besides. We Americans, indeed, may compete with them in mere locomotion, for our familiarity with magnificent distances at home makes us still more indifferent to them abroad; but this locomotion is generally in the way of business, and the result is rarely shown in a book, unless, indeed, it be the leger.

Yet John Bull is, on many accounts, less fitted than most of his neighbours for the duties of a traveller. However warm and hospitable in his own home, he has a cold reserve in his exterior, a certain chilling atmosphere, which he carries along with him, that freezes up the sympathies of strangers, and which is only to be completely thawed by long and intimate acquaintance. But the traveller has no time for intimate acquaintances. He must go forward, and trust to his first impressions, for they will also be his last. Unluckily, it rarely falls out that the first impressions of honest John are very favourable. There is too much pride, not to say *hauteur*, in his composition, which, with the best intentions in the world, will show itself in a way not particularly flattering to those who come in contact with him. He goes through a strange nation, treading on all their little irritable prejudices, shocking their self-love and harmless vanities—in short, going against the grain, and roughing up everything by taking it the wrong way. Thus he draws out the bad humours of the people among whom he moves, sees them in their most unamiable and by no means natural aspect—in short, looks on the wrong side of the tapestry. What wonder if his notions are somewhat awry as to what he sees! There are, it is true, distinguished exceptions to all this: English travellers, who cover the warm heart—as warm as it is generally true and manly—under a kind and sometimes cordial manner; but they are the exceptions. The Englishman undoubtedly appears best on his own soil, where his national predilections and prejudices, or, at least, the intimation of them, are somewhat mitigated in deference to his guest.

Another source of the disqualification of John Bull as a calm and philosophic traveller is the manner in which he has been educated at home; the soft luxuries by which he has been surrounded from his cradle have made luxuries necessaries, and, accustomed to perceive all the machinery of life glide along as noiselessly and as swiftly as the foot of Time itself, he becomes morbidly sensitive to every temporary jar or derangement in the working of it. In no country, since the world was made, have all the appliances for mere physical, and, we may add, intellectual indulgence, been carried to such perfection as in this little island nucleus of civilization. Nowhere can a man get such returns for his outlay. The whole organization of society is arranged so as to minister to the comforts of the wealthy; and an Englishman, with the golden talisman in his pocket, can bring about him genii to do his bidding, and transport himself over distances with a thought, almost as easy as if he were the possessor of Aladdin's magic lamp, and the fairy carpet of the Arabian Tales.

When he journeys over his little island, his comforts and luxuries cling as close to him as round his own fireside.   He rolls over roads as smooth and well-beaten as those in his own park; is swept onward by sleek and well-groomed horses, in a carriage as soft and elastic, and quite as showy as his own equipage; puts up at inns that may vie with his own castle in their comforts and accommodations, and is received by crowds of obsequious servants, more solicitous, probably, even than his own to win his golden smiles.   In short, wherever he goes, he may be said to carry with him his castle, park, equipage, establishment.   The whole are in movement together. He changes place, indeed, but changes nothing else For travelling, as it occurs in other lands—hard roads, harder beds, and hardest fare —he knows no more of it than if he had been passing from one wing of his castle to the other.

All this, it must be admitted, is rather an indifferent preparation for a tour on the Continent.   Of what avail is it that Paris is the most elegant capital, France the most enlightened country on the European *terra firma*, if one cannot walk in the streets without the risk of being run over for want of a *trottoir*, nor move on the roads without being half smothered in a lumbering vehicle, dragged by ropes, at the rate of five miles an hour ?   Of what account are the fine music and paintings, the architecture and art of Italy, when one must shiver by day for want of carpets and seacoal fires, and be thrown into a fever at night by the active vexations of a still

X x

more tormenting kind? The galled equestrian might as well be expected to feel nothing but raptures and ravishment at the fine scenery through which he is riding. It is probable he will think much more of his own petty hurts than of the beauties of nature. A travelling John Bull, if his skin is not off, is at least so thin-skinned that it is next door to being so.

If the European neighbourhood affords so many means of annoyance to the British traveller, they are incalculably multiplied on this side of the water, and that, too, under circumstances which dispose him still less to charity in his criticisms and constructions. On the Continent he feels he is among strange races, born and bred under different religious and political institutions, and, above all, speaking different languages. He does not necessarily, therefore, measure them by his peculiar standard, but allows them one of their own. The dissimilarity is so great in all the main features of national polity and society, that it is hard to institute a comparison. Whatever be his contempt for the want of progress and perfection in the science of living, he comes to regard them as a distinct race, amenable to different laws, and therefore licensed to indulge in different usages, to a certain extent, from his own. If a man travels in China, he makes up his mind to chop-sticks. If he should go to the moon, he would not be scandalized by seeing people walk with their heads under their arms. He has embarked on a different planet. It is only in things which run parallel to those in his own country that a comparison can be instituted, and charity too often fails where criticism begins.

Unhappily, in America, the Englishman finds these points of comparison forced on him at every step He lands among a people speaking the same language, professing the same religion, drinking at the same fountains of literature, trained in the same occupations of active life. The towns are built on much the same model with those in his own land. The brick houses, the streets, the "sidewalks," the in-door arrangements, all, in short, are near enough on the same pattern to provoke a comparison. Alas! for the comparison. The cities sink at once into mere provincial towns, the language degenerates into a provincial *patois*, the manners, the fashions, down to the cut of the clothes, and the equipages, all are provincial. The people, the whole nation — as independent as any, certainly, if not, as our orators fondly descant, the best and most enlightened upon earth — dwindle into a mere British colony. The traveller does not seem to understand that he is treading the soil of the New World, where everything is new, where antiquity dates but from yesterday, where the present and the future are all, and the past nothing, where hope is the watchword, and "Go ahead!" the principle of action. He does not comprehend that when he sets foot on such a land, he is no longer to look for old hereditary landmarks, old time-honoured monuments and institutions, old families that have vegetated on the same soil since the Conquest. He must be content to part with the order and something of the decorum incident to an old community, where the ranks are all precisely and punctiliously defined, where the power is deposited by prescriptive right in certain privileged hands, and where the great mass have the careful obsequiousness of dependants, looking for the crumbs that fall.

He is now among a new people, where everything is in movement, all struggling to get forward, and where, though many go adrift in their wild spirit of adventure, and a temporary check may be sometimes felt by all, the great mass still advances. He is landed on a hemisphere where fortunes are to be made, and men are employed in getting, not in spending— a difference which explains so many of the discrepancies between the structure of our own society and habits and those of the Old World. To know how to spend is itself a science; and the science of spending and that of getting are rarely held by the same hand.

In such a state of things, the whole arrangement of society, notwithstanding the apparent resemblance to that in his own country, and its real resemblance in minor points, is reversed. The rich proprietor, who does nothing but fatten on his rents, is no longer at the head of the scale, as in the Old World. The man of enterprise takes the lead in a bustling community, where action and progress, or at least change, are the very conditions of existence. The upper classes—if the term can be used in a complete democracy—have not the luxurious finish and accommodations to be found in the other hemisphere. The humbler classes have not the poverty-stricken,

cringing spirit of hopeless inferiority. The pillar of
society, if it want the Corinthian capital, wants also
the heavy and superfluous base. Every man not
only professes to be, but is practically, on a footing
of equality with his neighbour. The traveller must
not expect to meet here the deference, or even the
courtesies which grow out of distinction of castes.
This is an awkward dilemma for one whose nerves
have never been jarred by contact with the *profane*;
who has never been tossed about in the rough and
tumble of humanity. It is little to him that the poorest child in the community learns how to read and
write; that the poorest man can have—what Henry
the Fourth so good-naturedly wished for the humblest of his subjects—a fowl in his pot every day for
his dinner; that no one is so low but that he may
aspire to all the rights of his fellow-men, and find an
open theatre on which to display his own peculiar
talents.

As the tourist strikes into the interior, difficulties
of all sorts multiply, incident to a raw and unformed
country. The comparison with the high civilization
at home becomes more and more unfavourable, as he
is made to feel that in this land of promise it must
be long before promise can become the performance
of the Old World. And yet, if he would look beyond the surface, he would see that much here too
has been performed, however much may be wanting.
He would see lands over which the wild Indian
roamed as a hunting-ground, teeming with harvests
for the consumption of millions at home and abroad;

4   2 E

forests, which have shot up, ripened, and decayed on the same spot ever since the creation, now swept away to make room for towns and villages, thronged with an industrious population ; rivers, which rolled on in their solitudes, undisturbed except by the wandering bark of the savage, now broken and dimpled by hundreds of steamboats, freighted with the rich tribute of a country rescued from the wilderness. He would not expect to meet the careful courtesies of polished society in the pioneers of civilization, whose mission has been to recover the great continent from the bear and the buffalo. He would have some charity for their ignorance of the latest fashions of Bond-street, and their departure, sometimes, even from what, in the Old Country, is considered as the decorum, and, it may be, decencies of life. But not so ; his heart turns back to his own land, and closes against the rude scenes around him ; for he finds here none of the soft graces of cultivation, or the hallowed memorials of an early civilization ; no gray, weather-beaten cathedrals, telling of the Normans ; no Gothic churches in their groves of venerable oaks ; no moss-covered cemeteries, in which the dust of his fathers has been gathered since the time of the Plantagenets ; no rural cottages, half smothered with roses and honeysuckles, intimating that even in the most humble abodes the taste for the beautiful has found its way ; no trim gardens, and fields blossoming with hawthorn hedges and miniature culture ; no ring fences, enclosing well-shaven lawns, woods so disposed as to form a picture of

themselves, bright threads of silvery water, and
sparkling fountains. All these are wanting, and his
eyes turn with disgust from the wild and rugged features of nature, and all her rough accompaniments—
from man almost as wild; and his heart sickens as
he thinks of his own land, and all its scenes of beauty. He thinks not of the poor, who leave that land
for want of bread, and find in this a kindly welcome,
and the means of independence and advancement
which their own denies them.

He goes on, if he be a splenetic Sinbad, discharging his sour bile on everybody that he comes in contact with, thus producing an amiable ripple in the
current as he proceeds, that adds marvellously, no
doubt, to his own quiet and personal comfort. If he
have a true merry vein and hearty good nature, he
gets on, laughing sometimes in his sleeve at others,
and cracking his jokes on the unlucky pate of Brother Jonathan, who, if he is not very silly—which he
very often is—laughs too, and joins in the jest,
though it may be somewhat at his own expense. It
matters little whether the tourist be Whig or Tory
in his own land; if the latter, he returns, probably,
ten times the Conservative that he was when he left
it. If Whig, or even Radical, it matters not; his
loyalty waxes warmer and warmer with every step
of his progress among the Republicans; and he finds
that practical democracy, shouldering and elbowing
its neighbours as it "goes ahead," is no more like
the democracy which he has been accustomed to admire in theory, than the real machinery, with its

smell, smoke, and clatter, under full operation, is like the pretty toy which he sees as a model in the Patent Office at Washington.

There seems to be no people better constituted for travellers, at least for recording their travelling experiences, than the French. There is a mixture of frivolity and philosophy in their composition which is admirably suited to the exigencies of their situation. They mingle readily with all classes and races, discarding for the time their own nationality —at least their national antipathies. Their pleasant vanity fills them with the desire of pleasing others, which most kindly reacts by their being themselves pleased :

"Pleased with himself, whom all the world can please."

The Frenchman can even so far accommodate himself to habits alien to his own, that he can tolerate those of the savages themselves, and enter into a sort of fellowship with them, without either party altogether discarding his national tastes and propensities. It is Chateaubriand, if we are not mistaken, who relates that, wandering in the solitudes of the American wilderness, his ears were most unexpectedly saluted by the sounds of a violin. He had little doubt that one of his own countrymen must be at hand ; and in a wretched enclosure he found one of them, sure enough, teaching *Messieurs les sauvages* to dance. It is certain that this spirit of accommodation to the wild habits of their copper-coloured friends gave the French traders and missionaries formerly an ascendency over the Aborigines which was never obtained by any other of the white men.

The most comprehensive and truly philosophic work on the genius and institutions of this country, the best exposition of its social phenomena, its present condition, and probable future, are to be found in the pages of a Frenchman. It is in the French language, too, that by far the greatest work has been produced on the great Southern portion of our continent, once comprehended under New Spain.

To write a book of travels seems to most people to require as little preliminary preparation as to write a letter. One has only to jump into a coach, embark on board a steamboat, minute down his flying experiences and hair-breadth escapes, the aspect of the country as seen from the interior of a crowded *diligence* or a vanishing rail-car, note the charges of the landlords and the quality of the fare, a dinner or two at the minister's, the last new play or opera at the theatre, and the affair is done. It is very easy to do this, certainly ; very easy to make a bad book of travels, but by no means easy to make a good one. This requires as many and various qualifications as to make any other good book ; qualifications which must vary with the character of the country one is to visit. Thus, for instance, it requires a very different preparation and stock of accomplishments to make the tour of Italy, its studios and its galleries of art, or of Egypt, with its immortal pyramids and mighty relics of a primeval age, the great cemetery of antiquity, from what it does to travel understand-

4   2 E*

ingly in our own land, a new creation, as it were, without monuments, without arts, where the only study of the traveller—the noblest of all studies, it is true—is man. The inattention to this difference of preparation, demanded by different places, has led many a clever writer to make a very worthless book, which would have been remedied had he consulted his own qualifications instead of taking the casual direction of the first steamboat or mail-coach that lay in his way.

There is no country more difficult to discuss in all its multiform aspects than Mexico, or, rather, the wide region once comprehended under the name of New Spain. Its various climates, bringing to perfection the vegetable products of the most distant latitudes; its astonishing fruitfulness in its lower regions, and its curse of barrenness over many a broad acre of its plateau; its inexhaustible mines, that have flooded the Old World with an ocean of silver, such as Columbus in his wildest visions never dreamed of—and, unhappily, by a hard mischance, never lived to realize himself; its picturesque landscape, where the volcanic fire gleams amid wastes of eternal snow, and a few hours carry the traveller from the hot regions of the lemon and the cocoa to the wintry solitudes of the mountain fir; its motley population, made up of Indians, old Spaniards, modern Mexicans, meztizoes, mulattoes, and zambos; its cities built in the clouds; its lakes of salt water, hundreds of miles from the ocean; its people, with their wild and variegated costume, in keeping, as we

may say, with its extraordinary scenery; its stately
palaces, half furnished, where services of gold and
silver plate load the tables in rooms without a carpet, while the red dust of the bricks soils the dia-
mond-sprinkled robes of the dancer; the costly attire
of its higher classes, blazing with pearls and jewels;
the tawdry magnificence of its equipages, saddles
inlaid with gold, bits and stirrups of massy silver, all
executed in the clumsiest style of workmanship; its
lower classes—the men with their jackets glittering
with silver buttons, and rolls of silver tinsel round
their caps; the women with petticoats fringed with
lace, and white satin shoes on feet unprotected by a
stocking; its high-born fair ones crowding to the
cock-pit, and solacing themselves with the fumes of
a cigar; its churches and convents, in which all
those sombre rules of monastic life are maintained
in their primitive rigour, which have died away before the liberal spirit of the age on the other side of
the water; its swarms of *léperos*, the lazzaroni of
the land; its hordes of almost legalized banditti,
who stalk openly in the streets, and render the presence of an armed escort necessary to secure a safe
drive into the environs of the capital; its whole
structure of society, in which a Republican form is
thrown over institutions as aristocratic, and castes
as nicely defined, as in any monarchy of Europe;
in short, its marvellous inconsistencies and contrasts
in climate, character of the people, and face of the
land—so marvellous as, we trust, to excuse the unprecedented length of this sentence—undoubtedly

make modern Mexico one of the most prolific, original, and difficult themes for the study of the traveller.

Yet this great theme has found in Humboldt a writer of strength sufficient to grapple with it in nearly all its relations. While yet a young man, or, at least, while his physical as well as mental energies were in their meridian, he came over to this country with an enthusiasm for science which was only heightened by obstacles, and with stores of it already accumulated that enabled him to detect the nature of every new object that came under his eye, and arrange it in its proper class. With his scientific instruments in his hand, he might be seen scaling the snow-covered peaks of the Cordilleras, or diving into their unfathomable caverns of silver; now wandering through their dark forests in search of new specimens for his herbarium, now coasting the stormy shores of the Gulf, and penetrating its unhealthy streams, jotting down every landmark that might serve to guide the future navigator, or surveying the crested Isthmus in search of a practicable communication between the great seas on its borders, and then, again, patiently studying the monuments and manuscripts of the Aztecs in the capital, or mingling with the wealth and fashion in its saloons; frequenting every place, in short, and everywhere at home:

"Grammaticus, rhetor, geometres, ... omnia novit."

The whole range of these various topics is brought under review in his pages, and on all he sheds a ray, sometimes a flood of light. His rational philosophy content rather to doubt than to decide, points out the track which other adventurous spirits may follow up with advantage. No antiquary has done so much towards determining the original hives of the semi-civilized races of the Mexican plateau. No one, not even of the Spaniards, has brought together such an important mass of information in respect to the resources, natural products, and statistics generally, of New Spain. His explorations have identified more than one locality, and illustrated more than one curious monument of the people of Anahuac, which had baffled the inquiries of native antiquaries; and his work, while imbodying the results of profound scholarship and art, is, at the same time, in many respects, the very best *manuel du voyageur*, and, as such, has been most freely used by subsequent tourists. It is true, his pages are sometimes disfigured by pedantry, ambitious display, learned obscurity, and other affectations of the man of letters. But what human work is without its blemishes? His various writings on the subject of New Spain, taken collectively, are one of those monuments which may be selected to show the progress of the species. Their author reminds us of one of the ancient athletæ, who descended into the arena to hurl the discus with a giant arm, that distanced every cast of his contemporaries!

There is one branch of his fruitful subject which M. de Humboldt has not exhausted, and, indeed, has but briefly touched on. This is the social condition of the country, especially as found in its picturesque capital. This has been discussed by subsequent travellers more fully, and Ward, Bullock, Lyons, Poinsett, Tudor, Latrobe, have all produced works which have for their object, more or less, the social habits and manners of the people. With most of them this is not the prominent object; and others of them, probably, have found obstacles in effecting it, to any great extent, from an imperfect knowledge of the language—the golden key to the sympathies of a people—without which a traveller is as much at fault as a man without an eye for colour in a picture-gallery, or an ear for music at a concert. He may see and hear, indeed, in both, but *cui bono?* The traveller, ignorant of the language of the nation whom he visits, may descant on the scenery, the roads, the architecture, the outside of things, the rates and distances of posting, the dress of the people in the streets, and may possibly meet a native or two, half denaturalized, kept to dine with strangers at his banker's. But as to the interior mechanism of society, its secret sympathies, and familiar tone of thinking and feeling, he can know no more than he could of the contents of a library by running over the titles of strange and unknown authors packed together on the shelves.

It was to supply this deficiency that the work before us, no doubt, was given to the public, and it was composed under circumstances that afforded every possible advantage and facility to its author. Although the initials only of the name are given in the title-page, yet, from these and certain less equivocal

passages in the body of the work, it requires no
Œdipus to divine that the author is the wife of the
Chevalier Calderon de la Barca, well known in this
country during his long residence as Spanish minister at Washington, where his amiable manners and
high personal qualities secured him general respect,
and the regard of all who knew him. On the recognition of the independence of Mexico by the mother
country, Señor Calderon was selected to fill the
office of the first Spanish envoy to the Republic. It
was a delicate mission after so long an estrangement,
and it was hailed by the Mexicans with every demonstration of pride and satisfaction. Though twenty years had elapsed since they had established their
independence, yet they felt as a wayward son may
feel who, having absconded from the paternal roof
and set up for himself, still looks back to it with a
sort of reverence, and, in the plenitude of his prosperity, still feels the want of the parental benediction.
We, who cast off our allegiance in a similar way,
can comprehend the feeling. The new minister,
from the moment of his setting foot on the Mexican
shore, was greeted with an enthusiasm which attested the popular feeling, and his presence in the capital was celebrated by theatrical exhibitions, bull-
fights, illuminations, *fêtes* public and private, and
every possible demonstration of respect for the new
envoy and the country who sent him. His position
secured him access to every place of interest to an
intelligent stranger, and introduced him into the most
intimate recesses of society, from which the stranger

is commonly excluded, and to which, indeed, none but a Spaniard could, under any circumstances, have been admitted. Fortunately, the minister possessed, in the person of his accomplished wife, one who had both the leisure and the talent to profit by these uncommon opportunities, and the result is given in the work before us, consisting of letters to her family, which, it seems, since her return to the United States, have been gathered together and prepared for publication.*

* * * * * * *

The present volumes make no pretensions to enlarge the boundaries of our knowledge in respect to the mineral products of the country, its geography, its statistics, or, in short, to physical or political science. These topics have been treated with more or less depth by the various travellers who have written since the great publications of Humboldt. We have had occasion to become tolerably well acquainted with their productions; and we may safely assert, that for spirited portraiture of society—a society unlike anything existing in the Old World or the New —for picturesque delineation of scenery, for richness of illustration and anecdote, and for the fascinating graces of style, no one of them is to be compared with "Life in Mexico."

---

* The analysis of the work, with several pages of extracts from it, is here omitted, as containing nothing that is not already familiar to the English reader.

MOLIERE.

OCTOBER, 1828.

THE French surpass every other nation, indeed all the other nations of Europe put together, in the amount and excellence of their memoirs. Whence comes this manifest superiority? The important Collection relating to the History of France, commencing as early as the thirteenth century, forms a basis of civil history, more authentic, circumstantial, and satisfactory to an intelligent inquirer than is to be found among any other people; and the multitude of biographies, personal anecdotes, and similar scattered notices, which have appeared in France during the two last centuries, throw a flood of light on the social habits and general civilization of the period in which they were written. The Italian histories (and every considerable city in Italy, says Tiraboschi, had its historian as early as the thirteenth century) are fruitful only in wars, massacres, treasonable conspiracies, or diplomatic intrigues, matters that affect the tranquillity of the state. The rich body of Spanish chronicles, which maintain an unbroken succession from the reign of Alphonso the Wise to that of Philip the Second, are scarcely more personal or interesting in their details, unless it be in reference to the sovereign and his immediate

* " Histcire de la Vie et des Ouvrages de Molière. Par J. Taschereau." Paris 1825.

4

2 F

court. Even the English, in their memoirs and au-
tobiographies of the last century, are too exclusively
confined to topics of public notoriety, as the only
subject worthy of record, or which can excite a general interest in their readers. Not so with the French.
The most frivolous details assume in their eyes an
importance, when they can be made illustrative of
an eminent character; and even when they concern one of less note, they become sufficiently interesting, as just pictures of life and manners. Hence,
instead of exhibiting their hero only as he appears
on the great theatre, they carry us along with him
into retirement, or into those social circles where,
stripped of his masquerade dress, he can indulge in
all the natural gayety of his heart—in those frivolities and follies which display the real character
much better than all his premeditated wisdom; those
little nothings, which make up so much of the sum
of French memoirs, but which, however amusing,
are apt to be discarded by their more serious English neighbours as something derogatory to their
hero. Where shall we find a more lively portraiture of that interesting period, when feudal barbarism
began to fade away before the civilized institutions
of modern times, than in Philip de Comines' sketches of the courts of France and Burgundy in the latter half of the fifteenth century? Where a more
nice development of the fashionable intrigues, the
corrupt Machiavelian politics which animated the
little coteries, male and female, of Paris, under the
regency of Anne of Austria, than in the Memoirs of

De Retz? To say nothing of the vast amount of similar contributions in France during the last century, which, in the shape of letters and anecdotes, as well as memoirs, have made us as intimately acquainted with the internal movements of society in Paris, under all its aspects, literary, fashionable, and political, as if they had passed in review before our own eyes.

The French have been remarked for their excellence in narrative ever since the times of the *fabliaux* and the old Norman romances. Somewhat of their success in this way may be imputed to the structure of their language, whose general currency, and whose peculiar fitness for prose composition, have been noticed from a very early period. Brunetto Latini, the master of Dante, wrote his *Tesoro* in French, in preference to his own tongue, as far back as the middle of the thirteenth century, on the ground "that its speech was the most universal and most delectable of all the dialects of Europe." And Dante asserts in his treatise " on Vulgar Eloquence," that "the superiority of the French consists in its adaptation, by means of its facility and agreeableness, to narratives in prose." Much of the wild, artless grace, the *naïveté*, which characterized it in its infancy, has been gradually polished away by fastidious critics, and can scarcely be said to have survived Marot and Montaigne. But the language has gained considerably in perspicuity, precision, and simplicity of construction, to which the jealous labours of the French Academy must be admitted to have contributed essentially. This simplicity of construction, refusing those complicated inversions so usual in the other languages of the Continent, and its total want of prosody, though fatal to poetical purposes, have greatly facilitated its acquisition to foreigners, and have made it a most suitable vehicle for conversation. Since the time of Louis the Fourteenth, accordingly, it has become the language of the courts, and the popular medium of communication in most of the countries of Europe. Since that period, too, it has acquired a number of elegant phrases and familiar turns of expression, which have admirably fitted it for light, popular narrative, like that which enters into memoirs, letter-writing, and similar kinds of composition.

The character and situation of the writers themselves may account still better for the success of the French in this department. Many of them, as Joinville, Sully, Comines, De Thou, Rochefoucault, Torcy, have been men of rank and education, the counsellors or the friends of princes, acquiring from experience a shrewd perception of the character and of the forms of society. Most of them have been familiarized in those polite circles which, in Paris more than any other capital, seem to combine the love of dissipation and fashion with a high relish for intellectual pursuits. The state of society in France, or, what is the same thing, in Paris, is admirably suited to the purposes of the memoir-writer. The cheerful, gregarious temper of the inhabitants, which mingles all ranks in the common pursuit of pleasure;

the external polish, which scarcely deserts them in the commission of the grossest violence; the influence of the women, during the last two centuries, far superior to that of the sex among any other people, and exercised alike on matters of taste, politics, and letters; the gallantry and licentious intrigues so usual in the higher classes of this gay metropolis, and which fill even the life of a man of letters, so stagnant in every other country, with stirring and romantic adventure; all these, we say, make up a rich and varied panorama, that can hardly fail of interest under the hand of the most common artist.

Lastly, the vanity of the French may be considered as another cause of their success in this kind of writing; a vanity which leads them to disclose a thousand amusing particulars, which the reserve of an Englishman, and perhaps his pride, would discard as altogether unsuitable to the public ear. This vanity, it must be confessed, however, has occasionally seduced their writers, under the garb of confessions and secret memoirs, to make such a disgusting exposure of human infirmity as few men would be willing to admit, even to themselves.

The best memoirs of late produced in France seem to have assumed somewhat of a novel shape. While they are written with the usual freedom and vivacity, they are fortified by a body of references and illustrations that attest an unwonted degree of elaboration and research. Such are those of Rousseau, La Fontaine, and Molière, lately published. The last of these, which forms the subject of our article, is a compilation of all that has ever been recorded of the life of Molière. It is executed in an agreeable manner, and has the merit of examining, with more accuracy than has been hitherto done, certain doubtful points in his biography, and of assembling together in a convenient form what has before been diffused over a great variety of surface. But, however familiar most of these particulars may be to the countrymen of Molière (by far the greatest comic genius in his own nation, and, in very many respects, inferior to none in any other), they are not so current elsewhere as to lead us to imagine that some account of his life and literary labours would be altogether unacceptable to our readers.

Jean-Baptiste Poquelin (Molière) was born in Paris, January 15, 1622. His father was an upholsterer, as his grandfather had been before him; and the young Poquelin was destined to exercise the same hereditary craft, to which, indeed, he served an apprenticeship until the age of fourteen. In this determination his father was confirmed by the office which he had obtained for himself, in connexion with his original vocation, of *valet de chambre* to the king, with the promise of a reversion of it to his son on his own decease. The youth accordingly received only such a meager elementary education as was usual with the artisans of that day. But a secret consciousness of his own powers convinced him that he was destined by nature for higher purposes than that of quilting sofas and hanging tapestry. His occasional presence at the theatrical representations of the *Hôtel de*

Bourgogne is said also to have awakened in his mind, at this period, a passion for the drama. He therefore solicited his father to assist him in obtaining more liberal instruction; and when the latter at length yielded to the repeated entreaties of his son, it was with the reluctance of one who imagines that he is spoiling a good mechanic in order to make a poor scholar. He was accordingly introduced into the Jesuits' College of Clermont, where he followed the usual course of study for five years with diligence and credit. He was fortunate enough to pursue the study of philosophy under the direction of the celebrated Gassendi, with his fellow-pupils, Chapelle the poet, afterward his intimate friend, and Bernier, so famous subsequently for his travels in the East, but who, on his return, had the misfortune to lose the favour of Louis the Fourteenth by replying to him, that 'of all the countries he had ever seen, he preferred Switzerland.'

On the completion of his studies in 1641, he was required to accompany the king, then Louis the Thirteenth, in his capacity of *valet de chambre* (his father being detained in Paris by his infirmities), on an excursion to the south of France. This journey afforded him the opportunity of becoming intimately acquainted with the habits of the court, as well as those of the provinces, of which he afterward so repeatedly availed himself in his comedies. On his return he commenced the study of the law, and had completed it, it would appear, when his old passion for the theatre revived with increased ardour, and, after some hesitation, he determined no longer to withstand the decided impulse of his genius. He associated himself with one of those city companies of players with which Paris had swarmed since the days of Richelieu—a minister who aspired after the same empire in the republic of letters which he had so long maintained over the state, and whose ostentatious patronage eminently contributed to develop that taste for dramatic exhibition which has distinguished his countrymen ever since.

The consternation of the elder Poquelin, on receiving the intelligence of his son's unexpected determination, may be readily conceived. It blasted at once all the fair promise which the rapid progress the latter had made in his studies justified him in forming, and it degraded him to an unfortunate profession, esteemed at that time even more lightly in France than it has been in other countries. The humiliating dependance of the comedian on the popular favour, the daily exposure of his person to the caprice and insults of an unfeeling audience, the numerous temptations incident to his precarious and unsettled life, may furnish abundant objections to this profession in the mind of every parent. But in France, to all these objections were superadded others of a graver cast, founded on religion. The clergy there, alarmed at the rapidly-increasing taste for dramatic exhibitions, openly denounced these elegant recreations as an insult to the Deity; and the pious father anticipated, in this preference of his son, his spiritual no less than his temporal perdition. He actually made an earnest remonstrance to him to this effect, through the intervention of one of his friends, who, however, instead of converting the youth, was himself persuaded to join the company then organizing under his direction. But his family were never reconciled to his proceeding; and even at a later period of his life, when his splendid successes in his new career had shown how rightly he had understood the character of his own genius, they never condescended to avail themselves of the freedom of admission to his theatre, which he repeatedly proffered. M. Bret, his editor, also informs us, that he had himself seen a genealogical tree in the possession of the descendants of this same family, in which the name of Molière was not even admitted! Unless it were to trace their connexion with so illustrious a name, what could such a family want of a genealogical tree! It was from a deference to these scruples that our hero annexed to his patronymic the name of Molière, by which alone he has been recognised by posterity.

During the three following years he continued playing in Paris, until the turbulent regency of Anne of Austria withdrew the attention of the people from the quiet pleasures of the drama to those of civil broil and tumult. Molière then quitted the capital for the south of France. From this period, 1646 to 1658, his history presents few particulars worthy of record. He wandered with his company through the different provinces, writing a few farces which have long since perished, performing at the princi

A A A

pal cities, and, wherever he went, by his superior talent withdrawing the crowd from every other spectacle to the exhibition of his own. During this period, too, he was busily storing his mind with those nice observations of men and manners so essential to the success of the dramatist, and which were to ripen there until a proper time for their development should arrive. At the town of Pezénas they still show an elbow-chair of Molière's (as at Montpelier they show the gown of Rabelais), in which the poet, it is said, ensconced in a corner of a barber's shop, would sit for the hour together, silently watching the air, gestures, and grimaces of the village politicians, who, in those days, before coffee-houses were introduced into France, used to congregate in this place of resort. The fruits of this study may be easily discerned in those original draughts of character from the middling and lower classes with which his pieces everywhere abound.

In the south of France he met with the Prince of Conti, with whom he had contracted a friendship at the college of Clermont, and who received him with great hospitality. The prince pressed upon him the office of his private secretary; but, fortunately for letters, Molière was constant in his devotion to the drama, assigning as his reason that "the occupation was of too serious a complexion to suit his taste; and that, though he might make a passable author, he should make a very poor secretary." Perhaps he was influenced in this refusal, also, by the fate of the preceding incumbent, who had lately died of a fever, in consequence of a blow from the fire-tongs, which his highness, in a fit of ill humour, had given him on the temple. However this may be, it was owing to the good offices of the prince that he obtained access to Monsieur, the only brother of Louis the Fourteenth, and father of the celebrated regent, Philip of Orleans, who, on his return to Paris in 1658, introduced him to the king, before whom, in the month of October following, he was allowed, with his company, to perform a tragedy of Corneille's and one of his own farces.

His little corps was now permitted to establish itself under the title of the " Company of Monsieur," and the theatre of the Petit-Bourbon was assigned as the place for its performances. Here, in the course of a few weeks, he brought out his *Etourdi* and *Le Dépit Amoureux*, comedies in verse and in five acts, which he had composed during his provincial pilgrimage, and which, although deficient in an artful *liaison* of scenes and in probability of incident, exhibit, particularly the last, those fine touches of the ridiculous, which revealed the future author of the *Tartuffe* and the *Misanthrope*. They indeed found greater favour with the audience than some of his later pieces ; for in the former they could only compare him with the wretched models that had preceded him, while in the latter they were to compare him with himself.

In the ensuing year Molière exhibited his celebrated farce of *Les Précieuses Ridicules* ; a piece in only one act, but which, by its inimitable satire, effected such a revolution in the literary taste of his country-men as has been accomplished by few works of a more imposing form, and which may be considered as the basis of the dramatic glory of Molière, and the dawn of good comedy in France. This epoch was the commencement of that brilliant period in French literature which is so well known as the age of Louis the Fourteenth; and yet it was distinguish-ed by such a puerile, meretricious taste, as is rarely to be met with except in the incipient stages of civ-ilization, or in its last decline. The cause of this melancholy perversion of intellect is mainly imputa-ble to the influence of a certain *coterie* of wits, whose rank, talents, and successful authorship had author-ized them, in some measure, to set up as the arbi-ters of taste and fashion. This choice assembly, consisting of the splenetic Rochefoucault; the *bel-esprit* Voiture; Balzac, whose letters afford the ear-liest example of numbers in French prose; the lively and licentious Bussy; Rabutin; Chapelain, who, as a wit has observed, might still have had a reputation had it not been for his " Pucelle;" the poet Bensé-rade; Ménage, and others of less note; together with such eminent women as Madame Lafayette, Mademoiselle Scudéri (whose eternal romances, the delight of her own age, have been the despair of every other), and even the elegant Sévigné, was ac-customed to hold its *réunions* principally at the *Hô-tel de Rambouillet*, the residence of the marchioness of that name, and which, from this circumstance, has acquired such ill-omened notoriety in the history of letters.

Here they were wont to hold the most solemn
discussions on the most frivolous topics, but especially on matters relating to gallantry and love, which
they debated with all the subtilty and metaphysical
refinement that centuries before had characterized
the romantic Courts of Love in the south of France.
All this was conducted in an affected jargon, in which
the most common things, instead of being called by
their usual names, were signified by ridiculous peri-
phrases ; which, while it required neither wit nor
ingenuity to invent them, could have had no other
merit, even in their own eyes, than that of being unintelligible to the vulgar. To this was superadded
a tone of exaggerated sentiment, and a ridiculous
code of etiquette, by which the intercourse of these
exclusives was to be regulated with each other, all
borrowed from the absurd romances of Calprenede
and Scudéri. Even the names of the parties underwent a metamorphosis, and Madame de Rambouillet's christian name of *Catherine* being found too
trite and unpoetical, was converted into *Arthénice*,
by which she was so generally recognised as to be
designated by it in Fléchier's eloquent funeral oration on her daughter.* These insipid affectations,
which French critics are fond of imputing to an
Italian influence, savour quite as much of the Spanish *cultismo* as of the *concetti* of the former nation,
and may be yet more fairly referred to the same

* How comes La Harpe to fall into the error of supposing that Fléchier
referred to Madame Montausier by this epithet of *Arthénice* ? The bishop's style in this passage is as unequivocal as usual. See *Cours de Littérature*, &c., tome vi., p. 167.

4   2 G

false principles of taste which distinguished the French Pleiades of the sixteenth century, and the more ancient compositions of their Provençal ancestors. Dictionaries were compiled, and treatises written illustrative of this precious vocabulary; all were desirous of being initiated into the mysteries of so elegant a science: even such men as Corneille and Bossuet did not disdain to frequent the saloons where it was studied; the spirit of imitation, more active in France than in other countries, took possession of the provinces; every village had its coterie of *précieuses* after the fashion of the capital, and a false taste and criticism threatened to infect the very sources of pure and healthful literature.

It was against this fashionable corruption that Molière aimed his wit in the little satire of the "Précieuses Ridicules," in which the valets of two noblemen are represented as aping their masters' tone of conversation for the purpose of imposing on two young ladies fresh from the provinces, and great admirers of the new style. The absurdity of these affectations is still more strongly relieved by the contemptuous incredulity of the father and servant, who do not comprehend a word of them. By this process Molière succeeded both in exposing and degrading these absurd pretensions, as he showed how opposite they were to common sense, and how easily they were to be acquired by the most vulgar minds. The success was such as might have been anticipated on an appeal to popular feeling, where nature must always triumph over the arts of affectation. The piece was welcomed with enthusiastic applause, and the disciples of the *Hôtel Rambouillet*, most of whom were present at the first exhibition, beheld the fine fabric which they had been so painfully constructing brought to the ground by a single blow. "And these follies," said Ménage to Chapelain, "which you and I see so finely criticised here, are what we have been so long admiring. We must go home and burn our idols." "Courage, Molière," cried an old man from the pit; "this is genuine comedy." The price of the seats was doubled from the time of the second representation. Nor were the effects of the satire merely transitory. It converted an epithet of praise into one of reproach; and a *femme précieuse*, a *style précieux*, a *ton précieux*, once so much admired, have ever since been used only to signify the most ridiculous affectation.

There was, in truth, however, quite as much luck as merit in this success of Molière, whose production exhibits no finer raillery or better sustained dialogue than are to be found in many of his subsequent pieces. It assured him, however, of his own strength, and disclosed to him the mode in which he should best hit the popular taste. "I have no occasion to study Plautus or Terence any longer," said he; "I must henceforth study the world." The world, accordingly, was his study; and the exquisite models of character which it furnished him will last as long as it shall endure.

In 1660 he brought out the excellent comedy of the *Ecole des Maris*, and in the course of the same

month, that of the *Fâcheux,* in three acts—compo
sed, learned, and performed within the brief space
of a fortnight; an expedition evincing the dexterity
of the manager no less than that of the author.
This piece was written at the request of Fouquet,
superintendent of finances to Louis the Fourteenth,
for the magnificent *fête* at Vaux, given by him to
that monarch, and lavishly celebrated in the memoirs of the period, and with yet more elegance in
a poetical epistle of La Fontaine to his friend De
Maucroix. This minister had been intrusted with
the principal care of the finances under Cardinal
Mazarine, and had been continued in the same
office by Louis the Fourteenth, on his own assump-
tion of the government. The monarch, however,
alarmed at the growing dilapidations of the revenue,
requested from the superintendent an *exposé* of its
actual condition, which, on receiving, he privately
communicated to Colbert, the rival and successor of
Fouquet. The latter, whose ordinary expenditure
far exceeded that of any other subject in the kingdom, and who, in addition to immense sums occasionally lost at play and daily squandered on his
debaucheries, is said to have distributed in pensions
more than four millions of livres annually, thought
it would be an easy matter to impose on a young
and inexperienced prince, who had hitherto shown
himself more devoted to pleasure than business, and
accordingly gave in false returns, exaggerating the
expenses, and diminishing the actual receipts of the
treasury. The detection of this peculation deter-

mined Louis to take the first occasion of dismissing
his powerful minister; but his ruin was precipitated
and completed by the discovery of an indiscreet
passion for Madame de la Vallière, whose fascinating
graces were then beginning to acquire for her that
ascendency over the youthful monarch which has
since condemned her name to such unfortunate celebrity. The portrait of this lady, seen in the apart-
ments of the favourite on the occasion to which we
have adverted, so incensed Louis, that he would
have had him arrested on the spot but for the seasonable intervention of the queen-mother, who reminded him that Fouquet was his host. It was for
this *fête* at Vaux, whose palace and ample domains,
covering the extent of three villages, had cost their
proprietor the sum, almost incredible for that period,
of eighteen million livres, that Fouquet put in requisition all the various talents of the capital, the
dexterity of its artists, and the invention of its finest
poets. He was particularly lavish in his preparations for the dramatic portion of the entertainment.
Le Brun passed for a while from his victories of
Alexander to paint the theatrical decorations; To-
relli was employed to contrive the machinery; Pe-
lisson furnished the prologue, much admired in its
day, and Molière his comedy of the *Fâcheux*.

This piece, the hint for which may have been
suggested by Horace's ninth satire, *Ibam forte viâ
Sacrâ*, is an amusing caricature of the various *bores*
that infest society, rendered the more vexatious by
their intervention at the very moment when a young

4 2 G *

lover is hastening to the place of assignation with his mistress. Louis the Fourteenth, after the performance, seeing his master of the hunts near him, M. Soyecour, a personage remarkably absent, and inordinately devoted to the pleasures of the chase, pointed him out to Molière as an original whom he had omitted to bring upon his canvass. The poet took the hint, and the following day produced an excellent scene, where this Nimrod is made to go through the *technics* of his art, in which he had himself, with great complaisance, instructed the mischievous satirist, who had drawn him into a conversation for that very purpose on the preceding evening.

This play was the origin of the *comédie-ballet*, afterward so popular in France. The residence at Vaux brought Molière more intimately in contact with the king and the court than he had before been; and from this time may be dated the particular encouragement which he ever after received from this prince, and which eventually enabled him to triumph over the malice of his enemies. A few days after this magnificent entertainment, Fouquet was thrown into prison, where he was suffered to languish the remainder of his days, "which," says the historian from whom we have gathered these details, "he terminated *in sentiments of the most sincere piety :*"* a termination by no means uncommon in France with that class of persons, of either sex, respectively, who have had the misfortune to survive their fortune or their beauty.

* Histoire de la Vie, &c., de La Fontaine, par M. Valckenaer. Paris, 1824.

In February, 1662, Molière formed a matrimonial connexion with Mademoiselle Béjart, a young comedian of his company, who had been educated under his own eye, and whose wit and captivating graces had effectually ensnared the poet's heart, but for which he was destined to perform doleful penance the remainder of his life. The disparity of their ages, for the lady was hardly seventeen, might have afforded in itself a sufficient objection; and he had no reason to flatter himself that she would remain uninfected by the pernicious example of the society in which she had been educated, and of which he himself was not altogether an immaculate member. In his excellent comedy of the *Ecole des Femmes*, brought forward the same year, the story turns upon the absurdity of an old man's educating a young woman for the purpose, at some future time, of marrying her, which wise plan is defeated by the unseasonable apparition of a young lover, who in five minutes undoes what it had cost the veteran so many years to contrive. The pertinency of this moral to the poet's own situation shows how much easier it is to talk wisely than to act so.

This comedy, popular as it was on its representation, brought upon the head of its author a tempest of parody, satire, and even slander, from those of his own craft who were jealous of his unprecedented success, and from those literary *petits-maîtres* who still smarted with the stripes inflicted on them in some of his previous performances. One of this latter class, incensed at the applauses bestowed upon the piece on the night of its first representation, indignantly exclaimed, *Ris donc, parterre! ris donc!* "Laugh then, pit, if you will!" and immediately quitted the theatre.

Molière was not slow in avenging himself of these interested criticisms, by means of a little piece entitled *La Critique de l'Ecole des Femmes,* in which he brings forward the various objections made to his comedy, and ridicules them with unsparing severity. These objections appear to have been chiefly of a verbal nature. A few such familiar phrases as *Tarte à la crême, Enfans par l'oreille,* &c., gave particular offence to the purists of that day, and, in the prudish spirit of French criticism, have since been condemned by Voltaire and La Harpe as unworthy of comedy. One of the personages introduced into the *Critique* is a marquis, who, when repeatedly interrogated as to the nature of his objections to the comedy, has no other answer to make than by his eternal *Tarte à la crême.* The Duc de Feuillade, a coxcomb of little brains but great pretension, was the person generally supposed to be here intended. The peer, unequal to an encounter of wits with his antagonist, resorted to a coarser remedy. Meeting Molière one day in the gallery at Versailles, he advanced as if to embrace him; a civility which the great lords of that day occasionally condescended to bestow upon their inferiors. As the unsuspecting poet inclined himself to receive the salute, the duke, seizing his head between his hands, rubbed it briskly against the buttons of his coat, repeating, at the same time,

Tarte à la crême, Monsieur, tarte à la crême. The king, on receiving intelligence of this affront, was highly indignant, and reprimanded the duke with great asperity. He, at the same time, encouraged Molière to defend himself with his own weapons; a privilege of which he speedily availed himself, in a caustic little satire in one act, entitled *Impromptu de Versailles.* " The marquis," he says in this piece, " is nowadays the droll (*le plaisant*) of the comedy ; and as our ancestors always introduced a jester to furnish mirth for the audience, so we must have recourse to some ridiculous marquis to divert them."

It is obvious that Molière could never have maintained this independent attitude if he had not been protected by the royal favour. Indeed, Louis was constant in giving him this protection; and when, soon after this period, the character of Molière was blackened by the vilest imputations, the monarch testified his conviction of his innocence by publicly standing godfather to his child—a tribute of respect equally honourable to the prince and the poet. The king, moreover, granted him a pension of a thousand livres annually; and to his company, which henceforth took the title of "comedians of the king," a pension of seven thousand. Our author received his pension, as one of a long list of men of letters, who experienced a similar bounty from the royal hand. The curious estimate exhibited in this document of the relative merits of these literary stipendiaries affords a striking evidence that the decrees of contemporaries are not unfrequently to be reversed by pos-

terity. The obsolete Chapelain is there recorded
" as the greatest French poet who has ever existed ;"
in consideration of which, his stipend amounted to
three thousand livres, while Boileau's name, for which
his satires had already secured an imperishable existence, is not even noticed ! It should be added, however, on the authority of Boileau, that Chapelain
himself had the principal hand in furnishing this
apocryphal scale of merit to the minister.

In the month of September, 1665, Molière produced his *L'Amour Médecin*, a *comédie-ballet*, in three
acts, which, from the time of its conception to that
of its performance, consumed only five days. This
piece, although displaying no more than his usual
talent for caustic raillery, is remarkable as affording
the earliest demonstration of those direct hostilities
upon the medical faculty, which he maintained at
intervals during the rest of his life, and which he
may be truly said to have died in maintaining. In
this he followed the example of Montaigne, who, in
particular, devotes one of the longest chapters in his
work to a *tirade* against the profession, which he en-
forces by all the ingenuity of his wit, and his usual
wealth of illustration. In this, also, Molière was
subsequently imitated by Le Sage, as every reader
of Gil Blas will readily call to mind. Both Montaigne and Le Sage, however, like most other libel-
lers of the healing art, were glad to have recourse
to it in the hour of need. Not so with Molière.
His satire seems to have been without affectation.
Though an habitual valetudinarian, he relied almost

wholly on the temperance of his diet for the re-establishment of his health. " What use do you make of your physician ?" said the king to him one day. " We chat together, sire," said the poet; " he gives me his prescriptions; I never follow them, and so I get well."

An ample apology for this infidelity may be found in the state of the profession at that day, whose members affected to disguise a profound ignorance of the true principles of science under a pompous exterior, which, however it might impose upon the vulgar, could only bring them into deserved discredit with the better portion of the community. The physicians of that time are described as parading the streets of Paris on mules, dressed in a long robe and bands, holding their conversation in bad Latin, or, if they condescended to employ the vernacular, mixing it up with such a jargon of scholastic phrase and scientific *technics* as to render it perfectly unintelligible to vulgar ears. The following lines, cited by M. Taschereau, and written in good earnest at the time, seem to hit off most of these peculiarities.

> "Affecter un air pédantesque,
> Cracher du Grec et du Latin,
> Longue perruque, habit grotesque,
> De la fourrure et du satin,
> Tout cela réuni fait presque
> Ce qu'on appelle un médecin."*

* A gait and air somewhat pedantic,
And scarce to spit but Greek or Latin,
A long peruke and habit antic,
Sometimes of fur, sometimes of satin,
Form the receipt by which 'tis showed
How to make doctors *à la mode.*

In addition to these absurdities, the physicians of that period exposed themselves to still farther derision by the contrariety of their opinions, and the animosity with which they maintained them. The famous consultation in the case of Cardinal Mazarine was well known in its day; one of his four medical attendants affirming the seat of his disorder to be the liver, another the lungs, a third the spleen, and a fourth the mesentery. Molière's raillery, therefore, against empirics, in a profession where mistakes are so easily made, so difficult to be detected, and the only one in which they are irremediable, stands abundantly excused from the censures which have been heaped upon it. Its effects were visible in the reform which, in his own time, it effected in their manners, if in nothing farther. They assumed the dress of men of the world, and gradually adopted the popular forms of communication; an essential step to improvement, since nothing cloaks ignorance and empiricism more effectually with the vulgar than an affected use of learned phrase and a technical vocabulary.

We are now arrived at that period of Molière's career when he composed his *Misanthrope*, a play which some critics have esteemed his masterpiece, and which all concur in admiring as one of the noblest productions of the modern drama. Its literary execution, too, of paramount importance in the eye of a French critic, is more nicely elaborated than in any other of the pieces of Molière, if we except the *Tartuffe*, and its didactic dialogue displays a matu-

rity of thought equal to what is found in the best satires of Boileau. It is the very didactic tone of this
comedy, indeed, which, combined with its want of
eager, animating interest, made it less popular on its
representation than some of his inferior pieces. A
circumstance which occurred on the first night of its
performance may be worth noticing. In the second
scene of the first act, a man of fashion, it is well
known, is represented as soliciting the candid opinion of *Alceste* on a sonnet of his own enditing, though
he flies into a passion with him, five minutes after,
for pronouncing an unfavourable judgment. This
sonnet was so artfully constructed by Molière, with
those dazzling epigrammatic points most captivating
to common ears, that the gratified audience were
loud in their approbation of what they supposed intended in good faith by the author. How great was
their mortification, then, when they heard Alceste
condemn the whole as puerile, and fairly expose the
false principles on which it had been constructed.
Such a rebuke must have carried more weight with
it than a volume of set dissertation on the principles
of taste.

Rousseau has bitterly inveighed against Molière
for exposing to ridicule the hero of his *Misanthrope*
a high-minded and estimable character. It was told
to the Duc de Montausier, well known for his austere virtue, that he was intended as the original of
the character. Much offended, he attended a representation of the piece, but, on returning, declared
that " he dared hardly flatter himself the poet had

intended him so great an honour." This fact, as has been well intimated by La Harpe, furnishes the best reply to Rousseau's invective.

The relations in which Molière stood with his wife at the time of the appearance of this comedy gave to the exhibition a painful interest. The levity and extravagance of this lady had for some time transcended even those liberal limits which were conceded at that day by the complaisance of a French husband, and they deeply affected the happiness of the poet. As he one day communicated the subject to his friend Chapelle, the latter strongly urged him to confine her person; a remedy much in vogue then for refractory wives, and one, certainly, if not more efficacious, at least more gallant than the "moderate flagellation" authorized by the English law. He remonstrated on the folly of being longer the dupe of her artifices. "Alas!" said the unfortunate poet to him, "you have never loved!" A separation, however, was at length agreed upon, and it was arranged that, while both parties occupied the same house, they should never meet except at the theatre. The respective parts which they performed in this piece corresponded precisely with their respective situations: that of *Célimène*, a fascinating, capricious coquette, insensible to every remonstrance of her lover, and selfishly bent on the gratification of her own appetites; and that of *Alceste*, perfectly sensible of the duplicity of his mistress, whom he vainly hopes to reform, and no less so of the unworthiness of his own passion, from which he as vainly hopes to extricate himself. The coincidences are too exact to be considered wholly accidental.

If Molière in his preceding pieces had hit the follies and fashionable absurdities of the age, in the *Tartuffe* he flew at still higher game, the most odious of all vices, religious hypocrisy. The result showed that his shafts were not shot in the dark. The first three acts of the *Tartuffe*, the only ones then written, made their appearance at the memorable *fêtes* known under the name of "The Pleasures of the Enchanted Isle," given by Louis the Four teenth at Versailles, in 1664, and of which the inquisitive reader may find a circumstantial narrative in the twenty-fifth chapter of Voltaire's history of that monarch. The only circumstance which can give them a permanent value with posterity is their having been the occasion of the earliest exhibition of this inimitable comedy. Louis the Fourteenth, who, notwithstanding the defects of his education, seems to have had a discriminating perception of literary beauty, was fully sensible of the merits of this production. The *Tartuffes*, however, who were present at the exhibition, deeply stung by the sarcasms of the poet, like the foul birds of night whose recesses have been suddenly invaded by a glare of light, raised a fearful cry against him, until Louis even, whose solicitude for the interests of the Church was nowise impaired by his own personal derelictions, complied with their importunities for imposing a prohibition on the public performance of the play.

It was, however, privately acted in the presence of Monsieur, and afterward of the great Condé. Copies of it were greedily circulated in the societies of Paris; and although their unanimous suffrage was an inadequate compensation to the author for the privations he incurred, it was sufficient to quicken the activity of the false zealots, who, under the mask of piety, assailed him with the grossest libels. One of them even ventured so far as to call upon the king to make a public example of him with fire and fagot; another declared that it would be an offence to the Deity to allow Molière, after such an enormity, " to participate in the sacraments, to be admitted to confession, or even to enter the precincts of a church, considering the anathemas which it had fulminated against the authors of indecent and sacrilegious spectacles !" Soon after his sentence of prohibition, the king attended the performance of a piece entitled *Scaramouche Hermite*, a piece abounding in passages the most indelicate and profane. " What is the reason," said he, on retiring, to the Prince of Condé, " that the persons so sensibly scandalized at Molière's comedy take no umbrage at this ?" " Because," said the prince, " the latter only attacks religion, while the former attacks themselves:" an answer which may remind one of a remark of Bayle in reference to the *Decameron*, which, having been placed on the Index on account of its immorality, was, however, allowed to be published in an edition which converted the names of the ecclesiastics into those of laymen : " a conces-

sion," says the philosopher, "which shows the priests
to have been much more solicitous for the interests
of their own order than for those of heaven"

Louis, at length convinced of the interested motives of the enemies of the *Tartuffe*, yielded to the
importunities of the public and removed his prohibition of its performance. It accordingly was represented, for the first time in public, in August, 1667,
before an overflowing house, extended to its full
complement of five acts, but with alterations of the
names of the piece, the principal personages in it,
and some of its most obnoxious passages. It was
entitled *The Impostor*, and its hero was styled *Pa-
nulfe*. On the second evening of the performance,
however, an interdict arrived from the president of
the Parliament against the repetition of the performance, and, as the king had left Paris in order to join
his army in Flanders, no immediate redress was to
be obtained. It was not until two years later, 1669,
that the *Tartuffe*, in its present shape, was finally
allowed to proceed unmolested in its representations.
It is scarcely necessary to add, that these were attended with the most brilliant success which its author could have anticipated, and to which the intrinsic merits of the piece, and the unmerited persecutions he had undergone, so well entitled him.
Forty-four successive representations were scarcely
sufficient to satisfy the eager curiosity of the public:
and his grateful company forced upon Molière a
double share of the profits during every repetition
of its performance for the remainder of his life. Pos-

terity has confirmed the decision of his contemporaries, and it still remains the most admired comedy of the French theatre, and will always remain so, says a native critic, "as long as taste and hypocrites shall endure in France."

We have been thus particular in our history of these transactions, as it affords one of the most interesting examples on record of undeserved persecution with which envy and party spirit have assailed a man of letters. No one of Molière's compositions is determined by a more direct moral aim ; nowhere has he stripped the mask from vice with a more intrepid hand ; nowhere has he animated his discourses with a more sound and practical piety. It should be added, in justice to the French clergy of that period, that the most eminent prelates at the court acknowledged the merits of this comedy, and were strongly in favour of its representation.

It is generally known that the amusing scene in the first act, where *Dorine* enlarges so eloquently on the good cheer which *Tartuffe* had made in the absence of his host, was suggested to Molière some years previous in Lorraine, by a circumstance which took place at the table of Louis the Fourteenth, whom Molière had accompanied in his capacity of *valet de chambre*. Perefixe, bishop of Rhodez, entering while the king was at his evening meal, during Lent, was invited by him to follow his example ; but the bishop declined on the ground that he was accustomed to eat only once during the days of vigil and fast. The king, observing one of his attendants to smile, inquired of him the reason as soon as the prelate had withdrawn.   The latter informed his master that he need be under no apprehensions for the health of the good bishop, as he himself had assisted at his dinner on that day, and then recounted to him the various dishes which had been served up. The king, who listened with becoming gravity to the narration, uttered an exclamation of "Poor man!" at the specification of each new item, varying the tone of his exclamation in such a manner as to give it a highly comic effect.   The humour was not lost upon our poet, who has transported the same ejaculations, with much greater effect, into the above-mentioned scene of his play.   The king, who did not at first recognise the source whence he had derived it, on being informed of it, was much pleased, if we may believe M. Taschereau, in finding himself even thus accidentally associated with the work of a man of genius.

In 1668 Molière brought forward his *Avare*, and in the following year his amusing comedy of the *Bourgeois Gentilhomme*, in which the folly of unequal alliances is successfully ridiculed and exposed. This play was first represented in the presence of the court at Chambord.   The king maintained during its performance an inscrutable physiognomy, which made it doubtful what might be his real sentiments respecting it.   The same deportment was maintained by him during the evening towards the author, who was in attendance in his capacity of *valet de chambre*.   The quick-eyed courtiers, the counts and marquises, who had so often smarted under the lash of the poet, construing this into an expression of royal disapprobation, were loud in their condemnation of him, and a certain duke boldly affirmed " that he was fast sinking into his second childhood, and that, unless some better writer soon appeared, French comedy would degenerate into mere Italian farce." The unfortunate poet, unable to catch a single ray of consolation, was greatly depressed during the interval of five days which preceded the second representation of his piece ; on returning from which, the monarch assured him that " none of his productions had afforded him greater entertainment, and that, if he had delayed expressing his opinion on the preceding night, it was from the apprehension that his judgment might have been influenced by the excellence of the acting." Whatever we may think of this exhibition of royal caprice, we must admire the suppleness of the courtiers, one and all of whom straightway expressed their full conviction of the merits of the comedy, and the duke above mentioned added, in particular, that " there was a *vis comica* in all that Molière ever wrote, to which the ancients could furnish no parallel!" What exquisite studies for his pencil must Molière not have found in this precious assembly !

We have already remarked that the profession of a comedian was but lightly esteemed in France at this period. Molière experienced the inconveniences resulting from this circumstance even after his splendid literary career had given him undoubted claims

to consideration. Most of our readers, no doubt, are
acquainted with the anecdote of Belloc, an agreeable poet of the court, who, on hearing one of the
servants in the royal household refuse to aid the author of the *Tartuffe* in making the king's bed, cour-
teously requested "the poet to accept his services for
that purpose." Madame Campan's anecdote of a
similar courtesy on the part of Louis the Fourteenth
is also well known, who, when several of these functionaries refused to sit at table with the comedian,
kindly invited him to sit down with him, and, calling in some of his principal courtiers, remarked that
"he had requested the pleasure of Molière's company at his own table, as it was not thought quite good
enough for his officers." This rebuke had the desired effect. However humiliating the reflection
may be, that genius should have, at any time, stood
in need of such patronage, it is highly honourable to
the monarch who could raise himself so far above
the prejudices of his age as to confer it.

It was the same unworthy prejudice that had so
long excluded Molière from that great object and
recompense of a French scholar's ambition, a seat in
the Academy; a body affecting to maintain a jealous watch over the national language and literature,
which the author of the *Misanthrope* and the *Tartuffe*, perhaps more than any other individual of his
age, had contributed to purify and advance. Sensible of this merit, they at length offered him a place
in their assembly, provided he would renounce his
profession of a player, and confine himself in future

D d d

to his literary labours. But the poet replied to his friend Boileau, the bearer of this communication, that "too many individuals of his company depended on his theatrical labours for support to allow him for a moment to think of it;" a reply of infinitely more service to his memory than all the academic honours that could have been heaped upon him. This illustrious body, however, a century after his decease, paid him the barren compliment (the only one then in their power) of decreeing to him an *éloge*, and of admitting his bust within their walls, with this inscription upon it :

"Nothing is wanting to his glory : he was wanting to ours."

The catalogue of Academicians contemporary with Molière, most of whom now rest in sweet oblivion, or, with Cotin and Chapelain, live only in the satires of Boileau, shows that it is as little in the power of academies to confer immortality on a writer as to deprive him of it.

We have not time to notice the excellent comedy of the *Femmes Savantes*, and some inferior pieces, written by our author at a later period of his life, and must hasten to the closing scene. He had been long affected by a pulmonary complaint, and it was only by severe temperance, as we have before stated, that he was enabled to preserve even a moderate degree of health. At the commencement of the year 1673, his malady sensibly increased. At this very season he composed his *Malade Imaginaire*—the most whimsical, and, perhaps, the most amusing of the compositions in which he has indulged his railery against the faculty. On the seventeenth of February, being the day appointed for its fourth representation, his friends would have dissuaded him from appearing, in consequence of his increasing indisposition ; but he persisted in his design, alleging "that more than fifty poor individuals depended for their daily bread on its performance." His life fell a sacrifice to his benevolence. The exertions which he was compelled to make in playing the principal part of *Argan* aggravated his distemper, and as he was repeating the word *juro* in the concluding ceremony, he fell into a convulsion, which he vainly endeavoured to disguise from the spectators under a forced smile. He was immediately carried to his house in the *Rue de Richelieu*, now No. 34. A violent fit of coughing, on his arrival, occasioned the rupture of a blood-vessel ; and seeing his end approaching, he sent for two ecclesiastics of the parish of St. Eustace, to which he belonged, **to** administer to him the last offices of religion. But these worthy persons refused their assistance ; and before a third, who had been sent for, could arrive, Molière, suffocated with the effusion of blood, had expired in the arms of his family.

Harlay de Champvalon, at that time archbishop of Paris, refused the rites of sepulture to the deceased poet because he was a comedian, and had had the misfortune to die without receiving the sacraments. This prelate is conspicuous, even in the chronicles of that period, for his bold and infamous debaucheries. It is of him that Madame de Sévigné observes, in one of her letters: "There are two little inconveniences which make it difficult for any one to undertake his funeral oration—his life and his death." Father Gaillard, who at length consented to undertake it, did so on the condition that he should not be required to say anything of the character of the deceased. The remonstrance of Louis the Fourteenth having induced this person to remove his interdict, he privately instructed the curate of St. Eustace not to allow the usual service for the dead to be recited at the interment. On the day appointed for this ceremony, a number of the rabble assembled before the deceased poet's door, determined to oppose it. "They knew only," says Voltaire, "that Molière was a comedian, but did not know that he was a philosopher and a great man." They had, more probably, been collected together by the Tartuffes, his unforgiving enemies. The widow of the poet appeased these wretches by throwing money to them from the windows. In the evening, the body, escorted by a procession of about a hundred individuals, the friends and intimate acquaintances of the deceased poet, each of them bearing a flambeau in his hand, was quietly deposited in the cemetery of St. Joseph, without the ordinary chant, or service of any kind. It was not thus that Paris followed to the tomb the remains of her late distinguished comedian, Talma. Yet Talma was only a comedian, while Molière, in addition to this, had the merit of being the most eminent comic writer whom France had ever produced. The different degree of popular civilization which this difference of conduct indicates may afford a subject of contemplation by no means unpleasing to the philanthropist.

In the year 1792, during that memorable period in France when an affectation of reverence for their illustrious dead was strangely mingled with the persecution of the living, the Parisians resolved to exhume the remains of La Fontaine and Molière, in order to transport them to a more honourable place of interment. Of the relics thus obtained, it is certain that no portion belonged to La Fontaine, and it is extremely probable that none did to Molière. Whosesoever they may have been, they did not receive the honours for which their repose had been disturbed. With the usual fickleness of the period, they were shamefully transferred from one place to another, or abandoned to neglect for seven years, when the patriotic conservator of the *Monumens Français* succeeded in obtaining them for his collection at the *Petits Augustins*. On the suppression of this institution in 1817, the supposed ashes of the two poets were, for the last time, transported to the spacious cemetery of *Père de la Chaise*, where the tomb of the author of the *Tartuffe* is designated by an inscription in Latin, which, as if to complete the scandal of the proceedings, is grossly mistaken in the only fact which it pretends to record, namely, the age of the poet at the time of his decease.

Molière died soon after entering upon his fifty-second year. He is represented to have been somewhat above the middle stature, and well proportioned; his features large, his complexion dark, and his black, bushy eyebrows so flexible as to admit of his giving an infinetely comic expression to his physiognomy. He was the best actor of his own generation, and, by his counsels, formed the celebrated Baron, the best of the succeeding. He played all the range of his own characters, from *Alceste to Sganarelle*, though he seems to have been peculiarly fitted for broad comedy. He composed with rapidity, for which Boileau has happily complimented him:

> "Rare et sublime esprit, dont la fertile vein
> Ignore en écrivant le travail et la peine."

Unlike in this to Boileau himself, and to Racine, the former of whom taught the latter, if we may credit his son, "the art of rhyming with difficulty." Of course, the verses of Molière have neither the correctness nor the high finish of those of his two illustrious rivals.

He produced all his pieces, amounting to thirty, in the short space of fifteen years. He was in the habit of reading these to an old female domestic by the name of La Forêt, on whose unsophisticated judgment he greatly relied. On one occasion, when he attempted to impose upon her the production of a brother author, she plainly told him that he had never written it. Sir Walter Scott may have had this habit of Molière's in his mind when he introduced a similar expedient into his " Chronicles of the Canongate." For the same reason, our poet used to request the comedians to bring their children with them when he recited a new play. The peculiar advantage of this humble criticism in dramatic compositions is obvious. Alfieri himself, as he informs us, did not disdain to resort to it.

Molière's income was very ample, probably not less than twenty-five or thirty thousand francs—an immense sum for that day—yet he left but little property. The expensive habits of his wife and his own liberality may account for it. One example of this is worth recording, as having been singularly opportune and well directed. When Racine came up to Paris as a young adventurer, he presented to Molière a copy of his first crude tragedy, long since buried in oblivion. The latter discerned in it, amid all its imperfections, the latent spark of dramatic genius, and he encouraged its author by the present of a hundred Louis. This was doing better for him than Corneille did, who advised the future author of *Phédre* to abandon the tragic walk, and to devote himself altogether to comedy. Racine recompensed this benefaction of his friend, at a later period of his life, by quarrelling with him.

Molière was naturally of a reserved and taciturn temper, insomuch that his friend Boileau used to call him the *Contemplateur*. Strangers who had expected to recognise in his conversation the sallies of wit which distinguished his dramas, went away disappointed. The same thing is related of La Fontaine. The truth is, that Molière went into society as a spectator, not as an actor; he found there the studies for the characters which he was to transport upon the stage, and he occupied himself with observing them. The dreamer, La Fontaine, lived, too, in a world of his own creation. His friend, Madame de la Sablière, paid to him this untranslatable compliment: " En vérité, mon cher La Fontaine, vous seriez bien bête, si vous n'aviez pas tant d'esprit." These unseasonable reveries brought him, it may be imagined, into many whimsical adventures. The great Corneille, too, was distinguished by the same apathy. A gentleman dined at the same table with him for six months without suspecting the author of the " Cid."

The literary reputation of Molière, and his amiable personal endowments, naturally led him into an intimacy with the most eminent wits of the golden age in which he lived, but especially with Boileau, La Fontaine, and Racine; and the confidential intercourse of these great minds, and their frequent *réunions* for the purposes of social pleasure, bring to mind the similar associations at *the Mermaid's, Will's Coffee-house*, and *Button's*, which form so pleasing a picture in the annals of English literature. It was common on these occasions to have a volume of the unfortunate Chapelain's epic, then in popular repute, lie open upon the table, and if one of the party fell into a grammatical blunder, to impose upon him the reading of some fifteen or twenty verses of it: " a whole page," says Louis Racine, " was sentence of death." La Fontaine, in his *Psyché*, has painted his reminiscences of these happy meetings in the colouring of fond regret; where, "freely discussing such topics of general literature or personal gossip as might arise, they touched lightly upon all, like bees passing on from flower to flower, criticising the works of others without envy, and of one another, when any one chanced to fall into the malady of the age, with frankness." Alas! that so rare a union of minds, destined to live together through all ages, should have been dissolved by the petty jealousies incident to common men.

In these assemblies frequent mention is made of Chapelle, the most intimate friend of Molière, whose agreeable verses are read with pleasure in our day, and whose cordial manners and sprightly conversation made him the delight of his own. His mercurial spirits, however, led him into too free an indulgence of convivial pleasures, and brought upon him the repeated, though unavailing remonstrances of his friends. On one of these occasions, as Boileau was urging upon him the impropriety of this indulgence, and its inevitable consequences, Chapelle, who received the admonition with great contrition, invited his Mentor to withdraw from the public street in which they were then walking into a neighbouring house, where they could talk over the matter with less interruption. Here wine was called for, and, in the warmth of discussion, a second bottle being soon followed by a third, both parties at length found themselves in a condition which made it advisable to adjourn the lecture to a more fitting occasion.

Molière enjoyed also the closest intimacy with the great Condé, the most distinguished ornament of the court of Louis the Fourteenth ; to such an extent, indeed, that the latter directed that the poet should never be refused admission to him, at whatever hour he might choose to pay his visit. His regard for his friend was testified by his remark, rather more candid than courteous, to an abbé of his acquaintance, who had brought him an epitaph of his own writing upon the deceased poet. "Would to Heaven," said the prince, "that he were in a condition to bring me yours !"

We have already wandered beyond the limits which we had assigned to ourselves for an abstract of Molière's literary labours, and of the most interesting anecdotes in his biography. Without entering, therefore, into a criticism on his writings, of which the public stand in no need, we shall dismiss the subject with a few brief reflections on their probable influence, and on the design of the author in producing them.

The most distinguished French critics, with the overweening partiality in favour of their own nation, so natural and so universal, placing Molière by common consent at the head of their own comic writers, have also claimed for him a pre-eminence over those of every other age and country. A. W. Schlegel, a very competent judge in these matters, has degraded him, on the other hand, from the walks of high comedy to the writer of "buffoon farces, for which his genius and inclination seem to have essentially fitted him ;" adding, moreover, that "his characters are not drawn from nature, but from the fleeting and superficial forms of fashionable life." This is a hard sentence, accommodated to the more forcible illustration of the peculiar theory which the German writer has avowed throughout his work, and which, however reasonable in its first principles, has led him into as exaggerated an admiration of the romantic models which he prefers, as disparagement of the classical school which he detests. It is a sentence, moreover, upon which some eminent critics in his own country, who support his theory in the main, have taken the liberty to demur.

That a large proportion of Molière's pieces are conceived in a vein of broad, homely merriment, rather than in that of elevated comedy, abounding in forced situations, high caricature, and practical jokes; in the knavish, intriguing valets of Plautus and Terence; in a compound of that good-nature and irritability, shrewdness and credulity, which make up the dupes of Aristophanes, is very true; but that a writer, distinguished by his deep reflection, his pure taste, and nice observation of character, should have preferred this to the higher walks of his art, is absolutely incredible. He has furnished the best justification of himself in an apology, which a contemporary biographer reports him to have made to some one who censured him on this very ground: "If I wrote simply for fame," said he, "I should manage very differently; but I write for the support of my company. I must not address myself, therefore, to a few people of education, but to the mob. And this latter class of gentry take very little interest in a continued elevation of style and sentiment." With all these imperfections and lively absurdities, however, there is scarcely one of Molière's minor pieces which does not present us with traits of character that come home to every heart, and felicities of expression that, from their truth, have come to be proverbial.

With regard to the objection that his characters are not so much drawn from nature as from the local manners of the age, if it be meant that they are not acted upon by those deep passions which engross the whole soul, and which, from this intensity, have more of a tragic than a comic import in them, but are rather drawn from the foibles and follies of ordinary life, it is true; but then these last are likely to be quite as permanent, and, among civilized nations, quite as universal as the former. And who has exposed them with greater freedom, or with a more potent ridicule than Molière? Love, under all its thousand circumstances, its quarrels, and reconciliations; vanity, humbly suing for admiration under the guise of modesty; whimsical contradictions of profession and habitual practice; the industry with which the lower classes ape, not the virtues, but the follies of their superiors; the affectation of fashion, taste, science, or anything but what the party actually possesses; the *esprit de corps*, which leads us to feel an exalted respect for our own profession, and a sovereign contempt for every other; the friendly adviser, who has an eye to his own interest; the author, who seeks your candid opinion, and quarrels with you

when you have given it ; the fair friend, who kindly
sacrifices your reputation for a jest ; the hypocrite,
under every aspect, who deceives the world or himself—these form the various and motley panorama of
character which Molière has transferred to his canvass, and which, though mostly drawn from cultivated life, must endure as long as society shall hold
together.

Indeed, Molière seems to have possessed all the
essential requisites for excelling in genteel comedy :
a pure taste, an acute perception of the ridiculous,
the tone of elegant dialogue, and a wit brilliant and
untiring as Congreve's, but which, instead of wasting itself like his, in idle flashes of merriment, is uniformly directed with a moral or philosophical aim.
This obvious didactic purpose, in truth, has been
censured as inconsistent with the spirit of the drama,
and as belonging rather to satire ; but it secured to
him an influence over the literature and the opinions
of his own generation which has been possessed by
no other comic writer of the moderns.

He was the first to recall his countrymen from
the vapid hyperbole and puerile conceits of the ancient farces, and to instruct them in the maxim
which Boileau has since condensed into a memorable verse, that "nothing is beautiful but what is natural." We have already spoken of the reformation
which one of his early pieces effected in the admirers of the *Hôtel de Rambouillet* and its absurdities ;
and when this confederacy afterward rallied under
an affectation of science, as it had before done of

letters, he again broke it with his admirable satire of the *Femmes Savantes.* We do not recollect any similar revolution effected by a single effort of genius, unless it be that brought about by the *Baviad* and *Mæviad.* But Mr. Gifford, in the Della-Cruscan school, but " broke a butterfly upon the wheel," in comparison with those enemies, formidable by rank and talent, whom Molière assailed. We have noticed, in its proper place, the influence which his writings had in compelling the medical faculty of his day to lay aside the affected deportment, technical jargon, and other mummeries then in vogue, by means of the public derision to which he had deservedly exposed them. In the same manner, he so successfully ridiculed the miserable dialectics, pedantry, and intolerance of the schoolmen, in his diverting dialogues between *Dr. Marphurius* and *Dr. Pancrace*, that he is said to have completely defeated the serious efforts of the University for obtaining a confirmation of the decree of 1624, which had actually prohibited, *under pain of death*, the promulgation of any opinion contrary to the doctrines of Aristotle. The *arrêt burlesque* of his friend Boileau at a later period, if we may trust the *Menagiana*, had a principal share in preventing a decree of the Parliament against the philosophy of Descartes. It is difficult to estimate the influence of our poet's satire on the state of society in general, and on those higher ranks in particular whose affectations and pretensions he assailed with such pertinacious hostility. If he did not reform them, he at least deprired them of their fascination and much of their mischievous influence, by holding them up to the contempt and laughter of the public. Sometimes, it must be admitted, though very rarely, in effecting this object, he so far transgressed the bounds of decorum as to descend even to personalities.

From this view of the didactic purpose proposed by Molière in his comedies, it is obviously difficult to institute a comparison between them and those of our English dramatists, or, rather, of Shakspeare, who may be taken as their representative. The latter seems to have had no higher end in view than mere amusement; he took a leaf out of the great volume of human nature as he might find it; nor did he accommodate it to the illustration of any moral or literary theorem. The former, on the other hand, manifests such a direct perceptive purpose as to give to some of his pieces the appearance of satires rather than of comedies; argument takes place of action, and the *pro* and *con* of the matter are discussed with all the formality of a school exercise. This essentially diminishes the interest of some of his best plays, the *Misanthrope* and the *Femmes Savantes*, for example, which for this reason seem better fitted for the closet than the stage, and have long since ceased to be favourites with the public. This want of interest is, moreover, aggravated by the barrenness of action visible in many of Molière's comedies, where he seems only to have sought an apology for bringing together his *coteries* of gentlemen and ladies for the purpose of exhibiting their gladiatorial dexterity in conversation. Not so with the English dramatist, whose boundless invention crowds his scene with incidents that hurry us along with breathless interest, but which sadly scandalize the lover of the unities.

In conformity with his general plan, too, Shakspeare brings before us every variety of situation—the court, the camp, and the cloister; the busy hum of populous cities, or the wild solitude of the forest —presenting us with pictures of rich and romantic beauty, which could not fall within the scope of his rival, and allowing himself to indulge in the unbounded revelry of an imagination which Molière did not possess. The latter, on the other hand, an attentive observer of man as he is found in an over-refined state of society, in courts and crowded capitals, copied his minutest lineaments with a precision that gives to his most general sketches the air almost of personal portraits; seasoning, moreover, his discourses with shrewd hints and maxims of worldly policy. Shakspeare's genius led him rather to deal in bold touches than in this nice delineation. He describes classes rather than individuals; he touches the springs of the most intense passions. The daring of ambition, the craving of revenge, the deep tenderness of love, are all materials in his hands for comedy; and this gives to some of his admired pieces—his "Merchant of Venice" and his "Measure for Measure," for example—a solemnity of colouring that leaves them only to be distinguished from tragedy by their more fortunate termination. Molière, on the contrary, sedulously excludes from his plays whatever can impair their comic interest. And when, as he has done very rarely, he aims directly at vice instead of folly (in the *Tartuffe*, for instance), he studies to exhibit it under such ludicrous points of view as shall excite the derision rather than the indignation of his audience.

But whatever be the comparative merits of these great masters, each must be allowed to have attained complete success in his way. Comedy, in the hands of Shakspeare, exhibits to us man, not only as he is moved by the petty vanities of life, but by deep and tumultuous passion; in situations which it requires all the invention of the poet to devise and the richest colouring of eloquence to depict. But if the object of comedy, as has been said, be " to correct the follies of the age, by exposing them to ridicule," who then has equalled Molière ?

ITALIAN NARRATIVE POETRY.*

OCTOBER, 1824.

THE characteristics of an Italian school are no-where so discernible in English literary history as under the reign of Elizabeth. At the period when England was most strenuous in breaking off her spiritual relations with Italy, she cultivated most closely her intellectual. It is hardly necessary to name either the contemporary dramatists, or Surrey, Sidney, and Spenser, the former of whom derived the plots of many of their most popular plays, as the latter did the forms, and frequently the spirit of their poetical compositions, from Italian models. The translations of the same period were, in several instances, superior to any which have been since produced. Harrington's version of the "Orlando Furioso," with all its inaccuracy, is far superior to the cumbrous monotony of Hoole. Of Fairfax, the elegant translator of Tasso, it is enough to say that he is styled by Dryden "the poetical father of Waller," and quoted by him, in conjunction with Spenser, as "one of the great masters in our language." The popularity of the Italian was so great even in Ascham's day, who did not survive the first half of Elizabeth's reign, as to draw from the learned schoolmaster much peevish

* 1. "The Orlando Innamorato; translated into prose and verse, from the Italian of Francesco Berni. By W. S. Rose." 8vo, p. 279. London, 1823.

2. "The Orlando Furioso; translated into verse from the Italian of Ludovico Ariosto. By W. S. Rose." Vol. i., 8vo. London, 1823.

animadversion upon what he terms "the enchantments of Circe, fond books of late translated out of
Italian into English, and sold in every shop in London." It gradually lost this wide authority during
the succeeding century. This was but natural. Before the time of Elizabeth, all the light of learning
which fell upon the world had come from Italy, and
our own literature, like a young and tender plant, insensibly put forth its branches most luxuriantly in the
direction whence it felt this invigorating influence.
As it grew in years and hardihood, it sent its fibres
deeper into its own soil, and drew thence the nourishment which enabled it to assume its fair and full
proportions. Milton, it is true, the brightest name on
the poetical records of that period, cultivated it with
eminent success. Any one acquainted with the writings of Dante, Pulci, and Tasso, will understand the
value and the extent of Milton's obligations to the Italian. He was far from desiring to conceal them, and
he has paid many a tribute "of melodious verse" to the
sources from which he drew so much of the nourishment of his exalted genius. " To imitate, as he has
done," in the language of Boileau, " is not to act the
part of a plagiary, but of a rival." Milton is, moreover, one of the few writers who have succeeded so
far in comprehending the niceties of foreign tongue
as to be able to add something to its poetical wealth,
and his Italian sonnets are written with such purity
as to have obtained commendations from the Tuscan
critics.*

* Milton, in his treatise on *The Reason of Church Government*, alludes

Boileau, who set the current of French taste at this period, had a considerable contempt for that of his neighbours. He pointed one of his antithetical couplets at the " tinsel of Tasso" (" *clinquant du Tasse*"*), and in another he ridiculed the idea of epics, in which "the devil was always blustering against the heavens."† The English admitted the sarcasm of Boileau with the cold commentary of Addison ;‡ and the "clinquant du Tasse" became a cant term of reproach upon the whole body of Italian letters. The French went still farther, and afterward, applying the sarcasm of their critic to Milton as well as to Tasso, rejected both the poets upon the same principles. The French did the English as much justice as they did the Italians. No great change of opinion in this matter took place in England during the last century. The Wartons and Gray had a just estimation of this beautiful tongue, but Dr. Johnson, the dominant critic of that day, seems to have understood the language but imperfectly, and not to have much relished in it what he understood.

In the present age of intellectual activity, attention is so generally bestowed on all modern languages which are ennobled by a literature, that it is not singular an acquaintance with the Italian in particular

modestly enough to his Italian pieces, and the commendations bestowed upon them. " Other things, which I had shifted in scarcity of books and conveniencies to hatch up among them, were received with written encomiums, which the Italian is not forward to bestow on men of this side the Alps."   * Satire IX.

　　† L'Art Poetique, c. III.　　　　　　　　‡ Spectator, No. VI.

should be widely diffused.   Great praise, however, is due to the labours of Mr. Roscoe.   There can be little doubt that his elaborate biographies of the Medici, which contain as much literary criticism as historical narrative, have mainly contributed to the promotion of these studies among his countrymen. These works have of late met with much flippant criticism in some of their leading journals.   In Italy they have been translated, are now cited as authorities, and have received the most encomiastic notices from several eminent scholars.   These facts afford conclusive testimony of their merits.   The name of Mathias is well known to every lover of the Italian tongue ; his poetical productions rank with those of Milton in merit, and far exceed them in quantity. To conclude, it is not many years since Cary gave to his countrymen his very extraordinary version of the father of Tuscan poetry, and Rose is now swelling the catalogue with translations of the two most distinguished chivalrous epics of Italy.

Epic romance has continued to be a great favourite in that country ever since its first introduction into the polished circles of Florence and Ferrara, towards the close of the fifteenth century.   It has held much the same rank in its ornamental literature which the drama once enjoyed in the English, and which historical novel-writing maintains now.   It hardly seems credible that an enlightened people should long continue to take great satisfaction in poems founded on the same extravagant fictions, and spun out to the appalling length of twenty, thirty, nay, forty cantos of a thousand verses each. But the Italians, like most Southern nations, delight exceedingly in the uncontrolled play of the imagination, and they abandon themselves to all its brilliant illusions, with no other object in view than mere recreation. An Englishman looks for a moral, or, at least, for some sort of instruction, from the wildest work of fiction. But an Italian goes to it as he would go to the opera—to get impressions rather than ideas. He is extremely sensible to the fine tones of his native language, and, under the combined influence produced by the colouring of a lavish fancy and the music of a voluptuous versification, he seldom stoops to a cold analysis of its purpose or its probability.

Romantic fiction, however, which flourished so exuberantly under a warm Southern sky, was transplanted from the colder regions of Normandy and England. It is remarkable that both these countries, in which it had its origin, should have ceased to cultivate it at the very period when the perfection of their respective languages would have enabled them to do so with entire success. We believe this remark requires no qualification in regard to France. Spenser affords one illustrious exception among the English.*

---

* The *influence*, however, of the old Norman romances may be discovered in the productions of a much later period. Their incredible length required them to be broken up into *fyttes*, or cantos, by the minstrel, who recited them with the accompaniment of a harp, in the same manner as the epics of Homer, broken into *rhapsodies*, were chanted by the bards of Ionia. The minstrel who could thus beguile the tedium of

It was not until long after the extinction of this species of writing in the North that it reappeared in Italy. The commercial habits, and the Republican institutions of the Italians in the twelfth and thirteenth centuries, were most unfavourable to the spirit of chivalry, and, consequently, to the fables which grew out of it. The three patriarchs of their literature, moreover, by the light which, in this dark period, they threw over other walks of imagination, turned the attention of their countrymen from those of romance. Dante, indeed, who resembled Milton in so many other particulars, showed a similar predilection for the ancient tales of chivalry. His *Commedia* contains several encomiastic allusions to them, but, like the English bard, he contented himself with these, and chose a subject better suited to his ambitious genius and inflexible temper.* His poem, it is true, was of too eccentric a character to be widely

a winter's evening was a welcome guest at the baronial castle and in the hall of the monastery. As Greek and Roman letters were revived, the legends of chivalry fell into disrepute, and the minstrel gradually retreated to the cottage of the peasant, who was still rude enough to relish his simple melody. But the long romance was beyond the comprehension or the taste of the rustic. It therefore gave way to less complicated narratives, and from its wreck may be fairly said to have arisen those Border songs and ballads which form the most beautiful collection of rural minstrelsy that belongs to any age or country.

* Milton's poetry abounds in references to the subjects of romantic fable; and in his " *Epitaphium Damonis*," he plainly intimates his intention of writing an epic on the story of Arthur. It may be doubted whether he would have succeeded on such a topic. His austere character would seem to have been better fitted to feel the impulses of religious enthusiasm than those of chivalry; and England has no reason to regret that her most sublime poet was reserved for the age of Cromwell instead of the romantic reign of Elizabeth.

imitated,* and both Boccaccio and Petrarch, with less talent, had a more extensive influence over the taste of their nation. The garrulous graces of the former and the lyrical finish of the latter are still solicited in the lighter compositions of Italy. Lastly, the discoveries of ancient manuscripts at home, and the introduction of others from Constantinople, when that rich depository of Grecian science fell into the hands of the barbarian, gave a new direction to the intellectual enterprise of Italian scholars, and withdrew them almost wholly from the farther cultivation of their infant literature.

Owing to these circumstances, the introduction of the chivalrous epoque was protracted to the close of the fifteenth century, when its first successful specimens were produced at the accomplished court of the Medici. The encouragement extended by this illustrious family to every branch of intellectual culture has been too often the subject of encomium to require from us any particular animadversion. Lorenzo, especially, by uniting in his own person the scholarship and talent which he so liberally rewarded in others, contributed more than all to the effectual promotion of an enlightened taste among his countrymen. Even his amusements were sub-

---

* The best imitation of the "*Divina Commedia*" is probably the "*Cantiba in morte di Ugo Basville*," by the most eminent of the living Italian poets, Monti. His talent for vigorous delineation by a single *coup de vinceau* is eminently *Dantesque*, and the plan of his poem is the exact counterpart of that of the "*Inferno*." Instead of a mortal descending into the regions of the damned, one of their number (the spirit of Basville, a Frenchman) is summoned back to the earth, to behold the crimes and miseries of his native country during the period of the Revolution.

·servient to it, and the national literature may be
fairly said, at this day, to retain somewhat of the
character communicated to it by his elegant recreations. His delicious villas at Fiesole and Cajano
are celebrated by the scholars, who, in the silence
of their shades, pursued with him the studies of his
favourite philosophy and of poetry. Even the sensual pleasures of the banquet were relieved by the
inventions of wit and fancy. Lyrical composition,
which, notwithstanding its peculiar adaptation to the
flexible movements of the Italian tongue, had fallen
into neglect, was revived, and, together with the first
eloquent productions of the romantic muse, was recited at the table of Lorenzo.

Of the guests who frequented it, Pulci and Politian are the names most distinguished, and the only
ones connected with our present subject. The latter of these was received into the family of Lorenzo
as the preceptor of his children, an office for which
he seems to have been better qualified by his extraordinary attainments than by his disposition. Whatever may have been the asperity of his temper, however, his poetical compositions breathe the perfect
spirit of harmony. The most remarkable of these,
distinguished as the " Verses of Politian" (Stanzè di
Poliziano), is a brief fragment of an epic, whose
purpose was to celebrate the achievements of Julian
de Medici, a younger brother of Lorenzo, at a tournament exhibited at Florence in 1468. This would
appear but a meager basis for the structure of a
great poem. Politian, however, probably in conse-

G g g

quence of the untimely death of Julian, his hero, abandoned it in the middle of the second canto, even before he had reached the event which was to constitute the subject of his story.

The incidents of the poem thus abruptly terminated are of no great account. We have a portrait of Julian, a hunting expedition, a love adventure, a digression into the island of Venus, which takes up about half the canto, and a vision of the hero, which ends just as the tournament, the subject of the piece, is about to begin, and with it, like the " fabric of a vision," ends the poem also. In this short space, however, the poet has concentrated all the beauties of his art, the melody of a musical ear, and the inventions of a plastic fancy. His island of love, in particular, is emblazoned with those gorgeous splendours, which have since been borrowed for the enchanted gardens of Alcina, Armida, and Acrasia.

But this little fragment is not recommended, at least to an English reader, so much by its Oriental pomp of imagery as by its more quiet and delicate pictures of external nature. Brilliancy of imagination is the birthright of the Italian poet, as much as a sober, contemplative vein is of the English. This is the characteristic of almost all their best and most popular poetry during the sixteenth and seventeenth centuries. The two great poets of the fourteenth approach much nearer to the English character. Dante shows not only deeper reflection than is common with his countrymen, but in parts of his

work, in the *Purgatorio* more especially, manifests
a sincere relish for natural beauty, by his most accurate pictures of rural objects and scenery. Petrarch
cherished the recollections of an unfortunate passion, until, we may say, without any mystical perversion of language, it became a part of his intellectual existence.* This gave a tender and melancholy
expression to his poems, more particularly to those
written after the death of Laura, quite as much

* Whatever may be thought of the speculations of the Abbé de Sade,
no doubt can be entertained of the substantial existence of Laura, or of
Petrarch's passion for her. Indeed, independently of the internal evidence afforded by his poetry, such direct notices of his mistress are scattered through his "Letters" and serious prose compositions, that it is
singular there should ever have existed a skepticism on these points.
Ugo Foscolo, the well-known author of "*Jacobo Ortis*," has lately published an octavo volume, entitled "*Essays on Petrarch.*" Among other
particulars, showing the unbounded influence that Laura de Sade obtained
over the mind of her poetical lover, he quotes the following memoran-
dum, made by Petrarch two months after her decease, in his private
manuscript copy of Virgil, now preserved in the Ambrosian library at
Milan:

"It was in the early days of my youth, on the sixth of April, in the
morning, and in the year 1327, that Laura, distinguished by her own virtues, and celebrated in my verses, first blessed my eyes in the Church
of Santa Clara, at Avignon; and it was in the same city, on the sixth
of the very same month of April, at the very same hour in the morning,
in the year 1348, that this bright luminary was withdrawn from our sight,
when I was at Verona, alas! ignorant of my calamity. The remains of
her chaste and beautiful body were deposited in the Church of the Cor-
deliers on the evening of the same day. To preserve the afflicting re-
membrance, I have taken a bitter pleasure in recording it, particularly in
this book, which is most frequently before my eyes, in order that nothing
in this world may have any farther attraction for me; that this great
attachment to life being dissolved, I may, by frequent reflection, and a
proper estimation of our transitory existence, be admonished that it is
high time for me to think of quitting this earthly Babylon, which I trust it
will not be difficult for me, with a strong and manly courage, to accomplish."—P. 35

English as Italian. Love furnishes the great theme
and impulse to the Italian poet. It is not too much
to say that all their principal versifiers have written
under the inspiration of a real or pretended passion.
It is to them what a less showy and less exclusive
sensibility is to an Englishman. The latter ac-
knowledges the influence of many other affections
and relations in life. The death of a friend is far
more likely to excite his muse than the smiles or
frowns of his mistress. The Italian seldom dwells
on melancholy reminiscences, but writes under the
impulse of a living and ardent passion. Petrarch
did both; but in the poetry which he composed after
the death of his mistress, exalted as it is by devotional sentiment, he deviated from the customs of
his nation, and adopted an English tone of feeling.
A graver spirit of reflection and a deeper sympathy
for the unobtrusive beauties of nature are observable
in some of their later writers; but these are not
primitive elements in the Italian character. Gay,
brilliant, imaginative, are the epithets which best
indicate the character of their literature during its
most flourishing periods; and the poetry of Italy
seems to reflect as clearly her unclouded skies and
glowing landscape, as that of England does the tranquil and somewhat melancholy complexion of her
climate.

The verses of Politian, to return from our digression, contain many descriptions distinguished by the
calm, moral beauty of which we have been speaking. Resemblances may be traced between these

passages and the writings of some of our best English poets. The descriptive poetry of Gray and of Goldsmith, particularly, exhibits a remarkable coincidence with that of Politian in the enumeration of rural images. The stanza CXXI., setting forth the descent of Cupid into the island of Venus, may be cited as having suggested a much admired simile in Gay's popular ballad, *Black-eyed Susan*, since the English verse is almost a metaphrase of the Italian:

> "Or poi che ad ail tese ivi pervenne,
> Forte le scosse, e giù calossi a piombo.
> Tutto serrato nelle sacre penne,
> Come a suo nido fa lieto colombo."

> "So the sweet lark, high poised in air,
> Shuts close his pinions to his breast,
> If chance his mate's shrill call he hear,
> And drops at once into her nest."

These "Stanze" were the first example of a happy cultivation of Italian verse in the fifteenth century. The scholars of that day composed altogether in Latin. Politian, as he grew older, disdained this abortive production of his youthful muse, and relied for his character with posterity on his Latin poems and his elaborate commentaries upon the ancient classics. Petrarch looked for immortality to his "Africa," as did Boccaccio to his learned Latin disquisition upon ancient mythology.* Could they now, after the lapse of more than four centuries, revisit the

---

* " *De Genealogia Deorum.*"—The Latin writings of Boccaccio and Petrarch may be considered the foundation of their fame with their contemporaries. The coronation of the latter in the Roman capitol was a homage paid rather to his achievements in an ancient tongue than to any in his own. He does not even notice his Italian lyrics in his " *Letters to Posterity.*"

world, how would they be astonished, perhaps mortified, the former to find that he was remembered only as the sonnetteer, and the latter as the novelist? The Latin prose of Politian may be consulted by an antiquary; his Latin poetry must be admired by scholars of taste; but his few Italian verses constitute the basis of his high reputation at this day with the great body of his countrymen. He wrote several lyrical pieces and a short pastoral drama (Orfèo), the first of a species which afterward grew into such repute under the hands of Tasso and Guarini. All of these bear the same print of his genius. One cannot but regret that so rare a mind should, in conformity with the perverse taste of his age, have abandoned the freshness of a living tongue for the ungrateful culture of a dead one. His "Stanze," the mere prologue of an epic, still survive amid the complete and elaborate productions of succeeding poets; they may be compared to the graceful portico of some unfinished temple, which time and taste have respected, and which remains as in the days of its architect, a beautiful ruin.

Luigi Pulci, the other eminent poet whom we mentioned as a frequent guest at the table of Lorenzo de' Medici, was of a noble family, and the youngest of three brothers, all of them even more distinguished by their accomplishments than by birth. There seems to be nothing worthy of particular record in his private history. He is said to have possessed a frank and merry disposition, and, to judge from his great poem, as well as from some lighter pieces of burlesque satire, which he bandied with one of his friends, whom he was in the habit of meeting at the house of Lorenzo, he was not particularly fastidious in his humour. His *Morgante Maggiore* is reported to have been written at the request of Lorenzo's mother, and recited at his table. It is a genuine epic of chivalry, containing twenty-eight cantos, founded on the traditionary defeat, the " dolorosa rotta" of Charlemagne and his peers in the Valley of Roncesvalles. It adheres much more closely than any of the other Italian romances to the lying chronicle of Turpin.

It may appear singular that the intention of the author should not become apparent in the course of eight-and-twenty cantos; but it is a fact, that scholars both at home and abroad have long disputed whether the poem is serious or satirical. Crescimbeni styles the author " modesto e moderato," while Tiraboschi expressly charges him with the deliberate design of ridiculing Scripture, and Voltaire, in his preface, cites the *Morgante* as an apology for his profligate " Pucelle." It cannot be denied that the story abounds in such ridiculous eccentricities as give it the air of a parody upon the marvels of romance. The hero, Morgante, is a converted infidel, " un gigante smisurato," whose formidable weapon is a bell-clapper, and who, after running through some twenty cantos of gigantic valour and mountebank extravagance, is brought to an untimely end by a wound in the heel, not from a Trojan arrow, but from the bite of a crab! We doubt, however, whether Pulci intended his satirical shafts for the Christian faith. Liberal allowance is to be conceded for the fashion of his age. Nothing is more frequent in the productions of that period than such irreverent freedoms with the most sacred topics as would be quite shocking in ours. Such freedoms, however, cannot reasonably be imputed to profanity, or even levity, since numerous instances of them occur in works of professed moral tendency, as in the mysteries and moralities, for example, those solemn deformities of the ancient French and English drama. The chronicle of Turpin, the basis of Pulci's epic, which, though a fraud, was a pious one, invented by some priest to celebrate the triumphs of the Christian arms, is tainted with the same indecent familiarities.*

Tempora mutantur. In a scandalous pasquinade published by Lord Byron in the first number of his Liberal, there is a verse describing St. Peter officiating as the doorkeeper of heaven. Pulci has a similar one in the Morgante (canto XXVI., st. 91), which, no doubt, furnished the hint to his lordship who has often improved upon the Italian poets. Both authors describe St. Peter's dress and vocation

---

* This spurious document of the twelfth century contains, in a copy which we have now before us, less than sixty pages. It has neither the truth of history nor the beauty of fiction. It abounds in commonplace prodigies, and sets forth Charlemagne's wars and his defeat in the valley of Roncesvalles, an event which probably never happened. Insignificant as it is in every other respect, however, it is the seed from which has sprung up those romantic fictions which adorned the rude age of the Normans, and which flourished in such wide luxuriance under Italian culture.

with the most whimsical minuteness. In the Italian, tne passage, introduced into the midst of a solemn, elaborate description, has all the appearance of being told in very good faith. No one will venture to put so charitable a construction upon his lordship's motives.

Whatever may have been the intention of Pulci in the preceding portion of the work, its concluding cantos are animated by the genuine spirit of Christian heroism. The rear of Charlemagne's army is drawn into an ambuscade by the treachery of his confidant Ganelon. Roncesvalles, a valley in the heart of the Pyrenees, is the theatre of action, and Orlando, with the flower of French chivalry, perishes there, overpowered by the Saracens. The battle is told in a sublime epic tone worthy of the occasion. The cantos xxvi., xxvii., containing it, are filled with a continued strain of high religious enthusiasm, with the varying, animating bustle of a mortal conflict, with the most solemn and natural sentiment suggested by the horror of the situation. Orlando's character rises into that of the divine warrior. His speech at the opening of the action, his lament over his unfortunate army, his melancholy reflections on the battle-field the night after the engagement, are conceived with such sublimity and pathos as attest both the poetical talent of Pulci and the grandeur and capacity of his subject. Yet the Morgante, the greater part of which is so ludicrous, is the only eminent Italian epic which has seriously described the celebrated rout at Roncesvalles.

Pulci's poem is not much read by the Italians. Its style, in general, is too unpolished for the fastidious delicacy of a modern ear, but as it abounds in the oldfashioned proverbialisms (*riboboli*) of Florence, it is greatly prized by the Tuscan purists. These familiar sayings, the elegant slang of the Florentine mob, have a value among the Italian scholars, at least among a large faction of them, much like that of old coins with a virtuoso : the more rare and rusty, the better. They give a high relish to many of their ancient writers, who, without other merit than their antiquity, are cited as authorities in their vocabulary.* These *riboboli* are to be met with most abundantly in their old *novelle* those, especially, which are made up of familiar dialogue between the lower classes of citizens. Boccaccio has very many such ; Sacchetti has more than all his prolific tribe, and it is impossible for a foreigner to discern or to appreciate the merits of such a writer. The lower classes in Florence retain to this day much of their antique picturesque phraseology,† and Alfieri tells us that " it was his great delight to stand in some unnoticed corner, and listen to the conversation of the mob in the market-place."

* This has been loudly censured by many of their scholars opposed to the literary supremacy of the Della-Cruscan Academy. See, in particular, the acute treatise of Cesarotti, " *Saggio sulla Filosofia delle Lingue,*" Parte IV.

† " The pure language of Boccaccio, and of other ancient writers, is preserved at this day much more among the lower classes of Florentine mechanics and of the neighbouring peasants than among the more polished Tuscan society, whose original dialect has suffered great mutations in their intercourse with foreigners."—*Pignotti,* " *Storia della Toscana,*" tom. ii., p. 167.

With the exception of Orlando, Pulci has shown no great skill in delineation of character. Charlemagne and Ganelon are the prominent personages. The latter is a parody on traitors; he is a traitor to common sense. Charlemagne is a superannuated dupe, with just credulity sufficient to dovetail into all the cunning contrivances of Gan. The women have neither refinement nor virtue. The knights have none of the softer graces of chivalry; they bully and swagger like the rude heroes of Homer, and are exclusively occupied with the merciless extermination of infidels. We meet with none of the imagery, the rich sylvan scenery, so lavishly diffused through the epics of Ariosto and Boiardo. The *machinery* bears none of the airy touches of an Arabian pencil, but is made out of the cold excrescences of Northern superstition, dwarfs, giants, and necromancers. Before quitting Pulci, we must point out a passage (canto xxv., st. 229, 230), in which a devil announces to Rinaldo the existence of another continent beyond the ocean, inhabited by mortals like himself. The theory of gravitation is also plainly intimated. As the poem was written before the voyages of Columbus, and before the physical discoveries of Galileo and Copernicus, the predictions are extremely curious.* The fiend, alluding

---

* Dante, two centuries before, had also expressed the same belief in an undiscovered quarter of the globe :

"De' vostri sensi, ch'è del rimanente,
   Non vogliate negar l'esperienza,
   Diretro al sol, del mondo senza gente."

Inferno, can xxvi., v 115

to the vulgar superstitions entertained of the Pillars
of Hercules, thus addresses his companion:

> " Know that this theory is false; his bark
> The daring mariner shall urge far o'er
> The Western wave, a smooth and level plain,
> Albeit the earth is fashion'd like a wheel.
> Man was in ancient days of grosser mould,
> And Hercules might blush to learn how far
> Beyond the limits he had vainly set,
> The dullest seaboat soon shall wing her way.
> Men shall descry another hemisphere,
> Since to one common centre all things tend;
> So earth, by curious mystery divine
> Well balanced, hangs amid the starry spheres.
> At our antipodes are cities, states,
> And thronged empires, ne'er divined of yore.
> But see, the sun speeds on his western path
> To glad the nations with expected light."

The dialogues of Pulci's devils respecting free-will
and necessity, their former glorious, and their present fallen condition, have suggested many hints for
our greater Milton to improve upon. The juggling
frolics of these fiends at the royal banquet in Sara-
gossa may have been the original of the comical marvels played off through the intervention of similar
agents by Dr. Faust.

Notwithstanding the good faith and poetical elevation of its concluding cantos, the Morgante, according to our apprehension, is anything but a serious romance. Not that it shows a disposition to
satire, above all, to the religious satire often imputed
to it; but there is a light banter, a vein of fun running through the greater portion of it, which is quite
the opposite of the lofty spirit of chivalry. Romantic fiction, among our Norman ancestors, grew so

directly out of the feudal relations and adventurous spirit of the age, that it was treated with all the gravity of historical record. When reproduced in the polite and artificial societies of Italy, the same fictions wore an air of ludicrous extravagance which would no longer admit of their being repeated seriously. Recommended, however, by a proper seasoning of irony, they might still amuse as ingenious tales of wonder. This may be kept in view in following out the ramifications of Italian narrative poetry; for they will all be found, in a greater or less degree, tinctured with the same spirit of ridicule.* The circle for whom Pulci composed his epic was peculiarly distinguished by that fondness for good-humoured raillery, which may be considered a national trait with his countrymen.

It seems to have been the delight of Lorenzo de' Medici, as it was afterward, in a more remarkable

* A distinction may be pointed out between the Norman and the Italian epics of chivalry. The former, composed in the rude ages of feudal heroism, are entitled to much credit as pictures of the manners of that period; while the latter, written in an age of refinement, have been carried by their poets into such beautiful extravagances of fiction as are perfectly incompatible with a state of society at any period. Let any one compare the feats of romantic valour recorded by Froissart, the turbulent, predatory habits of the barons and *ecclesiastics* under the early Norman dynasty, as reported by Turner in his late " History of *England*," with these old romances, and he will find enough to justify our remark. St. Pelaye, after a diligent study of the ancient epics, speaks of them as exhibiting a picture of society closely resembling that set forth in the chronicles of the period. Turner, after as diligent an examination of early historical documents, pronounces that the facts contained in them perfectly accord with the general portraiture of manners depicted in the romances.—*Mem. de l'Acad. des Inscriptions*, tom. xx, *Art. sur l'Ancient Chevalerie. Turner's " History of England from the Norman Conquest,"* &c vol. i., ch. vi.

degree, of his son Leo Tenth, to abandon himself to the most unreserved social freedoms with the friends whom he collected around his table. The satirical epigrams which passed there in perfect good humour between his guests, show, at least, full as much merriment as manners. Machiavelli concludes his history of Florence with an elaborate portrait of Lorenzo, in which he says that " he took greater delight in frivolous pleasures, and in the society of jesters and satirists, than became so great a man." The historian might have been less austere in his commentary upon Lorenzo's taste, since he was not particularly fastidious in the selection of his own amusements.*

At the close of the fifteenth century Italy was divided into a number of small but independent states, whose petty sovereigns vied with each other, not merely in the poor parade of royal pageantry, but in the liberal endowment of scientific institutions, and

---

* A letter written by Machiavelli, long unknown, and printed for the first time at Milan, 1810, gives a curious picture of his daily occupations when living in retirement, on his little patrimony, at a distance from Florence. Among other particulars, he mentions that it was his custom after dinner to repair to the tavern, where he passed his afternoon at cards with the company whom he ordinarily found there, consisting of the host, a miller, a butcher, and a lime-maker. Another part of the epistle exhibits a more pleasing view of the pursuits of the ex-secretary. " In the evening I return to my house and retire to my study. I then take off the rustic garments which I had worn during the day, and, having dressed myself in the apparel which I used to wear at court and in town, I mingle in the society of the great men of antiquity. I draw from them the nourishment which alone is suited to me, and during the four hours passed in this intercourse I forget all my misfortunes, and fear neither poverty nor death. In this manner I have composed a little work upon government." This *little work* was *The Prince.*

the patronage of learned men. Almost every Italian scholar was attached to some one or other of these courtly circles, and a generous, enlightened emulation sprung up among the states of Italy, such as had never before existed in any other age or country. Among the Republics of ancient Greece the rivalship was *political.* Their *literature*, from the time of Solon, was almost exclusively Athenian. An interesting picture of the cultivated manners and intellectual pleasures of these little courts may be gathered from the *Cortigiano* of Castiglione, which contains in the introduction a particular account of the pursuits and pastimes at the court of his sovereign, the Duke of Urbino.

None of these Italian states make so shining a figure in literary history as the insignificant duchy of Ferrara. The foul crimes which defile the domestic annals of the family of Este have been forgotten in the munificent patronage extended by them to letters. The librarians of the Biblioteca Estense, Muratori and Tiraboschi, have celebrated the virtues of their native princes with the encomiastic pen of loyalty; while Ariosto and Tasso, whose misfortunes furnish but an indifferent commentary upon these eulogiums, offering to them the grateful incense of poetic adulation, have extended their names still wider by inscribing them upon their immortal epics. Their patronage had the good fortune, not always attending patronage, of developing genius. Those models of the pastoral drama, the *Aminta* of Tasso, and the *Pastor Fido* of Guarini, whose luxury of expression, notwithstanding the *dictum* of Dr. Johnson,* it has been found as difficult to imitate in their own tongue as it is impossible to translate into any other; the comedies and Horatian satires of Ariosto; the *Secchia Rapita* of Tassoni, the acknowledged model of the mock-heroic poems of Pope and Boileau; and, finally, the three great epics of Italy, the *Orlando Innamorato*, the *Furioso*, and the *Gerusalemme Liberata*, were all produced in the brief compass of a century, within the limited dominions of the House of Este. Dante had reproached Ferrara, in the thirteenth century, with never having been illustrated by the name of a poet.

Boiardo, Count of Scandiano, the author of the Orlando Innamorato, the first-born of these epics, was a subject of Hercules First, Duke of Ferrara, and by him appointed governor of Reggio. His military conduct in that office, and his learned translations from the ancient classics, show him to have been equally accomplished as a soldier and as a scholar. In the intervals of war, to which his active life was devoted, he amused himself with the composition of his long poem. He had spun this out into the sixty-seventh canto without showing any disposition to bring it to a conclusion, when his literary labours were suddenly interrupted, as he informs us in his parting stanza, by the invasion of

* "Dione is a counterpart to *Aminta* and *Pastor Fido*, and other trifles of the same kind, easily imitated and unworthy of imitation."—*Life of Gay.*

the French into Italy in 1794, and in the same year the author died. The Orlando Innamorato, as it advanced, had been read by its author to his friends; but no portion of it was printed till after his death, and its extraordinary merits were not then widely estimated, in consequence of its antiquated phraseology and Lombard provincialisms. A *Rifacimento* some time after appeared, by one Domenichi, who spoiled many of the beauties, without improving the style of his original. Finally, Berni, in little more than thirty years after the death of Boiardo, new-moulded the whole poem,* with so much dexterity as to retain the substance of every verse in the original, and yet to clothe them in the seductive graces of his own classical idiom. Berni's version is the only one now read in Italy, and the original poem of Boiardo is so rare in that country, that it was found impossible to procure, for the library of Harvard University, any copy of the Innamorato more ancient than the reformed one by Domenichi.

The history of letters affords no stronger example of the power of *style* than the different fate of these two productions of Berni and Boiardo. We doubt whether the experiment would have been attended with the same result among a people by whom the nicer beauties of expression are less cul-

---

* Sismondi is mistaken in saying that Berni remodelled the *Innamorato* sixty years after the original. He survived Boiardo only forty-two years, and he had half completed his *Rifacimento* at least ten years before his own death, as is evident from his beautiful invocation to Verona and the Po (canto xxx.), on whose banks he was then writing it, and where he was living, 1526, in the capacity of secretary to the Bishop of Verona.

tivated, as with the English, for example. If we may judge from the few specimens which we have seen extracted from the Italian original, Chaucer exhibits a more obsolete and exotic phraseology than Boiardo. Yet the partial attempt of Dryden to invest the father of English poetry with a modernized costume has had little success, and the little epic of *Palamon and Arcite* (*The Knight's Tale*) is much more highly relished in the rude but muscular diction of Chaucer than in the polished version of his imitator.

Whatever may be the estimation of the style, the glory of the original delineation of character and incident is to be given exclusively to Boiardo. He was the first of the epic poets who founded a romance upon the love of Orlando; and a large portion of the poem is taken up with the adventures of this hero and his doughty Paladius, assembled in a remote province of China for the defence of his mistress, the beautiful Angelica :

> " When Agrican, with all his northern powers,
> Besieged Albracca, as romances tell,
> The city of Gallaphrone, from thence to win
> The fairest of her sex, Angelica
> His daughter, sought by many prowess knights
> Both Paynim, and the peers of Charlemagne."

Paradise Regained.

With the exception of the midnight combat between Agrican and Orlando, in which the conversion of the dying Tartar reminds one of the similar, but more affecting death of Clorinda, in the Jerusalem Delivered, there is very little moral interest attach-

ed to these combats of Boiardo, which are mere
gladiatorial exhibitions of hard fighting, and sharp,
jealous wrangling. The fairy gardens of Falerina
and Morgana, upon which the poet enters in the
second book, are much better adapted to the display
of his wild and exuberant imagination. No Italian
writer, not even Ariosto, is comparable to Boiardo
for exhibitions of fancy. Enchantment follows enchantment, and the reader, bewildered with the
number and rapidity of the transitions, looks in vain
for some clew, even the slender thread of allegory
which is held out by the poet, to guide him through
the unmeaning marvellous of Arabian fiction. Ariosto has tempered his imagination with more discretion. Both of these great romantic poets have
wrought upon the same characters, and afford, in
this respect, a means of accurate comparison. Without going into details, we may observe, in general,
that Boiardo has more strength than grace ; Ariosto,
the reverse. Boiardo's portraits are painted, or may
be rather said to be sculptured, with a clear, coarse
hand, out of some rude material. Ariosto's are
sketched with the volatile graces, nice shades, and
variable drapery of the most delicate Italian pencil.
In female portraiture, of course, Ariosto is far superior to his predecessor. The glaring coquetry of
Boiardo's Angelica is refined by the hand of his rival
into something like the coquetry of high life, and
tne ferocious tigress beauties of the original Marfisa
are softened into those of a more polished and courtly amazon. The Innamorato contains no examples

of the pure, deep feeling, which gives a soul to the females of the Furioso, and we look in vain for the frolic and airy scenes which enchant us so frequently in the latter poem.* We may remark, in conclusion, that the rapid and unintermitting succession of incidents in the Innamorato prevents the poet from indulging in those collateral beauties of sentiment and imagery which are prodigally diffused over the romance of Ariosto, and which give to it an exquisite finish.

Berni's *Rifacimento* of the Orlando Innamorato, as we have already observed, first made it popular with the Italians, by a magical varnish of versification, which gave greater lustre to the beauties of his original, and glossed over its defects. It has, however, the higher merit of exhibiting a great variety of *original* reflections, sometimes in the form of digressions, but more frequently as introductions to the cantos. These are enlivened by the shrewd wit and *elaborate artlessness* of expression, that form the peculiar attraction of Berni's poetry. In one of the prefatory stanzas to the fifty-first canto, the reader may recognise a curious coincidence with a well-known passage in Shakspeare; the more so, as Berni, we believe, was never turned into English before the present partial attempt of Mr. Rose:

> " Who steals a bugle-horn, a ring, a steed,
>   Or such like worthless thing, has some discretion;
> 'Tis petty larceny; not such his deed
>   Who robs us of our fame, our best possession.

---

* The chase of the Fairy Morgana, and the malicious dance of the Loves round Rinaldo (l. ii., c. viii., xv.), may, however, be considered good exceptions to this remark.

And he who takes our labour's worthiest meed
    May well be deem'd a felon by profession ;
Who so much more our hate and scourge deserves,
    As from the rule of right he wider swerves."

In another of these episodes the poet has introduced a portrait of himself. The whole passage is too long for insertion here ; but, as Mr. Rose has also translated it, we will borrow a few stanzas from his skilful version :

" His mood was choleric, and his tongue was vicious,
    But he was praised for singleness of heart ;
Not taxed as avaricious or ambitious,
    Affectionate and frank, and void of art ;
A lover of his friends, and unsuspicious ;
    But where he hated knew no middle part ;
And men his malice by his love might rate :
But then he was more prone to love than hate.

" To paint his person, this was thin and dry :
    Well sorting it, his legs were spare and lean ;
Broad was his visage, and his nose was high,
    While narrow was the space that was between
His eyebrows sharp ; and blue his hollow eye,
    Which for his bushy beard had not been seen
But that the master kept this thicket clear'd,
At mortal war with mustache and with beard.

" No one did ever servitude detest
    Like him, though servitude was still his dole ;
Since fortune or the devil did their best
    To keep him evermore beneath control.
While, whatsoever was his patron's hest,
    To execute it went against his soul ;
His service would he freely yield, unask'd,
But lost all heart and hope if he were task'd.

" Nor music, hunting match, nor mirthful measure,
    Nor play, nor other pastime, moved him aught ;
And if 'twas true that horses gave him pleasure,
    The simple sight of them was all he sought,
Too poor to purchase ; and his only treasure
    His naked bed ; his pastime to do naught

4   2 M *

> But tumble there, and stretch his weary length,
> And so recruit his spirits and his strength."
>
> *Rose's Innamorato*, p. 48.

The passage goes on to represent the dreamy and luxurious pleasures of this indolent pastime, with such an Epicurean minuteness of detail as puts the sincerity of the poet beyond a doubt. His smaller pieces, *Capitoli*, as they are termed, contain many incidental allusions, which betray the same lazy propensity.

The early part of Berni's life was passed in Rome, where he obtained a situation under the ecclesiastical government. He was afterward established in a canonry at Florence, where he led an easy, effeminate life, much caressed for his social talents by the Duke Alessandro de' Medici. His end was more tragical than was to have been anticipated from so quiet and unambitious a temper. He is said to have been secretly assassinated, 1536, by the order of Alexander, for refusing to administer poison to the duke's enemy, the Cardinal Hyppolito de' Medici. The story is told in many contradictory ways by different Italian writers, some of whom disbelieve it altogether. The imputation, however, is an evidence of the profligate character of that court, and, if true, is only one out of many examples of perfidious assassination, which, in that age, dishonoured some of the most polished societies in Italy.

Berni has had the distinction of conferring his name on a peculiar species of Italian composition.* The epithet "*Bernesco*" is not derived, how-

---

* He cannot be properly considered its *inventor*, however. He lived

ever, as has been incorrectly stated by some foreign scholars,* from his reformed version of the " Orlando," but from his smaller pieces, his Capitoli more especially. It is difficult to convey a correct and adequate notion of this kind of satirical trifling, since its chief excellence results from idiomatic felicities of expression, that refuse to be transplanted into a foreign tongue, and there is no imitation of it, that we recollect, in our own language. It is a misapplication of the term Bernesque to apply it, as has been sometimes done, to the ironical style supposed to have been introduced by Lord Byron in his Beppo and Don Juan. The clear, unequivocal vein of irony which plays through the sportive sallies of the Italian has no resemblance to the subdued but caustic sneer of the Englishman ; nor does it, in our opinion, resemble in the least Peter Pindar's burlesque satire, to which an excellent critic in Italian poetry has compared it.† Pindar is much too unrefined in versification and in diction to justify the parallel. Italian poetry always preserves the purity of its expression, however coarse or indecent may be the topic on which it is employed. The subjects of many of these poems are of the most whimsical and trivial nature. We find some in *Lode della Peste, del Debito*, &c. Several in commendation of

---

'n time to give the last polish to a species of familiar poetry, which had been long undergoing the process of refinement from the hands of his countrymen.

* Vide *Annotazioni alla Vita di Berni*, dal conte Mazzuchelli. Clas. Ital., p. xxxiv.

† Roscoe's " *Life of Loren. de' Medici*," vol. i., p. 392, *Note*.

the delicacies of the table, of "jellies," "eels," or any other dainty which pleased his epicurean palate. These *Capitoli*, like most of the compositions of this polished versifier, furnish a perfect example of the triumph of style. The sentiments, sometimes indelicate, and often puerile, may be considered, like the worthless insects occasionally found in amber, indebted for their preservation to the beautiful substance in which they are imbedded.

It is a curious fact, that, notwithstanding the apparent facility and fluent graces of Berni's style, it was wrought with infinite care. Some of his verses have been corrected twenty and thirty times. Many of his countrymen have imitated it, mistaking its familiarity of manner for facility of execution.

This fastidious revision has been common with the most eminent Italian poets. Petrarca devoted months to the perfecting of one of his exquisite sonnets.* Ariosto, as his son Virginius records of him, "was never satisfied with his verses, but was continually correcting and recorrecting them;" almost

---

* The following is a literal translation of a succession of memorandums in Latin at the head of one of his sonnets : "I began this by the impulse of the Lord (*Domino jubente*), tenth September, at the dawn of day, after my morning prayers."

"I must make these two verses over again, singing them, and I must transpose them. Three o'clock A.M., 19th October."

"I like this. (*Hoc placet*) 30th October."

"No, this does not please me. 20th December, in the evening."

"February 18th, towards noon. This is now well ; however, look at it again."

It was generally on Friday that he occupied himself with the painful labour of correction, and this was also set apart by him as a day of fast and penitence.—" *Essays*," *cit. sup.*

every stanza in the last edition of his poem published in his lifetime is altered from the original, and
one verse is pointed out (canto XVIII., st. 142) whose
variations filled many pages. Tasso's manuscripts,
preserved in the library at Modena, have been so
o'ten retouched by him that they are hardly intelligible ; and Alfieri was in the habit, not only of correcting verses, but of remoulding whole tragedies,
several of which, he tells us in his *Memoirs*, were
thus transcribed by him no less than three times.
It is remarkable, that in a country where the imagination has been most active, the labour of the file
should have been most diligently exerted on poetical
compositions. Such examples of the pains taken by
men of real genius might furnish a wholesome hint
to some of the rapid, dashing writers of our own day.
"Avec quelque talent qu'on puisse être né," says
Rousseau, in his Confessions, "l'art d'écrire ne se
prend pas tout d'un coup."

We have violated the chronological series of the
Italian epopee, in our notice of Berni, in order to
connect his poem with the model on which it was
cast. We will quit him with the remark, that for
his fame he seems to have been as much indebted to
good fortune as to desert. His countrymen have
affixed his name to an illustrious poem of which he
was not the author, and to a popular species of composition of which he was not the inventor.

In little more than twenty years after the death
of Boiardo, Ariosto gave to the world his first edition of the *Orlando Furioso*. The celebrity of the

K K K

Innamorato made Ariosto prefer building upon this
sure foundation to casting a new one of his own, and
as his predecessor had fortunately left all the dramatis personæ of his unfinished epic alive upon the
stage, he had only to continue their histories to the
end of the drama. " As the former of these two
poems has no termination, and the latter no regular
beginning, they may both be considered as forming
one complete epic."* The latter half was, however,
destined not only to supply the deficiencies, but to
eclipse the glories of the former.

Louis Ariosto was born of a respectable family at
Reggio, 1474. After serving a reluctant apprenticeship of five years in the profession of the law, his
father allowed him to pursue other studies better
adapted to his taste and poetical genius. The elegance of his lyrical compositions in Latin and Italian recommended him to the patronage of the Cardinal Hyppolito d'Este, and of his brother Alphonso,
who in 1505 succeeded to the ducal throne of Ferrara. Ariosto's abilities were found, however, not to
be confined to poetry, and, among other offices of
trust, he was employed by the duke in two important diplomatic negotiations with the court of Rome.
But the Muses still obtained his principal homage,
and all his secret leisure was applied to the perfecting of the great poem, which was to commemorate
at once his own gratitude and the glories of the
house of Este. After fourteen years assiduous labour, he presented to the Cardinal Hyppolito the

* *Tasso, Discorsi Poetici,* p. 29.

first copy of his Orlando Furioso. The well-known reply of the prelate, "*Messer Lodovico, dove mai avete trovate tante fanfaluche?*" "Master Louis, where have you picked up so many trifles?" will be remembered in Italy as long as the poem itself.*

Ariosto, speaking of his early study of jurisprudence in one of his Satires,† says that he passed five years *in quelle ciancie;* a word which signifies much the same with the epithet *fanfaluche* or *coglionerie,* whichever it might have been, imputed to the cardinal. Ariosto was a poet; the cardinal was a mathematician; and each had the very common failing of undervaluing a profession different from his own. The courtly librarian of the *Biblioteca Estense* endeavours to explain away this and the subsequent conduct of Ariosto's patron ;‡ but the poet's Satires, in which he alludes to the behaviour of the cardinal with the fine raillery, and to his own situation with the philosophic independence of Horace, furnish abundant evidence of the cold, ungenerous deportment of Hyppolito.§

* An interrogation, which might remind an Englishman of that put by the *great* Duke of Cumberland to Gibbon : "What, Mr. Gibbon, scribble, scribble, scribble still ?"

† A. M. Pietro Bembo Cardinale.

‡ *Storia della Lett. Ital.,* tom. vii., P. i., p. 42, 43.

§ In a satire addressed to Alessandro Ariosto, he speaks openly of the unprofitableness of his poetic labours :

> "Thanks to the Muses who reward
> So well the service of their bard,
> He almost may be said to lack
> A decent coat to clothe his back."

And soon after, in the same epistle, he adverts with undisguised indignation to the oppressive patronage of Hyppolito :

Notwithstanding the alienation of the cardinal the poet still continued in favour with Alphonso. The patronage bestowed upon him, however, seems to have been of a very selfish and sordid complexion. He was employed by the duke in offices most vexatious to one of his studious disposition, and he passed three years in reducing to tranquillity a barbarous, rebellious province of the duchy. His adventure there with a troop of banditti, who abandoned a meditated attack upon him when they learned that he was the author of the Orlando Furioso, is a curious instance of homage to literary talent, which may serve as a *pendant* to the similar anecdote recorded of Tasso.[*]

The latter portion of his life was passed on his

> " If the poor stipend I receive
> Has led his highness to believe
> He has a right to task my toil
> Like any serf's upon his soil,
> T' enthral me with a servile chain
> That grinds my soul, his hopes are vain.
> Sooner than be such household slave,
> The sternest poverty I'll brave,
> And from his pride and presents free,
> Resume my long-lost liberty."

[*] Ginguenè, whose facts are never to be suspected, whatever credit may be attached to his opinions, has related both these adventures without any qualification (*Histoire Littéraire d'Italie*, tom. iv., p. 359, *et* V. 291). This learned Frenchman professes to have compiled his history under the desire of vindicating Italian literature from the disparaging opinions entertained of it among his countrymen. This has led him to swell the trumpet of panegyric somewhat too stoutly—indeed, much above the modest tone of the Italian *savant*, who, upon his premature death, was appointed to continue the work. Ginguenè died before he had completed the materials for his ninth volume, and the hiatus supplied by Professor Salfi carries down the literary narrative only to the conclusion of the sixteenth century.

own estate in comparative retirement. He refused all public employment, and, with the exception of his satires, and a few comedies which he prepared for the theatre committed to his superintendence by Alphonso, he produced no new work. His hours were diligently occupied with the emendation and extension of his great poem; and in 1532, soon after the republication of it in forty-six cantos, as it now stands, he died of a disease induced by severe and sedentary application.

Ariosto is represented to have possessed a cheerful disposition, temperate habits, and their usual concomitant, a good constitution. Barotti has quoted, in his memoirs of the poet, some particulars respecting him, found among the papers of Virginius, his natural son. He is there said not to have been a great reader; Horace and Catullus were the authors in whom he took most delight. His intense meditation upon the subject of his compositions frequently betrayed him into fits of abstraction, one of which is recorded. Intending, on a fine morning, to take his usual walk, he set out from Carpi, where he resided, and reached Ferrara late in the afternoon, in his slippers and robe de chambre, uninterrupted by any one. His patrimony, though small, was equal to his necessities. An inscription which he placed over his door is indicative of that moderation and love of independence which distinguished his character:

" Parva, sed apta mihi, sed nulli obnoxia, sed non
    Sordida, parta meo sed tamen aere domus."

It does not appear probable that he was ever married. He frequently alludes in his poems to some object of his affections, but without naming her. His bronze inkstand, still preserved in the library at Ferrara, is surmounted by a *relievo* of a Cupid with his finger upon his lip, emblematic of a discreet silence not very common in these matters with his countrymen. He is said to have intended his mistress by the beautiful portrait of Ginevra (c. IV., v.), as Tasso afterward shadowed out Leonora in the affecting episode of Sophronia. This was giving them, according to Ariosto's own allusion, a glorious niche in the temple of immortality.*

There still existed a general affectation among the Italian scholars of writing in the Latin language when Ariosto determined to compose an epic poem. The most accomplished proficients in that ancient tongue flourished about this period, and Politian, Pontano, Vida, Sannazarius, Sadolet, Bembo, had revived, both in prose and poetry, the purity, precision, and classic elegance of the Augustan age. Politian and Lorenzo de Medici were the only writers of the preceding century who had displayed the fecundity and poetical graces of their vernacular tongue, and their productions had been too few and of too trifling a nature to establish a permanent precedent. Bembo, who wrote his elaborate history first in Latin, and who carried the complicated inversions, in fact, the idiom of that language, into his Italian compositions, would have persuaded Ariosto **to** write his poem in the same tongue; but he wise-

* O. F., can. xxxv., st. 15, 16.

ly replied that "he would rather be first among Tuscan writers than second among the Latin," and, following the impulse of his own more discriminating taste, he gave, in the Orlando Furioso, such an exhibition of the fine tones and flexible movements of his native language as settled the question of its precedence forever with his countrymen.

Ariosto at first intended to adopt the *terza rima* of Dante; indeed, the introductory verses of his poem in this measure are still preserved. He soon abandoned it, however, for the *ottava rima*, which is much better adapted to the light, rambling, picturesque narrative of the romantic epic.* Every stanza furnishes a little picture in itself, and the perpetual recurrence of the same rhyme produces not only a most agreeable melody to the ear, but is very favourable to a full and more powerful development of the poet's sentiments. Instances of the truth of this remark must be familiar to every reader of Ariosto. It has been applied by Warton, with equal justice, to Spenser, whom the similar repetition of identical cadences often leads to a copious and beautiful expansion of imagery.† Spenser's stanza dif-

---

* The Italians, since the failure of Trissino, have very generally adopted this measure for their epic poetry, while the *terza rima* is used for didactic and satirical composition. The graver subjects which have engaged the attention of some of their poets during the last century have made blank verse (*verso sciolto*) more fashionable among them. Cesarotti's Ossian, one of the earliest, may be cited as one of the most successful examples of it. No nation is so skilful in a nice adaptation of style to the subject, and *imitative harmony* has been carried by them to a perfection which it can never hope to attain in any other living language; for what other language is made so directly out of the elements of music?

† The following stanza from the "Faerie Queene," describing the

fers materially from the Italian *ottava rima,* in having one more rhyme, and in the elongated Alexandrine with which it is concluded. This gave to his verses " the long, majestic march," well suited to the sober sublimity of his genius; but the additional rhyme much increased its metrical difficulties, already, from the comparative infrequency of assonances in our language, far superior to those of the Italian. This has few compound sounds, but, rolling wholly upon the five open vowels, *a, e, i, o, u,* affords a prodigious number of corresponding terminations. Hence their facility of *improvisation.* Voltaire observes that, in the Jerusalem Delivered, not more than seven words terminate in *u,* and expresses his astonishment that we do not find a greater monotony in the constant recurrence of only four rhymes.* The reason may be, that, in Italian poetry, the rhyme falls both upon the penultima and the final syllable of each verse; and as these two syllables in the same word turn upon different vowels, a greater variety is given to the melody. This

habitation of Morpheus " drowned deep in drowsie fit," may serve as an exemplification of our meaning :

> " And more to lull him in his slumber soft,
>   A trickling streame from high rock tumbling downe,
> And ever drizling raine upon the loft,
>   Mixt with a murmuring winde much like the sowne
> Of swarming bees, did cast him in a swowne ;
>   No other noyes nor people's troublous cryes
> As still are wont to annoy the walled towne
>   Might there be heard ; but careless quiet lyes,
> Wrapt in eternall silence farre from enemyes."

* *Lettre à Deodati di Tovazzi.*

double rhyming termination, moreover, gives an inexpressible lightness and delicacy to Italian poetry, very different from the broad comic which similar compound rhymes, no doubt from the infrequency of their application to serious subjects, communicate to the English.

Ariosto is commonly most admired for the inexhaustible fertility of his fancy; yet a large proportion of his fictions are borrowed, copied, or continued from those of preceding poets. The elegant allegories of ancient superstition, as they were collected or invented by Homer and Ovid, the wild adventures of the Norman romances, the licentious merriment of the gossiping fabliaux, and the enchantments of Eastern fable, have all been employed in the fabric of Ariosto's epic. But, although this diminishes his claims to an inventive fancy, yet, on the whole, it exalts his character as a poet; for these same fictions under the hands of preceding romancers, even of Boiardo, were cold and uninteresting, or, at best, raised in the mind of the reader only a stupid admiration, like that occasioned by the grotesque and unmeaning wonders of a fairy tale. But Ariosto inspired them with a deep and living interest; he adorned them with the graces of sentiment and poetic imagery, and enlivened them by a vein of wit and shrewd reflection.

Ariosto's style is most highly esteemed by his countrymen. The clearness with which it expresses the most subtle and delicate beauties of sentiment may be compared to Alcina's

4

" Vel sottile e rado,
Che non copria dinanzi nè di dietro,
Piu che le rose o i gigli un chiaro vetro."—C. VII., s. 28.*

We recollect no English poet whose manner in any degree resembles him. La Fontaine, the most exquisite versifier of his nation, when in his least familiar mood, comes the nearest to him among the French. Spence remarks, that Spenser must have imagined Ariosto intended to write a serious romantic poem. The same opinion has been maintained by some of the Italian critics. Such, however, is not the impression we receive from it. Not to mention the broad farce with which the narrative is occasionally checkered, as the adventures of Giocondo, the Enchanted Cup, &c., a sly, suppressed smile seems to lurk at the bottom even of his most serious eflections; sometimes, indeed, it plays openly upon the surface of his narrative, but more frequently, after a beautiful and sober description, it breaks out, as it were, from behind a cloud, and lights up the whole with a gay and comic colouring. It would seem as if the natural acuteness of his poetic taste led him to discern in the *magnanime mensogne* of romantic fable abundant sources of the grand and beautiful, while the anti-chivalric character of his age, and, still more, the lively humour of his nation, led him to laugh at its extravagances. Hence the delicate intermixture of serious and comic, which gives a most agreeable variety, though somewhat of a curious perplexity to his style.

*
" A thin transparent veil,
That all the beauties of her form discloses,
As the clear crystal doth th' imprison'd roses "

The Orlando Furioso went through six editions in the author's lifetime, two of which he supervised, and it passed through sixty in the course of the same century. Its poetic pretensions were of too exalted a character to allow it to be regarded as a mere fairy tale; but it sorely puzzled the pedantic critics, both of that and of the succeeding age, to find out a justification for admitting it, with all its fantastic eccentricities, into the ranks of epic poetry. Multitudes have attacked and defended it upon this ground, and justice was not rendered to it until the more enlightened criticism of a later day set all things right by pointing out the distinction between the romantic and the classical.*

The cold and precise Boileau, who, like most of his countrymen, seems to have thought that beauty could wear only one form, and to have mistaken the beginnings of ancient art for its principles, quoted Horace to prove that no poet had the right to produce such grotesque combinations of the tragical and comic as are found in Ariosto.† In the last century, Voltaire, a critic of a much wider range of observation, objects to a narrow, exclusive definition of an epic poem, on the just ground " that works

* Hurd and T. Warton seem to have been among the earliest English writers who insisted upon the distinction between the Gothic and the classical. In their application of it to Spenser they display a philosophical criticism, guided not so much by ancient rules as by the peculiar genius of modern institutions. How superior this to the pedantic dogmas of the French school, or of such a caviller as Rymer, whom Dryden used to quote, and Pope extolled as " the best of English critics."

† Dissertation Critique sur l'Aventure de Joconde. *Œuvres de Boileau* tom. ii., p. 151.

of imagination depend so much on the different languages and tastes of the different nations among whom they are produced, that precise definitions must have a tendency to exclude all beauties that are unknown or unfamiliar to us."—(*Essay sur la Poesie Epique.*) In less than forty pages farther we find, however, that "the Orlando Furioso, although popular with the mass of readers, is very inferior to the *genuine epic poem.*" Voltaire's general reflections were those of a philosopher; their particular application was that of a Frenchman.

At a later period of his life he made a recantation of this precipitate opinion; and he even went so far, in a parallel between the Furioso and the Odyssey, which he considered the *model* of the Italian poem, as to give a decided preference to the former. Ariosto's imitations of the Odyssey, however, are not sufficient to authorize its being considered the model of his epic. Where these imitations do exist, they are not always the happiest efforts of his muse. The tedious and disgusting adventure of the Ogre, borrowed from that of the Cyclops Polypheme, is one of the greatest blemishes in the Furioso. Such "Jack the giant killing" horrors do not blend happily with the airy and elegant fictions of the East. The *familiarity* of Ariosto's manner has an apparent resemblance to the *simplicity* of Homer's, which vanishes upon nearer inspection. The unaffected ease common to both resembles, in the Italian, the fashionable breeding that grows out of a perfect intimacy with the forms of good society   In the

Greek it is rather an artlessness which results from never having been embarrassed by the conventional forms of society at all. Ariosto is perpetually ad- dressing his reader in the most familiar tone of con- versation : Homer pursues his course with the un- deviating dignity of an epic poet. He tells all his stories, even the incredible, with an air of confiding truth. The Italian poet frequently qualifies his with some sly reference or apology, as " I will not vouch for it; I repeat only what Turpin has told be- fore me :"

"Mettendo lo Turpin, lo metto anch' io."*

Ariosto's narratives are complicated and interrupt- ed in a most provoking manner. This has given of- fence to some of his warmest admirers, and to the severe taste of Alfieri in particular. Yet this fault, if indeed it be one, seems imputable to the art, not to the artist. He but followed preceding romancers and conformed to the laws of his peculiar species of poetry. This involution of the narrative may be even thought to afford a relief and an agreeable con- trast, by its intermixture of grave and comic inci- dents; at least, this is the apology set up for the same peculiarities of our own romantic drama. But, whatever exceptions may be taken by the acuteness or ignorance of critics at the conduct of the Orlando

* Voltaire, with all his aversion to local prejudices, was too national to relish the naked simplicity of Homer. One of his witty reflections may show how he esteemed him. Speaking of Virgil's obligations to the Greek poet, " Some say," he observes, " that Homer made Virgil ; if so, this is, without doubt, the best work he ever made !" *si cela est, c'est sans doute son plus bel ouvrage.*

Furioso, the sagacity of its general plan is best vindicated by its wide and permanent popularity in its own country. None of their poets is so universally read by the Italians; and the epithet *divine*, which the homage of an enlightened few had before appropriated to Dante, has been conferred by the voice of the whole nation upon the "Homer of Ferrara."* While those who copied the classical models of antiquity are forgotten, Ariosto, according to the beautiful eulogium of Tasso, "Partendo dalle vestigie degli Antichi Scrittori e dalle regole d'Aristotile, è letto e riletto da tutte l'età, da tutti i sessi, noto a tutte le lingue, ringiovanisce sempre nella sua fama, e vola glorioso per le lingue de' mortali."†

The name of Ariosto most naturally suggests this of Tasso, his illustrious but unfortunate rival in the same brilliant career of epic poetry; for these two seem to hold the same relative rank, and to shed a lustre over the Italian poetry of the sixteenth century, like that reflected by Dante and Petrarch upon the fourteenth. The interest always attached to the misfortunes of genius has been heightened, in the case of Tasso, by the veil of mystery thrown over them; and while his sorrows have been consecrated by the "melodious tear" of the poet, the causes of them have furnished a most fruitful subject of speculation to the historian.

He had been early devoted by his father to the study of jurisprudence, but, as with Ariosto, a love

* The name originally given to him by his rival Tasso.
† Discorsi Poetici, p. 33.

for the Muses seduced him from his severer duties.
His father remonstrated; but Tasso, at the age of
seventeen, produced his *Rinaldo*, an epic in twelve
cantos, and the admiration which it excited throughout Italy silenced all future opposition on the part
of his parent. In 1565, Tasso, then twenty-one
years of age, was received into the family of the
Cardinal Luigi d'Este, to whom he had dedicated
his precocious epic. The brilliant assemblage of
rank and beauty at the little court of Ferrara excited the visions of the youthful poet, while its richly
endowed libraries and learned societies furnished a
more solid nourishment to his understanding. Under these influences, he was perpetually giving some
new display of his poetic talent. His vein flowed
freely in lyrical composition, and he is still regarded
as one of the most perfect models in that saturated
species of national poetry. In 1573 he produced
his *Aminta*, which, in spite of its conceits and pastoral extravagances, exhibited such a union of literary finish and voluptuous sentiment as was to be
found in no other Italian poem. It was translated
into all the cultivated tongues in Europe, and was
followed, during the lifetime of its author, by more
than twenty imitations in Italy. No valuable work
ever gave birth to a more worthless progeny. The
Pastor Fido of Guarini is by far the best of these
imitations; but its elaborate luxury of wit is certainly not comparable to the simple, unsolicited beauties
of the original. Tasso was, however, chiefly occupied with the composition of his great epic. He

had written six cantos in a few months, but he was nearly ten years in completing it. He wrote with the rapidity of genius, but corrected with scrupulous deliberation. His *Letters* show the unwearied pains which he took to obtain the counsel of his friends, and his critical *Discourses* prove that no one could stand less in need of such counsel than himself. In 1575 he completed his *Jerusalem Delivered.* Thus, before he had reached his thirty-second year, Tasso, as a lyric, epic, and dramatic writer, may be fairly said to have earned a threefold immortality in the highest walks of his art. His subsequent fate shows that literary glory rests upon no surer basis than the accidental successes of worldly ambition.

The long and rigorous imprisonment of Tasso, by the sovereign over whose reign his writings had thrown such a lustre, has been as fruitful a source of speculation as the inexplicable exile of Ovid, and in like manner was, for a long time, imputed to an indiscreet and too aspiring passion in the poet. At length Tiraboschi announced, in an early edition of his history, that certain letters and original manuscripts of Tasso, lately discovered in the library of Modena, had been put into the hands of the Abbé Serassi for the farther investigation of the mysterious transaction. The abbé's work appeared in 1785, and the facts disclosed by it clearly prove that the poet's passion for Leonora was not, as formerly imagined, the origin of his misfortunes.* These may

---

* We are only acquainted with Serassi's " Life of Tasso" through the epitomes of Fabroni and Ginguenè. The latter writer seems to us to lay

be imputed to a variety of circumstances, none of
which, however, would have deeply affected a per
son of a less irritable or better disciplined fancy
The calumnies and petty insults which he experienced from his rivals at the court of Ferrara, a clan-
destine attempt to publish his poem, but, more than
ll, certain conscientious scruples which he entertained as to the orthodoxy of his own creed, gradually wrought upon his feverish imagination to such
a degree as in a manner to unsettle his reason. He
fancied that his enemies were laying snares for his
life, and that they had concerted a plan for accusing
him of heresy before the Inquisition.* He privately
absconded from Ferrara, returned to it again, but,
soon after, disquieted by the same unhappy suspicions, left it precipitately a second time, without his
manuscripts, without money, or any means of subsistence, and, after wandering from court to court,
and experiencing, in the sorrowful language of Dante,

> " Come sa di sale
> Lo pane altrui, e com' è duro calle,
> Lo scendere e 'l salir per l'altrui scale,"†

greater stress upon the poet's passion for Leonora than is warranted by
his facts. Tasso dedicated, it is true, many an elegant sonnet to her
charms, and distorted her name into as many ingenious puns as did Petrarch that of his mistress ; but when we consider that this sort of poet
ical tribute is very common with the Italians, that the lady was at least
ten years older than the poet, and that, in the progress of this passion, he
had four or five other well-attested subordinate flames, we shall have
little reason to believe it produced a deep impression on his character.

* His "Letters" betray the same timid jealousy. He is perpetually
complaining that his correspondence is watched and intercepted.

† "How salt the savour is of other's bread,
How hard the passage to descend and climb
By other's stairs."—CAREY.

he threw himself once more upon the clemency of Alphonso; but the duke, already alienated from him by his past extravagances, was incensed to such a degree by certain intemperate expressions of anger in which the poet indulged on his arrival at the court, that he caused him to be confined in a mad-house (*Hospital of St. Anne*).

Here, in the darkness and solitude of its meanest cell, disturbed only by the cries of the wretched in-mates of the mansion, he languished two years un-der the severest discipline of a refractory lunatic Montaigne, in his visit to Italy, saw him in this hu-miliating situation, and his reflections upon it are even colder than those which usually fall from the phlegmatic philosopher.* The genius of Tasso, however, broke through the gloom of his dungeon, and several of the lyrical compositions of his impris-oned muse were as brilliant and beautiful as in the day of her prosperity. The distempered state of his imagination seems never to have clouded the vivid-ness of his perceptions on the subjects of his com-position, and during the remaining five years of his confinement at St. Anne, he wrote, in the form of dialogues, several highly-esteemed disquisitions on philosophical and moral theorems. During this lat-

---

* "I felt even more spite than compassion to see him in so miserable a state, surviving, as it were, himself, unmindful either of himself or his works, which, without his concurrence, and before his eyes, were pub-lished to the world incorrect and deformed."—*Essais de Montaigne,* tom. v., p. 114. Montaigne doubtless exaggerated the mental degradation of Tasso, since it favoured a position which, in the vain love of paradox that has often distinguished his countrymen, he was then endeavouring to establish, viz., the superiority of stupidity and ignorance over genius

ter period Tasso had enjoyed a more commodious apartment, but the duke, probably dreading some literary reprisal from his injured prisoner, resisted all entreaties for his release. This was at length effected, through the intercession of the Prince of Mantua, in 1586.

Tasso quitted Ferrara without an interview with his oppressor, and spent the residue of his days in the south of Italy. His countrymen, affected by his unmerited persecutions, received him wherever he passed with enthusiastic triumph. The nobility and the citizens of Florence waited upon him in a body, as if to make amends for the unjust strictures of their academy upon his poem, and a day was appointed by the court of Rome for his solemn coronation in the capitol with the poetic wreath which had formerly encircled the brow of Petrarch. He died a few days before the intended ceremony. His body, attired in a Roman toga, was accompanied to the grave by nobles and ecclesiastics of the highest dignity, and his temples were decorated with the laurel, of which his perverse fortune had defrauded him when living.

The unhappy fate of Tasso has affixed a deep stain on the character of Alphonso the Second The eccentricities of his deluded fancy could not have justified seven years of solitary confinement, either as a medicine or as a punishment, least of all from the man whose name he had so loudly celebrated in one of the most glorious productions of modern genius. What a caustic commentary upon his unrelenting rigour must Alphonso have found in one of the opening stanzas of the Jerusalem:

" Tu, magnanimo Alfonso, il qual ritogli
Al furor di fortuna, e guidi in porto
Me peregrino errante, e fra gli scogli.
E fra l'onde agitato, e quasi assorto ;
Queste mie carte in lieta fronte accogli," &c.

The illiberal conduct of the princes of Este, both towards Ariosto and Tasso, essentially diminishes their pretensions to the munificent patronage so exclusively imputed to them by their own historians, and by the eloquent pen of Gibbon.* A more accurate picture, perhaps, of the second Alphonso may be found in the concluding canto of Childe Harold, where the poet, in the language of indignant sensibility, not always so judiciously directed, has rendered more than poetical justice to the "antique brood of Este."

The Jerusalem was surreptitiously published, for the first time, during Tasso's imprisonment, and, notwithstanding the extreme inaccuracy of its early editions, it went through no less than six in as many months. Others grew rich on the productions of an author who was himself languishing in the most ab-

* Muratori's *Antichità Estensi* are expressly intended to record the virtues of the family of Este. Tiraboschi's *Storia della Letteratura Italiana* is a splendid *panegyric* upon the intellectual achievements of the whole nation. More than a due share of this praise, however, is claimed for his native princes of Ferrara. It is amusing to see by what evasions the historian attempts to justify their conduct both towards Tasso and Ariosto. Gibbon, who had less apology for partiality, in his laborious researches into the "Antiquities of the House of Brunswick" has not tempered his encomiums of the Alphonsos with a single animadversion upon their illiberal conduct towards their two illustrious subjects.

ject poverty ; one example out of many of the insecurity of literary property in a country where the number of distinct independent governments almost defeats the protection of a copyright.*

Notwithstanding the general admiration which the Jerusalem excited throughout Italy, it was assailed, on its first appearance, with the coarsest criticism it ever experienced. A comparison was naturally suggested between it and the Orlando Furioso, and the Italians became divided into the factions of Tassisti and Ariostisti. The Della Cruscan Academy, just then instituted, in retaliation of some extravagant encomiums bestowed on the Jerusalem, entered into an accurate, but exceedingly intemperate analysis of it, in which they degraded it, not only below the rival epic, but, denying it the name of a *poem*, spoke of it as " a cold and barren compilation." It is a curious fact, that both the Della Cruscan and French Academies commenced their career of criticism with an unlucky attack upon two of the most extraordinary poems in their respective languages.†

Although Tasso was only one-and-twenty years of age when he set about writing his Jerusalem, yet it is sufficiently apparent, from the sagacious criticism exhibited in his letters, that he brought to it a mind

* " Foreigners," says Denina, " who ask if there are great writers in Italy now, as in times past, would be surprised at the number, were they to learn how much even the best of them are brought in debt by the publication of their own works."—*Vicende della Létteratura*, tom. ii , p. 326.

† It is hardly necessary to refer to Corneille's " *Cid*," so clumsily anatomized by the Académie Française at the jealous instigation of Cardinal Richelieu.

ripened by extensive studies and careful meditation.
He had, moreover, the advantage of an experience
derived both from his own previous labours and
those of several distinguished predecessors in the
same kind of composition. The learned Trissino
had fashioned, some years before, a regular heroic
poem, with pedantic precision, upon the models of
antiquity. From this circumstance, it was so formal
and tedious that nobody could read it. Bernardo
Tasso, the father of Torquato, who might apply to
himself, with *equal* justice, the reverse of the younger
Racine's lament,

" Et moi *père* inconnu d'un si glorieux fils,"

had commenced his celebrated Amadis with the
same deference to the rules of Aristotle. Finding
that the audiences of his friends, to whom he was
accustomed to read the epic as it advanced, gradually thinned off, he had the discretion to take the
hint, and new cast it in a more popular and romantic form. Notwithstanding these inauspicious examples, Tasso was determined to give to his national
literature what it so much wanted, a great heroic
poem; his fine eye perceived at once, however, all
the advantages to be derived from the peculiar institutions of the moderns, and, while he conformed, in
the general plan of his epic, to the precepts of antiquity, he animated it with the popular and more
exalted notions of love, of chivalry, and of religion.
His Jerusalem exhibits a perfect combination of the
romantic and the classical.

The subject which he selected was most happily

adapted to his complicated design. However gloomy a picture the Crusades may exhibit to the rational historian, they are one of the most brilliant and imposing ever offered to the eye of the poet. It is surprising that a subject so fruitful in marvellous and warlike adventure, and which displays the full triumph of Christian chivalry, should have been so long neglected by the writers of epical romance. The plan of the Jerusalem is not without defects, which have been pointed out by the Italians, and bitterly ridiculed by Voltaire, whose volatile sarcasms have led him into one or two blunders, that have excited much wrath among some of Tasso's countrymen.* The conceits which occasionally glitter on the surface of Tasso's clear and polished style have afforded another and a fair ground for censure. Boileau's metaphorical distich, however, has given to them an undeserved importance. The epithet *tinsel* (clinquant), used by him without any limitation, was quoted by his countrymen as fixing the value at once of all Tasso's compositions, and afterward, by an easy transition, of that of the whole body of Italian literature. Boileau subsequently diluted this censure of the Italian poet with some partial commendations ;† but its ill effects were visible

---

* Among other heinous slanders, he had termed the musical bird " di color vari" " e purpureo rostro" in Armida's gardens, a " *parrot*," and the " fatal Donzella" (canto xv.), " whose countenance was beautiful like that of the angels," an " *old woman*," which his Italian censor assures his countrymen " is much worse than a *vecchia donna*." For the burst of indignation which these and similar sins brought upon Voltaire's head, vide " *Annotazioni ai Canti*," xv., xvi. · *Clas. Ital.*

† Both Ginguenè and some Italian critics affect to consider these com-

in the unfavourable prejudices which it left on the minds of his own countrymen, and on those of the English for nearly a century.

The affectations imputed to Tasso are to be traced to a much more remote origin. Petrarch's best productions are stained with them, as are those of preceding poets, Cino da Pistoja, Guido Cavalcanti, and others,* and they seem to have flowed directly from the Provençale, the copious fountain of Italian lyrical poetry. Tiraboschi referred their introduction to the influence of Spanish literature under the viceroys of Naples during the latter part of the sixteenth century, which provoked a patriotic replication, in seven volumes, from the Spanish Abbé Lampillas. The Italian had the better of his adversary in temper, if not in argument. This false refinement was brought to its height during the first half of the seventeenth century, under Marini and his imitators, and it is somewhat maliciously intimated by Denina that the foundation of the Academy Della Crusca corresponds with the *commencement* of the decay of

---

mendations as an *amende honorable* on the part of Boileau. They, however, amount to very little, and, like the Frenchman's compliment to Yorick, have full as much of bitter as of sweet in them. The remarks quoted by D'Olivet (Histoire de l'Académie Française), as having been made by the critic a short time previous to his death, are a convincing proof, on the other hand, that he was tenacious to the last of his original heresy. "So little," said he, "have I changed, that, on reviewing Tasso of late, I regretted exceedingly that I had not been more explicit in my strictures upon him." He then goes on to supply the hiatus by taking up all the blemishes in detail which he had before only alluded to *en gros*.

* These veteran versifiers have been condensed into two volumes 8vo, in an edition published at Florence, 1816, under the title of *Poeti del Primo Secolo.*

good taste.* Some of their early publications prove that they have at least as good a claim to be considered its promoters as Tasso.†

Tasso is the most lyrical of all epic poets. This often weakens the significance and picturesque delineation of his narrative, by giving to it an ideal and too general character. His eight line stanza is frequently wrought up, as it were, into a miniature sonnet. He himself censures Ariosto for occasionally indulging this lyrical vein in his romance, and cites as an example the celebrated comparison of the virgin and the rose (can. i., s. 42). How many similar examples may be found in his own epic! The gardens of Armida are full of them. To this cause we may perhaps ascribe the glittering affectations, the *clinquant* so often noticed in his poetry. Dazzling and epigrammatic points are often solicited in sonnets. To the same cause may be referred, in part, the nicely-adjusted harmony of his verses.

* *Vicende della Letteratura*, tom. ii., p. 52.

† A distinction seems to be authorized between the ancients and the moderns in regard to what is considered *purity of taste*. The earliest writings of the former are distinguished by it, and it fell into decay only with the decline of the nation ; while a vicious taste is visible in the earliest stages of modern literature, and it has been corrected only by the corresponding refinement of the nation. The Greek language was written in classic purity from Homer until long after Greece herself had become tributary to the Romans, and the Latin tongue from the time of Terence till the nation had sacrificed its liberties to its emperors ; while the early Italian authors, as we have already seen, the Spaniards in the age of Ferdinand, the English in that of Elizabeth, and the French under Francis the First (the epochs which may fix the dawn of their respective literatures), seem to have been deeply infected with a passion for conceits and quibbles, which has been purified only by the diligent cultivation of ages.

N n n

It would almost seem as if each stanza was meant to be set to music, as Petrarch is known to have composed many of his odes with this view.* The melodious rhythm of Tasso's verse has none of the monotonous sweetness so cloying in Metastasio. It is diversified by all the modulations of an exquisitely sensible ear. For this reason, no Italian poet is so frequently in the mouths of the common people. Ariosto's familiar style and lively narrative are better suited to the popular apprehension; but the lyrical melody of Tasso triumphs over these advantages in his rival, and enables him literally *virûm volitare per ora.* It was once common for the Venetian gondoliers to challenge each other, and to respond in the verses of the Jerusalem, and this sort of musical contest might be heard for hours in the silence of a soft summer evening. The same beautiful ballads, if we may so call these fragments of an epic, are still occasionally chanted by the Italian peasant, who is less affected by the sublimity of their sentiments than the musical flow of the expression.†

Tasso's sentiments are distinguished, in our opinion, by a moral grandeur surpassing that of any other Italian poet. His devout mind seems to have been fully inspired with the spirit of his subject. We say in our opinion, for an eminent German critic, F.

---

* *Foscolo*, " *Essay*," &c., p. 93.

† " The influence of metrical harmony is visible in the lower classes, who commit to memory the stanzas of Tasso, and sing them without comprehending them. They even disfigure the language so as to make nonsense of it, their senses deceived all the while by the unmeaning melody."—*Pignotti, Storia*, &c., tom. iv., p. 192.

Schlegel, is disposed to deny him this merit. We think in this instance he must have proposed to himself what is too frequent with the Germans, an ideal and exaggerated standard of elevation. A few stanzas (st. 1 to 19) in the fourth canto of the Jerusalem may be said to contain almost the whole argument of the Paradise Lost. The convocation of the devils in the dark abyss,* the picture of Satan, whom he injudiciously names Pluto, his sublime address to his confederates, in which he alludes to their rebellion and the subsequent creation of man, were the germs of Milton's most glorious conceptions. Dante had before shadowed forth Satan, but it was only in the physical terrors of a hideous aspect and gigantic stature. The ancients had clothed the Furies in the same external deformities. Tasso, in obedience to the superstitions of his age, gave to the devil similar attributes, but he invested his character with a moral sublimity which raised it to the rank of divine intelligences:

> " Ebbero i più felici allor vittoria
> Rimase a noi d'invitto ardir la gloria."

> " Sia destin ciò ch'io voglio."

In the literal version of Milton,

> " What I will is fate."

Sentiments like these also give to Satan, in Paradise

---

* The semi-stanza, which describes the hoarse reverberations of the infernal trumpet in this Pandemonium, is cited by the Italians as a happy example of imitative harmony :

> " Chiama gli abitator dell'ombre eterne
> Il rauco suon della tartarea tromba.
> Treman le spaziose atre caverne,
> E l'aer cieco a quel romor rimbomba."

Lost, his superb and terrific majesty. Milton, however, gave a finer finish to the portrait, by dispensing altogether with the bugbear deformities of his person, and by depicting it as a form that

> "Had yet not lost
> All its original brightness, nor appear'd
> Less than archangel ruin'd."

It seems to us a capital mistake in Tasso to have made so little use of the *diablerie* which he has so powerfully portrayed. Almost all the machinations of the infidels in the subsequent cantos turn upon the agency of petty necromancers.

Tasso frequently deepens the expression of his pictures by some skilful moral allusion. How finely has he augmented the misery of the soldier, perishing under a consuming drought before the walls of Jerusalem, by recalling to his imagination the cool and crystal waters with which he had once been familiar:

> "Se alcun giammai tra frondeggianti rive
> Puro vide stagnar liquido argento,
> O giù precipitose ir acque vive
> Per Alpe, o'n piaggia erbosa a passo lento;
> Quelle al vago desio forma e descrive,
> E ministra materia al suo tormento;
> Che l'imagine lor gelida e molle
> L'asciuga e scalda, e nel pensier ribolle."*

Can. XIII., st. 60.

---

* "He that the gliding rivers erst had seen
Adown their verdant channels gently roll'd,
Or falling streams, which to the valleys green
Distill'd from tops of Alpine mountains cold,
Those he desired in vain, new torments been
Augmented thus with wish of comforts old;
Those waters cool he drank in vain conceit,
Which more increased his thirst, increased his heat."—*Fairfax*

In all the manifold punishments of Dante's " Hell"
we remember one only in which the *mind* is made
use of as a means of torture.   A counterfeiter (*bar-
ratiere*) contrasts his situation in these dismal regions
with his former pleasant residence in the green vale
of the Arno; an allusion which adds a new sting to
his anguish, and gives a fine moral colouring to the
picture.   Dante was the first great Christian poet
that had written; and when, in conformity with the
charitable spirit of his age, he assigned all the ancient heathens a place either in his *hell* or *purgatory*, he inflicted upon them corporeal punishments
which alone had been threatened by their poets.

Both Ariosto and Tasso elaborated the style of
their compositions with infinite pains.   This labour,
however, led them to the most opposite results.   It
gave to the Furioso the airy graces of elegant conversation; to the Gerusalemme a stately and imposing eloquence.   In this last you may often find a
consummate art carried into affectation, as in the
former natural beauty is sometimes degraded into
vulgarity, and even obscenity.   Ariosto has none of
the national vices of style imputed to his rival, but
he is tainted with the less excusable impurities of
sentiment.   It is stated by a late writer that the ex-
ceptionable passages in the Furioso were found
crossed out with a pen in a manuscript copy of the
author, showing his intention to have suppressed
them at some future period.   The fact does not appear probable, since the edition, as it now stands,
with all its original blemishes, was revised and published by himself the year of his death.

4   2 P

Tasso possessed a deeper, a more abstracted, and lyrical turn of thought. Ariosto infuses an active worldly spirit into his poetry; his beauties are social, while those of his rival are rather of a solitary complexion. Ariosto's muse seems to have caught the gossiping spirit of the *fabliaux*, and Tasso's the lyrical refinements of the *Provençale*. Ariosto is seldom sublime like the other. This may be imputed to his subject, as well as to the character of his genius. Owing to his subject, he is more generally entertaining. The easy freedom of his narrative often leads him into natural details much more affecting than the ideal generalization of Tasso. How pathetic is the dying scene of Brandimarte, with the half-finished name of his mistress, Fiordiligi, upon his lip:

> " Orlando, fa che ti raccordi
> Di me nell' orazion tue grate a Dio ;
> Nè men ti raccomando la mia Fiordi . . . .
> Ma dir non poté *ligi ;* e qui finío."*

Tasso could never have descended to this beautiful negligence of expression.†

* " Orlando, I implore thee
That in thy prayers my name may be commended,
And to thy care I leave my loved *Fiordi—*
Ligi he could not add ; but here he ended."

† The *ideal*, which we have imputed to Tasso, may be cited, however, as a characteristic of the national literature, and as the point in which their literature is most decidedly opposed to our own. With the exception of Dante and Parini, whose copies from life have all the precision of proof impressions, it would be difficult to find a picture in the compass of Italian poetry executed with the fidelity to nature so observable in our good authors, so apparent in every page of Cowper or Thomson, for example. It might be well, perhaps, for the English artist, if he could embellish the minute and literal details of his own school with some of the ideal graces of the Italian. Byron may be considered as having done this more effectualiy than any contemporary poet. Byron's love of the

Tasso challenged a comparison with his predecessor in his gardens of Armida. The indolent and languishing repose of the one, the brisk, amorous excitement of the other, are in some measure characteristic of their different pencils. The parallel has been too often pursued for us to weary our readers with it.

The Italians have a copious variety of narrative poetry, and are very nice in their subdivisions of it. Without attending to these, we have been guided by its chronological succession. We have hardly room to touch upon the "Secchia Rapita" (*Rape of the Bucket*) of Tassoni, the model of the mock-heroic poems afterward frequent in Italy,* of Boileau's *Lutrin*, and of the *Rape of the Lock*. Tassoni, its author, was a learned and noble Modenese, who, after a life passed in the heats of literary controversies, to which he had himself given rise, died 1635, aged seventy-one. The subject of the poem is a war be-

ideal, it must be allowed, however, has too often bewildered him in mysticism and hyperbole.

* The Italians long disputed with great acrimony whether this or the comic heroic poem of Bracciolini (*Lo Scherno degli Dei*) was precedent in point of age. It appears probable that Tassoni's was written first, although printed last. No country has been half so fruitful as Italy in literary quarrels, and in none have they been pursued with such bitterness and pertinacity. In some instances, as in that of Marini, they have even been maintained by assassination. The sarcastic commentaries of Galileo upon the "Jerusalem," quoted in the vulgar edition of the "Classics," were found sadly mutilated by one of the offended *Tassisti*, into whose hands they had fallen more than two centuries after they were written; so long does a literary faction last in Italy! The Italians, inhibited from a free discussion on political or religious topics, enter with incredible zeal into those of a purely abstract and often unimportant character.

tween Modena and Bologna, at the commencement of the thirteenth century, in consequence of a wooden bucket having been carried off from the market-place in the latter city by an invading party of the former. This memorable trophy has been preserved down to the present day in the Cathedral of Modena. Tassoni's epic will confer upon it a more lasting existence

> "The Bucket, which so sorely had offended,
> In the Great Tower, where yet it may be found,
> Was from on high by ponderous chain suspended,
> And with a marble cope environ'd round.
> By portals five the entrance is defended ;
> Nor cavalier of note is that way bound,
> Nor pious pilgrim, but doth pause to see
> The spoil so glorious of the victory."—Canto i., st. 63

Gironi, in his life of the poet, triumphantly adduces, in evidence of the superiority of the Italian epic over the French mock-heroic poem of Boileau, that the subject of the former is far more insignificant than that of the latter, and yet the poem has twelve cantos, being twice the number of the Lutrin. He might have added that each canto contains about six hundred lines instead of two hundred, the average complement of the French, so that Tassoni's epic has the glory of being twelve times as long as Boileau's, and all about a bucket ! This is somewhat characteristic of the Italians. What other people would good-humouredly endure such an interminable epic upon so trivial an affair, which had taken place more than four centuries before ? To make amends, however, for the want of pungency in a satire on transactions of such an antiquated date,

Tassoni has besprinkled his poem very liberally with allusions to living characters.

We may make one general objection to the poem, that it is often too much in earnest for the perfect keeping of the mock heroic. The cutting of throats and fighting regular pitched battles are too bloody a business for a joke. How much more in the genuine spirit of this species of poetry is the bloodless battle with the books in the Lutrin!

The machinery employed by Tassoni is composed of the ancient heathen deities. These are frequently brought upon the stage, and are travestied with the coarsest comic humour. But the burlesque which reduces great things to little is of a grosser and much less agreeable sort than that which magnifies little things into great. The "Rape of the Lock" owes its charms to the latter process. The importance which it gives to the elegant nothings of high life, its perpetual sparkling of wit, the fairy fretwork which constitutes its machinery, have made it superior, as a fine piece of irony, to either of its foreign rivals. A Frenchman would doubtless prefer the epic regularity, progressive action, and smooth seesaw versification of the Lutrin ;* while an Italian would find sufficient in the grand heroic sentiment and the voluptuous portraiture with which Tassoni's unequal poem is occasionally inlaid, to justify his

* The versification of the Lutrin is esteemed as faultless as any in the language. The tame and monotonous flow of the best of French rhyme, however, produces an effect, at least upon a foreign ear, which has been well likened by one of their own nation to "the drinking of cold water."

preference of it. There is no accounting for national taste. La Harpe, the Aristarchus of French critics, censures the gossamer *machinery* of the "Rape of the Lock" as the greatest defect in the poem. " La fable des Sylphes, que Pope a très inutilement empruntée du Conte de Gabalis, pour en faire le merveilleux de son poëme, n'y produit *rien d'agréable, rien d'intéressant !*"

Italy, in the sixteenth and seventeenth centuries, was inundated with crude and insipid romances, distributed into all the varieties of epic poetry. The last one, however, of sufficient importance to require our notice, namely, the *Ricciardetto* of Nicholas Fortiguerra, appeared as late as 1738. After two centuries of marvellous romance, Charlemagne and his paladins became rather insipid dramatis personæ. What could not be handled seriously, however, might be ridiculed; and the smile, half suppressed by Ariosto and Berni, broke out into broad buffoonery in the poem of Fortiguerra.

The *Ricciardetto* may be considered the Don Quixote of Italy; for although it did not bring about that revolution in the national taste ascribed to the Spanish romance, yet it is, like that, an unequivocal parody upon the achievements of knight errantry. It may be doubted whether Don Quixote itself was not the consequence rather than the cause of the revolution in the national taste. Fortiguerra pursued an opposite method to Cervantes, and, instead of introducing his crack-brained heroes into the realities of vulgar life, he made them equally ridiculous by involving them in the most absurd caricatures of romantic fiction. Many of these adventures are of a licentious, and sometimes of a disgusting nature; but the graceful though negligent beauties of his style throw an illusive veil over the grossness of the narrative. Imitations of Pulci may be more frequently traced than of any other romantic poet. But, although more celebrated writers are occasionally, and the extravagances of chivalry are perpetually parodied by Fortiguerra, yet his object does not seem to have been deliberate satire so much as good-humoured jesting. What he wrote was for the simple purpose of raising a laugh, not for the derision or the correction of the taste of his countrymen. The tendency of his poem is certainly satirical, yet there is not a line indicating such an intention on his part. The most pointed humour is aimed at the clergy.* Fortiguerra was himself a canon. He commenced his epic at the suggestion of some friends with whom he was passing a few weeks of the autumn at a hunting seat. The conversation turned upon the labour bestowed by Pulci, Berni, and Ariosto on their great

* One of the leading characters is Ferragus, who had figured in all the old epics as one of the most formidable Saracen chieftains. He turns hermit with Fortiguerra, and beguiles his lonely winter evenings with the innocent pastime of making candles.

> " E ne l'orrida bruma
> Quando l'aria è piu fredda, e piu crudele,
> Io mi diverto in far de le candele."—III., 53.

A contrast highly diverting to the Italians, who had been taught to associate very lofty ideas with the name of Ferragus. The conflict kept up between the devout scruples of the new saint and his old heathen appetites affords perpetual subjects for the profane comi.

poems; and Fortiguerra undertook to furnish, the
next day, a canto of good poetry, exhibiting some of
the peculiarities of their respective styles. He fulfilled his promise, and his friends, delighted with its
sprightly graces, persuaded him to pursue the epic
to its present complement of thirty cantos. Any
one acquainted with the facilities for *improvisation*
afforded by the flexible organization of the Italian
tongue will be the less surprised at the rapidity of
this composition. The "Ricciardetto" may be looked upon as a sort of improvisation.

In the following literal version of the two opening
stanzas of the poem we have attempted to convey
some notion of the sportive temper of the original :

> " It will not let my busy brain alone ;
>   The whim has taken me to write a tale
> In poetry, of things till now unknown,
>   Or if not wholly new, yet nothing stale.
> My muse is not a daughter of the Sun,
>   With harp of gold and ebony ; a hale
> And buxom country lass, she sports at ease,
> And, free as air, sings to the passing breeze
>
> " Yet, though accustom'd to the wood—its spring
>   Her only beverage, and her food its mast,
> She will of heroes and of battles sing,
>   The loves and high emprizes of the past.
> Then if she falter on so bold a wing,
>   Light be the blame upon her errors cast ;
> She never studied ; and she well may err,
> Whose home hath been beneath the oak and fir."

Fortiguerra's introductions to his cantos are seasoned with an extremely pleasant wit, which Lord
Byron has attentively studied, and, in some passages
of his more familiar poetry, closely imitated. The
stanza, for example, in Beppo, beginning

> "She was not old, nor young, nor at the years
> Which certain people call a *certain age*,
> Which yet the most uncertain age appears," &c.,

was evidently suggested by the following in Ricci-ardetto:

> "Quando si giugne ad una *certa età*,
> Ch'io non voglio descrivervi qual è,
> Bisogna stare allora a quel ch'un ha,
> Nè d'altro amante provar più la fè,
> Perchè, donne me care, la beltà
> Ha l' ali al capo, alle spalle, ed a' piè;
> E vola si, che non si scorge più
> Vestigio alcun ne' visi, dove fu."

Byron's wit, however, is pointed with a keener sarcasm, and his serious reflections show a finer perception, both of natural and moral beauty, than belong to the Italian. No two things are more remote from each other than sentiment and satire. In "Don Juan" they are found side by side in almost every stanza. The effect is disagreeable. The heart, warmed by some picture of extreme beauty or pathos, is suddenly chilled by a selfish sneer, a cold-blooded maxim, that makes you ashamed of having been duped into a good feeling by the writer even for a moment. It is a melancholy reflection, that the last work of this extraordinary poet should be the monument alike of his genius and his infamy. Voltaire's licentious epic, the "Pucelle," is written .n a manner, perhaps, more nearly corresponding to that of the Italian; but the philosophical irony, if we may so call it, which forms the substratum of the more familiar compositions of this witty and profligate author, is of somewhat too deep a cast for the light, superficial banter of Fortiguerra.

We have now traced the course of Italian narrative poetry down to the middle of the last century. It has by no means become extinct since that period, and, among others, an author well known here by his history of our Revolutionary war has contributed his share to the epopee of his country, in his "Camillo, o Vejo Conquistata." Almost every Italian writer has a poetic vein within him, which, if it does not find a vent in sonnets or canzones, will flow out into more formidable compositions.*

In glancing over the long range of Italian narrative poems, one may be naturally led to the reflection that the most prolific branch of the national literature is devoted *exclusively* to purposes of mere amusement. Brilliant inventions, delicate humour, and a beautiful colouring of language are lavished upon all; but with the exception of the "Jerusalem," we rarely meet with sublime or ennobling sentiment, and very rarely with anything like a moral or philosophical purpose. Madame de Staël has attempted to fasten a reproach on the whole body of Italian letters, "that, with the exception of their works on physical science, they have never been directed to *utility*."† The imputation applied in this almost unqualified manner is unjust. The language has been enriched by the valuable reflections of too many historians, the solid labours of too many antiquaries

---

* Boccaccio, Machiavelli, Bembo, Varchi, Castiglione, Pignotti, Botta, and a host of other *classic* prose writers of Italy, have all confessed the "impetus sacer," and given birth to epics, lyrics, or bucolics.

† "Tous les ouvrages des Italiens, excepté ceux qui traitent des sciences physiques. n'ont jamais pour but l'utilité."—*De la Littérature, &c.*

and critics, to be thus lightly designated. The learned lady may have found a model for her own comprehensive manner of philosophizing, and an ample refutation of her assertion in Machiavelli alone.* In their works of imagination, however, such an imputation appears to be well merited. The Italians seemed to demand from these nothing farther than from a fine piece of music, where the heart is stirred, the ear soothed, but the understanding not a whit refreshed. The splendid apparitions of their poet's fancy fade away from the mind of the reader, and, like the enchanted fabrics described in their romances, leave not a trace behind them.

In the works of fancy in our language, fiction is almost universally made subservient to more important and nobler purposes. The ancient drama, and novels, the modern prose drama, exhibit historical pictures of manners and accurate delineations of character. Most of the English poets in other walks, from the "moral Gower" to Cowper, Crabbe, and Wordsworth, have made their verses the elegant vehicles of religious or practical truth. Even

* We say *manner*, not spirit. The "Discors isopra T. Livio," however, require less qualification on the score of their principles. They obviously furnished the model to the "Grandeur et Décadence des Romains," and the same extended philosophy which Montesquieu imitated in civil history, Madame de Staël has carried into literary.

Among the historians, antiquaries, &c., whose names are known where the language is not read, we might cite Guicciardini, Bembo, Sarpi, Giannone, Nardi, Davila, Denina, Muratori, Tiraboschi, Gravina, Bettinelli, Algarotti, Beccaria, Filanghieri, Cesarotti, Pignotti, and many others; a hollow muster-roll of names that it would be somewhat ridiculous to run over, did not their wide celebrity expose, in a stronger light, Madame de Staël's sweeping assertion.

descriptive poetry in England interprets the silence of external nature into a language of sentiment and devotion. It is characteristic of this spirit in the nation that Spenser, the only one of their classic writers who has repeated the fantastic legends of chivalry, deemed it necessary to veil his Italian fancy in a cloud of allegory, which, however it may be thought to affect the poem, shows unequivocally the didactic intention of the poet.

These grave and extended views are seldom visible in the ornamental writing of the Italians. It rarely conveys useful information, or inculcates moral or practical truth; but it is too commonly an elegant, unprofitable pastime. Novelle, lyrical, and epic poetry may be considered as constituting three principal streams of their lighter literature. These have continued to flow, with little interruption, the two first from the "golden urns" of Petrarch and Boccaccio, the last from the early sources we have already traced down to the present day. Their multitudinous novelle, with all their varieties of tragic and comic incident, the last by far the most frequent, present few just portraitures of character, still fewer examples of sound ethics or wise philosophy.* In the exuberance of their sonnets and canzone, we find some, it is true, animated by an efficient spirit of re-

---

* The heavier charge of indecency lies upon many. The Novelle of Casti, published as late as 1804, make the foulest tales of Boccaccio appear fair beside them. They have run through several editions since their first appearance, and it tells not well for the land that a numerous class of readers can be found in it who take delight in banqueting upon such abominable offal.

ligion or patriotism; but too frequently they are of a purely amatory nature, the unsubstantial though brilliant exhalations of a heated fancy. The pastoral drama, the opera, and other beautiful varieties of invention, which, under the titles of Bernesco, Burlesco, Maccherónico, and the like, have been nicely classed according to their different modifications of style and humour, while they manifest the mercurial temper and the originality of the nation, confirm the justice of our position.

The native melody of the Italian tongue, by seducing their writers into an overweening attention to sound, has doubtless been in one sense prejudicial to their literature. We do not mean to imply, in conformity with a vulgar opinion, that the language is deficient in energy or compactness. Its harmony is no proof of its weakness. It allows more licenses of contraction than any other European tongue, and retains more than any other the vigorous inversions of its Latin original. Dante is the most concise of early moderns, and we know none superior to Alfieri in this respect among those of our own age. Davanzati's literal translation of Tacitus is condensed into a smaller compass than its original, the most sententious of ancient histories; but still the silver tones of a language that almost sets itself to music as it is spoken, must have an undue attraction for the harmonious ear of an Italian. Their very first classical model of prose composition is an obvious example of it.

The frequency of *improvisation* is another circum-

4   2 Q

stance that has naturally tended to introduce a less serious and thoughtful habit of composition. Above all, the natural perceptions of an Italian seem to be peculiarly sensible to *beauty*, independent of every other quality. Any one who has been in Italy must have recognised the glimpses of a pure taste through the rags of the meanest beggar. The musical pieces, when first exhibited at the theatre of St. Carlos, are correctly pronounced upon by the Lazzaroni of Naples, and the mob of Florence decide with equal accuracy upon the productions of their immortal school. Cellini tells us that he exposed his celebrated statue of Perseus in the public square by order of his patron, Duke Cosmo First, who declared himself perfectly satisfied with it on learning the commendations of the people.* It is not extraordinary that this exquisite sensibility to the beautiful should have also influenced them in literary art, and have led them astray sometimes from the substantial and the useful. Who but an Italian historian would, in this practical age, so far blend fact and fiction as, for the sake of rhetorical effect, to introduce into the mouths of his personages sentiments and speeches never uttered by them, as Botta has lately done in his history of the American War?

In justice, however, to the Italians, we must admit, that the reproach incurred by too concentrated an attention to beauty, to the exclusion of more enlarged and useful views in their lighter compositions, does not fall upon this or the last century. They

* *Vita di Benvo. Cellin.*, tom. ii., p. 339.

have imbibed a graver and more philosophical cast
of reflection, for which they seem partly indebted to
the influence of English literature. Several of their
most eminent authors have either visited or resided
in Great Britain, and the genius of the language has
been made known through the medium of skilful
translations. Alfieri has transported into his tragedies the solemn spirit and vigorous characterization
peculiar to the English. He somewhere remarks
that " he could not read the language ;" but we are
persuaded his stern pen would never have traced the
dying scene of Saul, had he not witnessed a representation of Macbeth. Ippolito Pindemonte, in his
descriptive pieces, has deepened the tones of his native idiom with the moral melancholy of Gray and
Cowper. Monti's compositions, both dramatic and
miscellaneous, bear frequent testimony to his avowed
admiration for Shakspeare ; and Cesarotti, Foscolo,
and Pignotti have introduced the " severer muses"
of the north to a still wider and more familiar acquaintance with their countrymen.* Lastly, among
the works of fancy which attest the practical scope
of Italian letters in the last century, we must not
omit the " Giorno" of Parini, the most curious and
nicely-elaborated specimen of *didactic* satire produced in any age or country. Its polished irony, point-

* Both the prose and poetry of Foscolo are pregnant with more serious meditation and warmer patriotism than is usual in the works of
the Italians. Pignotti, although his own national manner has been but
.ittle affected by his foreign erudition, has contributed more than any
other to extend the influence of English letters among his countrymen.
His works abound in allusions to them, and two of his principal poems
are dedicated to the memory of Shakspeare and of Pope.

ed at the domestic vices of the Italian nobility, indicates both the profligacy of the nation and the moral independence of the poet.

The Italian language, the first-born of those descended from the Latin, is also the most beautiful. It is not surprising that a people endowed with an exquisite sensibility to beauty should have been often led to regard this language rather as a means of pleasure than of utility. We must not, however, so far yield to the unqualified imputation of Madame de Staël as to forget that they have other claims to our admiration than what arise from the inventions of the poet, or from the ideal beauties which they have revived of Grecian art; that the light of *genius* shed upon the world in the fourteenth, and that of *learning* in the fifteenth century, was all derived from Italy; that her writers first unfolded the sublimity of Christian doctrines as applied to modern literature, and by their patient, philological labours restored to life the buried literature of antiquity; that her schools revived and expounded the ancient code of law, since become the basis of so important a branch of jurisprudence both in Europe and our own country; that she *originated* literary, and brought to a perfection unequalled in any other language, unless it be our own, civil and political history; that she led the way in physical science and in that of political philosophy; and, finally, that of the two enlightened navigators who divide the glory of adding a new quarter to the globe, the one was a Genoese and the other a Florentine.

In following down the stream of Italian narrative poetry, we have wandered into so many details, especially where they would tend to throw light on the intellectual character of the nation, that we have little room, and our readers, doubtless, less patience, left for a discussion of the poems which form the text of our article. The few stanzas descriptive of Berni, which we have borrowed from the Innamorato, may give some notion of Mr. Rose's manner. The translations have been noticed in several of the English journals, and we perfectly accord with the favourable opinion of them, which has been so often expressed that it needs not here be repeated.

The composite style of Ariosto owes its charms to the skill with which the delicate tints of his irony are mixed with the sober colouring of his narrative. His translators have spoiled the harmony of the composition by overcharging one or other of these ingredients. Harrington has caricatured his original into burlesque; Hoole has degraded him into a most melancholy proser. The popularity of this latter version has been of infinite disservice to the fame of Ariosto, whose aerial fancy loses all its buoyancy under the heavy hexameters of the English translator. The purity of Mr. Rose's taste has prevented him from exaggerating even the beauties of his original.

4   2 Q *

POETRY AND ROMANCE OF THE ITALIANS.*

JULY, 1831.

IT is not our intention to go into an analysis, or even to discuss the merits of the works at the head of this article, which we have selected only as a text for such reflections on the poetry and ornamental prose-writing of the Italians as might naturally suggest themselves to an English reader. The points of view from which a native contemplates his own literature and those from which it is seen by a foreigner are so dissimilar, that it would be hardly possible that they should come precisely to the same results without affectation or servility on the part of the latter. The native, indeed, is far better qualified than any foreigner can be to estimate the productions of his own countrymen; but as each is subjected to peculiar influences, truth may be more likely to be elicited from a collision of their mutual opinions than from those exclusively of either.

The Italian, although the first modern tongue to produce what still endure as classical models of composition, was, of all the Romance dialects, the last

* [The reader may find in this article some inadvertent repetitions of what had been said in two articles written some years before, and covering, in part, the same ground.]

1. " Della Letteratura Italiana, Di Camillo Ugoni."—3 tom. 12mo. Brescia, 1820.

2. " Storia della Letteratura Italiana. Del cavaliere Giuseppe Maffei."—3 tom. 12mo. Milano, 1825.

3. " Storia della Letteratura Italiana nel secolo XVIII. di Antonio Lombardi."—3 tom. 8vo. Modena, 1827-9

to be applied to literary purposes. The poem of the Cid, which, with all its rawness, exhibits the frank bearing of the age in a highly poetic aspect, was written nearly a century previously to this event. The northern French, which even some Italian scholars of that day condescended to employ as the most popular vehicle of thought, had been richly cultivated, indemnifying itself in anticipation, as it were, by this extraordinary precocity, for the poetic sterility with which it has been cursed ever since. In the South, and along the shores of the Mediterranean, every remote corner was alive with the voice of song. A beautiful poetry had ripened into perfection there, and nearly perished, before the first lispings of the Italian muse were heard, not in her own land, but at the court of a foreigner, in Sicily. The poets of Lombardy wrote in the Provençal. The histories—and almost every city had its historian, and some two or three—were composed in Latin, or in some half-formed, discordant dialect of the country. "The Italian of that age," says Tiraboschi, "more nearly resembled the Latin than the Tuscan does now any of her sister dialects." It seemed doubtful which of the conflicting idioms would prevail, when a mighty genius arose, who, collecting the scattered elements together, formed one of those wonderful creations which make an epoch in the history of civilization, and forever fixed the destinies of his language.

We shall not trouble our readers with a particular criticism on so popular a work as the Divine

Comedy, but confine ourselves to a few such desultory observations as have been suggested on a reperusal of it. The Inferno is more frequently quoted and eulogized than any other portion of the Commedia. It exhibits a more marked progress of the action, and, while it affects us by its deepened pictures of misery, it owes, no doubt, something to the piquant personalities which have to this day not entirely lost their relish. Notwithstanding this, it by no means displays the whole of its author's intellectual power, and so very various are the merits of the different portions of his epic, that one who has not read the whole may be truly said not to have read Dante. The poet has borrowed the hints for his punishments partly from ancient mythology, partly from the metaphorical denunciations of Scripture, but principally from his own inexhaustible fancy; and he has adapted them to the specific crimes with a truly frightful ingenuity. We could wish that he had made more use of the mind as a means of torture, and thus given a finer moral colouring to the picture. This defect is particularly conspicuous in his portraiture of Satan, who, far different from that spirit whose form had not yet lost all her original brightness, is depicted in the gross and superstitious terrors of a childish imagination. This decidedly bad taste must be imputed to the rudeness of the age in which Dante lived. The progress of refinement is shown in Tasso's subsequent portrait of this same personage, who, " towering like Calpe or huge Atlas," is sustained by that unconquerable temper which gives life to the yet more spiritualized conceptions of Milton. The faults of Dante were those of his age; but in his elevated conceptions, in the wild and desolating gloom which he has thrown around the city of the dead, the world saw, for the first time, the genius of modern literature fully displayed; and in his ripe and vigorous versification, it beheld also, for the first time, the poetical capacities of a modern idiom.*

The Purgatory relies for its interest on no strong emotion, but on a contemplative moral tone, and on such luxuriant descriptions of nature as bring it much nearer to the style of English poetry than any other part of the work. It is on the Paradise, however, that Dante has lavished all the stores of his fancy. Yet he has not succeeded in his attempt to exhibit there a regular gradation of happiness; for happiness cannot, like pain, be measured by any scale of physical sensations. Neither is he always successful in the notions which he has conveyed of the occupations of the blessed. There was no source whence he could derive this knowledge. The Scriptures present no determinate idea of such occupations, and the mythology of the ancients had so little that was consolatory in it, even to themselves, that the shade of Achilles is made to say, in the Odyssey, that "he had rather be the slave of the

* Dante anticipated the final triumph of the Italian with a generous confidence, not shared by the more timid scholars of his own or the succeeding age. See his eloquent apology for it in his Convito, especially p. 81, 82, tom. iv., ed. 1758. See, also, Purg., can. xxiv.

Q q q

meanest living man than rule as a sovereign among the dead."

Dante wisely placed the moral sources of happiness in the exercises of the mind. The most agreeable of these to himself, though, perhaps, to few of his readers, was metaphysical polemics. He had, unfortunately, in his youth gained a prize for successful disputation at the schools, and in every page of these gladiatorial exhibitions we discern the disciple of Scotus and Aquinas. His *matériel* is made up of light, music, and motion. These he has arranged in every possible variety of combination. We are borne along from one magnificent *fête* to another, and, as we rise in the scale of being, the motion of the celestial dance increases in velocity, the light shines with redoubled brilliancy, and the music is of a more ravishing sweetness, until all is confounded in the intolerable splendours of the Deity.

Dante has failed in his attempt to personify the Deity. Who, indeed, has not? No such personification can be effected without the aid of illustration from physical objects, and how degrading are these to our conceptions of Omnipotence! The repeated failures of the Italians who have attempted this in the arts of design are still more conspicuous. Even the genius of Raphael has only furnished another proof of the impotence of his art. The advancement of taste may be again seen in Tasso's representation of the Supreme Being by his attributes,* and, with similar discretion, Milton, like the

* Ger. Lib., cix., s. 56.

Grecian artist who drew a mantle over the countenance which he could not trust himself to paint, whenever he has introduced the Deity, has veiled his glories in a cloud.

The characters and conditions of Dante and Milton were too analogous not to have often invited the parallel. Both took an active part in the revolutions of their age; both lived to see the extinction of their own hopes and the ruin of their party: and it was the fate of both to compose their immortal poems in poverty and disgrace. These circumstances, however, produced different effects on their minds. Milton, in solitude and darkness, from the cheerful ways of men cut off, was obliged to seek inwardly that celestial light, which, as he pathetically laments, was denied to him from without. Hence his poem breathes a spirit of lofty contemplation, which is never disturbed by the impurities that disfigure the page of Dante. The latter poet, an exile in a foreign land, condemned to eat the bread of dependance from the hands of his ancient enemies, felt the iron enter more deeply into his soul, and, in the spirit of his age, has too often made his verses the vehicle of his vindictive scorn. Both stood forth the sturdy champions of freedom in every form, above all, of intellectual freedom. The same spirit which animates the controversial writings of Milton glows with yet fiercer heat in every page of the Divine Comedy. How does its author denounce the abuses, the crying abuses of the Church, its hypocrisies, and manifold perversions of Scripture! How boldly does he declare his determination to proclaim the truth, that he may live in the memory of the just hereafter! His Ghibelline connexions were indeed unfavourable to these principles; but these connexions were the result of necessity, not of choice. His hardy spirit had been nursed in the last ages of the Republic; and it may be truly said of him that he became a Ghibelline in the hope of again becoming a Florentine. The love of his native soil, as with most exiles, was a vital principle with him. How pathetically does he recall those good old times when the sons of Florence were sure to find a grave within her walls! Even the bitterness of his heart against her, which breaks forth in the very courts of heaven, proves, paradoxical as it may appear, the tenacity of his affection. It might not be easy to rouse the patriotism of a modern Italian even into this symptom of vitality.

The genius of both was of the severest kind. For this reason, any display of their sensibility, like the light breaking through a dark cloud, affects us the more by contrast. Such are the sweet pictures of domestic bliss in Paradise Lost, and the tender tale of Francesca di Rimini in the Inferno. Both are sublime in the highest signification of the term; but Milton is an ideal poet, and delights in generalization, while Dante is the most literal of artists, and paints everything in detail. He refuses no imagery, however mean, that can illustrate his subject. This is too notorious to require exemplification. He is, moreover, eminently distinguished by the power of depicting his thought by a single vigorous touch, a manner well known in Italy under the name of *Dantesque*. It would not be easy for such a verse as the following, without sacrifice of idiom, to be condensed within the same compass in our language:

" Con viso, che tacendo dicea, taci."

It would be interesting to trace the similarity of tastes in these great minds, as exhibited in their pleasures equally with their serious pursuits ; in their exquisite sensibility to music ; in their early fondness for those ancient romances which they have so often celebrated both in prose and verse ; but our limits will not allow us to pursue the subject farther.

Dante's epic was greeted by his countrymen in that rude age with the general enthusiasm with which they have ever welcomed the works of genius. A chair was instituted at Florence for the exposition of the Divine Comedy, and Boccaccio was the first who filled it. The bust of its author was crowned with laurels ; his daughter was maintained at the public expense ; and the fickle Florentines vainly solicited from Ravenna the ashes of their poet, whom they had so bitterly persecuted when living.

Notwithstanding all this, the father of Italian verse has had a much less sensible influence on the taste of his countrymen than either of the illustrious triumvirate of the fourteenth century. His bold, masculine diction and his concentrated thought were ill suited to the effeminacy of his nation. One or two clumsy imitators of him appeared in his own age ; and in ours a school has been formed, professing to be modelled on the severe principles of the *trecentisti;* but no one has yet arisen to bend the bow of Ulysses.

Several poets wrote in the Tuscan or Italian dialect at the close of the thirteenth century with tolerable purity; but their amorous effusions would, probably, like those in the Provençal, have rapidly passed into oblivion, had the language not been consecrated by some established work of genius like the Divina Commedia. It was fortunate that its author selected a subject which enabled him to exhibit the peculiar tendency of Christianity and of modern institutions, and to demonstrate their immense superiority for poetical purposes over those of antiquity. It opened a cheering prospect to those who doubted the capacities of a modern idiom; and, after ages of barbarism, it was welcomed as the sign that the waters had at length passed from the face of the earth.

We have been detained long upon Dante, though somewhat contrary to our intention of discussing classes rather than individuals, from the circumstance that he constitutes in himself, if we may so say, an entire and independent class. We shall now proceed, as concisely as possible, to touch upon some of the leading peculiarities in the lyrical poetry of the Italians, which forms with them a very important branch of letters.

Lyrical poetry is more immediately the offspring of imagination, or of deep feeling, than any other kind of verse, and there can be little chance of reaching to high excellence in it among a nation whose character is defective in these qualities. The Italians are, undoubtedly, the most prolific in this department, as the French are the least so, of any people in Europe. Nothing can be more mechanical than a French ode. Reason, wit, pedantry, anything but inspiration, find their way into it; and when the poet is in extremity, like the countryman in the fable, he calls upon the pagan gods of antiquity to help him out. The best ode in the language, according to La Harpe, is that of J. B. Rousseau on the Count de Luc, in which Phœbus, or the Fates, Pluto, Ceres, or Cybele, figure in every stanza. There is little of the genuine *impetus sacer* in all this. Lyrical compositions, the expression of natural sensibility, are generally most abundant in the earlier periods of a nation's literature. Such are the beautiful collections of rural minstrelsy in our own tongue, and the fine old ballads and songs in the Castilian; which last have had the advantage over ours of being imitated down to a late day by their most polished writers. But Italy is the only country in which lyrical composition, from the first, instead of assuming a plebeian garb, has received all the perfection of literary finish, and which, amid every vicissitude of taste, has been cultivated by the most polished writers of the age.

One cause of this is to be found in the circumstances and peculiar character of the father of Italian song. The life of Petrarch furnishes the most brilliant example of the triumph of letters in a country where literary celebrity has been often the path to political consequence. Princes and pontiffs, cities and universities, vied with each other in lavishing honours upon him. His tour through Italy was a sort of royal progress, the inhabitants of the cities thronging out to meet him, and providing a residence for him at the public expense.

The two most enlightened capitals in Europe contended with each other for the honour of his poetical coronation. His influence was solicited in the principal negotiations of the Italian States, and he enjoyed, at the same time, the confidence of the ferocious Visconti and the accomplished Robert of Naples. His immense correspondence connected him with the principal characters, both literary and political, throughout Europe, and his personal biography may be said to constitute the history of his age.

It must be confessed that the heart of Petrarch was not insensible to this universal homage, and that his writings occasionally betray the vanity and caprice which indicate the spoiled child of fortune; but, with this moderate alloy of humanity, his general deportment exhibits a purity of principle and a generous elevation of sentiment far above the degenerate politics of his time. He was, indeed, the first in an age of servility, as Dante had been the last in an age of freedom. If he was intimate with some of the petty tyrants of Lombardy, he never prostituted his genius to the vindication of their vices. His political negotiations were conducted with the most generous and extended views for the weal of all Italy. How independently did he remonstrate with Dandolo on his war with the Genoese! How did he lift his voice against the lawless banditti who, as foreign mercenaries, ravaged the fair plains of Lombardy! How boldly, to a degree which makes it difficult to account for his personal safety, did he thunder his invectives against the western Babylon!

Even his failings were those of a generous nature. Dwelling much of his time at a distance from his native land, he considered himself rather as a citizen of Italy than of any particular district of it. He contemplated her with the eye of an ancient Roman, and wished to see the Imperial City once more resume her supremacy among the nations. This led him for a moment to give in to the brilliant illusion of liberty which Rienzi awakened. "Who would not," he says, appealing to the Romans, "rather die a freeman than live a slave?"* But when he saw that he had been deceived, he did not attempt to conceal his indignation, and, in an animated expostulation with the tribune, he admonishes him that he is the minister, not the master of the Republic, and that treachery to one's country is a crime which nothing can expiate.†

As he wandered amid the ruins of Rome, he contemplated with horror the violation of her venerable edifices, and he called upon the pontiffs to return to the protection of their "widowed metropolis." He was, above all, solicitous for the recovery of the in-

* Epist. ad Nic. Laurentii.—Opera, p. 535.
† Famil. Epist., lib. vii., ep. 7, p. 677, Basil ed.

tellectual treasures of antiquity, sparing no expense or personal fatigue in this cause. Many of the mouldering manuscripts he restored or copied with his own hand; and his beautiful transcript of the epistles of Cicero is still to be seen in the Laurentian Library at Florence.

The influence of his example is visible in the generous emulation for letters kindled throughout Italy, and in the purer principles of taste which directed the studies of the schools.* His extensive correspondence diffused to the remotest corners of Europe the sacred flame which glowed so brightly in his own bosom; and it may be truly said that he possessed an intellectual empire such as was never before enjoyed, and probably never can be again, in the comparatively high state of civilization to which the world is arrived.

It is not, however, the antiquarian researches of Petrarch, nor those elaborate Latin compositions, which secured to him the laurel wreath of poetry in the capitol, that have kept his memory still green in the hearts of his countrymen, but those humbler effusions in his own language, which he did not even condescend to mention in his Letter to Posterity, and which he freely gave away as alms to ballad-singers. It was auspicious for Italian literature that

---

* In Florence, for example, with a population which Villani, at the middle of the fourteenth century, reckons at 90,000 souls, there were from eight to ten thousand children who received a liberal education (Istor. Fiorent., lib. xi., cap. 93), at a time when the higher classes in the rest of Europe were often uninstructed in the elementary principles of knowledge.

a poet like Dante should have been followed by one of so flexible a character as Petrarch. It was beauty succeeding vigour. The language to which Dante had given all its compactness and energy was far from having reached the full harmony of numbers of which it was capable. He had, moreover, occasionally distorted it into such Latinized inversions, uncouth phrases, Hebraisms and Grecisms, as were foreign to the genius of the tongue. These blemishes, of so little account in Dante's extensive poem, would have been fatal to the lyrical pieces of Petrarch, which, like miniatures, from their minuteness, demand the highest finish of detail. The pains which the latter poet bestowed on the correction of his verses are almost inconceivable. Some of them would appear, from the memoranda which he has left, to have been submitted to the file for weeks, nay, months, before he dismissed them. Nor was this fastidiousness of taste frivolous in one who was correcting, not for himself, but for posterity, and who, in these peculiar graces of style, was creating beautiful and permanent forms of expression for his countrymen. His acquaintance with the modern dialects, especially the Spanish and the Provençal, enriched his vocabulary with many exotic beauties. His fine ear disposed him to refuse all but the most harmonious combinations of sound. He was accustomed to try the melody of his verses by the lute, and, like the fabled Theban, built up his elegant fabric by the charms of music. By these means he created a style scarcely more antiquated than that of the present day, and which can hardly be said to contain an obsolete phrase; an assertion not to be ventured respecting any author in our language before the days of Queen Anne. Indeed, even a foreigner can hardly open a page of Petrarch without being struck with the precocity of a language which, like the vegetation of an arctic summer, seems to have ripened into full maturity at once. There is nothing analogous to this in any other tongue with which we are acquainted, unless it be the Greek, which, in the poems of Homer, appears to have attained its last perfection; a circumstance which has led Cicero to remark, in his Brutus, that "there must, doubtless, have existed poets antecedent to Homer, since invention and perfection can hardly go together."

The mass of Petrarch's Italian poetry is, as is well known, of an amorous complexion. He was naturally of a melancholy temperament, and his unfortunate passion became with him the animating principle of being. His compositions in the Latin, as well as those in the vulgar tongue, his voluminous correspondence, his private memoranda or confessions, which, from their nature, seem never to have been destined for the public eye, all exhibit this passion in one shape or another. Yet there have been those who have affected to doubt even the existence of such a personage as Laura.

His Sonnets and Canzoni, chronologically arranged, exhibit pretty fairly the progress of his life and love, and, as such, have been judiciously used by the Abbé de Sade. The most trivial event seems to have stirred the poetic feeling within him. We find no less than four sonnets indited to his mistress's gloves, and three to her eyes; which last, styled, *par excellence*, the "Three Sisters," are in the greatest repute with his countrymen; a judgment on which most English critics would be at issue with them. Notwithstanding the vicious affectation of style and the mysticism which occasionally obscure these and other pieces of Petrarch, his general tone exhibits a moral dignity unknown to the sordid appetites of the ancients, and an earnestness of passion rarely reflected from the cold glitter of the Provençal. But it is in the verses written after the death of his mistress that he confesses the inspiration of Christianity, in the deep moral colouring which he has given to his descriptions of nature, and in those visions of immortal happiness which he contrasts with the sad realities of the present life. He dwells rather on the melancholy pleasures of retrospection than those of hope; unlike most of the poets of Italy, whose warm, sunny skies seem to have scattered the gloom which hangs over the poetry of the North. In this and some other peculiarities, Dante and Petrarch appear to have borne greater resemblance to the English than to their own nation.

Petrarch's career, however brilliant, may serve rather as a warning than as a model. The querulous tone of some of his later writings, the shade of real sorrow, which seems to come across even his brightest moments, show the utter inefficacy of genius and of worldly glory to procure to their possessor a substantial happiness. It is melancholy to witness the aberrations of mind into which so fine a genius was led by unfortunate passion. The apparition of Laura haunted him by night as well as by day, in society and in solitude. He sought to divert his mind by travelling, by political or literary occupation, by reason and religion, but in vain. His letters and private confessions show, no less than his poetry, how incessantly his imagination was tortured by doubts, hopes, fears, melancholy presages, regrets, and despair. She triumphed over the decay of her personal charms, and even over the grave, for it was a being of the mind he worshipped. There is something affecting in seeing such a mind as Petrarch's feeding on this unrequited passion, and more than twenty years after his mistress's death, and when on the verge of the grave himself, depicting her in all the bright colouring of youthful fancy, and following her in anticipation to that Heaven where he hopes soon to be united to her.

Petrarch's example, even in his own day, was widely infectious. He sarcastically complains of the quantities of verses sent to him for correction, from the farthest north, from Germany and the British Isles, then the *Ultima Thule* of civilization. The pedants of the succeeding age, it is true, wasted their efforts in hopeless experiments upon the ancient lan guages, whose chilling influence seems to have entirely closed the hand of the native minstrel; and it was not until the time of Lorenzo de' Medici, whose correct taste led him to prefer the flexible movements of a living tongue, that the sweet tones of the Italian lyre were again awakened. The excitement, however, soon became general, affecting all ranks, from the purpled prelate down to the most humble artisan; and a collection of the *Beauties* (as we should call them) of this latter description of worthies has been gathered into a respectable volume, which Baretti assures us, with a good-natured criticism, may be compared with the verses of Petrarch. In all these the burden of the song is love. Those who did not feel could at least affect the tender passion. Lorenzo de' Medici pitched upon a mistress as deliberately as Don Quixote did on his Dulcinea; and Tasso sighed away his soul to a nymph so shadowy as sorely to have puzzled his commentators till the time of Serassi.

It would be unavailing to attempt to characterize those who have followed in the footsteps of the Laureate, or we might dwell on the romantic sweetness of Lorenzo de' Medici, the purity of Vittoria Colonna, the elaborate polish of Bembo, the vivacity of Marini, and the eloquence, the Platonic reveries, and rich colouring of Tasso, whose beauties and whose defects so nearly resemble those of his great original in this department. But we have no leisure to go minutely into the shades of difference between the imitators of Petrarch. One may regret that, amid their clouds of amorous incense, he can so rarely discern the religious or patriotic enthusiasm which animates the similar compositions of the Spanish poets, and which forms the noblest basis of lyrical poetry at all times. The wrongs of Italy, the common battle-field of the banditti of Europe for nearly a century, and at the very time when her poetic vein flowed most freely, might well have roused the indignation of her children. The comparatively few specimens on this theme from Petrarch to Filicaja are justly regarded as the happiest efforts of the Italian lyre.

The seventeenth century, so unfortunate for the national literature in all other respects, was marked by a bolder deviation from the eternal track of the Petrarchists ; a reform, indeed, which may be traced back to Casa. Among these innovators, Chiabrera, whom Tiraboschi styles both Anacreon and Pindar, but who may be content with the former of these appellations, and Filicaja, who has found in the Christian faith sources of a sublimity that Pindar could never reach, are the most conspicuous. Their salutary example has not been lost on the modern Italian writers.

Some of the ancients have made a distinct division of lyrical poetry, under the title of *melicus*.* If, as it would seem, they mean something of a more calm and uniform tenour than the impetuous dithyrambic flow ; something in which symmetry of form and melody of versification are chiefly considered : in which, in fine, the effeminate beauties of sentiment are preferred to the more hardy conceptions of fancy, the term may be significant of the great mass of Italian lyrics. But we fear that we have

* Ausonius, Edyl. IV., 54.—Cicero, De Opt. Gen. Oratorum, I.

insisted too far on their defects. Our criticism has been formed rather on the average than on the highest specimens of the art. In this way the very luxuriance of the soil is a disadvantage to it. The sins of exuberance, however, are much more corrigible than those of sterility, which fall upon this department of poetry in almost every other nation. We must remember, too, that no people has exhibited the passion of love under such a variety of beautiful aspects, and that, after all, although the amount be comparatively small, no other modern nation can probably produce so many examples of the very highest lyrical inspiration.

But it is time that we should return to the Romantic Epics, the most important, and, perhaps, the most prolific branch of the ornamental literature of the Italians. They have been distributed into a great variety of classes by their own critics. We shall confine our remarks to some of their most eminent models, without regard to their classification.

Those who expect to find in these poems the same temper which animates the old English tales of chivalry, will be disappointed. A much more correct notion of their manner may be formed from Mr. Ellis's *Bernesque* (if we may be allowed a significant term) recapitulations of these latter. In short, they are the marvels of an heroic age, told with the fine incredulous air of a polite one. It is this contrast of the dignity of the matter with the familiarity of the manner of narration that has occasioned among their countrymen so many animated disputes respecting the serious or satirical intentions of Pulci, Ariosto, Berni, and the rest.

The Italians, although they have brought tales of chivalry to higher perfection than any other people in the world, are, of all others, in their character the most anti-chivalrous. Their early Republican institutions, which brought all classes nearly to the same level, were obviously unfavourable to the spirit of chivalry. Commerce became the road to preferment. Wealth was their pedigree, and their patent of nobility. The magnificent Medici were bankers and merchants; and the ancient aristocracy of Venice employed their capital in traffic until an advanced period of the Republic. Courage, so essential in the character of a knight, was of little account in the busy communities of Italy. Like Carthage of old, they trusted their defence to mercenaries, first foreign, and afterward native, but who in every instance fought for hire, not honour, selling themselves, and often their employers, to the highest bidder; and who, cased in impenetrable mail, fought with so little personal hazard, that Machiavelli has related more than one infamous encounter in which the only lives lost were from suffocation under their ponderous panoplies. So low had the military reputation of the Italians declined, that in the war of the Neapolitan succession in 1502, it was thought necessary for thirteen of their body to vindicate the national character from the imputation of cowardice by solemn defiance and battle against an equal number of French knights, in presence of the hostile armies.

Hence other arts came to be studied than that of war—the arts of diplomacy and intrigue. Hence statesmen were formed, but not soldiers. The campaign was fought in the cabinet instead of the field. Every spring of cunning and corruption was essayed, and an insidious policy came into vogue, in which, as the philosopher, who has digested its principles into a system, informs us, "the failure, not the atrocity of a deed, was considered disgraceful."* The law of honour became different with the Italians from what it was with other nations. Conspiracy was preferred to open defiance, and assassination was a legitimate method of revenge. The State of Venice condescended to employ a secret agent against the life of Francis Sforza; and the noblest escutcheons in Italy, those of Este and the Medici, were stained with the crimes of fratricide and incest

In this general moral turpitude, the literature of Italy was rapidly rising to its highest perfection. There was scarcely a petty state which, in the fourteenth, fifteenth, and beginning of the sixteenth centuries, had not made brilliant advances in elegant prose, poetry, or the arts of design. Intellectual culture was widely diffused, and men of the highest rank devoted themselves with eagerness to the occupation of letters; this, too, at a time when learning in other countries was banished to colleges and cloisters; when books were not always essential in the education of a gentleman. Du Guesclin, the flower of French chivalry in the fourteenth century,

* Machiavelli, Istor. Fior., l. vi.

could not read a word. Castiglione, in his Cortegiano, has given us so pleasing a picture of the recreations of the little court of Urbino, one of the
many into which Italy was distributed at the close
of the fifteenth century, as to suggest an exalted notion of its taste and cultivated habits; and Guicciardini has described, with all the eloquence of regret, the flourishing condition of his country at the
same period, ere the storm had descended on her
beautiful valleys. In all this we see the characteristics of a highly polished state of society, but none
of the hardy virtues of chivalry.

It was precisely in such a state of society, light,
lively, and licentious, possessed of a high relish for
the beauties of imagination, but without moral dignity, or even a just moral sense, that the Muse of
romance first appeared in Italy; and it was not to
be expected that she would retain there her majestic
Castilian port, or the frank, cordial bearing which
endeared her to our Norman ancestors. In fact, the
Italian fancy seems to have caught rather the gay,
gossiping temper of the *fabliaux*. The most familiar and grotesque adventures are mixed in with the
most serious, and even these last are related in a
fine tone of ironical pleasantry. Magnificent inventions are recommended by agreeable illusions of
style; but they not unfrequently furnish a flimsy
drapery for impurity of sentiment. The high devotion and general moral aspect of our English Faerie
Queene are not characteristic, with a few eminent
exceptions, of Italian tales of chivalry, in which we

too often find the best interests of our nature exposed to all the license of frivolous banter. Pulci, who has furnished an apology for the infamous Pucelle,* and Fortiguerra, with their school of imitators, may afford abundant examples to the curious in these matters.

The first successful models of the romantic epic were exhibited at the table of Lorenzo de' Medici; that remarkable man, who, as Machiavelli says of him, "seemed to unite in his person two distinct natures"—who could pass from the severe duties of the council-chamber to mingle in the dances of the people, and from the abstractions of his favourite philosophy to the broad merriment of a convivial table. Amid all the elegance of the Medici, however—of Lorenzo and Leo X.—there seems to have been a lurking appetite for vulgar pleasure, at least if we may judge from the coarse, satirical repartee which Franco and his friend Pulci poured out upon one another for the entertainment of their patron, and the still more bald buffoonery which enlightened the palace of his pontifical son.

The Stanze of Politian, however, exhibit no trace of this obliquity of taste. This fragment of an epic, almost too brief for criticism, like a prelude to some beautiful air, seems to have opened the way to those delightful creations of the Muse which so rapidly followed, and to have contained within itself their

---

* See Voltaire's preface to it. Chapelain's prosy poem on the same subject, La Pucelle d'Orleans, lives now only in the satire of Boileau. It was the hard fate of the Heroine of Orleans to be canonized in a dull epic, and damned in a witty one.

2 S*

various elements of beauty: the invention of Boiardo, the picturesque narrative of Ariosto, and Tasso's flush of colour. Every stanza is music to the ear, and affords a distinct picture to the eye. Unfortunately, Politian was soon seduced by the fashion of the age from the culture of his native tongue. Probably no Italian poet of equal promise was ever sacrificed to the manes of antiquity. His voluminous Latin labours are now forgotten, and this fragment of an epic affords almost the only point from which he is still contemplated by posterity.

Pulci's Morgante is the first thorough-bred romance of chivalry which the Italians have received as *text of the tongue.* It is fashioned much more literally than any of its successors, on Turpin's Chronicle, that gross medley of fact and fable, too barren for romance, too false for history; the dunghill from which have shot up, nevertheless, the bright flowers of French and Italian fiction. In like manner as in this, religion, not love, is the principle of Pulci's action. The theological talk of his devils may remind one of the prosy conference of Roland and Ferracute; and, strange to say, he is the only one of the eminent Italian poets who has adopted from the chronicle the celebrated rout at Roncesvalles. In his concluding cantos, which those who have censured him as a purely satirical or burlesque poet can have hardly reached, Pulci, throwing off the vulgar trammels which seem to have oppressed his genius, rises into the noblest conceptions of poetry, and describes the tragical catastrophe with all the eloquence of pathos and moral grandeur. Had he written often thus, the Morgante would now be resorted to by native purists, not merely as the well of Tuscan undefiled, but as the genuine fount of epic inspiration.

From the rank and military profession of Boiardo, it might be expected that his poem, the Orlando Innamorato, would display more of the lofty tone of chivalry than is usual with his countrymen; but, with some exceptions, the portrait of Ruggiero, for example, it will be difficult to discern this. He, however, excels them all in a certain force of characterizing, and in an inexhaustible fertility of invention. His *dramatis personæ*, continued by Ariosto, might afford an excellent subject for a parallel, which we have not room to discuss. In general, he may be said to sculpture where Ariosto paints. His heroes assume a fiercer and more indomitable aspect, and his Amazonian females a more glaring and less fastidious coquetry. But it is in the regions of pure fancy that his muse delights to sport, where, instead of the cold conceptions of a Northern brain, which make up the machinery of Pulci, we are introduced to the delicate fairies of the East, to gardens blooming in the midst of the desert, to palaces of crystal, winged steeds, enchanted armour, and all the gay fabric of Oriental mythology. It has been the singular fate of Boiardo to have had his story continued and excelled by one poet, and his style reformed by another, until his own original work, and even his name, have passed into comparative oblivion. Berni's *rifacimento* is perhaps the most remarkable instance of the triumph of style on record. Every stanza reflects the sense of the original; yet such is the fascination of his diction, compared with the provincial barbarism of his predecessor, as to remind one of those mutations in romance where some old and withered hag is suddenly transformed into a blooming fairy. It may be doubted whether this could have succeeded so completely in a language where the beauties of style are less appreciated. Dryden has made a similar attempt in the Canterbury Tales; but who does not prefer the racy, romantic sweetness of Chaucer?

The Orlando Furioso, from its superior literary execution, as well as from its union of all the peculiarities of Italian tales of chivalry, may be taken as the representative of the whole species. Some of the national critics have condemned, and some have endeavoured to justify these peculiarities of the romantic epopee; its complicated narrative and provoking interruptions, its transitions from the gravest to the most familiar topics, its lawless extravagance of fiction, and other deviations from the statutes of antiquity—but very few have attempted to explain them on just and philosophical principles. The romantic eccentricities of the Italian poets are not to be imputed either to inattention or ignorance. Most of them were accomplished scholars, and went to their work with all the forecast of consummate artists. Boiardo was so well versed in the ancient tongues as to have made accurate translations of

Herodotus and Apuleius. Ariosto was such an elegant Latinist, that even the classic Bembo did not disdain to learn from him the mysteries of Horace. He consulted his friends over and over again on the disposition of his fable, assigning to them the most sufficient reasons for its complicated texture. In like manner, Tasso shows, in his Poetical Discourses, how deeply he had revolved the principles of his art, and his Letters prove his dexterity in the application of these principles to his own compositions. These illustrious minds understood well the difference between copying the ancients and copying nature. They knew that to write by the rules of the former is not to write like them; that the genius of our institutions requires new and peculiar forms of expression; that nothing is more fantastic than a modern antique; and they wisely left the attempt and the failure to such spiritless pedants as Trissino.

The difference subsisting between the ancients and moderns, in the constitution of society, amply justifies the different principles on which they have proceeded in their works of imagination. Religion, love, honour—what different ideas are conveyed by these terms in these different periods of history!* The love of country was the pervading feeling

How feeble, as an operative principle, must religion have been among a people who openly avowed it to be the creation of their own poets. "Homer and Hesiod," says Herodotus, "created the theogony of the Greeks, assigning to the gods their various titles, characters, and forms." —Herod., ii., 63. Religion, it is well known, was a principal basis of modern chivalry.

T T T

which, in the ancient Greek or Roman, seems to have absorbed every other, and to have obliterated, as it were, the moral idiosyncrasy of the individual, while with the moderns it is the *individual* who stands forward in principal relief. His loves, his private feuds and personal adventures, form the object almost of exclusive attention. Hence, in the classical fable, strict unity of action and concentration of interest are demanded, while in the romantic, the object is best attained by variety of action and diversity of interest, and the threads of personal adventure separately conducted, and perpetually intersecting each other, make up the complicated texture of the fable. Hence it becomes so exceedingly difficult to discern who is the real hero, and what the main action, in such poems as the Innamorato and Furioso. Hence, too, the episode, the accident, if we may so say, of the classical epic, becomes the essence of the romantic. On this explication, Tasso's delightful excursions, his adventures of Sophronia and Erminia, so often condemned as excrescences, may be admired as perfectly legitimate beauties.

The poems of Homer were intended as historical compositions. They were revered and quoted as such by the most circumspect of the national writers, as Thucydides and Strabo, for example. The romantic poets, on the other hand, seem to have intended nothing beyond a mere *délassement* of the imagination. The old Norman epics, it is true, exhibit a wonderful coincidence in their delineations of manners with the contemporary chronicles. But this is not the spirit of Italian romance, which has rarely had any higher ostensible aim than that of pure amusement.

> " Scritta così come la penna getta,
> Per fuggir l'ozio, e non per cercar gloria,"

and which was right, therefore, in seeking its materials in the wildest extravagances of fiction, the *magnanime menzogne* of chivalry, and the brilliant chimeras of the East.

The immortal epics of Ariosto and Tasso are too generally known to require from us any particular analysis. Some light, however, may be reflected on these poets from a contrast of their peculiarities. The period in which Tasso wrote was one of high religious fermentation. The Turks, who had so long overawed Europe, had recently been discomfited in the memorable sea-fight of Lepanto, and the kindling enthusiasm of the nations seemed to threaten for a moment to revive the follies of the Crusades. Tasso's character was of a kind to be peculiarly sensible to these influences. His soul was penetrated with religious fervour, to which, as Serassi has shown, more than to any cause of mysterious passion, are to be imputed his occasional mental aberrations. He was distinguished, moreover, by his chivalrous personal valour, put to the test in more than one hazardous encounter; and he was reckoned the most expert swordsman of his time. Tasso's peculiarities of character were singularly suited to his subject. He has availed himself of this to the full in exhibiting the resources and triumphs of

Christian chivalry. The intellectual rather than the physical attributes of his supernatural agents, his solemn meditations on the fragility of earthly glory, and the noble ardour with which he leads us to aspire after an imperishable crown, give to his epic a moral grandeur which no preceding poet had ever reached. It has been objected to him, however, that he preferred the intervention of subordinate agents to that of the Deity; but the God of the Christians cannot be introduced like those of pagan mythology. They espoused the opposite sides of the contest; but, wherever He appears, the balance is no longer suspended, and the poetical interest is consequently destroyed.

> "Victrix causa Diis placuit, sed victa Catoni."

This might be sublime with the ancients, but would be blasphemous and absurd with the moderns, and Tasso judged wisely in availing himself of inferior and intermediate ministers.

Ariosto's various subject,

> "Le donne, i cavalier', l'arme, gli amori,"

was equally well suited with Tasso's to his own various and flexible genius. It did not, indeed, admit of the same moral elevation, in which he was himself perhaps deficient, but it embraced within its range every variety of human passion and portraiture. Tasso was of a solitary, as Ariosto was of a social temper. He had no acquaintance with affairs, and Gravina accuses him of drawing his knowledge from books instead of men. He turned his thoughts inward, and matured them by deep and serious meditation. He had none of the volatile talents of his rival, who seems to have parted with his brilliant fancies as readily as the tree gives up its leaves in autumn. Ariosto was a man of the world, and in his philosophy may be styled an Epicurean. His satires show a familiarity with the practical concerns of life, and a deep insight into the characters of men. His conceptions, however, were of the earth; and his pure style, which may be compared with Alcina's transparent drapery, too often reveals to us the grossest impurity of thought.

The muse of Tasso was of a heavenly nature, and nourished herself with celestial visions and ideal forms of beauty. He was a disciple of Plato, and hence the source of his general elevation of thought, and too often of his mystical abstraction. The healthful bloom of his language imparts an inexpressible charm to the purity of his sentiments, and it is truly astonishing that so chaste and dignified a composition should have been produced in an age and court so corrupt.

Both of these great artists elaborated their style with the utmost care, but with totally different results. This frequently gave to Tasso's verse the finish of a lyrical, or, rather, of a musical composition; for many of his stanzas have less resemblance to the magnificent rhythm of Petrarch than to the melodious monotony of Metastasio. This must be considered a violation of the true epic style. It is singular that Tasso himself, in one of his poetical criticisms, should have objected this very defect to his

4

2 T

rival.* The elaboration of Ariosto, on the other hand, resulted in that exquisite negligence, or, rather, artlessness of expression, so easy in appearance, but so difficult in reality to be imitated:

"Facil' versi che costan tanta pena."

The Jerusalem Delivered is placed, by the nice discrimination of the Italian critics, at the head of their heroic epics. In its essence, however, it is strictly romantic, though in its form it is accommodated to the general proportions of the antique. In Ariosto's complicated fable it is difficult to discern either a leading hero or a predominant action. Sismondi applauds Ginguené for having discovered this hero in Ruggiero. But both these writers might have found this discovery, where it was revealed more than two centuries ago, in Tasso's own Discourses.† We doubt, however, its accuracy, and cannot but think that the prominent part assigned to Orlando, from whom the poem derives its name, manifests a different intention in the author.

The stately and imposing beauties of Tasso's epic have rendered it generally the most acceptable to foreigners, while the volatile graces of Ariosto have made him most popular with his own nation. Both poets have had the rare felicity, not only of obtaining the applause of the learned, but of circulating among the humblest classes of their countrymen Fragments of the Furioso are still recited by the *lazzaroni* of Naples, as those of the Jerusalem once were by the gondoliers of Venice, where this beau-

* Discorsi Poetici, iii.   † Ibid., ii

*ti*ful epic, broken up into ballads, might be heard for miles along the canals on a tranquil summer evening. Had Boileau, who so bitterly sneers at the *clinquant* of Tasso, "heard these musical contests," says Voltaire, "he would have had nothing to say." It is worthy of remark, that these two celebrated poems, together with the Aminta, the Pastor Fido, and the Secchia Rapita, were all produced within the brief compass of a century, in the petty principality of the house of Este, which thus seemed to indemnify itself for its scanty territory by its ample acquisitions in the intellectual world.

The mass of epical imitations in Italy, both of Ariosto and Tasso, especially the former, is perfectly overwhelming. Nor is it easy to understand the patience with which the Italians have resigned themselves to these interminable poems of seventy, eighty, or even ninety thousand verses each. Many of them, it must be admitted, are the work of men of real genius, and, in a literature less fruitful in epic excellence, would have given a wide celebrity to their authors; and the amount of others of less note, in a department so rarely attempted in other countries, shows in the nation at large a wonderful fecundity of fancy.

The Italians, desirous of combining as many attractions as possible, and extremely sensible to harmony, have not, as has been the case in France and England, divested their romances of the music of verse. They have rarely adopted a national subject for their story, but have condescended to borrow those of the old Norman minstrels; and in conformity with the characteristic temperament of the nation, they have almost always preferred the mercurial temper of the court of Charlemagne to the more sober complexion of the Round Table.*

With a few exceptions, the romantic poets, since the time of Ariosto, appear to have gained as little in elevation of sentiment as in national feeling. The nice classification of their critics seems to relate only to their varieties of comic character, and as we descend to a later period, the fine, equivocal raillery of the older romances degenerates into a broad and undisguised burlesque. In the latter class, the Ricciardetto of Fortiguerra is a jest rather than a satire upon tales of chivalry. The singular union which this work exhibits of elegance of style and homeliness of subject, may have furnished, especially in its introduction, the model of that species of poetry which Lord Byron has familiarized us with in Don Juan, where the contrast of sentiment and satire, of vivid passion and chill misanthropy, of images of beauty and splenetic sarcasm, may remind one of the whimsical combinations in Alpine scenery, where the strawberry blooms on the verge of a snow-wreath.

The Italians claim to have given the first models of mock heroic poetry in modern times. The Secchia Rapita of Tassoni has the merit of a graceful versification, exhibiting many exquisite pictures of

---

* The French antiquary, Tressan, furnishes an exception to the general criticism of his countrymen, in admitting the superiority of this latter class of romances over those of Charlemagne.

voluptuous repose, and some passages of an imposing
grandeur. But these accord ill with the vulgar mer
riment and general burlesque tone of the piece,
which, on the whole, presents a strange medley of
beauties and blemishes mixed up promiscuously together. Twelve cantos of hard fighting and cutting
of throats are far too serious for a joke. The bloodless battle of the books in the Lutrin, or those of
the pot-valiant heroes of Knickerbocker, are in much
better keeping. The Italians have no poetry of a
mezzo carattere like our Rape of the Lock,* where
a fine atmosphere of irony pervades the piece, and
gives life to every character in it. They appear to
delight in that kind of travestie which reduces great
things into little, but which is of a much less spiritual nature than that which exalts little things into
great. Parini's exquisite Giorno, if the satire had
not rather too sharp an edge, might furnish an exception to both these remarks.

But it is time that we should turn to the *Novelle*,
those delightful " tales of pleasantry and love," which
form one of the most copious departments of the
national literature. And here we may remark two
peculiarities: first, that similar tales in France and
England fell entirely into neglect after the fifteenth
century, while in Italy they have been cultivated
with the most unwearied assiduity from their earliest appearance to the present hour; secondly, that
in both the former countries the *fabliaux* were almost
universally exhibited in a poetical dress, while in

* Pignotti, Stor. del. Toscana, tom. x., p 132.

Italy, contrary to the popular taste on all other occasions, they have been as uniformly exhibited in prose. These peculiarities are undoubtedly to be imputed to the influence of Boccaccio, whose transcendent genius gave a permanent popularity to this kind of composition, and finally determined the forms of elegant prose with his nation.

The appearance of the Decameron is, in some points of view, as remarkable a phenomenon as that of the Divine Comedy. It furnishes the only example on record of the almost simultaneous development of prose and poetry in the literature of a nation. The earliest prose of any pretended literary value in the Greek tongue, the most precocious of any of antiquity, must be placed near four centuries after the poems of Homer. To descend to modern times, the Spaniards have a little work, "El Conde Lucanor," nearly contemporary with the Decameron, written on somewhat of a similar plan, but far more didactic in its purport. Its style, though marked by a certain freshness and *naïveté*, the healthy beauties of an infant dialect, has nothing of a classical finish ; to which, indeed, Castilian prose, notwithstanding its fine old chronicles and romances, can make no pretension before the close of the fifteenth century. In France, a still later period must be assigned for this perfection. Dante, it is true, speaks of the peculiar suitableness of the French language in his day for prose narration, on account of its flexibility and freedom ;* but Dante had few

* De Vulg. Eloq., lib. i., cap. x.

and very inadequate standards of comparison, and experience has shown how many ages of purification it was to undergo before it could become the vehicle of elegant composition. Pascal's Provincial Letters furnish, in the opinion of the national critics, the earliest specimen of good prose. It would be more difficult to agree upon the author, or the period that arrested the fleeting forms of expression in our own language; but we certainly could not venture upon an earlier date than the conclusion of the seventeenth century.

The style of the Decameron exhibits the full maturity of an Augustan age. The finish of its periods, its long, Latinized involutions, but especially its redundancy and Asiatic luxury of expression, vices imputed to Cicero by his own contemporaries, as Quintilian informs us, reveal to us the model on which Boccaccio diligently formed himself. In the more elevated parts of his subject he reaches to an eloquence not unworthy of the Roman orator himself. The introductions to his novels, chiefly descriptive, are adorned with all the music and the colouring of poetry; much too poetic, indeed, for the prose of any other tongue. It cannot be doubted that this brilliant piece of mechanism has had an immense influence on the Italians, both in seducing them into a too exclusive attention to mere beauties of style, and in leading them to solicit such beauties in graver and less appropriate subjects than those of pure invention.

In the celebrated description of the Plague, how

ever, Boccaccio has shown a muscular energy of diction quite worthy of the pen of Thucydides. Yet there is no satisfactory evidence that he had read the similar performance of the Greek historian, and the conjecture of Baldelli to that effect is founded only on a resemblance of some detached passages, which might well occur in treating of a similar disease.* In the delineation of its fearful moral consequences, Boccaccio has undoubtedly surpassed his predecessor. It is singular that of the three celebrated narratives of this distemper, that by the Englishman, De Foe, is by far the most circumstantial in its details, and yet that he was the only one of the three historians who was not an eyewitness to what he relates.† The Plague of London happened in the year succeeding his birth.

The Italian novelists have followed so closely in the track of Boccaccio, that we may discuss their general attributes without particular reference to him, their beauties and their blemishes varying only in degree. They ransacked every quarter for their inventions : Eastern legends, Norman *fabliaux;* domestic history, tradition, and vulgar, contemporary anecdote. They even helped themselves, *plenis manibus,* to one another's fancies, particularly filching from the Decameron, which has for this reason been pleasantly compared to a pawnbroker's shop. But no exceptions seem to be taken at such plagia-

* Vita di Boccaccio, lib. ii., s. 2, note.

† It seems probable, however, from a passage in Boccaccio, cited by Bandelli, that he witnessed the plague in some other city of Italy than Florence.

rism, and, as long as the story could be disguised in a different dress, they cared little for the credit of the invention. These fictions are oftentimes of the most grotesque and improbable character, exhibiting no great skill in the *liaison* of events, which are strung together with the rude artlessness of a primitive *trouveur*, while most promising beginnings are frequently brought up by flat and impotent conclusions. Many of the *novelle* are made up of mere personal anecdote, proverbialisms, and Florentine table-talk, the ingredients of an encyclopedia of wit. In all this, however, we often find less wit than merriment, which shows itself in the most puerile practical jokes, played off upon idiots, unfortunate pedants, and other imbeciles, with as little taste as feeling.

The *novelle* wear the usual light and cheerful aspect of Italian literature. They seldom aim at a serious or didactic purpose. Their tragical scenes, though very tragical, are seldom affecting. We recollect in them no example of the passion of love treated with the depth and tenderness of feeling so frequent in the English dramatists and novelists. They can make little pretension, indeed, to accurate delineation of character of any sort. Even Boccaccio, who has acquired, in our opinion, a somewhat undeserved celebrity in this way, paints professions rather than individuals. The brevity of the Italian tale, which usually affords space only for the exhibition of a catastrophe, is an important obstacle to a gradual development of character.

A remarkable trait in these *novelle* is the extreme boldness with which the reputations of the clergy are handled. Their venality, lechery, hypocrisy, and abominable impositions are all exposed with a reckless independence. The head of the Church himself is not spared. It is not easy to account for this authorized latitude in a country where so jealous a *surveillance* has been maintained over the freedom of the press in relation to other topics. Warton attempts to explain it, as far as regards the Decameron, by supposing that the ecclesiastics of that age had become tainted with the dissoluteness so prevalent after the Plague of 1348; and Madame de Staël suggests that the government winked at this license as the jesting of children, who are content to obey their masters so they may laugh at them. But neither of these solutions will suffice; for the license of Boccaccio has been assumed more or less by nearly every succeeding novelist, and the jests of this merry tribe have been converted into the most stinging satire on the clergy, in the hands of the gravest and most powerful writers of the nation, from Dante to Monti.

It may be truly objected to the Italian novelists, that they have been as little solicitous about purity of sentiment as they have been too much so about purity of style. The reproach of indecency lies heavily upon most of their writings, from the Decameron to the infamous tales of Casti, which, reeking with the corruption of a brothel, have passed into several surreptitious editions during the present century. This indecency is not always a mere excrescence, but deeply ingrained in the body of the piece. It is not conveyed in innuendo, or softened under the varnish of sentiment, but is exhibited in all the nakedness of detail which a debauched imagination can divine. Petrarch's encomiastic letter to his friend Boccaccio, written at the close of his own life, in which he affects to excuse the licentiousness of the Decameron from the youth of the author,* although he was turned of forty when he composed it, has been construed into an ample apology for their own transgressions by the subsequent school of novelists.

It is true that some of the popes, of a more fastidious conscience, have taken exceptions at the license of the Decameron, and have placed it on the Index; but an expurgated edition, whose only alteration consisted in the substitution of lay names for those of the clergy, set all things right again.

Such adventures as the seduction of a friend's wife, or the deceptions practised upon a confiding husband, are represented as excellent pieces of wit in these fictions—in some of the best of them, even; and often when their authors would be moral, they betray, in their confused perceptions of right and wrong, the most deplorable destitution of a moral sense. Grazzini (*il Lasca*), one of the most popular of the tribe of the sixteenth century, after invoking, in the most solemn manner, the countenance of the Deity upon his labours, and beseeching him

* Petrarca Op., ed. Basil., p. 540

to inspire his mind with " such thoughts only as may redound to his praise and glory," enters immediately, in the next page, upon one of the most barefaced specimens of "bold bawdry," to make use of the plain language of Roger Ascham, that is to be found in the whole work. It is not easy to estimate the demoralizing influence of writings, many of which, being possessed of the beauties of literary finish, are elevated into the rank of classics, and thus find their way into the most reserved and fastidious libraries.

The literary execution of these tales is, however, by no means equal. In some it is even neglected, and in all falls below that of their great original. Still, in the larger part the graces of style are sedulously cultivated, and in many constitute the principal merit. Some of their authors, especially the more ancient, as Sacchetti and Ser Giovanni, derive great repute from their picturesque proverbialisms (*riboboli*), the racy slang of the Florentine mob; pearls of little price with foreigners, but of great estimation with their own countrymen. On these qualities, however, as on all those of mere external form, a stranger should pronounce with great diffidence; but the intellectual and moral character of a composition, especially the last, are open to univer-sal criticism. The principles of taste may differ in different nations; but, however often obscured by education or habit, there can be only one true standard of morality.

We may concede, then, to many of the *novelle*, the merits of a delicate work of art, gracefulness, nay, eloquence of style, agreeable facility of narrative, pleasantry that sometimes rises into wit, occasional developments of character, and an inexhaustible novelty of situation. But we cannot help regretting that, while so many of the finest wits of the nation have amused themselves with these compositions, they should not have exhibited virtue in a more noble and imposing attitude, or studied a more scientific delineation of passion, or a more direct moral aim or practical purpose. How rarely do we find, unless it be in some few of the last century, the didactic or even satirical tone of the English essayists, who seldom assume the Oriental garb, so frequent in Italian tales, for any other purpose than that of better conveying a prudential lesson. Goldsmith and Hawkesworth may furnish us with pertinent examples of this. How rarely do we recognise in these *novelle* the living portraiture of Chaucer, or the philosophical point which sharpens the pleasantry of La Fontaine; both competitors in the same walk. Without any higher object than that of present amusement, these productions, like many others of their elegant literature, seem to be thrown off in the mere gayety of the heart.

Chaucer, in his peculiarities, represents as faithfully those of the English nation as his rival and contemporary, Boccaccio, represents the Italian. In a searching anatomy of the human heart, he as far excels the latter, as in rhetorical beauty he is surpassed by him. The prologue to his Canterbury Tales alone contains a gallery of portraits, such as

4   2 U

is not to be found in the whole compass of the Decameron; his friar, for example,

> " That somewhat lisped from his wantonnesse
> To make his English sweete upon his tonge;"

his worthy parson, "glad to teche and glad to lerne;"
his man of law, who

> "Though so besy a man as he ther n' as,
> Yet seemed besier than he was;"

and his inimitable wag of a host, breaking his jests,
like Falstaff, indiscriminately upon every one he
meets. Chaucer was a shrewd observer of the realities of life. He did not indulge in day-dreams of
visionary perfection. His little fragment of Sir
Thopaz is a fine quiz upon the *incredibilia* of chivalry. In his conclusion of the story of the patient
Griselde, instead of adopting the somewhat *fade* eulogiums of Boccaccio, he good-naturedly jests at the
ultra perfection of the heroine. Like Shakspeare
and Scott, his successors and superiors in the school
of character, he seems to have had too vivid a perception of the vanities of human life to allow him
for a moment to give into those extravagances of
perfection which have sprung from the brain of so
many fond enthusiasts.

Chaucer's genius was every way equal to that of
Boccaccio, yet the direct influence of the one can
scarcely be discerned beyond his own age, while
that of the other has reached to the present generation. A principal cause of this is the difference of
their style; that of the former exhibiting only the
rude graces of a primitive dialect, while Boccaccio's

may be said to have reached the full prime of a cultivated period. Another cause is discernible in the new and more suitable forms which came to be adopted for that delineation of character which constitutes the essence of Chaucer's fictions, viz., those of the drama and the extended novel, in both of which Italian literature has, until very recently, been singularly deficient. Boccaccio made two elaborate essays in novel-writing, but his genius seems to have been ill adapted to it, and in his strange and prolix narrative, which brings upon the stage again the obsolete deities of antiquity, even the natural graces of his style desert him. The attempt has scarcely been repeated until our day, when the impulse communicated by the English, in romance and historical novel-writing, to other nations on the Continent, seems to have extended itself to Italy; and the extraordinary favour which has been shown there to the first essays in this way, may perhaps lead eventually to more brilliant successes.

The Spaniards, under no better circumstances than the Italians, made, previously to the last-mentioned period, a nearer approach to the genuine novel. Cervantes has furnished, amid his caricatures of chivalry, many passages of exquisite pathos and pleasantry, and a rich variety of national portraiture. The same, though in a less degree, may be affirmed of his shorter tales, *Novelas exemplares*, which, however inferior to those of the Decameron in rhetorical elegance, certainly surpass them in their practical application. But the peculiar property of the Spaniards is their *picaresco* novel, a mere chronicle of the adventures and mischievous pranks of young pickpockets and *chevaliers d'industrie*, invented, whimsically enough, by a Castilian grandee, one of the proudest of his *caste*, and which, notwithstanding the glaring contrast it affords to the habitual gravity of the nation, has, perhaps from this very circumstance, been a great favourite with it ever since.

The French have made other advances in novel-writing. They have produced many specimens of wit and of showy sentiment, but they seldom afford any wide range of observation, or searching views of character. The conventional breeding that universally prevails in France has levelled all inequalities of rank, and obliterated, as it were, the moral physiognomy of the different classes, which, however salutary in other respects, is exceedingly unpropitious to the purposes of the novelist. Molière, the most popular character-monger of the French, has penetrated the *superficies* of the most artificial state of society. His spirited sketches of fashionable folly, though very fine, very Parisian, are not always founded on the universal principles of human nature, and, when founded on these, they are sure to be carried more or less into caricature. The French have little of the English talent for humour. They have buffoonery, a lively wit, and a *naïveté* beyond the reach of art—Rabelais, Voltaire, La Fontaine—everything but humour. How spiritless and affected are the caricatures so frequently stuck up at their shop-windows, and which may be considered as the popular expression in this way, compared with those of the English. It is impossible to conceive of a French Goldsmith or Fielding, a Hogarth or a Wilkie. They have, indeed, produced a Le Sage, but ne seems to have confessed the deficiency of his own nation by deriving his models exclusively from a foreign one.

On the other hand, the freedom of the political and social institutions, both in this country and in England, which has encouraged the undisguised expansion of intellect and of peculiarities of temper, has made them the proper theatre for the student of his species. Hence man has been here delineated with an accuracy quite unrivalled in any ancient or modern nation, and, as the Greeks have surpassed every later people in statuary, from their familiarity with the visible, naked forms of manly beauty, so the English may be said, from an analogous cause, to have excelled all others in moral portraiture. To this point their most eminent artists have directed their principal attention. We have already noticed it in Chaucer. It formed the essence of the drama in Elizabeth's time, as it does that of the modern novel. Shakspeare and Scott, in their respective departments, have undoubtedly carried this art to the highest perfection of which it is capable, sacrificing to it every minor consideration of probability, incident, and gradation of plot, which they seem to have valued only so far as they might be made subservient to the main purpose of a clearer exposition of character.

But it is time to return from the digression into which we have been led by a desire of illustrating certain peculiarities of Italian literature, which can in no way be done so well as by comparing them with those of corresponding departments in other languages. Such a comparison abundantly shows how much deeper and more philosophical have been the views proposed by prose fiction in England than in Italy.

We have reserved the Drama for the last, as, until a very recent period, it has been less prolific in eminent models than either of the great divisions of Italian letters. Yet it has been the one most assiduously cultivated from a very early period, and this, too, by the ripest scholars and most approved wits. The career was opened by such minds as Ariosto and Machiavelli, at a time when the theatres in other parts of Europe had given birth only to the unseemly abortions of mysteries and moralities. Bouterwek has been led into a strange error in imputing the low condition of the Italian drama to the small number of men, of even moderate abilities, who have cultivated it.* A glance at the long muster-roll of eminent persons employed upon it, from Machiavelli to Monti, will prove the contrary.† The unprecedented favour bestowed on the most successful of the dramatic writers may serve to show, at least, the aspirations of the people. The Merope

* See the conclusion of his History of Spanish Literature.

† See Allacci's Drammaturgia, passim, and Riccoboni Theatre Ital., tom. i., p. 187–208. Allacci's catalogue, as continued down to the middle of the eighteenth century, occupies nearly a thousand quarto pages

of Maffei, which may be deemed the first dawn of improvement in the tragic art, passed through sixty editions. Notwithstanding all this, the Italians, in comedy, and still more in tragedy, until the late apparition of Alfieri, remained far below several of the other nations of Europe.

A principal cause of their repeated failures has been often referred to the inherent vices of their system, which required a blind conformity with the supposed rules of Aristotle. Under the cumbrous load of antiquity, the freedom and grace of natural movement were long impeded. Their first attempts were translations, or literal imitations of the Latin theatre; some of these, though objectionable in form, contain the true spirit of comedy. Those of Ariosto and Machiavelli, in particular, with even greater licentiousness of detail, and a more immoral conclusion than belong either to Plautus or Terence, fully equal, perhaps surpass them, in their spirited and whimsical draughts of character. Ariosto is never more a satirist than in his comedies; and Machiavelli, in his Mandragola, has exposed the hypocrisies of religion with a less glaring caricature than Molière has shown in his Tartuffe. The spirit of these great masters did not descend to their immediate successors. Goldoni, however, the Molière of Italy, in his numerous comedies or farces, has succeeded in giving a lively, graphic portraiture of local manners, with infinite variety and comic power, but no great depth of interest. He has seldom risen to refined and comprehensive views of society, and his

pieces, we may trust, are not to be received as faithfully reflecting the national character, which they
would make singularly deficient both in virtue and
the principle of honour. The writers who have
followed in the footsteps of Goldoni, exhibit, for the
most part, similar defects, with far inferior comic
talent. Their productions, on the whole, however,
may be thought to maintain an advantageous comparison with those of any other people in Europe
during the same period, although some of them, to
judge from the encomiastic tone of their critics, appear to have obtained a wider celebrity with their
contemporaries than will be probably conceded to
them by posterity. The *comedies of art* which Goldoni superseded, and which were, perhaps, more indicative of the national taste than any other dramatic performances, can hardly come within the scope
of literary criticism.

The Italian writers would seem not even to have
agreed upon a suitable measure for comedy, some
using the common *versi sciolti*, some the *sdruccioli*,
others, again, the *martelliani*, and many more pre-
ferring prose.* Another impediment to their success is the great variety of dialects in Italy, as numerous as her petty states, which prevents the recognition of any one uniform style of familiar conversation for comedy. The greater part of the
pieces of Goldoni are written, more or less, in the

* Professor Salfi affirms prose to be the most suitable, indeed the only
proper dress for Italian comedy. See his sensible *critique* on the Italian
comic drama, prefixed to the late edition of Alberto Nota's Commedie,
Parigi, 1829.

local idiom of one of the extremities of Italy; an inconvenience which cannot exist, and which can hardly be appreciated in a country where one acknowledged capital has settled the medium of polite intercourse.

The progress of the nation in the tragic art, until a late period, has been yet more doubtful. Some notion may be formed of its low state in the last century from the circumstance that, when the players were in want of a serious piece, they could find none so generally acceptable as an opera of Metastasio, stripped of its musical accompaniments. The appearance of Alfieri at this late season, of a genius so austere, in the midst of the voluptuous, Sybarite effeminacy of the period, is a remarkable phenomenon. It was as if the severe Doric proportions of a Pæstum temple had been suddenly raised up amid the airy forms of Palladian architecture. The reserved and impenetrable character of this man has been perfectly laid open to us in his own autobiography. It was made up of incongruity and paradox. To indomitable passions he joined the most frigid exterior. With the fiercest aristocratic nature, he yet quitted his native state that he might enjoy unmolested the sweets of liberty. He published one philippic against kings, and another against the people. His theoretic love of freedom was far from being warmed by the genuine glow of patriotism. Of all his tragedies, he condescended to derive two only from Italian history; and when, in his prefaces, dedications, or elsewhere, he takes occasion to notice

Y y y

his countrymen, he does it in the bitterness of irony and insult.

When he first set about his tragedies, he could compose only in a sort of French and Piedmontese *patois*. He was unacquainted with any written dramatic literature, though he had witnessed the theatrical exhibitions of the principal capitals of Europe. He was, therefore, to form himself all fresh upon such models as he might prefer. His haughty spirit carried him back to the *trecentisti*, especially to Dante, whose stern beauties he sedulously endeavoured to transfuse into his own style. He studied Tacitus, moreover, with diligence, and made three entire translations of Sallust. He was greatly afraid of falling into the *cantilena* of Metastasio, and sought to avoid this by sudden abruptions of language, by an eccentric use of the articles and pronouns, by dislocating the usual structure of verse, and by distributing the emphatic words with exclusive reference to the sense.*

This unprecedented manner brought upon Alfieri a host of critics, and he was compelled, in a subsequent edition, to soften down its most offensive asperities. He imputes to himself as many different styles of composition as distinguish the works of Raphael, and it is pretty evident that he considers the last as near perfection as he could well hope to attain. It is, indeed, a noble style : with the occasional turbulence of a mighty rapid, it has all its ful-

---

* See a summary of these peculiarities in Casalbigi's Letter, prefixed to the late editions of Alfieri's tragedies.

ness and magnificent flow; and it shows how utterly impossible it is, by any effort of art, to repress the natural melody of the Tuscan.

Alfieri effected a still more important revolution in the intellectual character of the drama, arousing it from the lethargy into which it had fallen, and making it the vehicle of generous and heroic sentiment.   He forced his pieces sometimes, it is true, by violent contrast, but he brought out his characters with a fulness of relief, and exhibited a dexterous combat of passion, that may not unfrequently remind us of Shakspeare.   He dismissed all supernumeraries from his plays, and put into action what his predecessors had coldly narrated.   He dispensed, moreover, with the curious coincidences, marvellous surprises, and all the *bei colpi di scena* so familiar in the plays of Metastasio.   He disdained even the poetical aid of imagery, relying wholly for effect on the dignity of his sentiments, and the imposing character of his agents.

Alfieri has been thought to have made a nearer approach to the Greek tragedy than any of the moderns.   He, indeed, disclaims the imitation of any foreign model, and he did not learn the Greek till late in life; but the drama of his own nation had always been servilely accommodated to the rules of the ancients, and he himself had rigorously adhered to the same code.   His severe genius, too, wears somewhat of the aspect of that of the father of Grecian tragedy, with which it has been repeatedly compared; but any apparent resemblance in their compositions vanishes on a closer inspection. The assassination of Agamemnon, for example, forms the subject of a tragedy with both these writers; but on what different principles is it conducted by each! The larger proportion of the play of Æschylus is taken up with the melancholy monologues of Cassandra and the chorus, which, boding the coming disasters of the house of Atreus, or mourning over the destiny of man, are poured forth in a lofty dithyrambic eloquence, that gives to the whole the air of a lyrical rather than a dramatic composition. It was this lyrical enthusiasm which, doubtless, led Plutarch to ascribe the inspiration of Æschylus to the influence of the grape.* The dialogue of the piece is of a most inartificial texture, and to an English audience might sometimes appear flat. The action moves heavily, and the principal, indeed, with the exception of Agamemnon, the only attempt at character, is in the part of Clytemnestra, whose gigantic stature overshadows the whole piece, and who appals the spectator by avowing the deed of assassination with the same ferocity with which she had executed it.

Alfieri, on the other hand, refuses the subsidiary aids of poetical imagery. He expressly condemns, in his criticisms, a confounding of the lyric and the dramatic styles. He elaborated his dialogue with the nicest art, and with exclusive reference to the

---

* Sympos. LVII., Prob. 10. In the same spirit, a critic of a more polished age has denounced Shakspeare's Hamlet as the work of a drunken savage! See Voltaire's Dissertation sur la Tragédie, &c., addressed to Cardinal Querini.

final catastrophe. *Scenæ non levis artifex.* His principal aim is to exhibit the collision of passions. The conflicts between passion and principle in the bosom of Clytemnestra, whom he has made a subordinate agent, furnish him with his most powerful scenes. He has portrayed the Iago-like features of Ægisthus in the darkest colours of Italian vengeance. The noble nature of Agamemnon stands more fully developed than in the Greek, and the sweet character of Electra is all his own. The assassination of the king of men in his bed, at the lonely hour of midnight, must forcibly remind the English reader of the similar scene in Macbeth; but, though finely conceived, it is far inferior to the latter in those fearful poetical accompaniments which give such an air of breathless horror to the story. In solemn, mysterious imaginings, who indeed can equal Shakspeare? He is the only modern poet who has succeeded in introducing the dim form of an apparition on the stage with any tolerable effect. Yet Voltaire accuses him of mistaking the horrible for the terrible. When Voltaire had occasion to raise a ghost upon the French stage (a ticklish experiment), he made him so amiable in his aspect that Queen Semiramis politely desires leave to "throw herself at his feet and to embrace them."[*]

It has been a matter of debate whether Italian tragedy, as reformed by Alfieri, is an improvement on the French. Both are conducted on the same general principles. A. W. Schlegel, a competent

[*] Semiramis, acte iii., s. 6.

critic whenever his own prejudices are not involved, decides in favour of the French. We must confess ourselves inclined to a different opinion. The three master-spirits in French tragedy seem to have contained within themselves all the elements of dramatic creation, yet their best performances have something tame and unsatisfactory in them. We see the influence of that fine-spun web of criticism which in France has bound the wing of genius to the earth, and which no one has been hardy enough to burst asunder. Corneille, after a severe lesson, submitted to it, though with an ill grace. The flexible character of Racine moved under it with more freedom, but he was of too timid a temper to attempt to contravene established prejudices. His reply to one who censured him for making Hippolyte in love, in his Phédre, is well known: " What would our *petits-maîtres* have said had I omitted it?" Voltaire, although possessed of a more enterprising and revolutionary spirit, left the essential principles of the drama as he found them. His multifarious criticisms exhibit a perpetual paradox. His general principles are ever at variance with their particular application. No one lauds more highly the scientific system of his countrymen; witness his numerous dramatic prefaces, dedications, and articles in the encyclopedia. He even refines upon it with hypercritical acumen, as in his commentaries on Corneille. But when he feels its tyrannical pressure on himself, he is sure to wince; see, for example, his lamentable protest in his Preface to Brutus.

Alfieri acknowledged the paramount authority of the ancients equally with the French dramatic writers. He has but thrice violated the unity of place, and very rarely that of time; but, with all his deference for antiquity, the Italian poet has raised himself far above the narrow code of French criticism. He has relieved tragedy from that eternal chime of love-sick damsels, so indispensable in a French piece, that, as Voltaire informs us, out of four hundred which had appeared before his time, there were not more than twelve which did not turn upon love. He substituted in its place a more pure and exalted sentiment. It will be difficult to find, even in Racine, such beautiful personifications of female loveliness as his Electra and Micol, to name no others. He has, moreover, dispensed with the *confidantes*, those insipid shadows that so invariably walk the round of the French stage. Instead of insulated axioms, and long, rhetorical pleadings, he has introduced a brisk, moving dialogue; and instead of the ceremonious breeding, the *perruque* and *chapeau bordé* of Louis XIV.th's court, his personages, to borrow an allusion from a sister art, are sculptured with the bold, natural freedom which distinguishes the school of Michael Angelo.

It is true that they are apt to show too much of the same fierce and sarcastic temper, too much of a family likeness with himself and with one another; that he sometimes mistakes passion for poetry; that ne has left this last too naked of imagery and rhetorical ornament; that he is sometimes stilted when he would be dignified; and that his affected energy is too often carried into mere muscular contortions His system has, indeed, the appearance of an aspiration after some ideal standard of excellence which he could not wholly attain. It is sufficient proof of his power, however, that he succeeded in establishing it, in direct opposition to the ancient taste of his countrymen, to their love of poetic imagery, of verbal melody, and voluptuousness of sentiment. It is the triumph of genius over the prejudices, and even the constitutional feelings of a nation.

We have dwelt thus long on Alfieri, because, like Dante, he seems himself to constitute a separate department in Italian literature. It is singular that the two poets who present the earliest and the latest models of surpassing excellence in this literature should bear so few of its usual characteristics. Alfieri's example has effected a decided revolution in the theatrical taste of his countrymen. It has called forth the efforts of some of their most gifted minds Monti, perhaps the most eminent of this school, surpasses him in the graces of an easy and brilliant elocution, but falls far below him in energy of conception and character. The stoical system of Alfieri would seem, indeed, better adapted to his own peculiar temperament than to that of his nation; and the successful experiment of Manzoni in discarding the unities, and otherwise relaxing the unnatural rigidity of this system, would appear to be much better suited to the popular taste as well as talent.

Our limits, necessarily far too scanty for our sub-

ject, will not allow us to go into the Opera and the
Pastoral Drama, two beautiful divisions in this department of Italian letters. It is singular that the
former, notwithstanding the natural sensibility of the
Italians to harmony, and the melody of their language, which almost sets itself to music as it is spoken, should have been so late in coming to its perfection under Metastasio. Nothing can be more
unfair than to judge of this author, or, indeed, of
any composer of operas, by the effect produced on
us in the closet. Their pieces are intended to be
exhibited, not read. The sentimental *ariettes* of the
heroes, the romantic bombast of the heroines, the
racks, ropes, poisoned daggers, and other fee-faw-fum
of a nursery tale, so plentifully besprinkled over
them, have certainly, in the closet, a very *fade* and
ridiculous aspect; but an opera should be considered as an appeal to the senses, by means of the illu
sions of music, dancing, and decorations. The poetry, wit, sentiment, intrigue, are mere accessories,
and of value only as they may serve to promote this
illusion. Hence the necessity of love—love, the
vivifying principle of the opera, the only passion in
perfect accordance with its voluptuous movements.
Hence the propriety of exhibiting character in exaggerated colour of light and shadow, the *chiar' os-
curo* of poetry, as the imagination is most forcibly
affected by powerful contrast. Yet this has been
often condemned in Metastasio. On the above
principle, too, the seasonable disclosures, miraculous
escapes, and all the other magical apparatus before

4 . 2 V *

alluded to, may be defended. The mind of the spectator, highly stimulated through the medium of the senses, requires a corresponding extravagance, if we may so say, in the creations of the poet. In this state, a veracious copy of nature would fall flat and powerless; to reach the heart, it must be raised into gigantic proportions, and adorned with a brighter flush of colouring than is to be found in real life. As a work of art, then, but not as a purely intellectual exhibition, we may criticise the opera, and, in this view of it, the peculiarities so often condemned in the artist may be, perhaps, sufficiently justified.

The Pastoral Drama, that attempt to shadow forth the beautiful absurdities of a golden age, claims to be invented by the Italians. It was carried to its ultimate perfection in two of its earliest specimens, the poems of Tasso and Guarini. Both these writers have adorned their subject with the highest charms of versification and imagery. With Tasso all this seems to proceed spontaneously from the heart, while Guarini's Pastor Fido, on the other hand, has the appearance of being elaborated with the nicest preparation. It may, in truth, be regarded as the solitary monument of his genius, and as such he seems to have been desirous to concentrate within it every possible variety of excellence. During his whole life he was employed in retouching and enriching it with new beauties. This great variety and finish of details somewhat impair its unity, and give it too much the appearance of a curious collection of specimens. Yet there are those, and very competent critics, too, who prefer the splendid patchwork of Guarini to the sweet, unsolicited beauties of his rival. Dr. Johnson has condemned both the Aminta and Pastor Fido as " trifles easily imitated and unworthy of imitation." The Italians have not found them so. Out of some hundred specimens cited by Serassi, only three or four are deemed by him worthy of notice. An English critic should have shown more charity for a kind of composition that has given rise to some of the most exquisite creations of Fletcher and Milton.

We have now reviewed the most important branches of the ornamental literature of the Italians. We omit some others, less conspicuous, or not essentially differing in their characteristics from similar departments in the literatures of other European nations. An exception may perhaps be made in favour of satirical writing, which, with the Italians, assumes a peculiar form, and one quite indicative of the national genius. Satire, in one shape or another, has been a great favourite with them, from Ariosto, or, indeed, we may say Dante, to the present time. It is, for the most part, of a light, vivacious character, rather playful than pointed. Their critics, with their usual precision, have subdivided it into a great variety of classes, among which the *Bernesque* is the most original. This epithet, derived not, as some have supposed, from the *rifacimento* but from the Capitoli of Berni, designates a style of writing compounded of the beautiful and the burlesque, of which it is nearly impossible to convey an adequate notion, either by translation or description, in a foreign language. Even so mature a scholar as Mr. Roscoe has failed to do this, when, in one of his histories, he compares this manner to that of Peter Pindar, and in the other to that of Sterne. But the Italian has neither the coarse diction of the former nor the sentiment of the latter. It is generally occupied with some frivolous topic, to which it ascribes the most extravagant properties, descanting on it through whole pages of innocent irony, and clothing the most vulgar and oftentimes obscene ideas in the polished phrase or idiomatic graces of expression that never fail to disarm an Italian critic. A foreigner, however, not so sensible to the seductions of style, will scarcely see in it anything more than a puerile debauch of fancy.

Historians are fond of distributing the literature of Italy into masses, chronologically arranged in successive centuries. The successive revolutions in this literature justify the division to a degree unknown in that of any other country, and a brief illustration of it may throw some additional light on our subject.

Thus the fourteenth century, the age of the *trecentisti*, as it is called, the age of Dante, Petrarch, and Boccaccio, is the period of high and original invention. These three great writers, who are alone capable of attracting our attention at this distance of time, were citizens of a free state, and were early formed to the contemplation and practice of public virtue. Hence their works manifest an independence and a generous self-confidence that we seek in vain in the productions of a later period, forced in the artificial atmosphere of a court. Their writings are marked, moreover, by a depth of reflection not to be discerned in the poets of a similar period of antiquity, the pioneers of the civilization of their times. The human mind was then in its infancy; but in the fourteenth century it seemed to awake from the slumber of ages, with powers newly invigorated, and a memory stored with the accumulated wisdom of the past. Compare, for example, the Divine Comedy with the poems of Homer and Hesiod, and observe how much superior to these latter writers is the Italian in moral and intellectual science, as well as in those higher speculations which relate to our ultimate destiny.* The rhetorical beauties of the great works of the fourteenth century have equally contributed to their permanent popularity and influence. While the early productions of other countries, the poems of the Niebelungen, of the Cid, of the Norman *trouveurs*, and those of Chaucer, even, have passed, in consequence of their colloquial barbarisms, into a certain degree of oblivion, the writings of the *trecentisti* are still revered as the models of purity and elegance, to be forever imitated, though never equalled.

The following age exhibits the reverse of all this. It was as remarkable for the general diffusion of

* Hesiod, it is true, has digested a compact body of ethics, wonderfully mature for the age in which he wrote; but the best of it is disfigured with those childish superstitions which betray the twilight of civilization. See, in particular, the concluding portion of his Works and Days.

learning as the preceding had been for the concentration of talent. The Italian, which had been so successfully cultivated, came to be universally neglected for the ancient languages. It would seem as if the soil, exhausted by too abundant harvests, must lie fallow another century before it could be capable of reproduction. The scholars of that day disdained any other than the Latin tongue for the medium of their publications, or even of their private epistolary correspondence. They thought, with Waller, that

> "Those who lasting marble seek,
> Must carve in Latin or in Greek."

But the marble has crumbled into dust, while the natural beauties of their predecessors are still green in the memory of their countrymen. To make use of a simile which Dr. Young applied to Ben Jonson, they "pulled down, like Samson, the temple of antiquity on their shoulders, and buried themselves under its ruins."

But let us not err by despising these men as a race of unprofitable pedants. They lived on the theatre of ancient art, in an age when new discoveries were daily making of the long-lost monuments of intellectual and material beauty, and it is no wonder that, dazzled with the contemplation of these objects, they should have been blind to the modest merits of their contemporaries. We should be grateful to men whose indefatigable labours preserved for us the perishable remains of classic literature, and who thus opened a free and familiar converse with the great minds of antiquity; and we may justly feel some degree of reverence for the enthusiasm of an age in which the scholar was willing to exchange his learned leisure for painful and perilous pilgrimages, when the merchant was content to barter his rich freights for a few mouldering, worm-eaten folios, and when the present of a single manuscript was deemed of sufficient value to heal the dissensions of two rival states. Such was the fifteenth century in Italy; and Tiraboschi, warming as he approaches it, in his preface to the sixth volume of his history, has accordingly invested it with more than his usual blaze of panegyric.

The genius of the Italians, however, was sorely fettered by their adoption of an ancient idiom, and, like Tasso's Erminia, when her delicate form was enclosed in the iron mail of the warrior, lost its elasticity and grace. But at the close of the century the Italian muse was destined to regain her natural freedom in the court of Lorenzo de' Medici. His own compositions, especially, are distinguished by a romantic sweetness, and his light, popular pieces— Carnascialeschi, Contadineschi—so abundantly imitated since, have a buoyant, exhilarating air, wholly unlike the pedantic tone of his age. Under these new auspices, however, the Italian received a very different complexion from that which had been imparted to it by the hand of Dante.

The sixteenth century is the healthful, the Augustan age of Italian letters. The conflicting principles of an ancient and a modern school are, however, to be traced throughout almost the whole course of it. A curious passage from Varchi, who flourished about the middle of this century, informs us that, when he was at school, it was the custom of the instructers to interdict to their pupils the study of any vernacular writer, even Dante and Petrarch.* Hence the Latin came to be cultivated almost equally with the Italian, and both, singularly enough, attained simultaneously their full development.

There are few phrases more inaccurately applied than that of the Age of Leo X., to whose brief pontificate we are accustomed to refer most of the magnificent creations of genius scattered over the sixteenth century, although very few, even of those produced in his own reign, can be imputed to his influence. The nature of this influence in regard to Italian letters may even admit of question. His early taste led him to give an almost exclusive attention to the ancient classics. The great poets of that century, Ariosto, Sanazzaro, the Tassos, Rucellai, Guarini, and the rest, produced their immortal works far from Leo's court. Even Bembo, the oracle of his day, retired in disgust from his patron, and composed his principal writings in his retreat. Ariosto, his ancient friend, he coldly neglected,† while he pensioned the infamous Aretin. He surrounded his table with buffoon literati and parasit-

* Ercolano, ques. VIII.

† Roscoe attempts to explain away this conduct of Leo, but the satires of the poet furnish a bitter commentary upon it, not to be misunderstood.

ical poets, who amused him with feats of improvisation, gluttony, and intemperance, some of whom, after expending on them his convivial wit, he turned over to public derision, and most of whom, debauched in morals and constitution, were abandoned, under his austere successor, to infamy and death. He collected about him such court-flies as Berni and Molza; but, as if the papal atmosphere were fatal to high continued effort, even Berni, like Trissino and Rucellai, could find no leisure for his more elaborate performance till after his patron's death. He magnificently recompensed his musical retainers, making one an archbishop, another an archdeacon; but what did he do for his countryman Machiavelli, the philosopher of his age ?* He hunted, and hawked, and caroused; everything was a jest; and while the nations of Europe stood aghast at the growing heresy of Luther, the merry pontiff and his ministers found strange matter of mirth in witnessing the representation of comedies that exposed the impudent mummeries of priestcraft. With such an example, and under such an influence, it is no wonder that nothing better should have been produced than burlesque satire, licentious farces, and frivolous impromptus. Contrast all this with the elegant recreations of the little court of Urbino, as described in the Cortegiano; or compare the whole result on Italian letters of the so much vaunted patronage of

---

* Machiavelli, after having suffered torture on account of a suspected conspiracy against the Medici, in which his participation was never proved, was allowed to linger out his days in poverty and disgrace.

this luxurious pontiff with the splendid achievements of the petty state of Este alone, during the first half of this century, and it will appear that there are few misnomers which convey grosser misconceptions than that of the age of Leo X.

The seventeenth century (*seicento*) is one of humiliation in the literary annals of Italy; one in which the Muse, like some dilapidated beauty, endeavoured to supply the loss of natural charms by all the aids of coquetry and meretricious ornament. It is the prodigal use of "these false brilliants," as Boileau terms them, in some of their best writers, which has brought among foreigners an undeserved discredit on the whole body of Italian letters, and which has made the condemned age of the *seicentisti* a by-word of reproach even with their own countrymen. The principles of a corrupt taste are, however, to be discerned at an earlier period, in the writings of Tasso especially, and still more of Guarini; but it was reserved for Marini to reduce them into a system, and by his popularity and foreign residence to diffuse the infection among the other nations of Europe. To this source, therefore, most of these nations have agreed to refer the impurities which, at one time or another, have disfigured their literatures. Thus the Spaniard Lampillas has mustered an array of seven volumes to prove the charge of original corruption on the Italians, though Marini openly affected to have formed himself upon a Spanish model.* In like manner, La Harpe imputes to

* Obras suelt. de Lope de Vega, tom. xxi., p. 17.

them the sins of Jodelle and the contemporary wits, though these last preceded, by some years, the literary existence of Marini ; and the vices of the English *metaphysical* school have been expressly referred, by Dr. Johnson, to Marini and his followers.

A nearer inspection, however, might justify the opinion that these various affectations bear too much of the physiognomy of the respective nations in which they are found, and are capable of being traced to too high a source in each, to be thus exclusively imputed to the Italians. Thus the elements of the *cultismo* of the Spaniards, that compound of flat pedantry and Oriental hyperbole, so different from the fine *concetti* of the Italian, are to be traced through some of their most eminent writers up to the fugitive pieces of the fifteenth century, as collected in their Cancioneros ; and, in like manner, the elements of the metaphysical jargon of Cowley, whose intellectual combinations and far-fetched analogies show too painful a research after wit for the Italian taste, may be traced in England through Donne and Ben Jonson, to say nothing of the " unparalleled John Lillie," up to the veteran versifiers of the fifteenth and fourteenth centuries. Thus, also, some features of the *style précieux* of the Hôtel de Rambouillet, so often lashed by Boileau and laughed at by Molière, may be imputed to the malign influence of the constellation of pedants, celebrated in France under the title of Pleiades, in the sixteenth century.

The Greek is the only literature which, from the

first, seems to have maintained a sound and healthful
state. In every other, the barbaric love of ornament,
so discernible even in the best of the early writers,
has been chastised only by long and assiduous criticism ; but the principle of corruption still remains,
and the season of perfect ripeness seems to be only
that of the commencement of decay. Thus it was
in Italy, in the perverted age of the *seicentisti*, an
age yet warm with the productions of an Ariosto
and a Tasso.

The literature of the Italians assumed in the last
century a new and highly improved aspect. With
less than its usual brilliancy of imagination, it displayed an intensity, and, under the circumstances in
which it has been produced, we may add, intrepidity of thought quite worthy of the great spirits of
the fourteenth century, and a freedom and nature in
its descriptions altogether opposed to the heartless
affectations of the seventeenth. The prejudicial influence of their neighbours threatened at one time,
indeed, to precipitate the language into a French
machéronico ; but a counter-current, equally exclusive, in favour of the *trecentisti*, contributed to check
the innovation, and to carry them back to the ancient models of purity and vigour. The most eminent writers of this period seem to have formed
themselves on Dante, in particular, as studiously as
those of the preceding age affected the more effemi-
inate graces of Petrarch. Among these, Monti, who,
in the language of his master, may be truly said to
have inherited from him "Lo bello stile, che l'ha

fatto onore," is thought most nearly to resemble Dante in the literary execution of his verses; while Alfieri, Parini, and Foscolo approach him still nearer in the rugged virtue and independence of their sentiments. There seems to be a didactic import in much of the poetry of this age, too, and in its descriptions of external nature, a sober, contemplative vein, that may remind us of writers in our own language. Indeed, an English influence is clearly discernible in some of the most eminent poets of this period, who have either visited Great Britain in person, or made themselves familiar with its language.* The same influence may be, perhaps, recognised in the moral complexion of many of their compositions, the most elegant specimen of which is probably Parini's satire, which disguises the sarcasm of Cowper in the rich, embroidered verse which belongs to the Italians.

In looking back on the various branches of literature which we have been discussing, we are struck with the almost exclusive preference given to poetry over prose, with the great variety of beautiful forms which the former exhibits, with its finished versification, its inexhaustible inventions, and a wit that never tires. But in all this admirable mechanism we too often feel the want of an informing soul, of a nobler, or, at least, some more practical object than mere amusement. Their writers too rarely seem to feel,

> "Divinity within them, breeding wings
> Wherewith to spurn the earth."

* Among these may be mentioned Monti, Pindemonte, Cesarotti, Mazza, Alfieri, Pignotti, and Foscolo.

4

2 W *

They have gone beyond every other people in painting the intoxication of voluptuous passion; but how rarely have they exhibited it in its purer and more ethereal form! How rarely have they built up their dramatic or epic fables on national or patriotic recollections! Even satire, disarmed of its moral sting, becomes in their hands a barren, though perhaps a brilliant jest—the harmless electricity of a summer sky.

The peculiar inventions of a people best show their peculiar genius. The romantic epic has assumed with the Italians a perfectly original form, in which, stripped of the fond illusions of chivalry, it has descended, through all the gradations of mirth, from well-bred raillery to broad and bald buffoonery. In the same merry vein their various inventions in the burlesque style have been conceived. Whole cantos of these puerilities have been strung together with a patience altogether unrivalled, except by that of their indefatigable commentators.* Even the most austere intellects of the nation, a Machiavelli and a Galileo, for example, have not disdained to revel in this frivolous debauch of fancy, and may remind one of Michael Angelo, at the instance of Pietro de' Medici, employing his transcendent talents in sculpturing a perishable statue of snow!

The general scope of our vernacular literature, as contrasted with that of the Italian, will set the peculiarities of the latter in a still stronger light. In

* The annotations upon Lippi's burlesque poem of the Malmantile Racquistata are inferior in bulk to those only on the Divine Comedy.

the English, the drama and the novel, which may be considered as its staples, aiming at more than a vulgar interest, have always been made the theatre of a scientific dissection of character. Instead of the romping merriment of the *novelle*, it is furnished with those periodical essays which, in the form of apologue, of serious disquisition or criticism, convey to us lessons of practical wisdom. Its pictures of external nature have been deepened by a sober contemplation not familiar to the mercurial fancy of the Italians. Its biting satire, from Pierce Plowman's Visions to the Baviad and Mæviad of our day, instead of breaking into vapid jests, has been sharpened against the follies or vices of the age, and the body of its poetry, in general, from the days of "moralle Gower" to those of Cowper and Wordsworth, breathes a spirit of piety and unsullied virtue Even Spenser deemed it necessary to shroud the eccentricities of his Italian imagination in sober allegory; and Milton, while he adopted in his Comus the beautiful and somewhat luxurious form of the Aminta and Pastor Fido, animated it with the most devotional sentiments.

The political situation of Italy may afford a key to some of the peculiarities of her literature. Oppressed by foreign or domestic tyrants for more than five centuries, she has been condemned, in the indignant language of her poet,

" Per servir sempre, o vincitrice o vinta."

Her citizens, excluded from the higher walks of public action, have too often resigned themselves to corrupt and effeminate pleasure, and her writers, inhibited from the free discussion of important topics, have too frequently contented themselves with an impotent play of fancy. The histories of Machiavelli and of Guicciardini were not permitted to be published entire until the conclusion of the last century. The writings of Alemanni, from some umbrage given to the Medici, were burned by the hands of the common hangman. Marchetti's elegant version of Lucretius was long prohibited on the ground of its epicurean philosophy, and the learned labours of Giannone were recompensed with exile. Under such a government, it is wonderful that so many, rather than so few writers, should have been found with intrepidity sufficient to raise the voice of unwelcome truth. It is not to be wondered at that they should have produced so few models of civil or sacred eloquence, the fruit of a happier and more enlightened system; that they should have been too exclusively devoted to mere beauties of form; have been more solicitous about style than thought; have studied rather to amuse than to instruct. Hence the superabundance of their philological treatises and mere verbal criticisms, of their tomes of commentaries, with which they have illustrated or obscured their most insignificant poets, where a verse furnishes matter for a lecture, and a *canzone* becomes the text for a volume. This is no exaggeration.*

---

* Benedetto of Ravenna wrote ten lectures on the fourth sonnet of Petrarch. Pico della Mirandola devoted three whole books to the illustration of a *canzone* of his friend Benivieni, and three Arcadians publish-

Hence, too, the frequency and ferocity of their literary quarrels, into which the Italians, excluded too often from weightier disquisition, enter with an enthusiasm which in other nations can be roused only by the dearest interests of humanity. The comparative merit of some obscure classic, the orthography of some obsolete term, a simple sonnet, even, has been sufficient to throw the whole community into a ferment, in which the parties have not always confined themselves to a war of words.

The influence of academies on Italian literature is somewhat doubtful. They have probably contributed to nourish that epicurean sensibility to mere verbal elegance so conspicuous in the nation. The great variety of these institutions scattered over every remote district of the country, the whimsicality of their titles, and still more of those of their members, have an air sufficiently ridiculous.* Some of them have been devoted to the investigation of science. But a license, refused to individuals, will hardly be conceded to public associations; and the persecution of some of the most eminent has proved an effectual warning to confine their speculations within the inoffensive sphere of literary criticism. Hence the exuberance of *prose* and *lezioni*, endless dissertations

---

ed a volume in defence of the *Tre Sorelle* of Petrarch! It would be easy to multiply similar examples of critical prodigality.

* Take at hazard some of the most familiar, the "Ardent," the "Frozen," the "Wet," the "Dry," the "Stupid," the "Lazy." The Cruscan takes its name from Crusca (bran); and its members adopted the corresponding epithets of "Brown bread," "white bread," "the kneaded," &c. Some of the Italians, as Lasca, La Bindo, for instance, are better known by their frivolous academic names than by their own.

4 B

on barren rhetorical topics; and those vapid attempts at academic wit, which should never have transcended the bounds of the Lyceum.

It is not in such institutions that the great intellectual efforts of a nation are displayed. All that any academy can propose to itself is to keep alive the flame which genius has kindled, and in more than one instance they have gone near to smother it. The French academy, as is well known, opened its career with its celebrated attack upon Corneille; and the earliest attempt of the Cruscan was upon Tasso's Jerusalem, which it compelled its author to remodel, or, in other words, to reduce, by the extraction of its essential spirit, into a flat and insipid decoction. Denina has sarcastically intimated that the era of the foundation of this latter academy corresponds exactly with that of the commencement of the decline of good taste. More liberal critics concede, however, that this body has done much to preserve the integrity of the tongue, and that a pure spirit of criticism was kept alive within its bosom when it had become extinct in almost every other part of Italy.* Their philological labours have, in truth, been highly valuable, though perhaps not so completely successful as those of the French academicians. We do not allude to any capricious principle on which their vocabulary may have been constructed, an affair of their own critics; but to the fact that, after all, they have not been able to settle

---

* See, in particular, the treatise of Parini, himself a Lombard, De' principi delle Belle Lettere, part ii., cap. v.

the language with the same precision and uniformity with which it has been done in France, from the want of some great metropolis, like Paris, whose authority would be received as paramount throughout the country. No such universal deference has been paid to the Cruscan academy; and the Italian language, far from being accurately determined, is even too loose and inexact for the common purposes of business. Perhaps it is for this very reason better adapted to the ideal purposes of poetry.

The exquisite mechanism of the Italian tongue, made up of the very elements of music, and picturesque in its formation beyond that of any other living language, is undoubtedly a cause of the exaggerated consequence imputed to style by the writers of the nation. The author of the Dialogue on Orators points out, as one of the symptoms of depraved eloquence in Rome, that "voluptuous artificial harmony of cadence, which is better suited to the purposes of the musician or the dancer than of the orator." The same vice has infected Italian prose from its earliest models, from Boccaccio and Bembo down to the most ordinary book-wright of the present day, who hopes to disguise his poverty of thought under his melodious redundancy of diction. Hence it is that their numerous Letters, Dialogues, and their specimens of written eloquence, are too often defective both in natural force and feeling. Even in those graver productions which derive almost their sole value from their facts, they are apt to be far more solicitous about style and ingenious turns of thought, as one of their own critics has admitted, than either utility or sound philosophy.*

A principal cause, after all, of the various peculiarities of Italian literature, of which we have been speaking, is to be traced to that fine perception of the beautiful, so inherent in every order of the nation, whether it proceed from a happier physical organization, or from an early familiarity with those models of ideal beauty by which they are everywhere surrounded. Whoever has visited Italy must have been struck with a sensibility to elegant pleasure, and a refinement of taste in the very lowest classes, that in other countries belong only to the more cultivated. This is to be discerned in the most trifling particulars; in their various costume, whose picturesque arrangement seems to have been studied from the models of ancient statuary; in the flowers and other tasteful ornaments with which, on *fête* days, they decorate their chapels and public temples; in the eagerness with which the peasant and the artisan, after their daily toil, resort to the theatre, the opera, or similar intellectual amusements, instead of the bear-baitings, bull-fights, and drunken orgies so familiar to the populace of other countries; and in the quiet rapture with which they listen for hours, in the public squares, to the strains of an *improvisatore*, or the recitations of a story-teller, without any other refreshment than a glass of water. Even the art of improvisation, carried to such perfection by the Italians, is far less imputable to the facilities of their

---

* Bettinelli, Risorgim. d'Italia, Introd., p. 14.

verse than to the poetical genius of the people; an evidence of which is the abundance of *improvisatori* in Latin in the sixteenth century, when that language came to be widely cultivated.

It is time, however, to conclude our remarks, which have already encroached too liberally on the patience of our readers. Notwithstanding our sincere admiration, as generally expressed, for the beautiful literature of Italy, we fear that some of our reflections may be unpalatable to a people who shrink with sensitive delicacy from the rude touch of foreign criticism. The most liberal opinions of a foreigner, it is true, coming through so different a medium of prejudice and taste, must always present a somewhat distorted aspect to the eye of a native. On those finer shades of expression which constitute, indeed, much of the value of poetry, none but a native can pronounce with accuracy; but on its intellectual and moral character a foreign critic is better qualified to decide. He may be more perspicacious, even, than a native, in detecting those obliquities from a correct standard of taste, to which the latter has been reconciled by prejudice and long example, or which he may have learned to reverence as beauties.

There must be so many exceptions, too, to the sweeping range of any general criticism, that it will always carry with it a certain air of injustice. Thus, while we object to the Italians the diluted, redundant style of their compositions, may they not refer us to their versions of Tacitus and Perseus, the most

4   2 X

condensed writers in the most condensed language
in the world, in a form equally compact with that
of the originals? May they not object to us Dante
and Alfieri, scarcely capable of translation into any
modern tongue, in the same compass, without a violence to idiom? And may they not cite the same
hardy models in refutation of an unqualified charge
of effeminacy? Where shall we find examples of
purer and more exalted sentiment than in the writings of Petrarch and Tasso? Where of a more
chastised composition than in Casa or Caro? And
where more pertinent examples of a didactic aim
than in their numerous poetical treatises on hus-
bandry, manufactures, and other useful arts, which
in other countries form the topics of bulky disquisitions in prose? This is all just. But such exceptions, however imposing, in no way contravene the
general truth of our positions, founded on the *prevalent* tone and characteristics of Italian literature.

Let us not, however, appear insensible to the
merits of a literature, pre-eminent above all others
for activity of fancy and beautiful variety of form, or
to those of a country so fruitful in interesting recollections to the scholar and the artist; in which the
human mind has displayed its highest energies un-
tired through the longest series of ages; on which
the light of science shed its parting ray, and where
it first broke again upon the nations; whose history
is the link that connects the past with the present,
the ancient with the modern, and whose enterprising
genius enlarged the boundaries of the Old World

by the discovery of a New; whose scholars opened
to mankind the intellectual treasures of antiquity;
whose schools first expounded those principles of
law which have become the basis of jurisprudence
in most of the civilized nations of Europe; whose
cities gave the earliest example of free institutions,
and, when the vision of liberty had passed away,
maintained their empire over the mind by those ad
mirable productions of art that revive the bright period of Grecian glory; and who, even now, that her
palaces are made desolate and her vineyards trodden
down under the foot of the stranger, retains within
her bosom all the fire of ancient genius. It would
show a strange insensibility indeed did we not sympathize in the fortunes of a nation that has manifested, in such a variety of ways, the highest intellectual power; of which we may exclaim, in the
language which a modern poet has applied to one
of the most beautiful of her cities,

"O Decus, O Lux
Ausoniæ, per quam libera turba sumus,
Per quam Barbaries nobis non imperat, et Sol
Exoriens nostro clarius orbe nitet!"

SCOTTISH SONG.*

JULY, 1826.

IT is remarkable that poetry, which is esteemed so much more difficult than prose among cultivated people, should universally have been the form which man, in the primitive stages of society, has adopted for the easier development of his ideas. It may be that the infancy of nations, like that of individuals, is more taken up with imagination and sentiment than with reasoning, and is thus instinctively led to verse, as best suited, by its sweetness and harmony, to the expression of passionate thought. It may be, too, that the refinements of modern criticism have multiplied rather than relieved the difficulties of the art. The ancient poet poured forth his *carmina incondita* with no other ambition than that of accommodating them to the natural music of his own ear, careless of the punctilious observances which the fastidious taste of a polished age so peremptorily demands. However this may be, it is certain that poetry is more ancient than prose in the records of every nation, and that this poetry is found in its earliest stages almost always allied with music. Thus the Rhapsodies of Homer were chanted to the sound of the lyre by the wandering bards of Ionia ; thus the cithæroedi of the ancient Romans, the Welsh

* "The Songs of Scotland, Ancient and Modern, with an Introduction and Notes, Historical and Critical, and the Characters of the Lyric Poets. By Allan Cunningham." In four volumes. London, 1825. 12mo.

harper, the Saxon gleeman, the Scandinavian scald, and the Norman minstrel, soothed the sensual appetites of an unlettered age by the more exalted charms of poetry and music. This precocious poetical spirit seems to have been more widely diffused among the modern than the ancient European nations. The astonishing perfection of the Homeric epics makes it probable, it is true, that there must have been previously a diligent cultivation of the divine art among the natives.[*]

The introduction of the bards Phemius and Demodocus into the Odyssey shows also that minstrelsy had long been familiar to Homer's countrymen. This, however, is but conjecture, as no undisputed fragments of this early age have come down to us. The Romans, we know, were not, till a very late period, moved by the *impetus sacer*. One or two devotional chants and a few ribald satires are all that claim to be antiquities in their prosaic literature.

It was far otherwise with the nations of modern Europe. Whether the romantic institutions of the age, or the warmth of classic literature not wholly extinguished, awakened this general enthusiasm, we know not; but no sooner had the thick darkness, which for centuries had settled over the nations, begun to dissipate, than the voice of song was heard in the remotest corners of Europe, where heathen civilization had never ventured; from the frozen isles of Britain and Scandinavia, no less than from

---

[*] " Nec dubitari debet quin fuerint ante Homerum poetæ."—*Cic.*, *Brut.*, 18.

the fertile shores of Italy and Provence. We do not mean that the light of song was totally extinguished, even at the darkest period. It may be faintly discerned in the barbaric festivals of Attila, himself the theme of more than one venerable German romance; and, at a later period, in the comparatively refined courts of Alfred and Charlemagne.

But it was not until the eleventh or twelfth century that refinement of taste was far advanced among the nations of Europe; that, in spite of all the obstacles of a rude, unconcocted dialect, the foundations and the forms of their poetical literature were cast, which, with some modification, they have retained ever since. Of these, the ballads may be considered as coming more immediately from the body of the people. In no country did they take such deep root as in Spain and Scotland, and, although cultivated more or less by all the Northern nations, yet nowhere else have they had the good fortune, by their own intrinsic beauty, and by the influence they have exerted over the popular character, to constitute so important a part of the national literature. The causes of this are to be traced to the political relations of these countries. Spain, divided into a number of petty principalities, which contended with each other for pre-eminence, was obliged to carry on a far more desperate struggle for existence, as well as religion, with its Saracen invaders; who, after advancing their victorious crescent from the Arabian desert to the foot of the Pyrenees, had established a solid empire over the fairest portions of the Peninsula. Seven long centuries was the ancient Spaniard reclaiming, inch by inch, this conquered territory; thus a perpetual crusade was carried on, and the fertile fields of Andalusia and Granada became the mimic theatre of exploits similar to those performed by the martial enthusiasts of Europe, on a much greater scale, indeed, on the plains of Palestine. The effect of all this was to infuse into their popular compositions a sort of devotional heroism, which is to be looked for in vain in any other. The existence of the Cid, so early as the eleventh century, was a fortunate event for Spanish poetry. The authenticated actions of that chief are so nearly allied to the marvellous, that, like Charlemagne he forms a convenient *nucleus* for the manifold fictions in which successive bards have enveloped him. The ballads relating to this doughty hero have been collected into a sort of patchwork epic, whose fabrication thus resembles that imputed to those ancient poems which some modern critics have determined to be but a tissue of rhapsodies executed by different masters. But, without comparing them with the epics of Homer in symmetry of design or perfection of versification, we may reasonably claim for them a moral elevation not inferior, and a tone of courtesy and generous gallantry altogether unknown to the heroes of the Iliad.

The most interesting of the Spanish ballads are those relating to the Moors. This people, now so degraded in every intellectual and moral aspect, were, as is well known, in the ninth and tenth centuries the principal depositaries of useful science and elegant art. This is particularly true of the Spanish caliphate; and more than one Christian prelate is on record who, in a superstitious age, performed a literary pilgrimage to the schools of Cordova, and drank from these profane sources of wisdom. The peculiarities of Oriental costume; their showy military exercises; their perilous bull-feasts and canefights; their chivalric defiance and rencounters with the Christian knights on the plains before the assembled city; their brilliant revels, romantic wooings, and midnight serenades, afforded rich themes for the muse; above all, the capture and desolation of Granada, that "city without peer," the "pride of heathendom," on which the taste and treasures of the Western caliphs had been lavished for seven centuries, are detailed in a tone of melancholy grandeur, which comes over us like the voice of an expiring nation.*

One trait has been pointed out in these poems most honourable to the Spanish character, and in which, in later times, it has been lamentably deficient, that of religious toleration; we find none of the fierce bigotry which armed the iron hand of the

---

* An ancient Arabian writer concludes a florid eulogium on the architecture and local beauties of Granada in the fourteenth century, with likening it, in Oriental fashion, to "a richly-wrought vase of silver, filled with jacinths and emeralds."—*Historia de los Arabes de Espana*, tom. iii., p. 147. Among the ballads relating to the Moorish wars, two of the most beautiful are the "Lament over Alhama," indifferently translated by Byron, and that beginning with "En la ciudad de Granada," rendered by Lockhart with his usual freedom and vivacity.—*Hita*, i., 464, and *Depping*, 240.

Inquisition; which coolly condemned to exile or the stake a numerous native population for an honest difference of religious opinion, and desolated with fire and sword the most flourishing of their Christian provinces.

The ancient Spaniard, on the contrary, influenced by a more enlightened policy, as well as by humanity, contracted familiar intimacies, nay, even matrimonial alliances, with his Mohammedan rivals, and the proudest of their nobles did not disdain, in an honest cause, to fight under the banners of the Infidel. It would be a curious study to trace the progress and the causes of this pitiable revolution in national feeling.

The Spaniards have good reason to cherish their ancient ballads, for nowhere is the high Castilian character displayed to such advantage. Haughty, it is true, jealous of insult, and without the tincture of letters, which throws a lustre over the polished court of Charles and Philip; but also without the avarice, the insatiable cruelty, and dismal superstition which deface the bright page of their military renown.* The Cid himself, whose authentic history may vindicate the hyperbole of romance, was the *beau idéal* of chivalry.†

* Sufficient evidence of this may be found in works of imagination, as well as the histories of the period. The plays of Lope de Vega, for instance, are filled with all manner of perfidy and assassination, which takes place as a matter of course, and without the least compunction. In the same spirit, the barbarous excesses of his countrymen in South America are detailed by Ercilla, in his historical epic, *La Araucana.* The flimsy pretext of conscience, for which these crimes are perpetrated, cannot veil their enormity from any but the eyes of the offender.

† The veracity of the traditionary history of the Cid, indeed his exist-

The peculiarities of early Scottish poetry may also be referred, in a great degree, to the political relations of the nation, which for many centuries was distracted by all the rancorous dissensions incident to the ill-balanced fabric of feudal government. The frequent and long regencies, always unfavourable to civil concord, multiplied the sources of jealousy, and armed with new powers the factious aristocracy. In the absence of legitimate authority, each baron sought to fortify himself by the increased number of his retainers, who, in their turn, willingly attached themselves to the fortunes of a chief who secured to them plunder and protection. Hence a system of clanship was organized, more perfect and more durable than has existed in any other country, which is not entirely effaced at the present day. To the nobles who garrisoned the Marches, still greater military powers were necessarily delegated for purposes of state defence, and the names of Home, Douglas, and Buccleuch make a far more frequent and important figure in national history than that of the reigning sovereign. Hence private feuds were inflamed and vindicated by national antipathies, and a pretext of patriotism was never wanting to justify perpetual hostility. Hence the scene of the old

ence, discussed and denied by Masdeu, in his *Historia Critica de Espana*, has been satisfactorily established by the learned Müller; and the conclusions of the latter writer are recently confirmed by Condé's posthumous publication of translated Arabian manuscripts of great antiquity, where the Cid is repeatedly mentioned as the chief known by the name of the Warrior, *el Campeador:* "the Cid whom Alla curse;" "the tyrant Cid;" "the accursed Cid," &c. See *Historia de los Arabes de Espana,* ii., 92.

ballads was laid chiefly on the borders, and hence the minstrels of the "North Countrie" obtained such pre-eminence over their musical brethren.

The odious passion of revenge, which seems adapted by nature to the ardent temperaments of the South, but which even there has been mitigated by the spirit of Christianity, glowed with fierce heat in the bosoms of those Northern savages. An offence to the meanest individual was espoused by his whole clan, and was expiated, not by the blood of the offender only, but by that of his whole kindred. The sack of a peaceful castle, and the slaughter of its sleeping inhabitants, seem to have been as familiar occurrences to these Border heroes as the lifting of a drove of cattle, and attended with as little compunction. The following pious invocation, uttered on the eve of an approaching foray, may show the acuteness of their moral sensibility :

> " He that ordained us to be born,
> Sent us mair meat for the morn.
> Come by right or come by wrang,
> Christ, let us not fast owre lang,
> But blithely spend what's gaily got.
> Ride, Rowland, hough 's i' the pot."

When superstition usurps the place of religion, there will be little morality among the people. The only law they knew was the command of their chief, and the only one he admitted was his sword. " By what right," said a Scottish prince to a marauding Douglas, " do you hold these lands ?" " By that of my sword," he answered.

From these causes the early Scottish poetry is

deeply tinged with a gloomy ferocity, and abounds
in details of cool, deliberate cruelty. It is true that
this is frequently set off, as in the fine old ballads of
Chevy Chase and Auld Maitland, by such deeds of
rude but heroic gallantry as, in the words of Sidney, "stir the soul like the sound of a trumpet."
But, on the whole, although the scene of the oldest
ballads is pitched as late as the fourteenth century,
the manners they exhibit are not much superior, in
point of refinement and humanity, to those of our
own North American savages.*

From wanton or vindictive cruelty, especially
when exercised on the defenceless or the innocent,
the cultivated mind naturally shrinks with horror
and disgust ; but it was long ere the stern hearts of
our English ancestors yielded to the soft impulses
of mercy and benevolence. The reigns of the Norman dynasty are written in characters of fire and
blood. As late as the conclusion of the fourteenth
century, we find the Black Prince, the "flower of
English knighthood," as Froissart styles him, super-
intending the butchery of three thousand unresisting
captives, men, women, and children, who vainly
clung to him for mercy. The general usage of sur-
rendering as hostages their wives and children,
whose members were mutilated or lives sacrificed on
the least infraction of their engagements, is a still

* For proof of this assertion, see "Minstrelsy of the Scottish Border,"
and in particular the ballads of "Jellon Grame," "Young Benjie," "Lord
William," "Duel of Wharton and Stuart," "Death of Featherstone-
haugh," "Douglas Tragedy," &c.

better evidence of the universal barbarism of the so much lauded age of chivalry.

Another trait in the old Scotch poetry, and of a very opposite nature from that we have been describing, is its occasional sensibility: touches of genuine pathos are found scattered among the cold, appalling passions of the age, like the flowers which, in Switzerland, are said to bloom alongside the avalanche. No state of society is so rude as to extinguish the spark of natural affection; tenderness for our offspring is but a more enlarged selfishness, perfectly compatible with the utmost ferocity towards others. Hence scenes of parental and filial attachment are to be met with in these poems which cannot be read without emotion. The passion of love appears to have been a favourite study with the ancient English writers, and by none, in any language we have read, is it managed with so much art and feeling as by the dramatic writers of Queen Elizabeth's day. The Scottish minstrels, with less art, seem to be entitled to the praise of possessing an equal share of tenderness. In the Spanish ballad love glows with the fierce ardour of a tropical sun. The amorous serenader celebrates the beauties of his Zayda (the name which, from its frequency, would seem to be a general title for a Spanish mistress) in all the florid hyperbole of Oriental gallantry, or, as a disappointed lover, wanders along the banks of the Guadalete, imprecating curses on her head and vengeance on his devoted rival. The calm dejection and tender melancholy which are diffused over the Scottish

4   2 Y

love-songs are far more affecting than all this turbulence of passion. The sensibility which, even in a rude age, seems to have characterized the Scottish maiden, was doubtless nourished by the solemn complexion of the scenery by which she was surrounded, by the sympathies continually awakened for her lover in his career of peril and adventure, and by the facilities afforded her for brooding over her misfortunes in the silence of rural solitude.

To similar physical causes may be principally referred those superstitions which are so liberally diffused over the poetry of Scotland down to the present day. The tendency of wild, solitary districts, darkened with mountains and extensive forests, to raise in the mind ideas of solemn, preternatural awe, has been noticed from the earliest ages. " Where is a lofty and deeply-shaded grove," writes Seneca, in one of his epistles, " filled with venerable trees, whose interlacing boughs shut out the face of heaven, the grandeur of the wood, the silence of the place, the shade so dense and uniform, infuse into the breast the notion of a divinity ;" and thus the speculative fancy of the ancients, always ready to supply the apparent void of nature, garrisoned each grove, fountain, or grotto, with some local and tutelary genius. These sylvan deities, clothed with corporeal figures, and endowed with mortal appetites, were brought near to the level of humanity ; but the Christian revelation, which assures us of another world, is the " evidence of things unseen," and, while it dissipates the gross and sensible creations of classic mythology, raises our conceptions to the spiritual and the infinite. In our eager thirst for communication with the world of spirits, we naturally imagine it can only be through the medium of spirits like themselves, and, in the vulgar creed, these apparitions never come from the abodes of the blessed, but from the tomb, where they are supposed to await the period of a final and universal resurrection, and whence they are allowed to " revisit the glimpses of the moon," for penance or some other inscrutable purpose. Hence the gloomy, undefined character of the modern apparition is much more appalling than the sensual and social personifications of antiquity.

The natural phenomena of a wild, uncultivated country greatly conspire to promote the illusions of the fancy. The power of clouds to reflect, to distort, and to magnify objects is well known, and on this principle many of the preternatural appearances in the German mountains and the Scottish Highlands, whose lofty summits and unreclaimed valleys are shrouded in clouds and exhalations, have been ingeniously and philosophically explained. The solitary peasant, as the shades of evening close around him, witnesses with dismay the gathering phantoms, and, hurrying home, retails his adventures with due amplification. What is easily believed is easily seen, and the marvellous incident is soon placed beyond dispute by a multitude of testimonies. The appetite, once excited, is keen in detecting other visions and prognostics, which as speedily circulate through the channels of rustic tradition, until in time each glen and solitary heath has its unearthly visitants, each family its omen or boding spectre, and superstition, systematized into a science, is expounded by indoctrinated wizards and gifted seers.

In addition to these fancies, common, though in a less degree, to other nations, the inhabitants of the North have inherited a more material mythology, which has survived the elegant fictions of Greece and Rome, either because it was not deemed of sufficient importance to provoke the arm of the Church, or because it was too nearly accommodated to the moral constitution of the people to be thus easily eradicated. The character of a mythology is always intimately connected with that of the scenery and climate in which it is invented. Thus the graceful Nymphs and Naiads of Greece; the Peris of Persia, who live in the colours of the rainbow, and on the odours of flowers; the Fairies of England, who in airy circles "dance their ringlets to the whistling wind," have the frail gossamer forms and delicate functions congenial with the beautiful countries which they inhabit; while the Elves, Bogles, Brownies, and Kelpies, which seem to have legitimately descended, in ancient Highland verse, from the Scandinavian Dvergar, Nisser, &c., are of a stunted and malignant aspect, and are celebrated for nothing better than maiming cattle, bewildering the benighted traveller, and conjuring out the souls of newborn infants. Within the memory of the present generauon, very well authenticated anecdotes of these ghostly kidnappers have been circulated and greedily credited in the Scottish Highlands. But the sunshine of civilization is rapidly dispelling the lingering mists of superstition. The spirits of darkness love not the cheerful haunts of men, and the bustling activity of an increasing, industrious population allows brief space for the fears or inventions of fancy.

The fierce aspect of the Scottish ballad was mitigated under the general tranquillity which followed the accession of James to the united crowns of England and Scotland, and the Northern muse might have caught some of the inspiration which fired her Southern sister at this remarkable epoch, had not the fatal prejudices of her sovereign in favour of an English or even a Latin idiom diverted his ancient subjects from the cultivation of their own. As it was, Drummond of Hawthornden, whose melodious and melancholy strains, however, are to be enrolled among English verse, is the most eminent name which adorns the scanty annals of this reign. The civil and religious broils, which, by the sharp concussion they gave to the English intellect during the remainder of this unhappy century, seemed to have forced out every latent spark of genius, served only to discourage the less polished muse of the North. The austerity of the reformers chilled the sweet flow of social song, and the only verse in vogue was a kind of rude satire, sometimes pointed at the licentiousness of the Roman clergy, and sometimes at the formal affectation of the Puritans, but which, from

4   2 Y *

the coarseness of the execution, and the transitory interest of its topics, has for the most part been consigned to a decent oblivion.

The Revolution in 1688, and the subsequent union of the two kingdoms, by the permanent assurance they gave of civil and religious liberty, and, lastly, the establishment of parochial schools about the same period, by that wide diffusion of intelligence among the lower orders which has elevated them above every other European peasantry, had a most sensible influence on the moral and intellectual progress of the nation. Improvements in art and agriculture were introduced; the circle of ideas was expanded, and the feelings liberalized by a free communication with their southern neighbours, and religion, resigning much of her austerity, lent a prudent sanction to the hilarity of social intercourse. Popular poetry naturally reflects the habits and prevailing sentiments of a nation. The ancient notes of the border trumpet were exchanged for the cheerful sounds of rustic revelry; and the sensibility which used to be exhausted on subjects of acute but painful interest, now celebrated the temperate pleasures of domestic happiness, and rational though romantic love.

The rustic glee, which had put such mettle into the compositions of James the First and Fifth, those royal poets of the commonalty, as they have been aptly styled, was again renewed; ancient songs, purified from their original vices of sentiment or diction, were revived; new ones were accommodated to ancient melodies; and a revolution was gradually effected in Scottish verse, which experienced little variation during the remainder of the eighteenth century. The existence of a national music is essential to the entire success of lyrical poetry. It may be said, indeed, to give wings to song, which, in spite of its imperfections, is thus borne along from one extremity of the nation to the other, with a rapidity denied to many a nobler composition.

Thus allied, verse not only represents the present, but the past; and while it invites us to repose or to honourable action, its tones speak of joys which are gone, or wake in us the recollections of ancient glory.

It is impossible to trace the authors of a large portion of the popular lyrics of Scotland, which, like its native wild-flowers, seem to have sprung up spontaneously in the most sequestered solitudes of the country. Many of these poets, even, who are familiar in the mouths of their own countrymen, are better known south of the Tweed by the compositions which, under the title of "Scottish Melodies," are diligently thrummed by every miss in her teens, than by their names; while some few others, as Ramsay, Ferguson, &c., whose independent tomes maintain higher reputation, are better known by their names than their compositions, which, much applauded, are, we suspect, but little read.

The union of Scotland with England was unpropitious to the language of the former country; at least, it prevented it from attaining a classical perfection, which some, perhaps, may not regret, as being in its present state a better vehicle for the popular poetry, so consonant with the genius of the nation. Under Edward the First the two nations spoke the same language, and the formidable epics of Barbour and Blind Harry, his contemporaries, are cited by Warton as superior models of English versification. After the lapse of five centuries, the Scottish idiom retains a much greater affinity with the original stock than does the English; but the universal habit with the Scotch of employing the latter in works of taste or science, and of relinquishing their own idiom to the more humble uses of the people, has degraded it to the unmerited condition of a provincial dialect. Few persons care to bestow much time in deciphering a vocabulary which conceals no other treasures than those of popular fancy and tradition.

A genius like Burns certainly may do, and doubtless has done, much to diffuse a knowledge and a relish for his native idiom. His character as a poet has been too often canvassed by writers and biographers to require our panegyric. We define it, perhaps, as concisely as may be, by saying, that it consisted of an acute sensibility, regulated by uncommon intellectual vigour. Hence his frequent visions of rustic love and courtship never sink into mawkish sentimentality, his quiet pictures of domestic life are without insipidity, and his mirth is not the unmeaning ebullition of animal spirits, but is pointed with the reflection of a keen observer of human nature. This latter talent, less applauded in him than some others, is in our opinion his most eminent. Without the grace of La Fontaine, or the broad buffoonery of Berni, he displays the same facility of illuminating the meanest topics, seasons his humour with as shrewd a moral, and surpasses both in a generous sensibility, which gives an air of truth and cordiality to all his sentiments. Lyrical poetry admits of less variety than any other species; and Burns, from this circumstance, as well as from the flexibility of his talents, may be considered as the representative of his whole nation. Indeed, his universal genius seems to have concentrated within itself the rays which were scattered among his predecessors : the simple tenderness of Crawford, the fidelity of Ramsay, and careless humour of Ferguson. The Doric dialect of his country was an instrument peculiarly fitted for the expression of his manly and unsophisticated sentiments. But no one is more indebted to the national music than Burns : embalmed in the sacred melody, his songs are familiar to us from childhood, and, as we read them, the silver sounds with which they have been united seem to linger in our memory, heightening and prolonging the emotions which the sentiments have excited.

Mr. Cunningham, to whom it is high time we should turn, in some prefatory reflections on the condition of Scottish poetry, laments exceedingly the improvements in agriculture and mechanics, the multiplication of pursuits, the wider expansion of

4 E

knowledge, which have taken place among the peasantry of Scotland during the present century.

"Change of condition, increase of knowledge," says he, "the calling in of machinery to the aid of human labour, and the ships which whiten the ocean with their passing and repassing sails, wafting luxuries to our backs and our tables, are all matters of delight to the historian or the politician, but of sorrow to the poet, who delights in the primitive glory of a people, and contemplates with pain all changes which lessen the original vigour of character, and refine mankind till they become too sensitive for enjoyment. Man has now to labour harder and longer to shape out new ways to riches, and even bread, and feel the sorrows of the primeval curse, a hot and sweaty brow, more frequently and more severely than his ancestors. All this is uncongenial to the creation of song, where many of our finest songs have been created, and to its enjoyment, where it was long and fondly enjoyed, among the peasantry of Scotland."—*Preface.*

These circumstances certainly will be a matter of delight to the historian and politician, and we doubt if they afford any reasonable cause of lamentation to the poet. An age of rudeness and ignorance is not the most propitious to a flourishing condition of the art, which indulges quite as much in visions of the past as the present, in recollections as in existing occupations; and this is not only true of civilized, but of ruder ages: the forgotten bards of the Niebelungen and the Heldenbuch, of the roman-

ces of Arthur and of Charlemagne, looked back
through the vista of seven hundred years for their
subjects, and the earliest of the Border minstrelsy
celebrates the antique feuds of a preceding century
On the other hand, a wider acquaintance with speculative and active concerns may be thought to open
a bolder range of ideas and illustrations to the poet.
Examples of this may be discerned among the Scottish poets of the present age; and if the most eminent, as Scott, Campbell, Joanna Baillie, have deserted their natural dialect and the humble themes
of popular interest for others better suited to their
aspiring genius, and for a language which could diffuse and perpetuate their compositions, it can hardly
be matter for serious reproach even with their own
countrymen. But this is not true of Scott, who has
always condescended to illuminate the most rugged
and the meanest topics relating to his own nation,
and who has revived in his " Minstrelsy" not merely
the costume, but the spirit of the ancient Border
muse of love and chivalry.

In a similar tone of lamentation, Mr. Cunningham deprecates the untimely decay of superstition
throughout the land. But the seeds of superstition
are not thus easily eradicated; its grosser illusions,
indeed, may, as we have before said, be scattered by
the increasing light of science; but the principal
difference between a rude and a civilized age, at
least as regards poetical fiction, is that the latter requires more skill and plausibility in working up the
matériel than the former. The witches of Macbeth

are drawn too broadly to impose on the modern spectator, as they probably did on the credulous age of Queen Bess; but the apparition in Job, or the Bodach Glas in Waverley, is shadowed with a dim and mysterious portraiture, that inspires a solemn interest sufficient for the purposes of poetry. The philosophic mind may smile with contempt at popular fancies, convinced that the general experience of mankind contradicts the existence of apparitions; that the narratives of them are vague and ill authenticated; that they never or rarely appeal to more than one sense, and that the most open to illusion; that they appear only in moments of excitement, and in seasons of solitude and obscurity; that they come for no explicable purpose, and effect no perceptible result; and that, therefore, they may in every case be safely imputed to a diseased or a deluded imagination. But if, in the midst of these solemn musings, our philosopher's candle should chance to go out, it is not quite certain that he would continue to pursue them with the same stoical serenity. In short, no man is quite so much a hero in the dark as in broad daylight, in solitude as in society, in the gloom of the churchyard as in the blaze of the drawing-room. The season and the place may be such as to oppress the stoutest heart with a mysterious awe, which, if not fear, is near akin to it. We read of adventurous travellers, who, through a sleepless night, have defied the perilous nonentities of a haunted chamber, and the very interest we take in their exploits proves that the superstitious principle is not wholly extinguished in our own bosoms. So, indeed, do the mysterious inventions of Mrs. Radcliffe and her ghostly school; of our own Brown, in a most especial manner; and Scott, ever anxious to exhibit the speculative as well as practical character of his countrymen, has more than once appealed to the same general principle. Doubtless few in this enlightened age are disposed boldly to admit the existence of these spiritual phenomena; but fewer still there are who have not enough of superstitious feeling lurking in their bosoms for all the purposes of poetical interest.

Mr. Cunningham's work consists of four volumes of lyrics, in a descending series from the days of Queen Mary to our own. The more ancient, after the fashion of Burns and Ramsay, he has varnished over with a colouring of diction that gives greater lustre to their faded beauties, occasionally restoring a mutilated member, which time and oblivion had devoured. Our author's prose, consisting of a copious preface and critical notices, is both florid and pedantic; it continually aspires to the vicious affectation of poetry, and explains the most common sentiments by a host of illustrations and images, thus perpetually reminding us of the children's play of What is it like?" As a poet, his fame has long been established, and the few original pieces which he has introduced into the present collection have the ease and natural vivacity conspicuous in his former compositions. We will quote one or two, which we presume are the least familiar to our readers:

4   2 Z

"A wet sheet and a flowing sea,
    A wind that follows fast,
And fills the white and rustling sail,
    And bends the gallant mast!
And bends the gallant mast, my boys,
    While, like the eagle free,
Away the good ship flies, and leaves
    Old England on the lea.

"O for a soft and gentle wind!
    I heard a fair one cry;
But give to me the swelling breeze,
    And white waves heaving high;
And white waves heaving high, my lads,
    The good ship tight and free;
The world of waters is our home,
    And merry men are we.

"There's tempest in yon horned moon,
    And lightning in yon cloud;
And hark the music, mariners!
    The wind is wakening loud.
The wind is wakening loud, my boys,
    The lightning flashes free;
The hollow oak our palace is,
    Our heritage the sea."—Vol. iv., p. 208.

This spirited water-piece, worthy of Campbell, is
one evidence among others of the tendency of the
present improved condition of the Scottish peasantry
to expand the beaten circle of poetical topics and
illustrations. The following is as pretty a piece of
fairy gossamer as has been spun out of this skeptical age:

"SONG OF THE ELFIN MILLER.

"Full merrily rings the millstone round,
    Full merrily rings the wheel,
Full merrily gushes out the grist—
    Come, taste my fragrant meal.
As sends the lift its snowy drift,
    So the meal comes in a shower;
Work, fairies, fast, for time flies past-
    I borrow'd the mill an hour

"The miller he's a worldly man,
  And maun hae double fee;
So draw the sluice of the churl's dam,
  And let the stream come free.
Shout, fairies, shout! see, gushing out,
  The meal comes like a river;
The top of the grain on hill and plain
  Is ours, and shall be ever.

"One elf goes chasing the wild bat's wing
  And one the white owl's horn;
One hunts the fox for the white o' his tail,
  And we winna hae him till morn.
One idle fay, with the glow-worm's ray,
  Runs glimmering 'mang the mosses;
Another goes tramp wi' the will-o-wisp's lamp,
  To light a lad to the lasses.

"O haste, my brown elf, bring me corn
  From bonnie Blackwood plains
Go, gentle fairy, bring me grain
  From green Dalgonar mains;
But, pride of a' at Closeburn ha',
  Fair is the corn and fatter;
Taste, fairies, taste, a gallanter grist
  Has never been wet with water.

"Hilloah! my hopper is heaped high;
  Hark to the well-hung wheels!
They sing for joy; the dusty roof
  It clatters and it reels.
Haste, elves, and turn yon mountain burn—
  Bring streams that shine like siller;
The dam is down, the moon sinks soon,
  And I maun grind my meller.

"Ha! bravely done, my wanton elves,
  That is a foaming stream;
See how the dust from the mill-ee flies,
  And chokes the cold moon-beam.
Haste, fairies, fleet come baptized feet,
  Come sack and sweep up clean,
And meet me soon, ere sinks the moon,
  In thy green vale, Dalveen."—Vol. iv., p. 327.

The last we can afford is a sweet, amorous effusion, in the best style of the romantic muse of the

Lowlands. It has before found a place in the "Niths-dale and Galloway" collection:

"Thou hast vow'd by thy faith, my Jeanie,
  By that pretty white hand of thine,
And by all the lowing stars in heaven
  That thou wouldst aye be mine;
And I have sworn by my faith, my Jeanie,
  And by that kind heart of thine,
By all the stars sown thick o'er heaven,
  That thou shalt aye be mine.

"Foul fa' the hands wad loose sic bands
  And the heart wad part sic love;
But there's nae hand can loose the band
  But the finger of Him above.
Though the wee wee cot maun be my bield
  And my clothing e'er sae mean,
I should lap me up rich in the faulds of love
  Heaven's armfu' of my Jean.

"Thy white arm wad be a pillow to me,
  Far softer than the down,
And Love wad winnow o'er us his kind, kind wings
  And sweetly we'd sleep and soun'.
Come here to me, thou lass whom I love,
  Come here and kneel wi' me,
The morning is full of the presence of God,
  And I cannot pray but thee.

"The wind is sweet amang the new flowers,
  The wee birds sing saft on the tree,
Our goodman sits in the bonnie sunshine,
  And a blithe old bodie is he;
The Beuk maun be ta'en when he comes hame,
  Wi' the holie psalmodie,
And I will speak of thee when I pray,
  And thou maun speak of me."—Vol. iv., p. 308.

Our readers may think we have been detained too long by so humble a theme as old songs and ballads; yet a wise man has said, "Give me the making of the ballads, and I care not who makes the laws of a nation." Indeed, they will not be lightly regarded by those who consider their influence on the character of a simple, susceptible people, particularly in a rude age, when they constitute the authentic records of national history. Thus the wandering minstrel kindles in his unlettered audience a generous emulation of the deeds of their ancestors, and while he sings the bloody feuds of the Zegris and Abencerrages, the Percy and the Douglas, artfully fans the flame of an expiring hostility. Under these animating influences, the ancient Spaniard and the Border warrior displayed that stern military enthusiasm which distinguished them above every other peasantry in Europe. Nor is this influence altogether extinguished in a polite age, when the narrow attachments of feudal servitude are ripened into a more expanded patriotism; the generous principle is nourished and invigorated in the patriot by the simple strains which recount the honourable toils, the homebred joys, the pastoral adventures, the romantic scenery, which have endeared to him the land of his fathers. There is no moral cause which operates more strongly in infusing a love of country into the mass of the people than the union of a national music with popular poetry.

But these productions have an additional value in the eyes of the antiquarian to what is derived from their moral or political influence, as the repertory of the motley traditions and superstitions that have descended for ages through the various races of the North. The researches of modern scholars have discovered   urprising affinity between the ancient

4   2 Z *

Scottish ballad and the Teutonic, Scandinavian, and even Calmuck romance. Some of the most eminent of the old Border legends are almost literal versions of those which inflamed the martial ardour of our Danish ancestors.* A fainter relationship had before been detected between them and Southern and Oriental fable. Thus, in a barbarous age, when the nearest provinces of Europe had but a distant intercourse with each other, the electric spark of fancy seems to have run around the circle of the remotest regions, animating them with the same wild and original creations.

Even the lore of the nursery may sometimes ascend to as high an antiquity. The celebrated Whittington and his Cat can display a Teutonic pedigree of more than eight centuries; "Jack, commonly called the Giant Killer, and Thomas Thumb," says an antiquarian writer, "landed in England from the very same keels and war-ships which conveyed Hengist and Horsa, and Ebba the Saxon;" and the nursery-maid who chants the friendly monition to the "Lady-bird," or narrates the "fee-faw-fum" adventure of the carnivorous giant, little thinks she has purloined the stores of Teutonic song and Scandinavian mythology.† The ingenious Blanco White,

---

* Such are "The Childe of Elle," "Catharine and Janfarie," "Cospatric," "Willie's Lady," &c.

> "Lady-bird, lady-bird, fly away home,
> Your house is on fire, your children will roam."

This fragment of a respectable little poem has soothed the slumbers of the German infant for many ages. The giant who so cunningly scented the "blood of an Englishman" is the counterpart of the personage

who, under the name of Doblado, has thrown great light on the character and condition of modern Spain, has devoted a chapter to tracing out the genealogies of the games and popular pastimes of his country. Something of the same kind might be attempted in the untrodden walks of nursery literature. Ignorance and youth are satisfied at no great cost of invention. The legend of one generation answers, with little variation, for the next, and, within the precincts of the nursery, obtains that imperishable existence which has been the vain boast of many a loftier lyric. That the mythology of one age should be abandoned to the "Juvenile Cabinet" of another, is indeed curious. Thus the doctrines most venerated by man in the infancy of society become the sport of infants in an age of civilization, furnishing a pleasing example of the progress of the human intellect, and a plausible colouring for the dream of perfectibility.

recorded in the collection of Icelandic mythology made by Snorro in the thirteenth century.—*Edda*, Fable 23.

DA PONTE'S OBSERVATIONS.*

JULY, 1825.

THE larger part of the above work is devoted to strictures upon an article on "Italian Narrative Poetry," which appeared in October, 1824. The author is an eminent Italian teacher at New-York. His poetical abilities have been highly applauded in his own country, and were rewarded with the office of Cæsarean poet at the court of Vienna, where he acquired new laurels as successor to the celebrated Metastasio. His various fortunes in literary and fashionable life while in Europe, and the eccentricities of his enthusiastic character, furnish many interesting incidents for an autobiography, published by him two years since at New-York, and to this we refer those of our readers who are desirous of a more intimate acquaintance with the author.

We regret that our remarks, which appeared to us abundantly encomiastic of Italian letters, and which certainly proceeded from our admiration for them, should have given such deep offence to the respectable author of the "Osservazioni," as to compel him, although a "veteran" in literature, to arm himself against us in defence of his "calumniated" country. According to him, "we judge too lightly of the Italians, and quote as axioms the absurd opin-

---

* "Alcune Osservazioni sull' Articulo Quarto publicato nel North American Review, il Mese d'Ottobre dell' Anno 1824. Da L. Da Ponte Nuova-Jcrca. Stampatori Gray e Bunce." 1825.

ions of their insane rivals (accaniti rivali), the
French. We conceal some things where silence
has the appearance of malice; we expose others
which common generosity should have induced us
to conceal; we are guilty of false and arbitrary ac-
cusations, that do a grievous wrong to the most
tender and most compassionate of nations; we are
wanting in a decent reverence for the illustrious men
of his nation; finally, we pry with the eyes of Argus
into the defects of Italian literature, and with one
eye only, and that, indeed. half shut (anche quello
socchiuso), into its particular merits." It is true, this
sour rebuke is sweetened once or twice with a compliment to the extent of our knowledge, and a "confession that many of our reasonings, facts, and reflections merit the gratitude of his countrymen; that
our intentions were doubtless generous, praisewor-
thy," and the like; but such vague commendations,
besides that they are directly inconsistent with some
of the imputations formerly alleged against us, are
too thinly scattered over sixty pages of criticism to
mitigate very materially the severity of the censure.
The opinions of the author of the Osservazioni on
this subject are undoubtedly entitled to great respect;
but it may be questioned whether the excitable temperament usual with his nation, and the local partiality which is common to the individuals of every
nation, may not have led him sometimes into extravagance and error. This seems to us to have been
the case; and as he has more than once intimated
the extreme difficulty of forming a correct estimate

of a foreign literature, " especially of the Italian," we shall rely exclusively for the support of our opinions on the authorities of his own countrymen, claiming one exception only in favour of the industrious Ginguené, whose opinions he has himself recommended to " the diligent study of all who would form a correct notion of Italian literature."*

His first objection is against what he considers the unfair view which we exhibited of the influence of Italy on English letters. This influence, we had stated, was most perceptible under the reign of Elizabeth, but had gradually declined during the succeeding century, and, with a few exceptions, among whom we cited Milton and Gray, could not be said to be fairly discerned until the commencement of the present age. Our censor is of a different opinion. "Instead of confining *himself*" (he designates us always by this humble pronoun) " to Milton," he says, "for which exception *I acknowledge no obligation to him*, since few there are who were not previously acquainted with it, I would have had him acknowledge that many English writers not only loved and admired, but studiously imitated our authors, from the time of Chaucer to that of the great Byron; for the *clearest evidence* of which it will suffice to read the compositions of this last poet, of Milton, and of Gray. He then censures us for not specifying the obligations which Shakspeare was

* " Ma bisognava aver l'anima di Ginguené, conoscer la lingua e la letteratura Italiana, come Ginguené, e amar il vero come Ginguené per sentire," &c.—*Osservazioni*, p. 115, 116.

under to the early Italian novelists for the plots of
many of his pieces; "which silence" he deems "as
little to be commended as would be an attempt to
conceal the light, the most beautiful prerogative of
the sun, from one who had never before seen it.
And," he continues, "these facts should, for two reasons, have been especially communicated to Americans: first, to animate them more and more to study
the Italian tongue; and, secondly, in order not to
imitate, by what may appear a malicious silence, the
example of another nation [the French], who, after
drawing their intellectual nourishment from us, have
tried every method of destroying the reputation of
their earliest masters."—P. 74–79.

We have extracted the leading ideas diffused by
the author of the *Osservazioni* over half a dozen pages. Some of them have at least the merit of novelty. Such are not, however, those relating to Chaucer, whom we believe no one ever doubted to have
found in the Tuscan tongue—the only one of that
rude age in which

"The pure well-head of poesie did dwell"—

one principal source of his premature inspiration.
We acknowledged that the same sources nourished
the genius of Queen Elizabeth's writers, among
whom we particularly cited the names of Surrey,
Sidney, and Spenser. And if we did not distinguish Shakspeare amid the circle of contemporary
dramatists whom we confessed to have derived the
designs of many of their most popular plays from
Italian models, it was because we did not think the

extent of his obligations, amounting to half a dozen imperfect skeletons of plots, required any such specification; more especially as several of his *great minor* contemporaries, as Fletcher, Shirley, and others, made an equally liberal use of the same materials. The obligations of Shakspeare, such as they were, are, moreover, notorious to every one. The author of the *Osservazioni* expressly disclaims any feelings of gratitude towards us for mentioning those of Milton, because they were notorious. It is really very hard to please him. The literary enterprise which had been awakened under the reign of Elizabeth was in no degree diminished under her successor; but the intercourse with Italy, so favourable to it at an earlier period, was, for obvious reasons, at an end. A Protestant people, but lately separated from the Church of Rome, would not deign to resort to what they believed her corrupt fountains for the sources of instruction. The austerity of the Puritan was yet more scandalized by the voluptuous beauties of her lighter compositions, and Milton, whose name we cited in our article, seems to have been a solitary exception on the records of that day, of an eminent English scholar thoroughly imbued with a relish for Italian letters.

After the days of civil and religious faction had gone by, a new aspect was given to things under the brilliant auspices of the Restoration. The French language was at that time in the meridian of its glory. Boileau, with an acute but pedantic taste, had draughted his critical ordinances from the most

perfect models of classical antiquity. Racine, working on these principles, may be said to have put into
action the poetic conceptions of his friend Boileau;
and, with such a model to illustrate the excellence of
his theory, it is not wonderful that the code of the
French legislator, recommended, as it was, too, by
the patronage of the most imposing court in Europe,
should have found its way into the rival kingdom,
and have superseded there every other foreign influence.* It did so. "French criticism," says Bishop
Hurd, speaking of this period, "has carried it before
the Italian with the rest of Europe. This dexterous
people have found means to lead the taste, as well
as set the fashions, of their neighbours." Again :
"The exact but cold Boileau happened to say something of the *clinquant* of Tasso, and the magic of
this word, like the report of Astolfo's horn in Ariosto, overturned at once the solid and well-built foundation of Italian poetry : it became a sort of watchword among the critics." Mr. Gifford, whose acquaintance with the ancient literature of his nation
entitles him to perfect confidence on this subject,
whatever we may be disposed to concede to him on
some others, in his introduction to Massinger remarks, in relation to this period, that "criticism,
which in a former reign had been making no incon-

* Boileau's sagacity in fully appreciating the merits of Phèdre and of
Athalie, and his independence in supporting them against the fashionable
factions of the day, are well known. But he conferred a still greater obligation on his friend. Racine the younger tells us that "his father, in
his youth, was given to a vicious taste (*concetti*), and that Boileau led him
back to nature, and taught him to rhyme with labour (*rimer difficilement*)."

4   3 A

siderable progress under the great masters of Italy, was now diverted into a new channel, and only studied under the puny and jejune canons of their degenerate followers, the French." Pope and Addison, the legislators of their own and a future age, cannot be exempted from this reproach. The latter conceived and published the most contemptuous opinion of the Italians. In a very early paper of the Spectator bearing his own signature (No. 6), he observes, "The finest writers among the modern Italians [in contradistinction to the ancient Romans] express themselves in such a florid form of words, and such tedious circumlocutions, as are used by none but pedants in our own country, and at the same time fill their writings with such poor imaginations and conceits as our youths are ashamed of before they have been two years at the University." In the same paper he adds, "I entirely agree with Monsieur Boileau, that one verse of Virgil is worth all the tinsel of Tasso." This is very unequivocal language, and our censor will do us the justice to believe that we do not quote it from any "malicious intention," but simply to show what must have been the popular taste, when sentiments like these were promulgated by a leading critic of the day, in the most important and widely-circulated journal in the kingdom.*

* Addison tells us, in an early number of the Spectator, that three thousand copies were daily distributed; and Chalmers somewhere remarks, that this circulation was afterward increased to fourteen thousand; an amount, in proportion to the numerical population and intellectual culture of that day, very far superior to that of the most popular journals at the present time.

In conformity with this anti-Italian spirit, we find that no translation of Ariosto was attempted subsequent to the very imperfect one by Harrington in Elizabeth's time. In the reign of George the Second a new version was published by one Huggins. In his preface he observes, "After this work was pretty far advanced, I was informed there had been a translation published in the reign of Elizabeth, and dedicated to that queen; whereupon I requested a friend to obtain a sight of that book, for it is, it seems, very scarce, and the *glorious original* much more so in this country." Huggins was a learned scholar, although he made a bad translation. Yet it seems he had never met with, or even heard of, the version of his predecessor Harrington. But, without encumbering ourselves with authorities, a glance at the compositions of the period in question would show how feeble are the pretensions of an Italian influence, and we are curious to know what important names, or productions, or characteristics can be cited by the author of the *Osservazioni* in support of it. Dryden, whom he has objected to us, versified, it is true, three of his Fables from Boccaccio; but this brief effort is the only evidence we can recall, in the multitude of his miscellaneous writings, of a respect for Italian letters, and he is well known to have powerfully contributed to the introduction of a French taste in the drama. The only exception which occurs to our general remark is that afforded by the Metaphysical School of Poets, whose vicious propensities have been referred by Dr. Johnson to Marini and his followers. But as an ancient English model for this affectation may be found in Donne, and as the doctor was not prodigal of golden opinions towards Italy, we will not urge upon our opponent what may be deemed an ungenerous, perhaps an unjust imputation. The same indifference appears to have lasted the greater portion of the eighteenth century, and with few exceptions, enumerated in our former article, the Tuscan spring seems to have been almost hermetically sealed against the English scholar. The increasing thirst for every variety of intellectual nourishment in our age has again invited to these early sources, and while every modern tongue has been anxiously explored by the diligence of critics, the Italian has had the good fortune to be more widely and more successfully cultivated than at any former period.

We should apologize to our readers for afflicting them with so much commonplace detail, but we know no other way of rebutting the charge, which, according to the author of the *Osservazioni*, might be imputed to us, of a "malicious silence" in our account of the influence of Italian letters in England.

But if we have offended by saying too little on the preceding head, we have given equal offence on another occasion by saying too much; our antagonist attacks us from such opposite quarters that we hardly know where to expect him. We had spoken, and in terms of censure, of Boileau's celebrated sarcasm upon Tasso; and we had added that, notwithstanding an affected change of opinion. "he ad-

hered until the time of his death to his original heresy." "As much," says our censor, "as it would
have been desirable in him [the reviewer] to have
spoken on these other matters, so it would have been
equally proper to have suppressed all that Boileau
wrote upon Tasso, together with the remarks made
by him in the latter part of his life, as having a tendency to prejudice unfavourably the minds of such
as had not before heard them. Nor should he have
coldly styled it his 'original heresy;' but he should
have said that, in spite of all the heresies of Boileau
and all the blunders of Voltaire, the *Jerusalem* has
been regarded for more than two centuries and a
half, and will be regarded, as long as the earth has
motion, by *all* the nations of the civilized world, as
the most noble, most magnificent, most sublime epic
produced for more than eighteen centuries; that
this consent and this duration of its splendour are
the strongest and most authentic seal of its incontro-
vertible merit; that this unlucky *clinquant*, that de-
faces at most a hundred verses of this poem, and
which, in fact, is nothing but an excess of over-
wrought beauty, is but the merest flaw in a mountain of diamonds; that these hundred verses are compensated by more than three thousand, in which are
displayed all the perfection, grace, learning, eloquence, and colouring of the loftiest poetry." In the
same swell of commendation the author proceeds
for half a page farther. We know not what inad-
vertence on our part can have made it necessary, by
way of reproof to us, to pour upon Tasso's head such

4   3 A*

a pelting of pitiless panegyric. Among all the Italian poets, there is no one for whom we have ever felt so sincere a veneration, after

"quel signor dell' altissimo canto
Che sovra gli altri, com' aquila vola,"

as for Tasso. In some respects he is even superior to Dante. His writings are illustrated by a purer morality, as his heart was penetrated with a more genuine spirit of Christianity. Oppression, under which they both suffered the greater part of their lives, wrought a very different effect upon the gentle character of Tasso and the vindictive passions of the Ghibelline. The religious wars of Jerusalem, exhibiting the triumphs of the Christian chivalry, were a subject peculiarly adapted to the character of the poet, who united the qualities of an accomplished knight with the most unaffected piety. The vulgar distich, popular in his day with the common people of Ferrara, is a homely but unsuspicious testimony to his opposite virtues.* His greatest fault was an ill-regulated sensibility, and his greatest mis-

---

* "Colla penna e colla spada,
Nessun val quanto Torquato."

This elegant couplet was made in consequence of a victory obtained by Tasso over three cavaliers, who treacherously attacked him in one of the public squares of Ferrara. His skill in fencing is notorious, and his passion for it is also betrayed by the frequent, circumstantial, and masterly pictures of it in his "Jerusalem." See, in particular, the mortal combat between Tancred and Argante, can. xix., where all the evolutions of the art are depicted with the accuracy of a professed sword-player. In the same manner, the numerous and animated allusions to field-sports betray the favourite pastime of the author of Waverley; and the falcon, the perpetual subject of illustration and simile in the "Divina Commedia," might lead us to suspect a similar predilection in Dante.

fortune was to have been thrown among people who knew not how to compassionate the infirmities of genius. In contemplating such a character, one may, without affectation, feel a disposition to draw a veil over the few imperfections that tarnished it, and in our notice of it, expanded into a dozen pages, there are certainly not the same number of lines devoted to his defects, and those exclusively of a literary nature. This is but a moderate allowance for the transgressions of any man; yet, according to Mr. Da Ponte, "we close our eyes against the merits of his countrymen, and pry with those of Argus into their defects."

But why are we to be debarred the freedom of criticism enjoyed even by the Italians themselves? To read the *Osservazioni*, one would conclude that Tasso, from his first appearance, had united all suffrages in his favour; that, by unanimous acclamation, his poem had been placed at the head of all the epics of the last eighteen centuries, and that the only voice raised against him had sprung from the petty rivalries of French criticism, from which source we are more than once complimented with having recruited our own forces. Does our author reckon for nothing the reception with which the first academy in Italy greeted the Jerusalem on its introduction into the world, when they would have smothered it with the kindness of their criticism? Or the volumes of caustic commentary by the celebrated Galileo, almost every line of which is a satire? Or, to descend to a later period, when the lapse of more

than a century may be supposed to have rectified
the caprice of contemporary judgments, may we not
shelter ourselves under the authorities of Andres,[*]
whose favourable notice of Italian letters our author
cites with deference; of Metastasio, the avowed admirer and eulogist of Tasso;[†] of Gravina, whose
philosophical treatise on the principles of poetry, a
work of great authority in his own country, exhibits
the most ungrateful irony on the literary pretensions
of Tasso, almost refusing to him the title of a poet.[‡]

But, to proceed no farther, we may abide by the
solid judgment of Ginguené, that second Daniel,
whose opinions we are advised so strenuously "to
study and to meditate." "As to florid images, frivolous thoughts, affected turns, conceits, and *jeux de
mots*, they are to be found in greater abundance in
Tasso's poem than is commonly imagined. The
enumeration of them would be long, if one should
run over the Jerusalem and cite all that could be
classed under one or other of these heads, &c. Let
us content ourselves with a few examples." He
then devotes ten pages to these few examples (our
author is indignant that we should have bestowed as
many lines), and closes with this sensible reflection:
"I have not promised a blind faith in the writers I
admire the most; I have not promised it to Boileau,
I have not promised it to Tasso; and in literature
we all owe our faith and homage to the eternal laws
of truth, of nature, and of taste."[§]

* Dell' Origine, &c., d'Ogni Lett., tom. iv., p. 250.
† Opere Postume di Metastasio, tom. iii , p. 30.
‡ Ragion Poetica, p. 161, 162.   § Tom. v., p. 368. 378.

But, in order to relieve Tasso from an undue responsibility, we had stated in our controverted article that "the affectations imputed to him were to be traced to a much more remote origin;" that "Petrarch's best productions were stained with them, as were those of preceding poets, and that they seemed to have flowed directly from the Provençale, the fountain of Italian lyric poetry." This transfer of the sins of one poet to the door of another is not a whit more to the approbation of our censor, and he not only flatly denies the truth of our remark, as applied to "Petrarch's best productions," but gravely pronounces it "one of the most solemn, the most horrible literary blasphemies that ever proceeded from the tongue or pen of mortal!"* "I maintain," says he, "that not one of those that are truly Petrarch's best productions, and there are very many, can be accused of such a defect; let but the critic point me out a single affected or vicious expression in the three patriotic Canzoni, or in the *Chiare fresche e dolci acque,* or in the *Tre Sorelle,*" &c. (he names several others), "or, in truth, in any of the rest, excepting one or two only." He then recommends to us that, "instead of hunting out the errors and blemishes of these masters of our intellects, and occupying ourselves with unjust and unprofitable criticism, we should throw over them the mantle of gratitude, and recompense them with our eulogiums

* "Dirò essere questa una delle più solenni, delle più orribili letterarie bestemmie, che sia stata mai pronunziata o scritta da lingua o penna mortale."—P. 94.

4 H

and applause." In conformity with which, the author proceeds to pour out his grateful tribute on the head of the ancient laureate for two pages farther, but which, as not material to the argument, we must omit.

We know no better way of answering all this than by taking up the gauntlet thrown down to us, and we are obliged to him for giving us the means of bringing the matter to so speedy an issue. We will take one of the first Canzoni, of which he has challenged our scrutiny. It is in Petrarch's best manner, and forms the first of a series, which has received κατ' ἐξοχὴν, the title of the *Three Sisters* (*Tre Sorelle*). It is indited to his mistress's eyes, and the first stanza contains a beautiful invocation to these sources of a lover's inspiration; but in the second we find him relapsing into the genuine Provençale heresy:

> " When I become *snow* before their *burning rays*,
>   Your noble pride
> Is perhaps offended with my unworthiness.
> Oh ! if this my apprehension
> Should not *temper the flame that consumes me*,
> Happy should I be *to dissolve*; since in their presence
> It is dearer to me to die than to live without them.
> Then, that I do *not melt*,
> Being so frail an object, before so *potent a fire*,
> It is not my own strength which saves me from it,
> But principally fear,
> Which *congeals* the blood wandering through my veins,
> And mends the heart that it may *burn* a long time."*

---

* " Quando agli ardenti rai neve divegno ;
    Vostro gentile sdegno
    Forse ch' allor mia indegnitate offende.
    O, se questa temenza

This melancholy parade of cold conceits, of fire and snow, thawing and freezing, is extracted, be it observed, from one of those choice productions which is recommended as without a blemish; indeed, not only is it one of the best, but it was esteemed by Petrarch himself, together with its two sister odes, the very best of his lyrical pieces, and the decision of the poet has been ratified by posterity. Let it not be objected that the spirit of an ode must necessarily evaporate in a prose translation. The ideas may be faithfully transcribed, and we would submit it to the most ordinary taste whether ideas like those above quoted can ever be ennobled by any artifice of expression.

We think the preceding extract from one of the " best of Petrarch's compositions" may sufficiently vindicate us from the imputation of unprecedented "blasphemy" on his poetical character; but, lest an appeal be again made, on the ground of a diversity in national taste, we will endeavour to fortify our feeble judgment with one or two authorities among his own countrymen, whom Mr. Da Ponte may be more inclined to admit.

The Italians have exceeded every other people in

Non temprasse l' arsura che m' incende ;
Beato venir men ! che 'n lor presenza
M' è più caro il morir, che 'l viver senza.
Dunque ch' i' non mi sfaccia,
Si frale oggetto a si possente foco,
Non è proprio valor, che me ne scampi ;
Ma la paura un poco,
Che 'l sangue vago per le vene agghiaccia,
Risalda 'l cor, perchè più tempo avvampi."

Canzone vii., *nell' Edizione di Muratori.*

the grateful tribute of commentaries which they have paid to the writings of their eminent men ; some of these are of extraordinary value, especially in verbal criticism, while many more, by the contrary lights which they shed over the path of the scholar, serve rather to perplex than to enlighten it.* Tassoni and Muratori are accounted among the best of Petrarch's numerous commentators, and the latter, in particular, has discriminated his poetical character with as much independence as feeling. We cannot refrain from quoting a few lines from Muratori's preface, as exceedingly pertinent to our present purpose: "Who, I beg to ask, is so pedantic, so blind an admirer of Petrarch, that he will pretend that no defects are to be found in his verses, or, *being found, will desire they should be respected with a religious silence?* Whatever may be our rule in regard to moral defects, there can be no doubt that, in those of art and science, the public interest requires that truth should be openly unveiled, since it is important that all should distinguish the beautiful from the bad, in order to imitate the one and to avoid the other."† In

* A single ode has furnished a repast for a volume. The number of Petrarch's commentators is incredible ; no less than a dozen of the most eminent Italian scholars have been occupied with annotations upon him at the same time. Dante has been equally fortunate. A noble Florentine projected an edition of a hundred volumes for the hundred cantos of the "Commedia," which should embrace the different illustrations. One of the latest of the fraternity, Biagioli, in an edition of Dante, published at Paris, 1818, not only claims for his master a foreknowledge of the existence of America, but of the celebrated Harveian discovery of the circulation of the blood !—Tom. i., p. 18, note. After this, one may feel less surprise at the bulk of these commentaries.

† Le Rime di F. Petrarca; con le Osservazioni di Tassoni. Muzio, e Muratori. Pref., p. ix.

the same tone speaks Tiraboschi, tom. v., p. 474.
Yet more to the purpose is an observation of the
Abbé Denina upon Petrarch, "who," says he, "not
only in his more ordinary sonnets affords obvious examples of affectation and coldness, but in his *most
tender and most beautiful* compositions approaches
the conceited and inflated style of which I am now
speaking."* And the "impartial Ginguené," a name
we love to quote, confesses that "Petrarch could not
deny himself those puerile antitheses of cold and
heat, of ice and flames, which occasionally *disfigure
his most interesting and most agreeable pieces.*"† It
would be easy to marshal many other authorities of
equal weight in our defence, but obviously superfluous, since those we have adduced are quite competent to our vindication from the reproach, somewhat
severe, of having uttered "the most horrible blasphemy which ever proceeded from the pen of mortal."

The age of Petrarch, like that of Shakspeare,
must be accountable for his defects, and in this manner we may justify the character of the poet where
we cannot that of his compositions. The Provençale, the most polished European dialect of the Middle Ages, had reached its last perfection before the
fourteenth century. Its poetry, chiefly amatory and
lyrical, may be considered as the homage offered by
the high-bred cavaliers of that day at the shrine of
beauty, and, of whatever value for its literary execu-

* Vicende della Letteratura, tom. ii., p. 55.
† Hist. Lit., tom ii., p. 566.

4   3 B

tion, is interesting for the beautiful grace it diffuses over the iron age of chivalry. It was, as we have said, principally devoted to love; those who did not feel could at least affect the tender passion; and hence the influx of subtle metaphors and frigid conceits, that give a meretricious brilliancy to most of the Provençale poetry. The fathers of Italian verse, Guido, Cino, &c., seduced by the fashion of the period, clothed their own more natural sentiments in the same vicious forms of expression; even Dante, in his admiration, often avowed for the Troubadours, could not be wholly insensible to their influence; but the less austere Petrarch, both from constitutional temperament and the accidental circumstances of his situation, was more deeply affected by them. In the first place, a pertinacious attachment to a mistress whose heart was never warmed, although her vanity may have been gratified by the adulation of the finest poet of the age, seems to have maintained an inexplicable control over his affections, or his fancy, during the greater portion of his life. In the amatory poetry of the ancients, polluted with coarse and licentious images, he could find no model for the expression of this sublimated passion. But the Platonic theory of love had been imported into Italy by the fathers of the Church, and Petrarch, better schooled in ancient learning than any of his contemporaries, became early enamoured of the speculative doctrines of the Greek philosophy. To this source he was indebted for those abstractions and visionary ecstasies which sometimes give a generous elevation, but very often throw a cloud over his conceptions. And again, an intimate familiarity with the Provençale poetry was the natural consequence of his residence in the south of France. There, too, he must often have been a spectator at those metaphysical disputations in the courts of love, which exhibited the same ambition of metaphor, studied antithesis, and hyperbole, as the written compositions of Provence. To all these causes may be referred those defects which, under favour be it spoken, occasionally offend us, even "in his most perfect compositions." The rich finish which Petrarch gave to the Tuscan idiom has perpetuated these defects in the poetry of his country. *Decipit exemplar vitiis imitabile.* His beauties were inimitable, but to copy his errors was in some measure to tread in his footsteps, and a servile race of followers sprang up in Italy, who, under the emphatic name of Petrarchists, have been the object of derision or applause, as a good or a bad taste predominated in their country. Warton, with apparent justice, refers to the same source some of the early corruptions in English poetry; and Petrarch—we hope it is not "blasphemy" to say it—becomes, by the very predominance of his genius, eminently responsible for the impurities of diction which disfigure some of the best productions both in English literature and his own.

We trust that the free manner in which we have spoken will not be set down by the author of the *Osservazioni* to a malicious desire of "calumniating" the literature of his country. We have been neces-

sarily led to it in vindication of our former assertions. After an interval of nearly five centuries, the
dispassionate voice of posterity has awarded to Petrarch the exact measure of censure and applause.
We have but repeated their judgment. No one of
the illustrious triumvirate of the fourteenth century
can pretend to have possessed so great an influence
over his own age and over posterity. Dante, sacrificed by a faction, was, as he pathetically complains,
a wandering mendicant in a land of strangers; Boccaccio, with the interval of a few years in the meridian of his life, passed from the gayety of a court
to the seclusion of a cloister; but Petrarch, the
friend, the minister of princes, devoted, during the
whole of his long career, his wealth, his wide authority, and his talents, to the generous cause of
philosophy and letters. He was unwearied in his
researches after ancient manuscripts, and from the
most remote corners of Italy, from the obscure recesses of churches and monasteries, he painfully collected the mouldering treasures of antiquity. Many
of them he copied with his own hand—among the
rest, all the works of Cicero; and his beautiful transcript of the epistles of the Roman orator is still preserved in the Laurentian library at Florence. In
his numerous Latin compositions he aspired to revive the purity and elegance of the Augustan age
and, if he did not altogether succeed in the attempt,
he may claim the merit of having opened the soil
for the more successful cultivation of later Italian
scholars.

His own efforts, and the generous impulse which his example communicated to his age, have justly entitled him to be considered the restorer of classical learning. His greatest glory, however, is derived from the spirit of life which he breathed into modern letters. Dante had fortified the Tuscan idiom with the vigour and severe simplicity of an ancient language, but the graceful genius of Petrarch was wanting to ripen it into that harmony of numbers which has made it the most musical of modern dialects. His knowledge of the Provençale enabled him to enrich his native tongue with many foreign beauties ; his exquisite ear disposed him to refuse all but the most melodious combinations ; and, at the distance of five hundred years, not a word in him has become obsolete, not a phrase too quaint to be used. Voltaire has passed the same high eulogium upon Pascal ; but Pascal lived three centuries later than Petrarch. It would be difficult to point out the writer who so far fixed the ἔπεα πτερόεντα ; we certainly could not assign an earlier period than the commencement of the last century. Petrarch's brilliant success in the Italian led to most important consequences all over Europe by the evidence which it afforded of the capacities of a modern tongue. He relied, however, for his future fame on his elaborate Latin compositions, and, while he dedicated these to men of the highest rank, he gave away his Italian lyrics to ballad-mongers, to be chanted about the streets for their own profit. His contemporaries authorized this judgment, and it was for his Latin

4   3 B*

eclogues, and his epic on Scipio Africanus, that he received the laurel wreath of poetry in the Capitol. But nature must eventually prevail over the decisions of pedantry or fashion. By one of those fluctuations, not very uncommon in the history of letters, the author of the Latin "*Africa*" is now known only as the lover of Laura and the father of Italian song.

We have been led into this long, we fear tedious exposition of the character of Petrarch, partly from the desire of defending the justice of our former criticism against the heavy imputations of the author of the *Osservazioni*, and partly from reluctance to dwell only on the dark side of a picture so brilliant as that of the laureate, who, in a barbarous age, with

> " his rhetorike so swete
> Enluminid all Itaile of poetrie."

Our limits will compel us to pass lightly over some less important strictures of our author.

About the middle of the last century a bitter controversy arose between Tiraboschi and Lampillas, a learned but intemperate Spaniard, respecting which of their two nations had the best claim to the reproach of having corrupted the other's literature in the sixteenth century. In alluding to it, we had remarked that "the Italian had the better of his adversary in temper, if not in argument." The author of the *Osservazioni* styles this "a dry and dogmatic decision, which so much displeased a certain Italian letterato that he had promised him a confutation of it." We know not who the indignant letterato may be whose thunder has been so long hanging over us, but we must say that, so far from a "dogmatic decision," if ever we made a circumspect remark in our lives, this was one. As far as it went, it was complimentary to the Italians; for the rest, we waived all discussion of the merits of the controversy, both because it was impertinent to our subject, and because we were not sufficiently instructed in the details to go into it. One or two reflections, however, we may now add. The relative position of Italy and Spain, political and literary, makes it highly probable that the predominant influence, of whatever kind it may have been, proceeded from Italy. 1. She had matured her literature to a high perfection while that of every other nation was in its infancy, and she was, of course, much more likely to communicate than to receive impressions. 2. Her political relations with Spain were such as particularly to increase this probability in reference to her. The occupation of an insignificant corner of her own territory (for Naples was very insignificant in every literary aspect) by the house of Aragon opened an obvious channel for the transmission of her opinions into the sister kingdom. 3. Any one, even an Italian, at all instructed in the Spanish literature, will admit that this actually did happen in the reign of Charles the Fifth, the golden age of Italy; that not only, indeed, the latter country influenced, but changed the whole complexion of Spanish letters, establishing, through the intervention of her high-priests, Boscan and Garcilaso, what is universally recognised under the name of an Italian school. This was an era of good taste; but when, only fifty years later, both languages were overrun with those deplorable affectations which, in Italy particularly, have made the very name of the century (*seicento*) a term of reproach, it would seem probable that the same country, which but so short a time before had possessed so direct an influence over the other, should through the same channels have diffused the poison with which its own literature was infected. As Marini and Gongora, however, the reputed founders of the school, were contemporaries, it is extremely difficult to adjust the precise claims of either to the melancholy credit of originality, and, after all, the question to foreigners can be one of little interest or importance.

Much curiosity has existed respecting the source of those affectations which, at different periods, have tainted the modern languages of Europe. Each nation is ambitious of tracing them to a foreign origin, and *all* have at some period or other agreed to find this in Italy. From this quarter the French critics derive their *style précieux*, which disappeared before the satire of Molière and Boileau; from this the English derive their *metaphysical* school of Cowley; and the *cultismo*, of which we have been speaking, which Lope and Quevedo condemned by precept, but authorized by example, is referred by the Spaniards to the same source. The early celebrity of Petrarch and his vicious imitators may afford a specious justification of all this; but a generous criticism may perhaps be excused in referring them to a more ancient origin. The Provençale for three centuries was the most popular, and, as we have before said, the most polished dialect in Europe. The language of the people all along the fertile coasts of the Mediterranean, it was also the language of poetry in most of the polite courts in Europe; in those of Toulouse, Provence, Sicily, and of several in Italy; it reached its highest perfection under the Spanish nobles of Aragon; it passed into England in the twelfth century with the dowry of Eleanor of Guienne and Poictou; even kings did not disdain to cultivate it, and the lion-hearted Richard, if report be true, could embellish the rude virtues of chivalry with the milder glories of a Troubadour.* When this precocious dialect had become extinct, its influence still remained. The early Italian poets gave a sort of classical sanction to its defects; but while their genius may thus, with justice, be accused of scattering the seeds of corruption, the soil must be confessed to have been universally prepared for their reception at a more remote period.

Thus the metaphysical conceits of Cowley's

* Every one is acquainted with Sismondi's elegant treatise on the Provençale poetry. It cannot, however, now be relied on as of the highest authority. The subject has been much more fully explored since the publication of his work by Monsieur Raynouard, Secretary of the French Academy. His *Poésies des Troubadours* has now reached the sixth volume; and W. A. Schlegel, in a treatise of little bulk but great learning, entitled *Observations sur la Langue et la Littérature Provençale*, has pronounced it, by the facts it has brought to light, to have given the *coup de grace* to the theory of Father Andrés, whom Sismondi has chiefly followed.

school, which Dr. Johnson has referred to Marini, may be traced through the poetry of Donne, of Shakspeare and his contemporaries, of Surrey, Wyatt, and Chaucer, up to the fugitive pieces of the thirteenth and fourteenth centuries, which have been redeemed from oblivion by the diligence of the antiquarian. In the same manner, the religious and amatory poetry of Spain at the close of the thirteenth century, as exhibited in their *Cancioneros*, displays the same subtleties and barbaric taste for ornament, from which few of her writers, even in the riper season of her literature, have been wholly uncontaminated. Perhaps the perversities of Voiture and of Scudery may find as remote a genealogy in France. The corruptions of the Pleiades may afford one link in the chain, and any one who has leisure might verify our suggestions. Almost every modern literature seems to have contained, in its earliest germs, an active principle of corruption. The perpetual lapses into barbarism have at times triumphed over all efforts of sober criticism; and the perversion of intellect, for the greater part of a century, may furnish to the scholar an ample field for humiliating reflection. How many fine geniuses in the condemned age of the *seicentisti*, wandering after the false lights of Marini and his school, substituted cold conceits for wit, puns for thoughts, and wiredrawn metaphors for simplicity and nature! How many, with Cowley, exhausted a genuine wit in hunting out remote analogies and barren combinations; or with Lope, and even Calderon, devoted pages to curious distortions of rhyme, to echoes or acrostics, in scenes which invited all the eloquence of poetry ! Prostitutions of genius like these not merely dwarf the human mind, but carry it back centuries to the scholastic subtleties, the alliterations, anagrams, and thousand puerile devices of the Middle Ages.

But we have already rambled too far from the author of the " Osservazioni." Our next rock of offence is a certain inconsiderate astonishment which we expressed at the patience of his countrymen under the infliction of epics of thirty and forty cantos in length ; and he reminds us of our corresponding taste, equally unaccountable, for novels and romances, spun out into an interminable length, like those, for example, by the author of Waverley [p. 82 to 85]. A liberal criticism, we are aware, will be diffident of censuring the discrepancies of national tastes. Where the value of the thought is equal, the luxury of polished verse and poetic imagery may yield a great superiority to poetry over prose, particularly with a people so sensible to melody and of so vivacious a fancy as the Italians ; but, then, to accomplish all this requires a higher degree of skill in the artist, and mediocrity in poetry is intolerable.

> " Mediocribus esse poetis
> Non homines, non Di," &c.

Horace's maxim is not the less true for being somewhat stale. D'Alembert has uttered a sweeping denunciation against all long works in verse, as impossible to be read through without experiencing *ennui;* from which he does not except even the masterpieces of antiquity.* What would he have said to a second-rate Italian epic, wiredrawn into thirty or forty cantos, of the *incredibilia* of chivalry!

The English novel, if tolerably well executed, may convey some solid instruction in its details of life, of human character, and of passion; but the tales of chivalry—the overcharged pictures of an imaginary state of society; of "Gorgons, hydras, and chimeras dire"—can be regarded only as an intellectual *relaxation.* In a less polished dialect, and in a simpler age, they beguiled the tedious evenings of our unlettered Norman ancestors, and, as late as Elizabeth's day, they incurred their parting malediction from the worthy Ascham, as "stuff for wise men to laugh at, whose whole pleasure standeth in open manslaughter and bold bawdry." The remarks in our article, of course, had no reference to the *chef d'œuvres* of their romantic muse, many of which we had been diligently commending. It is the prerogative of genius, we all know, to consecrate whatever it touches.

Some other of our general remarks seem to have been barbed arrows to the patriot breast of the author of the "Osservazioni." Such are our reflections "on the want of a moral or philosophical aim in the ornamental writings of the Italians;" on "love, as suggesting the constant theme and impulse to their poets;" on the evil tendency of their language, in seducing their writers into "an overweening at-

---

* Œuvres Philosophiques, &c., tom. iv., p. 152.

tention to sound." There are few general reflections which have the good fortune not to require
many, and sometimes very important exceptions.
The physiognomy of a nation, whether moral or intellectual, must be made up of those features which
arrest the eye most frequently and forcibly on a
wide survey of them; yet how many individual portraits, after all, may refuse to correspond with the
prevailing one. The Bœotians were dull to a proverb;* yet the most inspired, in the most inspired region of Greek poetry, was a Bœotian. The most
amusing of Greek prose writers was a Bœotian.
Or, to take recent examples, when we find the " accurate Ginguené" speaking of " the *universal* corruption of taste in Italy during the seventeenth century," or Sismondi telling us that " the abuse of wit
extinguished there, during that age, *every other species of talent*," we are obviously not to nail them
down to a pedantic precision of language, or how
are we to dispose of some of the finest poets and
scholars Italy has ever produced; of Chiabrera, Filicaja, Galileo, and other names sufficiently numerous
to swell into a bulky quarto of Tiraboschi? The
same pruning principle applied to writers who, like
Montesquieu, Madame de Staël, and Schlegel, deal
in general views, would go near to strip them of all
respect or credibility.

But it is frivolous to multiply examples. Dante
Tasso, Alamanni, Guidi, Petrarch often, the generous Filicaja always, with, doubtless, very many oth-

* " Sus Bœotica, auris Bœotica, Bœoticum ingenium."

ers, afford an honourable exception to our remark
on the want of a moral aim in the lighter walks of
Italian letters, and to many of these, by indirect criticism, we accorded it in our article. But let any
scholar cast his eye over the prolific productions of
their romantic muse, which even Tiraboschi censures as " crude and insipid,"* and Gravina deplores
as having " excluded the light of truth" from his
countrymen ;† or on their thousand tales of pleasantry and love, which, since Boccaccio's example, have
agreeably perpetuated the ingenious inventions of a
barbarous age ;‡ or round " the circle of frivolous extravagances," as Salfi§ characterizes the burlesque
novelties with which the Italian wits have regaled
the laughter-loving appetite of their nation ; or on
their hecatombs of *amorous* lyrics alone, and he may
accept, in these saturated varieties of the national
literature, a decent apology, if not an ample justification for our assertion.

* Lett. Ital., tom. vii., P. iii., s. 42.   † Ragion Poetica, p. 14.

‡ The Italian Novelle, it is well known, were originally suggested by
the French Fabliaux of the 12th and 13th centuries. It may be worthy
of remark, that, while in Italy these amusing fictions have been diligently propagated from Boccaccio to the present day, in England, although
recommended by a genius like Chaucer, they have scarcely been adopted
by a single writer. The same may be said of them in France, their native soil, with perhaps a solitary exception in the modern imitations by
La Fontaine, himself inimitable.

§ This learned Italian is now employed in completing the unfinished
history of M. Ginguené. With deference to the opinions of the author
of the " Osservazioni" (vide p. 115, 116), we think he has shown in it a
more independent and impartial criticism than his predecessor. His
own countrymen seem to be of the same opinion, and in a recent flattering notice of his work they have qualified their general encomium with
more than one rebuke on the severity of his strictures. *Vide Antologia
for April*, 1824.

But are we not to speak of "love as furnishing the great impulse to the Italian poet," and "as prevailing in his bosom far over every other affection or relation in life?" Have not their most illustrious writers, Dante, Petrarch, Boccaccio, Sannazarius, Tasso, nay, philosophic prelates like Bembo, politic statesmen like Lorenzo, embalmed the names of their mistresses in verse, until they have made them familiar in every corner of Italy as their own? Is not nearly half of the miscellaneous selection of lyrics, in the vulgar edition of "Italian classics," exclusively amatory? Had Milton, Dryden, Pope, or, still more, such solid personages as Bishop Warburton or Dr. Johnson (whose "Tetty," we suspect, never stirred the doctor's poetic feeling), dedicated, not a passing sonnet, but whole volumes to their Beatrices, Lauras, and Leonoras, we think a critic might well be excused in regarding the tender passion as the *vivida vis* of the English author. Let us not be misunderstood, however, as implying that nothing but this amorous incense escapes from the Italian lyric muse. To the exceptions which the author of the *Osservazioni* has enumerated, he might have added, had not his modesty forbidden him, as inferior to none, the sacred melodies which adorn his own autobiography; above all, the magnificent canzone on the "Death of Leopold," which can derive nothing from our commendation, when a critic like Mathias has declared it to have "secured to its author a place on the Italian Parnassus, by the side of Petrarch and Chiabrera."*

* A letter from Mr. Mathias, which fell into our hands some time

As to our remark on the tendency of the soft Italian tones " to seduce their writers into an overweening attention to sound," we are surprised that this should have awakened two such grave pages of admonition from our censor. Why, we were speaking of

> " The Tuscan's siren tongue,
> That music in itself, whose sounds are song."

We thought the remark had been as true as it was old. We cannot but think there is something in it, even now, as we are occasionally lost in the mellifluous redundances of Bembo or Boccaccio, those celebrated models of Italian eloquence. At any rate, our remark fell far short of the candid confession of Bettinelli, who, in speaking of historical writing, observes that " in this, as in every other department of literature, his countrymen have been more solicitous about *style*, and ingenious turns of thought, than utility or good philosophy."*

But we must hasten to the last, not by any means the least offence recorded on the roll of our enormities. This is an ill-omened stricture on the poetical character of Metastasio, for which the author of the *Osservazioni*, after lavishing upon him a shower of golden compliments at our expense, proceeds to censure us as " wanting in respect to this famous man ; as perspicacious only in detecting blemishes ; as

since, concludes a complimentary analysis of the above canzone with this handsome eulogium : " After having read and reflected much on this wonderful production, I believe that, if Petrarch could have heard it, he would have assigned to its author a seat very near to his own, without requiring any other evidence of his vivacious, copious, and sublime genius."   * Risorg. d'Italia Introduz., tom. i., p. 14.

guilty of extravagant and unworthy expressions, which prove that we cannot have read or digested the works of this exalted dramatist, nor those of his biographers, nor of his critics."—P. 98–111. And what, think you, gentle reader, invited these unsavoury rebukes, with the dozen pages of panegyrical accompaniment on his predecessor? "The melodious rhythm of Tasso's verse has *none of the monotonous sweetness so cloying in Metastasio.*" In this italicised line lies the whole of our offending; no more.

We shall consult the comfort of our readers by disposing of this point as briefly as possible. We certainly do not feel, and we will not affect, that profound veneration for Metastasio which the author of the *Osservazioni* professes, and which may have legitimately descended to him with the inheritance of the Cæsarean laurel. We have always looked upon his *operas* as exhibiting an effeminacy of sentiment, a violent contrivance of incident, and an extravagance of character, that are not wholly to be vindicated by the constitution of the Musical Drama. But nothing of all this was intimated in our unfortunate suggestion; and as we are unwilling to startle anew the principles or prejudices of our highly respectable censor, we shall content ourselves with bringing into view one or two stout authorities, behind whom we might have intrenched ourselves, and resign the field to him.

The author has presented his readers with an abstract of about forty pages of undiluted commenda-

4   3 C*

tion on his favourite poet, by the Spaniard Arteaga. We have no objection to this; but, while he recommends them as the opinions of "a learned, judicious, and indubitably impartial critic," we think it would have been fair to temper these forty pages of commendation with some allusion to five-and-thirty pages of almost unmitigated censure which immediately follow them.* In the course of this censorious analysis, it may be noticed that the "impartial Arteaga," speaking of the common imputation of *monotony in the structure of Metastasio's verse, and of his periods,* far from acquitting him, expressly declines passing judgment upon it.

But we may find ample countenance for our "irreverent opinion" in that of Ugo Foscolo, a name of high consideration both as a poet and a critic, and whom, for his perspicacity in the latter vocation, our author, on another occasion, has himself cited and eulogized as his "magnus Apollo." Speaking incidentally of Metastasio, he observes: "To please the court of Vienna, the musicians, and the public of his day, and to gratify the delicacy of his own feminine taste, Metastasio has reduced his *language and versification to so limited a number of words, phrases, and cadences, that they seem always the same,* and in the end produce only the effect of a flute, which conveys rather delightful melody than quick and distinct sensations."† To precisely the same effect speaks W. A. Schlegel, in his eighth lecture

* Le Rivoluzioni del Teatro Musicale, &c., p. 375. 410.
† Essays on Petrarch, p. 93.

on Dramatic Literature, whose acknowledged excellence in this particular department of criticism may induce us to quote him, although a foreigner. These authorities are too pertinent and explicit to require the citation of any other, or to make it necessary, by a prolix but easy enumeration of extracts from the poet, more fully to establish our position.

" Hic aliquid plus
Quam satis est."

We believe we are quite as weary as our readers of the very disagreeable office of dwelling on the defects of a literature so beautiful, and for which we feel so sincere an admiration, as the Italian. The severe impeachment made, both upon the spirit and the substance of our former remarks, by so accomplished a scholar as the author of the *Osservazioni*, has necessarily compelled us to this course in self-defence. The tedious parade of citations must be excused by the necessity of buoying up our opinions in debatable matters of taste by those whose authority alone our censor is disposed to admit—that of his own countrymen. He has emphatically repeated his distrust of the capacity of foreigners to decide upon subjects of literary taste ; yet the extraordinary diversity of opinion manifest between him and those eminent authorities whom we have quoted might lead us to anticipate but little correspondence in the national criticism. An acquaintance with Italian history will not serve to diminish our suspicions; and the feuds which, from the learned but querulous scholars of the fifteenth century to those of our own time, have divided her republic of letters, have not been always carried on with the bloodless weapons of scholastic controversy.*

That some assertions too unqualified, some errors or prejudices should have escaped, in the course of fifty or sixty pages of remark, is to be expected from the most circumspect pen; but a benevolent critic, instead of fastening upon these, will embrace the spirit of the whole, and by this interpret and excuse any specific inaccuracy. It may not be easy to come up to the standard of our author's principles, it may be his partialities, in estimating the intellectual character of his country; but we think we can detect one source of his dissatisfaction with us, in his misconception of our views, which, according to him, were, that " a particular knowledge of the Italian should be widely diffused in America." This he quotes and requotes with peculiar emphasis, objecting it to us as perfectly inconsistent with our style of criticism. Now, in the first place, we made no such declaration. We intended only to give a veracious analysis of one branch of Italian letters. But, secondly, had such been our design, we doubt exceedingly, or, rather, we do not doubt, whether the best way of effecting it would be by indiscriminate

* Take two familiar examples: that of Caro and that of Marini. The adversary of the former poet, accused of murder, heresy, &c., was condemned by the Inquisition, and compelled to seek his safety in exile. The adversary of Marini, in an attempt to assassinate him, fortunately shot only a courtier of the King of Sardinia. In both cases, the wits of Italy, ranged under opposite banners, fought with incredible acrimony during the greater part of a century. The subject of fierce dispute, in both instances, was a *sonnet!*

panegyric. The amplification of beauties, and the prudish concealment of all defects, would carry with it an air of insincerity that must dispose the mind of every ingenuous reader to reject it. Perfection is not the lot of humanity more in Italy than elsewhere. Such intemperate panegyric is, moreover, unworthy of the great men who are the objects of it. They really shine with too brilliant a light to be darkened by a few spots; and to be tenacious of their defects is in some measure to distrust their genius. *Rien n'est beau, que le vrai,* is the familiar reflection of a critic, whose general maxims in his art are often more sound than their particular application.

Notwithstanding the difficulty urged by Mr. Da Ponte of forming a correct estimate of a foreign language, the science of general literary criticism and history, which may be said to have entirely grown up within the last fifty years, has done much to eradicate prejudice and enlarge the circle of genuine knowledge. A century and a half ago, "the best of English critics,"[*] in the opinion of Pope and Dryden, could institute a formal examination, and, of course, condemnation of the plays of Shakspeare "by the practice of the ancients." The best of French critics,[†] in the opinion of every one, could condemn the "Orlando Furioso" for wandering from the rules

---

[*] "The Tragedies of the last Age, considered and examined by the practice of the Ancients," &c. By Thomas Rymer. London, 1678.

[†] "Dissertation Critique sur l'Aventure de Joconde." Œuvres de Boileau, tom. ii.

of Horace; even Addison, in his triumphant vindication of the "Paradise Lost," seems most solicitous
to prove its conformity with the laws of Aristotle;
and a writer like Lope de Vega felt obliged to apologize for the independence with which he deviated
from the dogmas of the same school, and adapted his
beautiful inventions in the drama to the peculiar
genius of his own countrymen.* The magnificent
fables of Ariosto and Spencer were stigmatized as
barbarous, because they were not *classical;* and the
polite scholars of Europe sneered at "the bad taste
which could prefer an 'Ariosto to a Virgil, a Romance to an Iliad.'"† But the reconciling spirit of
modern criticism has interfered; the character, the
wants of different nations and ages have been consulted; from the local beauties peculiar to each, the
philosophic inquirer has deduced certain general
principles of beauty applicable to all; petty national
prejudices have been extinguished; and a difference
of taste, which for that reason alone was before

---

* "Arte de hacer Comedias." Obras Sueltas, tom. iv., p. 406.

> Y quando he de escribir una Comedia,
> Encierro los preceptos con seis llaves;
> Saco a Terencio y Plauto de mi estudio
> Para que no me den voces, que suele
> Dar gritos la verdad en libros mudos, &c.

† See Lord Shaftesbury's "Advice to an Author;" a treatise of great
authority in its day, but which could speak of the "*Gothic* Muse of
Shakspeare, Fletcher, and Milton as lisping with stammering tongues,
that nothing but the youth and rawness of the age could excuse!" Sir
William Temple, with a purer taste, is not more liberal. The term
Gothic, with these writers, is applied to much the same subjects with
the modern term *Romantic*, with this difference : the latter is simply dis-
tinctive, while the former was also an opprobrious epithet.

condemned as a deformity, is now admired as a beautiful variety in the order of nature.

The English, it must be confessed, can take little credit to themselves for this improvement. Their researches in literary history amount to little in their own language, and to nothing in any other. Warton, Johnson, and Campbell have indeed furnished an accurate inventory of their poetical wealth; but, except it be in the limited researches of Drake and of Dunlop, what record have we of all their rich and various prose? As to foreign literature, while other cultivated nations have been developing their views in voluminous and valuable treatises, the English have been profoundly mute.* Yet for several reasons they might be expected to make the best general critics in the world, and the collision of their

* The late translation of Sismondi's "Southern Europe" is the only one, we believe, which the English possess of a detailed literary history. The discriminating taste of this sensible Frenchman has been liberalized by his familiarity with the languages of the North. His knowledge, however, is not always equal to his subject, and the credit of his opinions is not unfrequently due to another. The historian of the "Italian Republics" may be supposed to be at home in treating of Italian letters, and this is undoubtedly the strongest part of his work; but in what relates to Spain, he has helped himself "manibus plenis" from Bouterwek, much too liberally, indeed, for the scanty acknowledgments made by him to the accurate and learned German. Page upon page is *literally translated* from him. Sismondi's work, however, is intrinsically valuable for its philosophical illustrations of the *character* of the Spaniards, by the peculiarities of their literature. His analysis of the national drama, as opposed to that of Schlegel, is also extremely ingenious. Is it not more sound than that of the German? We trust that this hitherto untrodden field in our language will be entered before long by one of our own scholars, whose researches have enabled him to go much more extensively into the Spanish department than either of his predecessors.

judgments in this matter with those of the other European scholars, might produce new and important results.

The author of the *Osservazioni* has accused us of being too much under the influence of his enemies, the French (p. 112). There are slender grounds for this imputation. We have always looked upon this fastidious people as the worst general critics possible; and we scarcely once alluded to their opinions in the course of our article without endeavouring to controvert them. The truth is, while they have contrived their own system with infinite skill, and are exceedingly acute in detecting the least violation of it, they seem incapable of understanding why it should not be applied to every other people, however opposite its character from their own. The consequence is obvious. Voltaire, whose elevated views sometimes advanced him to the level of the generous criticism of our own day, is by no means an exception. His Commentaries on Corneille are filled with the finest reflections imaginable on that eminent poet, or, rather, on the French drama; but the application of these same principles to the productions of his neighbours leads him into the grossest absurdities. "Addison's Cato is the only well-written tragedy in England." "Hamlet is a barbarous production, that would not be endured by the meanest populace in France or Italy." "Lope de Vega and Calderon familiarized their countrymen with all the extravagances of a gross and ridiculous drama." But the French theatre, modelled upon the ancient Greek, can boast "of more than twenty pieces which surpass their most admirable *chef d'œuvres*, without excepting those of Sophocles or Euripides." So in other walks of poetry, Milton, Tasso, Ercilla, occasionally fare no better. "Who would dare to talk to Boileau, Racine, Molière, of an epic poem upon Adam and Eve! Voltaire had one additional reason for the exaltation of his native literature at the expense of every other: he was himself at the head, or aspired to be of every department in it.

Madame de Staël is certainly an eminent exception, in very many particulars, to the general character of her nation. Her defects, indeed, are rather of an opposite cast. Instead of the narrowness of conventional precept, she may be sometimes accused of vague and visionary theory ; instead of nice specific details, of dealing too freely in abstract and independent propositions. Her faults are of the German school, which she may have in part imbibed from her intimacy with their literature (no common circumstance with her countrymen), from her residence in Germany, and from her long intimacy with one of its most distinguished scholars, who lived under the same roof with her for many years. But, with all her faults, she is entitled to the praise of having showed a more enlarged and truly philosophical spirit of criticism than any of her countrymen.

The English have never yielded to the arbitrary legislation of academies ; their literature has at different periods exhibited all the varieties of culture which have prevailed over the other European tongues; and their language, derived both from the Latin and the Teutonic idiom, affords them a much greater facility for entering into the spirit of foreign letters than can be enjoyed by any other European people, whose language is derived almost exclusively from one or the other of these elements. With all these peculiar facilities for literary history and criticism, why, with their habitual freedom of thought, have they remained in it, so far behind most other cultivated nations?

SPANISH LITERATURE.*

JANUARY, 1852.

LITERARY history is the least familiar kind of historical writing. It is, in some respects, the most difficult, requiring certainly far the most laborious study. The facts for civil history we gather from personal experience, or from the examination of a comparatively few authors, whose statements the historian transfers, with such modification and commentary as he pleases, to his own pages. But in literary history, the books are the facts, and pretty substantial ones in many cases, which are not to be mastered at a glance, or on the report of another. It is a tedious process to read through a library in order to decide that the greater part is probably not worth reading at all.

Literary history must come late in the intellectual development of a nation. It is the history of books, and there can be no history of books till books are written. It presupposes, moreover, a critical knowledge — an acquaintance with the principles of taste, which can come only from a wide study and comparison of models. It is, therefore, necessarily the product of an advanced state of civilization and mental culture.

Although criticism, in one form or another, was studied and exemplified by the ancients, yet they

---

* "History of Spanish Literature." By George Ticknor. New York. Harper & Brothers. 1849: 3 vols. 8vo.

made no progress in direct literary history. Neither has it been cultivated by all the nations of modern Europe. At least, in some of them it has met with very limited success. In England, one might have thought, from the free scope given to the expression of opinion, it would have flourished beyond all other countries. But Italy, and even Spain, with all the restraint imposed on intellectual movement, have done more in this way than the whole Anglo-Saxon race. The very freedom with which the English could enter on the career of political action has not only withdrawn them from the more quiet pursuits of letters, but has given them a decided taste for descriptions of those stirring scenes in which they or their fathers have taken part. Hence the great preponderance with them, as with us, of civil history over literary.

It may be further remarked, that the monastic institutions of Roman Catholic countries have been peculiarly favourable to this, as to some other kinds of composition. The learned inmates of the cloister have been content to solace their leisure with those literary speculations and inquiries which had no immediate connexion with party excitement and the turmoils of the world. The best literary histories, from whatever cause, in Spain and in Italy, have been the work of members of some one or other of the religious fraternities.

Still another reason of the attention given to this study in most of those countries may be found in the embarrassments existing there to the general pursuit of science, which have limited the powers to the more exclusive cultivation of works of imagination, and those other productions of elegant literature that come most properly within the province of taste and of literary criticism.

Yet in England, during the last generation, in which the mind has been unusually active, if there have been few elaborate works especially devoted to criticism, the electric fluid has been imperceptibly carried off from a thousand minor points, in the form of essays and periodical reviews, which cover nearly the whole ground of literary inquiry, both foreign and domestic. The student who has the patience to consult these scattered notices, if he cannot find a system ready made to his hands, may digest one for himself by a comparison of contradictory judgments on every topic under review. Yet it may be doubted if the multitude of cross lights thrown at random over his path will not serve rather to perplex than to enlighten him.

Wherever we are to look for the reasons, the fact will hardly be disputed, that, since Warton's learned fragment, no general literary history has been produced in England which is likely to endure, with the exception of Hallam's late work, that, under the modest title of an " Introduction," gives a general survey of the scientific and literary culture of Europe during three centuries. If the English have done so little in this way for their own literature, it can hardly be expected that they should do much for that of their neighbours. If

4   3 D *

they had extended their researches to the Continent, it might probably have been in the direction of Spain; for no country has been made with them the subject of so large historical investigation. One or two good histories devoted to Italy and Germany, as many to the revolutionary period of France—the country with which they are most nearly brought into contact—make up the sum of what is of positive value in this way. But for Spain, a series of writers—Robertson, Watson, Dunlop, Lord Mahon, Coxe, some of the highest order, all respectable—have exhibited the political annals of the monarchy under the Austrian and Bourbon dynasties. Even at the present moment, a still livelier interest seems to be awakened to the condition of this romantic land. Two excellent works, by Head and by Stirling—the latter of especial value—have made the world acquainted, for the first time, with the rich treasures of art in the Peninsula. And last, not least, Ford, in his Hand-book and other works, has joined to a curious erudition, that knowledge of the Spanish character and domestic institutions that can be obtained only from singular acuteness of observation combined with a long residence in the country he describes.

Spain, too, has been the favourite theme of more than one of our own writers, in history and romance; and now the long list is concluded by the attempt of the work before us to trace the progress of intellectual culture in the Peninsula.

No work on a similar extended plan is to be found in Spain itself. Their own literary histories have been chiefly limited to the provinces, or to particular departments of letters. We may except, indeed, the great work of Father Andres, which, comprehending the whole circle of European science and literature, left but a comparatively small portion to his own country. To his name may also be added that of Lampillas, whose work, however, from its rambling and its controversial character, throws but a very partial and unsatisfactory glance on the topics which he touches.

The only books on a similar plan, which cover the same ground with the one before us, are the histories of Bouterwek and Sismondi. The former was written as part of a great plan for the illustration of European art and science since the revival of learning—projected by a literary association in Göttingen. The plan, as is too often the case in such copartnerships, was very imperfectly executed. The best fruits of it were the twelve volumes of Bouterwek, on the elegant literature of modern Europe. That of Spain occupies one of these volumes.

It is written with acuteness, perspicuity, and candour. Notwithstanding the writer is perhaps too much under the influence of certain German theories then fashionable, his judgments, in the main, are temperate and sound, and he is entitled to great credit as the earliest pioneer in this untrodden field of letters. The great defect in the book is the want of proper materials on which to rest these judgments. Of this the writer more than once complains. It is a capital defect, not to be compensated by any talent or diligence in the author. For in this kind of writing, as we have said, books are facts, the very stuff out of which the history is to be made.

Bouterwek had command of the great library of Göttingen. But it would not be safe to rely on any one library, however large, for supplying all the materials for an extended literary history. Above all, this is true of Spanish literature. The difficulty of making a literary collection in Spain is far greater than in most other parts of Europe. The booksellers' trade there is a very different affair from what it is in more favoured regions. The taste for reading is not, or, rather, has not been, sufficiently active to create a demand for the republication always of even the best authors, the ancient editions of whose works have become scarce and most difficult to be procured. The impediment to a free expression of opinion has condemned many more works to the silence of manuscript. And these manuscripts are preserved, or, to say truth, buried, in the collections of old families, or of public institutions, where it requires no ordinary interest with the proprietors, private or public, to be allowed to disinter them. Some of the living Spanish scholars are now busily at work in these useful explorations, the result of which they are giving, from time to time, to the

world in the form of *livraisons* or numbers, which
seem likely to form an important contribution to
historical science. For the impulse thus given to
these patriotic labours the world is mainly indebted to the late venerable Navarrete, who, in his own
person, led the way by the publication of a series
of important historical documents. It is only from
these obscure and uncertain repositories, and from
booksellers' stalls, that the more rare and recondite works in which Spain is so rich can be procured; and it is only under great advantages that
the knowledge of their places of deposit can be obtained, and that, having obtained it, the works
can be had, at a price proportioned to their rarity.
The embarrassments caused by this circumstance
have been greatly diminished under the more liberal spirit of the present day, which, on a few occasions, has even unlocked the jealous archives
of Simancas, that Robertson, backed by the personal authority of the British ambassador, strove
in vain to penetrate.

Spanish literature occupies also one volume of
Sismondi's popular work on the culture of Southern Europe. But Sismondi was far less instructed
in literary criticism than his German predecessor,
of whose services he has freely availed himself in
the course of his work. Indeed, he borrows from
him, not merely thoughts, but language, translating from the German page after page, and incor-
porating it with his own eloquent commentary.
He does not hesitate to avow his obligations; but

they prove at once his own deficiencies in the performance of his critical labours, as well as in the
possession of the requisite materials. Sismondi's
ground was civil history, whose great lessons no
one had meditated more deeply; and it is in the
application of these lessons to the character of the
Spaniards, and in tracing the influence of that character on their literature, that a great merit of his
work consists. He was, moreover, a Frenchman
—or, at least, a Frenchman in language and education; and he was prepared, therefore, to correct
some of the extravagant theories of the German
critics, and to rectify some of their judgments by
a moral standard, which they had entirely over-
looked in their passion for the beautiful.

With all his merits, however, and the additional
grace of a warm and picturesque style, his work,
like that of Bouterwek, must be admitted to afford
only the outlines of the great picture, which they
have left to other hands to fill up in detail, and on
a far more extended plan. To accomplish this
great task is the purpose of the volumes before
us; we are now to inquire with what result. But,
before entering on the inquiry, we will give some
account of the preparatory training of the writer,
and the materials which he has brought together.

Mr. Ticknor, who now first comes before the
world in the avowed character of an author, has
long enjoyed a literary reputation which few authors who have closed their career might not envy.
While quite a young man, he was appointed to

fill the chair of Modern Literature in Harvard College, on the foundation of the late Abiel Smith, Esq., a distinguished merchant of Boston. When he received the appointment, Mr. Ticknor had been some time in Europe pursuing studies in philology. He remained there two or three years afterward, making an absence of above four years in all. A part of this period was passed in diligent study at Göttingen. In Paris, he explored, under able teachers, the difficult *romance* dialects, the medium of the beautiful Provençal.

During his residence in Spain, he perfected himself in the Castilian, and established an intimacy with her most eminent scholars, who aided him in the collection of rare books and manuscripts, to which he assiduously devoted himself. It is a proof of the literary consideration which, even at that early age, he had obtained in the society of Madrid, that he was elected a corresponding member of the Royal Academy of History. His acquisitions in the early literature of modern Europe attracted the notice of Sir Walter Scott, who, in a letter to Southey, printed in Lockhart's Life, speaks of his young guest (Mr. Ticknor was then at Abbotsford) as " a wonderful fellow for romantic lore."

On his return home, Mr. Ticknor entered at once on his academic labours, and delivered a series of lectures on the Castilian and French literatures, as well as on some portions of the English, before successive classes, which he continued to repeat, with the occasional variation of oral instruction, during the fifteen years he remained at the University.

We well remember the sensation produced on the first delivery of these Lectures, which served to break down the barrier which had so long confined the student to a converse with antiquity; they opened to him a free range among those great masters of modern literature who had hitherto been veiled in the obscurity of a foreign idiom. The influence of this instruction was soon visible in the higher education, as well as the literary ardour shown by the graduates. So decided was the impulse thus given to the popular sentiment, that considerable apprehension was felt lest modern literature was to receive a disproportionate share of attention in the scheme of collegiate education.

After the lapse of fifteen years so usefully employed, Mr. Ticknor resigned his office, and, thus released from his academic labours, paid a second visit to Europe, where, in a second residence of three years, he much enlarged the amount and the value of his literary collection. In the more perfect completion of this he was greatly assisted by the professor of Arabic in the University of Madrid, Don Pascual de Gayangos, a scholar to whose literary sympathy and assistance more than one American writer has been indebted, and who to a profound knowledge of Oriental literature unites one equally extensive in the European.

With these aids, and his own untiring efforts,

Mr. Ticknor succeeded in bringing together a body of materials in print and manuscript, for the illustration of the Castilian, such as probably has no rival either in public or private collections. This will be the more readily believed, when we find that nearly every author employed in the composition of this great work—with the exception of a few, for which he has made ample acknowledgments—is to be found on his own shelves. We are now to consider in what manner he has availed himself of this inestimable collection of materials.

The title of the book—the "History of Spanish Literature"—is intended to comprehend all that relates to the poetry of the country, its romances, and works of imagination of every sort, its criticism and eloquence—in short, whatever can be brought under the head of elegant literature. Even its chronicles and regular histories are included; for, though scientific in their import, they are still, in respect to their style and their execution as works of art, brought into the department of ornamental writing. In Spain, freedom of thought, or, at least, the free expression of it, has been so closely fettered that science, in its strictest sense, has made little progress in that unhappy country, and a history of its elegant literature is, more than in any other land, a general history of its intellectual progress.

The work is divided into three great periods, having reference to time rather than to any philosophical arrangement. Indeed, Spanish litera.

4   3 E

ture affords less facilities for such an arrangement than the literature of many other countries, as that of England and of Italy, for example, where, from different causes, there have been periods exhibiting literary characteristics that stamp them with a peculiar physiognomy. For example, in England we have the age of Elizabeth, the age of Queen Anne, our own age. In Italy, the philosophical arrangement seems to correspond well enough with the chronological. Thus, the Trecentisti, the Seicentisti, convey ideas as distinct and as independent of each other as the different schools of Italian art. But in Spain, literature is too deeply tinctured at its fountain-head not to retain somewhat of the primitive colouring through the whole course of its descent. Patriotism, chivalrous loyalty, religious zeal, under whatever modification, and under whatever change of circumstances, have constituted, as Mr. Ticknor has well insisted, the enduring elements of the national literature. And it is this obvious preponderance of these elements throughout which makes the distribution into separate masses on any philosophical principle extremely difficult. A proof of this is afforded by the arrangement now adopted by Mr. Ticknor himself, in the limit assigned to his first period, which is considerably shorter than that assigned to it in his original Lectures. The alteration, as we shall take occasion to notice hereafter, is, in our judgment, a decided improvement.

The first great division embraces the whole time

from the earliest appearance of a written document in the Castilian to the commencement of the sixteenth century, the reign of Charles the Fifth— a period of nearly four centuries.

At the very outset, we are met by the remarkable poem of the Cid, that primitive epic, which, like the Nieblungenlied or the Iliad, stands as the traditional legend of an heroic age, exhibiting all the freshness and glow which belong to the morning of a nation's existence. The name of the author, as is often the case with those memorials of the olden time, when the writer thought less of himself than of his work, has not come down to us. Even the date of its composition is uncertain— probably before the year 1200; a century earlier than the poem of Dante; a century and a half before Petrarch and Chaucer. The subject of it, as its name imports, is, the achievements of the renowned Ruy Diaz de Bivar—*the Cid, the Campeador*, " the lord, the champion," as he was fondly styled by his countrymen, as well as by his Moorish foes, in commemoration of his prowess, chiefly displayed against the infidel. The versification is the fourteen-syllable measure, artless, and exhibiting all the characteristics of an unformed idiom, but, with its rough melody, well suited to the expression of the warlike and stirring incidents in which it abounds. It is impossible to peruse it without finding ourselves carried back to the heroic age of Castile; and we feel that, in its simple and cordial portraiture of existing manners, we get

a more vivid impression of the feudal period than
is to be gathered from the more formal pages of
the chronicler.   Heeren has pronounced that the
poems of Homer were one of the principal bonds
which held the Grecian states together.   The assertion may seem extravagant; but we can well
understand that a poem like that of the Cid, with
all its defects as a work of art, by its proud historic recollections of an heroic age, should do much
to nourish the principle of patriotism in the bosoms
of the people.

From the "Cid" Mr. Ticknor passes to the review of several other poems of the thirteenth, and
some of the fourteenth century.   They are usually
of considerable length.   The Castilian muse, at
the outset, seems to have delighted in works of
longue haleine.   Some of them are of a satirical
character, directing their shafts against the clergy,
with an independence which seems to have marked also the contemporaneous productions of other
nations, but which, in Spain at least, was rarely
found at a later period.   Others of these venerable
productions are tinged with the religious bigotry
which enters so largely into the best portions of
the Castilian literature.

One of the most remarkable poems of the period is the *Danza General*—the "Dance of Death."
The subject is not original with the Spaniards, and
has been treated by the bards of other nations in
the elder time.   It represents the ghastly revels
of the dread monarch, to which all are summon-

ed, of every degree, from the potentate to the peasant.

"It is founded on the well-known fiction, so
often illustrated both in painting and in verse during the Middle Ages, that all men, of all conditions, are summoned to the Dance of Death; a
kind of spiritual masquerade, in which the different ranks of society, from the Pope to the young
child, appear dancing with the skeleton form of
Death. In this Spanish version it is striking and
picturesque—more so, perhaps, than in any other
—the ghastly nature of the subject being brought
into a very lively contrast with the festive tone
of the verses, which frequently recalls some of the
better parts of those flowing stories that now and
then occur in the 'Mirror for Magistrates.'

"The first seven stanzas of the Spanish poem
constitute a prologue, in which Death issues his
summons partly in his own person, and partly in
that of a preaching friar, ending thus:

> Come to the Dance of Death, all ye whose fate
> By birth is mortal, be ye great or small;
> And willing come, nor loitering, nor late,
> Else force shall bring you struggling to my thrall:
> For since yon friar hath uttered loud his call
> To penitence and godliness sincere,
> He that delays must hope no waiting here;
> For still the cry is, Haste! and, Haste to all!

"Death now proceeds, as in the old pictures and
poems, to summon, first, the Pope, then cardinals,
kings, bishops, and so on, down to day-labourers;
all of whom are forced to join his mortal dance,
though each first makes some remonstrance that

4   3 E *

indicates surprise, horror, or reluctance. The call to youth and beauty is spirited:

> Bring to my dance, and bring without delay,
>   Those damsels twain you see so bright and fair;
> They came, but came not in a willing way,
>   To list my chants of mortal grief and care:
> Nor shall the flowers and roses fresh they wear,
> Nor rich attire, avail their forms to save.
> They strive in vain who strive against the grave;
>   It may not be; my wedded brides they are."

Another poem, of still higher pretensions, but, like the last, still in manuscript, is the *Poema de José*—The "Poem of Joseph." It is probably the work of one of those Spanish Arabs who remained under the Castilian domination after the great body of their countrymen had retreated. It is written in the Castilian dialect, but in Arabic characters, as was not very uncommon with the writings of the Moriscoes. The story of Joseph is told, moreover, conformably to the version of the Koran, instead of that of the Hebrew Scriptures.

The manner in which the Spanish and the Arabic races were mingled together after the great invasion produced a strange confusion in their languages. The Christians, who were content to dwell in their old places under the Moslem rule, while they retained their own language, not unfrequently adopted the alphabetical characters of their conquerors. Even the coins struck by some of the ancient Castilian princes, as they recovered their territory from the invaders, were stamped with Arabic letters. Not unfrequently, the ar-

chives and municipal records of the Spanish cities,
for a considerable time after their restoration to
their own princes, were also written in Arabic
characters. On the other hand, as the great inundation gradually receded, the Moors who lingered behind under the Spanish sway often adopted the language of their conquerors, but retained
their own written alphabet. In other words, the
Christians kept their language, and abandoned
their alphabetical characters; while the Moslems
kept their alphabetical characters, and abandoned
their language. The contrast is curious, and may,
perhaps, be accounted for by the fact that the superiority conceded by the Spaniards to the Arabic
literature in this early period led the few scholars
among them to adopt, for their own compositions,
the characters in which that literature was written. The Moriscoes, on the other hand, did what
was natural, when they retained their peculiar
writing, to which they had been accustomed in
the works of their countrymen, while they conformed to the Castilian language, to which they
had become accustomed in daily intercourse with
the Spaniard. However explained, the fact is curious. But it is time we should return to the Spanish Arab poem.

We give the following translation of some of its
verses by Mr. Ticknor, with his few prefatory remarks :

" On the first night after the outrage, Jusuf, as
he is called in the poem, when travelling along

in charge of a negro, passes a cemetery on a hill-
side where his mother lies buried.

And when the negro heeded not, that guarded him behind,
From off the camel Jusuf sprang, on which he rode confined,
And hastened, with all speed, his mother's grave to find,
Where he knelt and pardon sought, to relieve his troubled mind.

He cried, ' God's grace be with thee still, O Lady mother dear!
O mother, you would sorrow, if you looked upon me here ;
For my neck is bound with chains, and I live in grief and feaɪ,
Like a traitor by my brethren sold, like a captive to the spear.

' They have sold me ! they have sold me ! though I never did them harm ;
They have torn me from my father, from his strong and living arm,
By art and cunning they enticed me, and by falsehood's guilty charm,
And I go a base-bought captive, full of sorrow and alarm.'

But now the negro looked about, and knew that he was gone
For no man could be seen, and the camel came alone ;
So he turned his sharpened ear, and caught the wailing tone,
Where Jusuf, by his mother's grave, lay making heavy moan.

And the negro hurried up, and gave him there a blow ;
So quick and cruel was it, that it instant laid him low ;
' A base-born wretch,' he cried aloud, ' a base-born thief art thou :
Thy masters, when we purchased thee, they told us it was so.'

But Jusuf answered straight, ' Nor thief nor wretch am I ;
My mother's grave is this, and for pardon here I cry ;
I cry to Allah's power, and send my prayer on high,
That, since I never wronged thee, his curse may on thee lie.'

And then all night they travelled on, till dawned the coming day,
When the land was sore tormented with a whirlwind's furious sway ;
The sun grew dark at noon, their hearts sunk in dismay,
And they knew not, with their merchandise, to seek or make their way."

The manuscript of the piece, containing about
1200 verses, though not entirely perfect, is in Mr.
Ticknor's hands, with its original Arabic characters converted into the Castilian.   He has saved
it from the chances of time by printing it at length
in his Appendix, accompanied by the following
commendations, which, to one practiced in the old

Castilian literature, will probably not be thought beyond its deserts.

" There is little, as it seems to me, in the early narrative poetry of any modern nation better worth reading than this old Morisco version of the story of Joseph. Parts of it overflow with the tenderest natural affection; other parts are deeply pathetic; and every where it bears the impress of the extraordinary state of manners and society that gave it birth. From several passages, it may be inferred that it was publicly recited; and even now, as we read it, we fall unconsciously into a long-drawn chant, and seem to hear the voices of Arabian camel-drivers, or of Spanish muleteers, as the Oriental or the romantic tone happens to prevail. I am acquainted with nothing in the form of the old metrical romance that is more attractive—nothing that is so peculiar, original, and separate from every thing else of the same class."

With these anonymous productions, Mr. Ticknor enters into the consideration of others from an acknowledged source, among which are those of the Prince Don Juan Manuel and Alfonso the Tenth, or Alfonso the Wise, as he is usually termed. He was one of those rare men who seem to be possessed of an almost universal genius. His tastes would have been better suited to a more refined period. He was, unfortunately, so far in advance of his age, that his age could not fully profit by his knowledge. He was raised so far above the general level of his time, that the light of his genius, though it reached to distant generations, left his own in a comparative obscurity. His great work was the code of the *Siete Partidas*—little heeded in his own day, though destined to become the basis of Spanish jurisprudence both in the Old World and in the New.

Alfonso caused the Bible, for the first time, to be translated into the Castilian. He was an historian, and led the way in the long line of Castilian writers in that department, by his *Cronica General*. He aspired also to the laurel of the Muses. His poetry is still extant in the Gallician dialect, which the monarch thought might in the end be the cultivated dialect of his kingdom. The want of a settled capital, or, to speak more correctly, the want of civilization, had left the different elements of the language contending, as it were, for the mastery. The result was still uncertain at the close of the thirteenth century. Alfonso himself did, probably, more than any other to settle it, by his prose compositions—by the *Siete Partidas* and his Chronicle, as well as by the vernacular version of the Scriptures. The Gallician became the basis of the language of the sister kingdom of Portugal, and the generous dialect of Castile became, in Spain, the language of the court and of literature.

Alfonso directed his attention also to mathematical science. His astronomical observations are held in respect at the present day. But, as Mariana sarcastically intimates, while he was gazing

at the stars he forgot the earth, and lost his kingdom. His studious temper was ill accommodated
to the stirring character of the times. He was
driven from his throne by his factious nobles ; and
in a letter written not long before his death, of
which Mr. Ticknor gives a translation, the unhappy monarch pathetically deplores his fate and
the ingratitude of his subjects. Alfonso the Tenth
seemed to have at command every science but that
which would have been of more worth to him than
all the rest—the science of government. He died
in exile, leaving behind him the reputation of being the wisest fool in Christendom.

In glancing over the list of works which, from
their anomalous character as well as their antiquity, are arranged by Mr. Ticknor in one class,
as introductory to his history, we are struck with
the great wealth of the period—not great, certainly, compared with that of an age of civilization,
but as compared with the productions of most other
countries in this portion of the Middle Ages. Much
of this ancient lore, which may be said to constitute the foundations of the national literature, has
been but imperfectly known to the Spaniards themselves ; and we have to acknowledge our obligations to Mr. Ticknor, not only for the diligence
with which he has brought it to light, but for the
valuable commentaries, in text and notes, which
supply all that could reasonably be demanded, both
in a critical and bibliographical point of view. To
estimate the extent of this information, we must

compare it with what we have derived on the same
subject from his predecessors ; where the poverty
of original materials, as well as of means for illustrating those actually possessed, is apparent at a
glance. Sismondi, with some art, conceals his poverty, by making the most of the little finery at his
command. Thus his analysis of the poem of the
Cid, which he had carefully read, together with
his prose translation of no inconsiderable amount,
covers a fifth of what he has to say on the whole
period, embracing more than four centuries. He
has one fine bit of gold in his possession, and he
makes the most of it, by hammering it out into a
superficial extent altogether disproportionate to its
real value.

Our author distributes the productions which occupy the greater part of the remainder of his first
period into four great classes : Ballads, Chronicles,
Romances of Chivalry, and the Drama. The mere
enumeration suggests the idea of that rude, romantic age, when the imagination, impatient to find
utterance, breaks through the impediments of an
unformed dialect, or, rather, converts it into an instrument for its purposes. Before looking at the
results, we must briefly notice the circumstances
under which they were effected.

The first occupants of the Peninsula who left
abiding traces of their peculiar civilization were
the Romans. Six tenths of the languages now
spoken are computed to be derived from them.
Then came the Visigoths, bringing with them the

peculiar institutions of the Teutonic races.   And
lastly, after the lapse of three centuries, came the
great Saracen inundation, which covered the whole
land up to the northern mountains, and, as it slowly
receded, left a fertilizing principle, that gave life
to much that was good as well as evil in the character and literature of the Spaniards.   It was near
the commencement of the eighth century that the
great battle was fought, on the banks of the Guadalete, which decided the fate of Roderic, the last
of the Goths, and of his monarchy.   It was to the
Goths—the Spaniards, as their descendants were
called—what the battle of Hastings was to the
English.   The Arab conquerors rode over the
country, as completely its masters as were the
Normans of Britain.   But they dealt more merci-
fully with the vanquished.   The Koran, tribute,
or the sword, were the terms offered by the victors.
Many were content to remain under Moslem rule,
in the tolerated enjoyment of their religion, and, to
some extent, of their laws.   Those of nobler metal
withdrew to the rocks of the Asturias ; and every
muleteer or water-carrier who emigrates from this
barren spot glories in his birth-place as of itself a
patent of nobility.

Then came the struggle against the Saracen invaders—that long crusade to be carried on for centuries—in which the ultimate triumph of a hand-
ful of Christians over the large and flourishing
empire of the Moslems is the most glorious of the
triumphs of the Cross upon record.   But it was the

4   3 F

work of eight centuries. During the first of these the Spaniards scarcely ventured beyond their fast-nesses. The conquerors occupied the land, and settled in greatest strength over the pleasant places of the South, so congenial with their own voluptuous climate in the East. Then rose the empire of Cordova, which, under the sway of the Omeyades, rivalled in splendour and civilization the caliphate of Bagdad. Poetry, philosophy, letters, every where flourished. Academies and gymnasiums were founded, and Aristotle was expounded by commentators who acquired a glory not inferior to that of the Stagirite himself. This state of things continued after the Cordovan empire had been broken into fragments, when Seville, Murcia, Malaga, and the other cities which still flourished among the ruins, continued to be centres of a civilization that shone bright amid the darkness of the Middle Ages.

Meanwhile, the Spaniards, strong in their religion, their Gothic institutions, and their poverty, had emerged from their fastnesses in the North, and brought their victorious banner as far as the Douro. In three centuries more, they had advanced their line of conquest only to the Tagus. But their progress, though slow, was irresistible, till at length the Moslems, of all their proud possessions, retained only the petty territory of Granada. On this little spot, however, they made a stand for more than two centuries, and bade defiance to the whole Christian power; while at the same time, though sunk in intellectual culture, they surpassed their best days in the pomp of their architecture and in the magnificence of living characteristic of the East. At the close of the fifteenth century, this Arabian tale—the most splendid episode in the Mohammedan annals — was brought to an end by the fall of Granada before the arms of Ferdinand and Isabella.

Such were the strange influences which acted on the Spanish character, and on the earliest development of its literature—influences so peculiar, that it is no wonder they should have produced results to which no other part of Europe has furnished a parallel. The Oriental and the European for eight centuries brought into contact with one another! yet, though brought into contact, too different in blood, laws, and religion ever to coalesce. Unlike the Saxons and Normans, who sprung from a common stock, with a common faith, were gradually blended into one people; in Spain, the conflicting elements could never mingle. No length of time could give the Arab a right to the soil. He was still an intruder. His only right was the right of the sword. He held his domain on the condition of perpetual war—the war of race against race, of religion against religion. This was the inheritance of the Spaniard, as well as of the Moslem, for eight hundred years. What remarkable qualities was this situation not calculated to call out! Loyalty, heroism, the patriotic feeling, and the loftier feeling of religious enthusiasm. What wonder that the soldier of the Cross should fancy that the arm of Heaven was stretched out to protect him? That St. Jago should do battle for him, with his celestial chivalry? That miracles should cease to be miracles? That superstition, in short, should be the element, the abiding element, of the national character? Yet this religious enthusiasm, in the early ages, was tempered by charity towards a foe whom even the Christian was compelled to respect for his superior civilization. But as the latter gained the ascendant, enthusiasm was fanned by the crafty clergy into fanaticism. As the Moslem scale became more and more depressed, fanaticism rose to intolerance, and intolerance ended in persecution when the victor was converted into the victim. It is a humiliating story—more humiliating even to the oppressors than to the oppressed.

The literature all the while, with chameleon-like sensibility, took the colour of the times; and it is for this reason that we have always dwelt with greater satisfaction on the earlier period of the national literature, rude though it be, with its cordial, free, and high romantic bearing, than on the later period of its glory—brilliant in an intellectual point of view, but in its moral aspect dark and unrelenting.

Mr. Ticknor has been at much pains to unfold these peculiarities of the Castilian character, in order to explain by them the peculiarities of the literature, and indeed to show their reciprocal action on each other. He has devoted occasional chapters to this subject, not the least interesting in his volumes, making the history of the literature a running commentary on that of the nation; and thus furnishing curious information to the political student, no less than to the student of letters. His acute, and at the same time accurate, observations, imbued with a spirit of sound philosophy, give the work a separate value, and raise it above the ordinary province of literary criticism.

But it is time that we should turn to the ballads —or *romances*, as they are called in Spain, the first of the great divisions already noticed. Nowhere does this popular minstrelsy flourish to the same extent as in Spain. The condition of the country, which converted every peasant into a soldier, and filled his life with scenes of stirring and romantic incident, may in part account for it. We have ballads of chivalry, of the national history, of the Moorish wars, mere domestic ballads — in short, all the varieties of which such simple poetical narratives are susceptible. The most attractive of these to the Spaniards, doubtless, were those devoted to the national heroes. The Cid here occupies a large space. His love, his loyalty, his invincible prowess against the enemies of God, are all celebrated in the frank and cordial spirit of a primitive age. They have been chronologically arranged into a regular series—as far as the date could be conjectured—like the Robin Hood ballads in England, so as to form a tolerably complete narrative of his life. It is interesting to observe with what fondness the Spaniards are ever ready to turn to their ancient hero, the very type of Castilian chivalry, and linked by so many glorious recollections with the heroic age of their country.

The following version of one of these ballads, by Mr. Ticknor, will give a fair idea of the original. The time chosen is the occasion of a summons made by the Cid to Queen Urraca to surrender her castle, which held out against the arms of the warrior's sovereign, Sancho the Brave

> "Away! away! proud Roderic!
> Castilian proud, away!
> Bethink thee of that olden time,
> That happy, honoured day,
> When, at St. James's holy shrine,
> Thy knighthood first was won;
> When Ferdinand, my royal sire,
> Confessed thee for a son.
> He gave thee then thy knightly arms,
> My mother gave thy steed;
> Thy spurs were buckled by these hands,
> That thou no grace might'st need.
> And had not chance forbid the vow,
> I thought with thee to wed;
> But Count Lozano's daughter fair,
> Thy happy bride was led.
> With her came wealth, an ample store,
> But power was mine, and state:
> Broad lands are good, and have their grace,
> But he that reigns is great.
> Thy wife is well; thy match was wise;
> Yet, Roderic! at thy side
> A vassal's daughter sits by thee,
> And not a royal bride!"

Our author has also given a pleasing version of the beautiful *romance* of "*Fonte frida, fonte frida*"

—" Cooling fountain, cooling fountain"—which we are glad to see rendered faithfully, instead of following the example of Dr. Percy, in his version of the fine old ballad in a similar simple style, "*Rio verde, rio verde*," which we remember he translates by " Gentle river, gentle river," &c. Indeed, to do justice to Mr. Ticknor's translations, we should have the text before us. Nowhere do we recall so close fidelity to the original, unless in Cary's Dante. Such fidelity does not always attain the object of conveying the best idea of the original. But in this humble poetry it is eminently successful. To give these rude gems a polish would be at once to change their character, and defeat the great object of our author—to introduce his readers to the peculiar culture of a primitive age.

A considerable difficulty presents itself in finding a suitable measure for the English version of the *romances*. In the original they are written in the eight-syllable line, with trochaic feet, instead of the iambics usually employed by us. But the real difficulty is in the peculiarity of the measure—the *asonante*, as it is called, in which the rhyme depends solely on the conformity of vowel sounds, without reference to the consonants, as in English verse. Thus the words *dedo, tiempo, viejos,* are all good *asonantes,* taken at random from one of these old ballads. An attempt has been made by more than one clever writer to transplant them into English verse. But it has had as little success as the attempt to naturalize the ancient hexameter, which neither the skill of Southey nor of Longfellow will, probably, be able to effect. The Spanish vowels have, for the most part, a clear and open sound, which renders the melody of the versification sufficiently sensible to the ear; while the middle station which it occupies between the perfect rhyme and blank verse seems to fit it, in an especial manner, for these simple narrative compositions. The same qualities have recommended it to the dramatic writers of Spain as the best medium of poetical dialogue, and as such it is habitually used by the great masters of the national theatre.

No class of these popular compositions have greater interest than the Moorish *romances*, affording glimpses of a state of society in which the Oriental was strangely mingled with the European. Some of them may have been written by the Moriscoes, after the fall of Granada. They are redolent of the beautiful land which gave them birth —springing up like wild flowers amid the ruins of the fallen capital. Mr. Ticknor has touched lightly on these in comparison with some of the other varieties, perhaps because they have been more freely criticised by preceding writers. Every lover of good poetry is familiar with Mr. Lockhart's picturesque version of these ballads, which has every merit but that of fidelity to the original.

The production of the Spanish ballads is evidence of great sensibility in the nation; but it must also be referred to the exciting scenes in which it was engaged. A similar cause gave rise to the beautiful border minstrelsy of Scotland. But the adventures of robber chieftains and roving outlaws excite an interest of a very inferior order to that created by the great contest for religion and independence which gave rise to the Spanish ballads. This gives an ennobling principle to these compositions, which raises them far above the popular minstrelsy of every other country. It recommended them to the more polished writers of a later period, under whose hands, if they have lost something of their primitive simplicity, they have been made to form a delightful portion of the national literature. We cannot do better than to quote on this the eloquent remarks of our author.

"Ballads, in the seventeenth century, had become the delight of the whole Spanish people. The soldier solaced himself with them in his tent, and the muleteer amid the *sierras;* the maiden danced to them on the green, and the lover sang them for his serenade; they entered into the low orgies of thieves and vagabonds, into the sumptuous entertainments of the luxurious nobility, and into the holiday services of the Church; the blind beggar chanted them to gather alms, and the puppet-showman gave them in recitative to explain his exhibition; they were a part of the very foundation of the theatre, both secular and religious, and the theatre carried them every where, and

added every where to their effect and authority.
No poetry of modern times has been so widely
spread through all classes of society, and none has
so entered into the national character. The ballads, in fact, seem to have been found on every
spot of Spanish soil. They seem to have filled
the very air that men breathed."

The next of the great divisions of this long period is the Chronicles—a fruitful theme, like the
former, and still less explored. For much of this
literature is in rare books, or rarer manuscripts.
There is no lack of materials, however, in the present work, and the whole ground is mapped out
before us by a guide evidently familiar with all
its intricacies.

The Spanish Chronicles are distributed into several classes, as those of a public and of a private
nature, romantic chronicles, and those of travels.
The work which may be said to lead the van of
the long array is the "*Chronica General*" of Alfonso the Wise, written by this monarch probably
somewhere about the middle of the thirteenth century. It covers a wide ground, from the creation
to the time of the royal writer. The third book
is devoted to the Cid, ever the representative of
the heroic age of Castile. The fourth records the
events of the monarch's own time. Alfonso's work
is followed by the "Chronicle of the Cid," in which
the events of the champion's life are now first detailed in sober prose.

There is much resemblance between large por-

tions of these two chronicles. This circumstance
has led to the conclusion that they both must have
been indebted to a common source, or, as seems
more probable, that the "Chronicle of the Cid"
was taken from that of Alfonso. This latter opinion Mr. Ticknor sustains by internal evidence not
easily answered. There seems no reason to doubt,
however, that both one and the other were indebted to the popular ballads, and that these, in their
turn, were often little more than a versification
of the pages of Alfonso's Chronicle; Mr. Ticknor
has traced out this curious process by bringing together the parallel passages, which are too numerous and nearly allied to leave any doubt on the
matter.

Sepulveda, a scholar of the sixteenth century,
has converted considerable fragments of the "General Chronicle" into verse, without great violence
to the original—a remarkable proof of the near
affinity that exists between prose and poetry in
Spain; a fact which goes far to explain the facility and astonishing fecundity of some of its pop
ular poets. For the Spaniards, it was nearly as
easy to extemporize in verse as in prose.

The example of Alfonso the Tenth was followed by his son, who appointed a chronicler to take
charge of the events of his reign. This practice
continued with later sovereigns, until the chronicle gradually rose to the pretensions of regular
history; when historiographers, with fixed salaries,
were appointed by the crowns of Castile and Ar-

agon; giving rise to a more complete body of contemporary annals, from authentic public sources,
than is to be found in any other country in Christendom.

Such a collection, beginning with the thirteenth
century, is of high value, and would be of far higher, were its writers gifted with any thing like a
sound spirit of criticism. But superstition lay too
closely at the bottom of the Castilian character to
allow of this; a superstition nourished by the
strange circumstances of the nation, by the legends
of the saints, by the miracles coined by the clergy
in support of the good cause, by the very ballads
of which we have been treating, which, mingling
fact with fable, threw a halo around both that
made it difficult to distinguish the one from the
other. So palpable to a modern age are many of
these fictions in regard to the Cid, that one ingenious critic doubts even the real existence of this
personage. But this is a degree of skepticism
which, as Mr. Ticknor finely remarks, "makes too
great a demand on our credulity."

This superstition, too deeply seated to be eradicated, and so repugnant to a philosophical spirit
of criticism, is the greatest blemish on the writings
of the Castilian historians, even of the ripest age
of scholarship, who show an appetite for the marvellous, and an easy faith scarcely to be credited
at the present day. But this is hardly a blemish
with the older chronicles, and was suited to the
twilight condition of the times. They are, indeed,

a most interesting body of ancient literature, with all the freshness and chivalrous bearing of the age; with their long, rambling episodes, that lead to nothing; their childish fondness for pageants and knightly spectacles; their rough dialect, which, with the progress of time, working off the impurities of an unformed vocabulary, rose, in the reign of John the Second and of Ferdinand and Isabella, into passages of positive eloquence. But we cannot do better than give the concluding remarks of our author on this rich mine of literature, which he has now, for the first time, fully explored and turned up to the public gaze.

" As we close it up," he says—speaking of an old chronicle he has been criticising—" we should not forget that the whole series, extending over full two hundred and fifty years, from the time of Alfonso the Wise to the accession of Charles the Fifth, and covering the New World as well as the Old, is unrivalled in richness, in variety, and in picturesque and poetical elements. In truth, the chronicles of no other nation can, on such points, be compared to them; not even the Portuguese, which approach the nearest in original and early materials; nor the French, which, in Joinville and Froissart, make the highest claims in another direction. For these old Spanish chronicles, whether they have their foundations in truth or in fable, always strike farther down than those of any other nation into the deep soil of the popular feeling and character. The old Spanish loyalty, the old

Spanish religious faith, as both were formed and
nourished in the long periods of national trial and
suffering, are constantly coming out; hardly less
in Columbus and his followers, or even amid the
atrocities of the conquests in the New World, than
in the half-miraculous accounts of the battles of
Hazinas and Tolosa, or in the grand and glorious
drama of the fall of Granada. Indeed, wherever
we go under their leading, whether to the court
of Tamerlane or to that of Saint Ferdinand, we
find the heroic elements of the national genius
gathered around us; and thus, in this vast, rich
mass of chronicles, containing such a body of antiquities, traditions, and fables as has been offered
to no other people, we are constantly discovering,
not only the materials from which were drawn a
multitude of the old Spanish ballads, plays, and
romances, but a mine which has been unceasing-
ly wrought by the rest of Europe for similar purposes, and still remains unexhausted."

We now come to the Romances of Chivalry, to
which the transition is not difficult from the romantic chronicles we have been considering. It
was, perhaps, the romantic character of these compositions, as well as of the popular minstrelsy of
the country, which supplied the wants of the
Spaniards in this way, and so long delayed the
appearance of the true Romance of Chivalry.

Long before it was seen in Spain, this kind of
writing had made its appearance, in prose and
verse, in other lands; and the tales of Arthur and

the Round Table, and of Charlemagne and his Peers, had beguiled the long evenings of our Norman ancestors, and of their brethren on the other side of the Channel. The first book of chivalry that was published in Spain even then was not indigenous, but translated from a Portuguese work, the Amadis de Gaula. But the Portuguese, according to the account of Mr. Ticknor, probably perished with the library of a nobleman, in the great earthquake at Lisbon, in 1755; so that Montalvan's Castilian translation, published in Queen Isabella's reign, now takes the place of the original. Of its merits as a translation who can speak? Its merits as a work of imagination, and, considering the age, its literary execution, are of a high order.

An English version of the book appeared early in the present century, from the pen of Southey, to whom English literature is indebted for more than one valuable contribution of a similar kind. We well remember the delight with which, in our early days, we pored over its fascinating pages— the bright scenes in which we revelled of Oriental mythology, the beautiful portraiture which is held up of knightly courtesy in the person of Amadis, and the feminine loveliness of Oriana. It was an ideal world of beauty and magnificence, to which the Southern imagination had given a far warmer colouring than was to be found in the ruder conceptions of the Northern minstrel. At a later period, we have read—tried to read—the same story in the pages of Montalvan himself. But the age of chivalry was gone.

The "Amadis" touched the right spring in the Castilian bosom, and its popularity was great and immediate. Edition succeeded edition; and, what was worse, a swarm of other knight-errants soon came into the world, claiming kindred with the Amadis. But few of them bore any resemblance to their prototype, other than in their extravagance. Their merits were summarily settled by the worthy curate in "Don Quixote," who ordered most of them to the flames, declaring that the good qualities of Amadis should not cloak the sins of his posterity.

The tendency of these books was very mischievous. They fostered the spirit of exaggeration, both in language and sentiment, too natural to the Castilian. They debauched the taste of the reader, while the voluptuous images, in which most of them indulged, did no good to his morals. They encouraged, in fine, a wild spirit of knight-errantry, which seemed to emulate the extravagance of the tales themselves. Sober men wrote, preachers declaimed against them, but in vain. The Cortes of 1553 presented a petition to the crown, that the publication of such works might be prohibited, as pernicious to society. Another petition of the same body, in 1555, insists on this still more strongly, and in terms that, coming as they do, from so grave an assembly, can hardly be read at the present day without a smile. Mr. Ticknor notices both these legislative acts, in an extract which we shall give. But he omits the words of the petition of 1555, which dwells so piteously on the grievances of the nation; and which we will quote, as they may amuse the reader. "Moreover," says the instrument, " we say that it is very notorious what mischief has been done to young men and maidens, and other persons, by the perusal of books full of lies and vanities, like Amadis, and works of that description, since young people especially, from their natural idleness, resort to this kind of reading, and becoming enamoured of passages of love or arms, or other nonsense which they find set forth therein, when situations at all analogous offer, are led to act much more extravagantly than they otherwise would have done. And many times the daughter, when her mother has locked her up safely at home, amuses herself with reading these books, which do her more hurt than she would have received from going abroad. All which redounds, not only to the dishonour of individuals, but to the great detriment of conscience, by diverting the affections from holy, true, and Christian doctrine, to those wicked vanities, with which the wits, as we have intimated, are completely bewildered. To remedy this, we entreat your majesty, that no book treating of such matters be henceforth permitted to be read, that those now printed be collected and burned, and that none be published hereafter without special license; by which measures your majesty will render great service to God, as well as to these king-doms," &c., &c.

But what neither the menaces of the pulpit noi the authority of the law could effect, was brought about by the breath of ridicule :

"That soft and summer breath, whose subtile power
Passes the strength of storms in their most desolate hour."

The fever was at its height when Cervantes sent his knight-errant into the world to combat the phantoms of chivalry; and at one touch of his lance, they disappeared forever. From the day of the publication of the "Don Quixote," not a book of chivalry was ever written in Spain. There is no other such triumph recorded in the annals of genius.

We close these remarks with the following ex-tract, which shows the condition of society in Cas-tile under the influence of these romances.

"Spain, when the romances of chivalry first ap-peared, had long been peculiarly the land of knight-hood. The Moorish wars, which had made every gentleman a soldier, necessarily tended to this re-sult; and so did the free spirit of the communities, led on as they were, during the next period, by barons, who long continued almost as independent in their castles as the king was on his throne. Such a state of things, in fact, is to be recognized as far back as the thirteenth century, when the Partidas, by the most minute and painstaking legislation, provided for a condition of society not easily to be distinguished from that set forth in the Amadis or the Palmerin. The poem and history of the Cid bear witness yet earlier, indirectly indeed, but very strongly, to a similar state of the country; and so do many of the old ballads and other records of the national feelings and traditions that had come from the fourteenth century.

"But in the fifteenth, the chronicles are full of it, and exhibit it in forms the most grave and imposing. Dangerous tournaments, in some of which the chief men of the time, and even the kings themselves, took part, occur constantly, and are recorded among the important events of the age. At the passage of arms near Orbigo, in the reign of John the Second, eighty knights, as we have seen, were found ready to risk their lives for as fantastic a fiction of gallantry as is recorded in any of the romances of chivalry; a folly of which this was by no means the only instance. Nor did they confine their extravagances to their own country. In the same reign, two Spanish knights went as far as Burgundy, professedly in search of adventures, which they strangely mingled with a pilgrimage to Jerusalem; seeming to regard both as religious exercises. And as late as the time of Ferdinand and Isabella, Fernando del Pulgar, their wise secretary, gives us the names of several distinguished noblemen, personally known to himself, who had gone into foreign countries, 'in order,' as he says, 'to try the fortune of arms with any cavalier that might be pleased to adventure with them, and so gain honour for themselves, and the fame of valiant and bold knights for the gentlemen of Castile.'

"A state of society like this was the natural result of the extraordinary development which the institutions of chivalry had then received in Spain. Some of it was suited to the age, and salutary; the rest was knight-errantry, and knight-errantry in its wildest extravagance. When, however, the imaginations of men were so excited as to tolerate and maintain, in their daily life, such manners and institutions as these, they would not fail to enjoy the boldest and most free representations of a corresponding state of society in works of romantic fiction. But they went farther. Extravagant and even impossible as are many of the adventures recorded in the books of chivalry, they still seemed so little to exceed the absurdities frequently witnessed or told of known and living men, that many persons took the romances themselves to be true histories, and believed them. Thus, Mexia, the trustworthy historiographer of Charles the Fifth, says, in 1545, when speaking of 'the Amadises, Lisuartes, and Clarions,' that 'their authors do waste their time and weary their faculties in writing such books, which are read by all and believed by many. For,' he goes on, 'there be men who think all these things really happened, just as they read or hear them, though the greater part of the things themselves are sinful, profane, and unbecoming.' And Castillo, another chronicler, tells us gravely, in 1587, that Philip the Second, when he married Mary of England, only forty years earlier, promised, that if King Arthur should return to claim the throne, he would peaceably yield to that prince all his rights; thus implying, at least in Castillo himself, and probably in many of his readers, a full faith in the stories of Arthur and his Round Table.

"Such credulity, it is true, now seems impossible, even if we suppose it was confined to a moderate number of intelligent persons; and hardly less so, when, as in the admirable sketch of an easy faith in the stories of chivalry by the innkeeper and Maritornes in Don Quixote, we are shown that it extended to the mass of the people. But before we refuse our assent to the statements of such faithful chroniclers as Mexia, on the ground that what they relate is impossible, we should recollect, that in the age when they lived, men were in the habit of believing and asserting every day things no less incredible than those recited in the old romances. The Spanish Church then countenanced a trust in miracles as of constant recurrence, which required of those who believed them more credulity than the fictions of chivalry; and yet how few were found wanting in faith! And how few doubted the tales that had come down to them of the impossible achievements of their fathers during the seven centuries of their warfare against the Moors, or the glorious traditions of all sorts, that still constitute the charm of their brave old chronicles, though we now see at a glance that many of them are as fabulous as any thing told of Palmerin or Launcelot!

" But whatever we may think of this belief in the romances of chivalry, there is no question that in Spain, during the sixteenth century, there prevailed a passion for them such as was never known elsewhere. The proof of it comes to us from all sides. The poetry of the country is full of it, from the romantic ballads that still live in the memory of the people, up to the old plays that have ceased to be acted and the old epics that have ceased to be read. The national manners and the national dress, more peculiar and picturesque than in other countries, long bore its sure impress. The old laws, too, speak no less plainly. Indeed, the passion for such fictions was so strong, and seemed so dangerous, that in 1553 they were prohibited from being printed, sold, or read in the American colonies; and in 1555 the Cortes earnestly asked that the same prohibition might be extended to Spain itself, and that all the extant copies of romances of chivalry might be publicly burned. And, finally, half a century later, the happiest work of the greatest genius Spain has produced bears witness on every page to the prevalence of an absolute fanaticism for books of chivalry, and becomes at once the seal of their vast popularity and the monument of their fate."

We can barely touch on the Drama, the last of the three great divisions into which our author has thrown this period. It is of little moment, for down to the close of the fifteenth century, the Castilian drama afforded small promise of the brilliant fortunes that awaited it. It was born under an Italian sky. Almost its first lispings were at the vice-regal court of Naples, and, under a foreign influence, it displayed few of the national characteristics which afterward marked its career. Yet the germs of future excellence may be discerned in the compositions of Encina and Naharro; and the "Celestina," though not designed for the stage, had a literary merit that was acknowledged throughout Europe.

Mr. Ticknor, as usual, accompanies his analysis with occasional translations of the best passages from the ancient masters. From one of these — a sort of dramatic eclogue, by Gil Vicente — we extract the following spirited verses. The scene represents Cassandra, the heroine of the piece, as refusing all the solicitations of her family to change her state of maiden freedom for married life:

> " They say, ' 'Tis time, go, marry! go!'
> But I'll no husband! not I! no!
> For I would live all carelessly,
> Amid these hills, a maiden free,
> And never ask, nor anxious be,
> Of wedded weal or wo.
> Yet still they say, ' Go, marry! go!'
> But I'll no husband! not I! no!
>
> "So, mother, think not I shall wed,
> And through a tiresome life be led,
> Or use, in folly's ways instead,
> What grace the heavens bestow.
> Yet still they say, ' Go, marry, go!'
> But I'll no husband! not I! no!

The man has not been born, I ween,
Who as my husband shall be seen;
And since what frequent tricks have been
Undoubtingly I know.
In vain they say, 'Go, marry! go!'
For I'll no husband! not I! no!"

She escapes to the woods, and her kinsmen, after in vain striving to bring her back, come in dancing and singing as madly as herself:

"She is wild! she is wild!
Who shall speak to the child?
On the hills pass her hours,
As a shepherdess free;
She is fair as the flowers,
She is wild as the sea!
She is wild! she is wild!
Who shall speak to the child?"

During the course of the period we have been considering there runs another rich vein of literature, the beautiful Provençal—those lays of love and chivalry poured forth by the Troubadours in the little court of Provence, and afterward of Catalonia. During the twelfth and thirteenth centuries, when the voice of the minstrel was hardly heard in other parts of Europe, the northern shores of the Mediterranean, on either side of the Pyrenees, were alive with song. But it was the melody of a too early spring, to be soon silenced under the wintry breath of persecution.

Mr. Ticknor, who paid, while in Europe, much attention to the Romance dialects, has given a pleasing analysis of this early literature, after it had fled from the storms of persecution to the south of Spain. But few will care to learn a lan-

guage which locks up a literature that was rather
one of a beautiful promise than performance—that
prematurely perished and left no sign.   And yet
it did leave some sign of its existence, in the in
fluence it exerted both on Italian and Castilian
poetry.

This was peculiarly displayed at the court of
John the Second of Castile, who flourished toward
the middle of the fifteenth century.   That prince
gathered around him a circle of wits and poets,
several of them men of the highest rank ; and the
intellectual spirit thus exhibited shows like a
bright streak in the dawn of that higher civilization which rose upon Castile in the beginning of
the following century.   In this literary circle King
John himself was a prominent figure, correcting
the verses of his loving subjects, and occasionally
inditing some of his own.   In the somewhat severe language of Mr. Ticknor, " he turned to letters to avoid the importunity of business, and to
gratify a constitutional indolence."   There was,
it is true, something ridiculous in King John's most
respectable tastes, reminding us of the character
of his contemporary, René of Anjou.   But still it
was something, in those rough times, to manifest
a relish for intellectual pleasures ; and it had its
effect in weaning his turbulent nobility from the
indulgence of their coarser appetites.

The same liberal tastes, with still better result,
were shown by his daughter, the illustrious Isabella the Catholic.   Not that any work of great

pretensions for its poetical merits was then produced. The poetry of the age, indeed, was pretty generally infected with the meretricious conceits of the Provençal and the old Castilian verse.
We must except from this reproach the "Coplas"
of Jorge Manrique, which have found so worthy
an interpreter in Mr. Longfellow, and which would
do honour to any age. But the age of Isabella
was in Castile what that of Poggio was in Italy.
Learned men were invited from abroad, and took
up their residence at the court. Native scholars
went abroad, and brought back the rich fruits of
an education in the most renowned of the Italian
universities. The result of this scholarship was
the preparation of dictionaries, grammars, and various philological works, which gave laws to the
language, and subjected it to a classic standard.
Printing was introduced, and, under the royal patronage, presses were put in active operation in various cities of the kingdom. Thus, although no
great work was actually produced, a beneficent
impulse was given to letters, which trained up the
scholar, and opened the way for the brilliant civilization of the reign of Charles the Fifth. Our
author has not paid the tribute to the reign of Isabella to which, in our judgment, it is entitled
even in a literary view. He has noticed with commendation the various efforts made in it to introduce a more liberal scholarship, but has by no
means dwelt with the emphasis they deserve on
the importance of the results.

With the glorious rule of Ferdinand and Isabella closes the long period from the middle of the twelfth to the beginning of the sixteenth century —a period which, if we except Italy, has no rival in modern history for the richness, variety, and picturesque character of its literature. It is that portion of the literature which seems to come spontaneously like the vegetation of a virgin soil, that must lose something of its natural freshness and perfume when brought under a more elaborate cultivation. It is that portion which is most thoroughly imbued with the national spirit, unaffected by foreign influences; and the student who would fully comprehend the genius of the Spaniards must turn to these pure and primitive sources of their literary culture.

We cannot do better than close with the remarks in which Mr. Ticknor briefly, but with his usual perspicuity, sums up the actual achievements of the period.

"Poetry, or at least the love of poetry, made progress with the great advancement of the nation under Ferdinand and Isabella; though the taste of the court in whatever regarded Spanish literature continued low and false. Other circumstances, too, favoured the great and beneficial change that was every where becoming apparent. The language of Castile had already asserted its supremacy, and, with the old Castilian spirit and cultivation, it was spreading into Andalusia and Aragon, and planting itself amid the ruins of the

Moorish power on the shores of the Mediterranean.
Chronicle-writing was become frequent, and had
begun to take the forms of regular history. The
drama was advanced as far as the 'Celestina' in
prose, and the more strictly scenic efforts of Tor-
res Naharro in verse. Romance-writing was at
the height of its success. And the old ballad
spirit — the true foundation of Spanish poetry —
had received a new impulse and richer materials
from the contests in which all Christian Spain had
borne a part amid the mountains of Granada, and
from the wild tales of the feuds and adventures
of rival factions within the walls of that devoted
city. Every thing, indeed, announced a decided
movement in the literature of the nation, and almost every thing seemed to favour and facilitate
it."

The second great division embraces the long interval between 1500 and 1700, occupied by the
Austrian dynasty of Spain. It covers the golden
age, as generally considered, of Castilian literature;
that in which it submitted in some degree to the
influences of the advancing European civilization
and which witnessed those great productions of
genius that have had the widest reputation with
foreigners; the age of Cervantes, of Lope de Vega, and of Calderon. The condition of Spain itself was materially changed. Instead of being
hemmed in by her mountain barrier, she had extended her relations to every court in Europe, and
established her empire in every quarter of the

globe. Emerging from her retired and solitary condition, she now took the first rank among the states of Christendom. Her literature naturally took the impress of this change, but not to the extent—or, at least, not in the precise manner—it would have done if left to its natural and independent action. But, unhappily for the land, the great power of its monarchs was turned against their own people, and the people were assailed, moreover, through the very qualities which should have entitled them to forbearance from their masters. Practicing on their loyalty, their princes trampled on their ancient institutions, and loyalty was degraded into an abject servility. The religious zeal of early days, which had carried them triumphant through the Moorish struggle, turned, under the influence of the priests, into a sour fanaticism, which opened the way to the Inquisition —the most terrible engine of oppression ever devised by man—not so terrible for its operation on the body as on the mind. Under its baneful influence, literature lost its free and healthy action ; and, however high its pretensions as a work of art, it becomes so degenerate in a moral aspect, that it has far less to awaken our sympathies than the productions of an earlier time. From this circumstance, as well as from that of its being much better known to the generality of scholars, we shall pass only in rapid review some of its most remarkable persons and productions. Before entering on this field, we will quote some important observa-

4   3 H *

tions of our author on the general prospects of the period he is to discuss. Thus to allow coming events to cast their shadows before, is better suited to the purposes of the literary historian than of the novelist. His remarks on the Inquisition are striking.

" The results of such extraordinary traits in the national character could not fail to be impressed upon the literature of any country, and particularly upon a literature which, like that of Spain, had always been strongly marked by the popular temperament and peculiarities. But the period was not one in which such traits could be produced with poetical effect. The ancient loyalty, which had once been so generous an element in the Spanish character and cultivation, was now infected with the ambition of universal empire, and was lavished upon princes and nobles who, like the later Philips and their ministers, were unworthy of its homage ; so that, in the Spanish historians and epic poets of this period, and even in more popular writers, like Quevedo and Calderon, we find a vainglorious admiration of their country, and a poor flattery of royalty and rank, that reminds us of the old Castilian pride and deference only by showing how both had lost their dignity. And so it is with the ancient religious feeling that was so nearly akin to this loyalty. The Christian spirit, which gave an air of duty to the wildest forms of adventure throughout the country, during its long contest with the power of misbelief, was now fallen away into a low and anxious bigotry, fierce and intolerant toward every thing that differed from its own sharply-defined faith, and yet so pervading and so popular, that the romances and tales of the time are full of it, and the national theatre, in more than one form, becomes its strange and grotesque monument.

"Of course, the body of Spanish poetry and eloquent prose produced during this interval—the earlier part of which was the period of the greatest glory Spain ever enjoyed—was injuriously affected by so diseased a condition of the national character. That generous and manly spirit which is the breath of intellectual life to any people, was restrained and stifled. Some departments of literature, such as forensic eloquence and eloquence of the pulpit, satirical poetry, and elegant didactic prose, hardly appeared at all; others, like epic poetry, were strangely perverted and misdirected; while yet others, like the drama, the ballads, and the lighter forms of lyrical verse, seemed to grow exuberant and lawless, from the very restraints imposed on the rest; restraints which, in fact, forced poetical genius into channels where it would otherwise have flowed much more scantily and with much less luxuriant results.

"The books that were published during the whole period on which we are now entering, and indeed for a century later, bore everywhere marks of the subjection to which the press and those who wrote for it were alike reduced. From the abject title-pages and dedications of the authors themselves, through the crowd of certificates collected from their friends to establish the orthodoxy of works that were often as little connected with religion as fairy tales, down to the colophon, supplicating pardon for any unconscious neglect of the authority of the Church or any too free use of classical mythology, we are continually oppressed with painful proofs, not only how completely the human mind was enslaved in Spain, but how grievously it had become cramped and crippled by the chains it had so long worn.

"But we shall be greatly in error, if, as we notice these deep marks and strange peculiarities in Spanish literature, we suppose they were produced by the direct action either of the Inquisition or of the civil government of the country, compressing, as if with a physical power, the whole circle of society. This would have been impossible. No nation would have submitted to it; much less so high-spirited and chivalrous a nation as the Spanish in the reign of Charles the Fifth and in the greater part of that of Philip the Second. This dark work was done earlier. Its foundations were laid deep and sure in the old Castilian character. It was the result of the excess and misdirection of that very Christian zeal which fought so fervently and gloriously against the intrusion of Mohammedanism into Europe, and of that military loyalty which sustained the Spanish princes so faithfully through the whole of that terrible contest;

both of them high and ennobling principles, which in Spain were more wrought into the popular character than they ever were in any other country.

" Spanish submission to an unworthy despotism, and Spanish bigotry, were, therefore, not the results of the Inquisition and the modern appliances of a corrupting monarchy ; but the Inquisition and the despotism were rather the results of a misdirection of the old religious faith and loyalty. The civilization that recognised such elements presented, no doubt, much that was brilliant, picturesque, and ennobling ; but it was not without its darker side ; for it failed to excite and cherish many of the most elevating qualities of our common nature—those qualities which are produced in domestic life, and result in the cultivation of the arts of peace.

" As we proceed, therefore, we shall find, in the full development of the Spanish character and literature, seeming contradictions, which can be reconciled only by looking back to the foundations on which they both rest. We shall find the Inquisition at the height of its power, and a free and immoral drama at the height of its popularity— Philip the Second and his two immediate successors governing the country with the severest and most jealous despotism, while Quevedo was writing his witty and dangerous satires, and Cervantes his genial and wise Don Quixote. But the more carefully we consider such a state of things, the more we shall see that these are moral contra-

dictions which draw after them grave moral mis-
chiefs. The Spanish nation and the men of genius
who illustrated its best days, might be light-heart-
ed because they did not perceive the limits within
which they were confined, or did not, for a time,
feel the restraints that were imposed upon them.
What they gave up might be given up with cheerful hearts, and not with a sense of discouragement
and degradation; it might be done in the spirit
of loyalty and with the fervor of religious zeal;
but it is not at all the less true that the hard limits were there, and that great sacrifices of the best
elements of the national character must follow.

"Of this time gave abundant proof. Only a
little more than a century elapsed before the government that had threatened the world with a universal empire was hardly able to repel invasion
from abroad, or maintain the allegiance of its own
subjects at home. Life—the vigorous, poetical
life which had been kindled through the country
in its ages of trial and adversity—was evidently
passing out of the whole Spanish character. As
a people they sunk away from being a first-rate
power in Europe, till they became one of altogether inferior importance and consideration; and
then, drawing back haughtily behind their mountains, rejected all equal intercourse with the rest
of the world, in a spirit almost as exclusive and
intolerant as that in which they had formerly refused intercourse with their Arab conquerors. The
crude and gross wealth poured in from their Amer-

ican possessions sustained, indeed, for yet another century the forms of a miserable political existence in their government; but the earnest faith, the loyalty, the dignity of the Spanish people, were gone; and little remained in their place but a weak subserviency to the unworthy masters of the state, and a low, timid bigotry in whatever related to religion. The old enthusiasm, rarely directed by wisdom from the first, and often misdirected afterward, faded away; and the poetry of the country, which had always depended more on the state of the popular feeling than any other poetry of modern times, faded and failed with it."

The first thing that strikes us, at the very commencement of this new period, is the attempt to subject the Castilian to Italian forms of versification. This attempt, through the perfect tact of Boscan, and the delicate genius of Garcilasso, who rivalled in their own walks the greatest masters of Italian verse, was eminently successful. It would, indeed, be wonderful if the intimate relations now established between Spain and Italy did not lead to a reciprocal influence of their literatures on each other. The two languages, descended from the same parent stock, the Latin, were nearest of kin to each other—in the relation, if we may so speak, of brother and sister. The Castilian, with its deep Arabic gutturals, and its clear, sonorous sounds, had the masculine character, which assorted well with the more feminine graces of the Italian, with its musical cadences and soft vowel terminations. The transition from one language to the other was almost as natural as from the dialect of one province of a country to that of its neighbour.

The revolution thus effected went far below the surface of Spanish poetry. It is for this reason that we are satisfied that Mr. Ticknor has judged wisely, as we have before intimated, in arranging the division lines of his two periods in such a manner as to throw into the former that primitive portion of the national literature which was untouched, at least to any considerable extent, by a foreign influence.

Yet, in the compositions of this second period, it must be admitted that by far the greater portion of what is really good rests on the original basis of the national character, though under the controlling influences of a riper age of civilization. And foremost of the great writers of this national school we find the author of "Don Quixote," whose fame seems now to belong to Europe, as much as to the land that gave him birth. Mr. Ticknor has given a very interesting notice of the great writer and of his various compositions. The materials for this are, for the most part, not very difficult to be procured; for Cervantes is the author whom his countrymen, since his death, with a spirit very different from that of his contemporaries, have most delighted to honour. Fortunately, the Castilian romancer has supplied us with materials for his own biography, which re mind us of the lamentable poverty under which we labour in all that relates to his contemporary, Shakspeare. In Mr. Ticknor's biographical notice, the reader will find some details probably not familiar to him, and a careful discussion of those points over which still rests any cloud of uncertainty.

He inquires into the grounds of the imputation of an unworthy jealousy having existed between Lope and his illustrious rival, and we heartily concur with him in the general results of his investigation.

" Concerning his relations with Lope de Vega there has been much discussion to little purpose. Certain it is that Cervantes often praises this great literary idol of his age, and that four or five times Lope stoops from his pride of place and compliments Cervantes, though never beyond the measure of praise he bestows on many whose claims were greatly inferior. But in his stately flight, it is plain that he soared much above the author of Don Quixote, to whose highest merits he seemed carefully to avoid all homage; and though I find no sufficient reason to suppose their relation to each other was marked by any personal jealousy or ill-will, as has been sometimes supposed, yet I can find no proof that it was either intimate or kindly. On the contrary, when we consider the good nature of Cervantes, which made him praise to excess nearly all his other literary contemporaries, as well as the greatest of them all, and when we allow for the frequency of hyperbole in such praises at that time, which prevented them from being what they would now be, we may perceive an occasional coolness in his manner, when he speaks of Lope, which shows that, without overrating his own merits and claims, he was not insensible to the difference in their respective positions, or to the injustice towards himself implied by it. Indeed, his whole tone, whenever he notices Lope, seems to be marked with much personal dignity, and to be singularly honourable to him."

Mr. Ticknor, in a note to the above, states that he has been able to find only five passages in all Lope de Vega's works where there is any mention of Cervantes, and not one of these written after the appearance of the " Don Quixote," during its author's lifetime—a significant fact. One of the passages to which our author refers, and which is from the " Laurel de Apolo," contains, he says, "a somewhat stiff eulogy on Cervantes." We quote the original couplet, which alludes to the injury inflicted on Cervantes' hand in the great battle of Lepanto.

> "Porque se diga que una mano herida
> Pudo dar á su dueño eterna vida."

Which may be rendered,

> The hand, though crippled in the glorious strife,
> Sufficed to gain its lord eternal life.

We imagine that most who read the distich—the Castilian, not the English—will be disposed to regard it as no inelegant, and certainly not a parsimonious tribute from one bard to another—at least, if made in the lifetime of the subject of it. Unfortunately, it was not written till some fourteen years after the death of Cervantes, when he was beyond the power of being pleased or profited by praise from any quarter.

Mr. Ticknor closes the sketch of Cervantes with some pertinent and touching reflections on the circumstances under which his great work was composed.

"The romance which he threw so carelessly from him, and which, I am persuaded, he regarded rather as a bold effort to break up the absurd taste of his time for the fancies of chivalry than as any thing of more serious import, has been established by an uninterrupted, and, it may be said, an unquestioned, success ever since, both as the oldest classical specimen of romantic fiction, and as one of the most remarkable monuments of modern genius. But though this may be enough to fill the measure of human fame and glory, it is not all to which Cervantes is entitled; for, if we would do him the justice that would have been dearest to his own spirit, and even if we would ourselves fully comprehend and enjoy the whole of his Don Quixote, we should, as we read it, bear in mind that this delightful romance was not the result of a youthful exuberance of feeling and a happy external condition, nor composed in his best years, when the spirits of its author were light and his hopes high; but that—with all its unquenchable and irresistible humour, with its bright views of the world, and its cheerful trust in goodness and virtue—it was written in his old age, at the conclusion of a life nearly every step of which had been marked with disappointed expectations, disheartening struggles, and sore calamities; that he began it in a prison, and that it was finished when he felt the hand of death pressing heavy and cold upon his heart. If this be remembered as we read, we may feel, as we ought to feel, what admiration and reverence are due, not only to the living power of Don Quixote, but to the character and genius of Cervantes."

The next name that meets us in the volume is that of Lope de Vega Carpio, the idol of his generation, who lived, in all the enjoyment of wealth and worldly honours, in the same city, and, as some accounts state, in the same street, where his illustrious rival was pining in poverty and neglect. If posterity has reversed the judgment of their contemporaries, still we cannot withhold our admiration at the inexhaustible invention of Lope, and the miraculous facility of his composition. His achievements in this way, perfectly well authenticated, are yet such as to stagger credibility. He wrote in all about eighteen hundred regular dramas, and four hundred autos—pieces of one act each. Besides this, he composed, at leisure intervals, no less than twenty-one printed volumes of miscellaneous poetry, including eleven narrative and didactic poems of much length, in *ottava rima*, and seven hundred sonnets, also in the Italian measure. His comedies, amounting to between two and three thousand lines each, were mostly rhymed, and interspersed with ballads, sonnets, and different kinds of versification. Critics have sometimes amused themselves with computing the amount of matter thus actually thrown off by him in the course of his dramatic career. The sum swells to twenty-one million three hundred thousand verses! He lived to the age of seventy-two, and if we allow him to have employed fifty years —which will not be far from the truth—in his theatrical compositions, it will give an average of something like a play a week, through the whole period, to say nothing of the epics and other miscellanies! He tells us farther, that, on one occasion, he produced five entire plays in a fortnight. And his biographer assures us that more than once he turned off a whole drama in twenty-four hours. These plays, it will be recollected, with their stores of invention and fluent versification, were the delight of all classes of his countrymen, and the copious fountain of supply to half the theatres of Europe. Well might Cervantes call him the "*monstruo de naturaleza*"—the "miracle of nature."

The vast popularity of Lope, and the unprecedented amount of his labours, brought with them, as might be expected, a substantial recompense. This remuneration was of the most honourable kind, for it was chiefly derived from the public

It is said to have amounted to no less than a hundred thousand ducats—which, estimating the ducat at its probable value of six or seven dollars of our day, has no parallel—or, perhaps, not more than one—upon record.

Yet Lope did not refuse the patronage of the great. From the Duke of Sessa he is said to have received, in the course of his life, more than twenty thousand ducats. Another of his noble patrons was the Duke of Alva; not the terrible duke of the Netherlands, but his grandson—a man of some literary pretensions, hardly claimed for his great ancestor. Yet with the latter he has been constantly confounded, by Lord Holland, in his life of the poet, by Southey, after an examination of the matter, and lastly, though with some distrust, by Nicholas Antonio, the learned Castilian biographer. Mr. Ticknor shows, beyond a doubt, from a critical examination of the subject, that they are all in error. The inquiry and the result are clearly stated in the notes, and are one among the many evidences which these notes afford of the minute and very accurate researches of our author into matters of historical interest, that have baffled even the Castilian scholars.

We remember meeting with something of a similar blunder in Schlegel's Dramatic Lectures, where he speaks of the poet Garcilasso de la Vega as descended from the Peruvian Incas, and as having lost his life before Tunis. The fact is, that the poet died at Nice, and that, too, some years before

the birth of the Inca Garcilasso, with whom Schlegel so strangely confounds him. One should be
charitable to such errors—though a dogmatic critic like Schlegel has as little right as any to demand such charity—for we well know how difficult it is always to escape them, when, as in Castile, the same name seems to descend, as an heir-
loom, from one generation to another; if it be not,
indeed, shared by more than one of the same generation. In the case of the Duke of Alva, there
was not even this apology.

Mr. Ticknor has traced the personal history of
Lope de Vega, so as to form a running commentary on his literary. It will be read with satisfaction, even by those who are familiar with Lord
Holland's agreeable life of the poet, since the publication of which more ample researches have been
made into the condition of the Castilian drama.
Those who are disposed to set too high a value
on the advantages of literary success may learn a
lesson by seeing how ineffectual it was to secure
the happiness of that spoiled child of fortune. We
give our author's account of his latter days, when
his mind had become infected with the religious
gloom which has too often settled round the evening of life with the fanatical Spaniard.

"But as his life drew to a close, his religious
feelings, mingled with a melancholy fanaticism,
predominated more and more. Much of his poetry
composed at this time expressed them; and at last
they rose to such a height, that he was almost

constantly in a state of excited melancholy, or, as it was then beginning to be called, of hypochondria. Early in the month of August, he felt himself extremely weak, and suffered more than ever from that sense of discouragement which was breaking down his resources and strength. His thoughts, however, were so exclusively occupied with his spiritual condition, that, even when thus reduced, he continued to fast, and on one occasion went through with a private discipline so cruel, that the walls of the apartment where it occurred were afterward found sprinkled with his blood. From this he never recovered. He was taken ill the same night; and, after fulfilling the offices prescribed by his Church with the most submissive devotion—mourning that he had ever been engaged in any occupations but such as were exclusively religious—he died on the 25th of August, 1635, nearly seventy-three years old.

"The sensation produced by his death was such as is rarely witnessed even in the case of those upon whom depends the welfare of nations. The Duke of Sessa, who was his especial patron, and to whom he left his manuscripts, provided for the funeral in a manner becoming his own wealth and rank. It lasted nine days. The crowds that thronged to it were immense. Three bishops officiated, and the first nobles of the land attended as mourners. Eulogies and poems followed on all sides, and in numbers all but incredible. Those written in Spain make one considerable volume, and end with a drama in which his apotheosis was brought upon the public stage. Those written in Italy are hardly less numerous, and fill an other. But more touching than any of them was the prayer of that much-loved daughter, who had been shut up from the world fourteen years, that the long funeral procession might pass by her convent and permit her once more to look on the face she so tenderly venerated ; and more solemn than any was the mourning of the multitude, from whose dense mass audible sobs burst forth, as his remains slowly descended from their sight into the house appointed for all living."

Mr. Ticknor follows up his biographical sketch of Lope with an analysis of his plays, concluding the whole with a masterly review of his qualities as a dramatic writer. The discussion has a wider import than at first appears. For Lope de Vega, although he built on the foundations of the ancient drama, yet did this in such a manner as to settle the forms of this department of literature forever for his countrymen.

It would be interesting to compare the great Spanish dramatist with Shakspeare, who flourished at the same period, and who, in like manner, stamped his own character on the national theatre. Both drew their fictions from every source indiscriminately, and neither paid regard to probabilities of chronology, geography, or scarcely history. Time, place, and circumstance were of little moment in their eyes. Both built their dramas

4 Q

on the romantic model, with its magic scenes of
joy and sorrow, in the display of which each was
master in his own way; though the English poet
could raise the tone of sentiment to a moral grandeur, which the Castilian, with all the tragic colouring of his pencil, could never reach. Both fascinated their audiences by that sweet and natural
flow of language, that seemed to set itself to music
as it was uttered. But, however much alike in
other points, there was one distinguishing feature
in each, which removed them and their dramas
far as the poles asunder.

Shakspeare's great object was the exhibition of
character. To this everything was directed. Situation, dialogue, story—all were employed only
to this great end. This was in perfect accordance
with the taste of his nation, as shown through
the whole of its literature, from Chaucer to Scott.
Lope de Vega, on the other hand, made so little
account of character that he reproduces the same
leading personages, in his different plays, over and
over again, as if they had been all cast in the
same mould. The *galan*, the *dama*, the *gracioso*,
or buffoon, recur as regularly as the clown in the
old English comedy, and their *rôle* is even more
precisely defined.

The paramount object with Lope was the intrigue — the story. His plays were, what Mr
Ticknor well styles them, dramatic novels. And
this, as our author remarks, was perfectly conformable to the prevalent spirit of Spanish literature

—clearly narrative—as shown in its long epics of the twelfth and thirteenth centuries, its host of ballads, its gossiping chronicles, its chivalrous romances. The great purpose of Lope was to excite and maintain an interest in the story. "Keep the *dénouement* in suspense," he says; "if it be once surmised, your audience will turn their backs on you." He frequently complicates his intrigues in such a manner that only the closest attention can follow them. He cautions his hearers to give this attention, especially at the outset.

Lope, with great tact, accommodated his theatre to the prevailing taste of his countrymen. "Plautus and Terence," he says, "I throw into the fire when I begin to write;" thus showing that it was not by accident, but on a settled principle that he arranged the forms of his dramas. It is the favourite principle of modern economists, that of consulting the greatest happiness of the greatest number. Lope did so, and was rewarded for it, not merely by the applause of the million, but by that of every Spaniard, high and low, in the country. In all this, Lope de Vega acted on strictly philosophical principles. He conformed to the romantic, although the distinction was not then properly understood; and he thought it necessary to defend his departure from the rules of the ancients. But, in truth, such rules were not suited to the genius and usages of the Spaniards, any more than of the English; and more than one experiment proved that they would be as little tolerated by the one people as the other.

It is remarkable that the Spaniards, whose language rests so broadly on the Latin, in the same manner as with the French and the Italians, should have refused to rest their literature, like them, on the classic models of antiquity, and have chosen to conform to the romantic spirit of the more northern nations of the Teutonic family. It was the paramount influence of the Gothic element in their character, co-operating with the peculiar, and most stimulating influences of their early history.

We close our remarks on Lope de Vega with some excellent reflections of our author on the rapidity of his composition, and showing to what extent his genius was reverenced by his contemporaries.

"Lope de Vega's immediate success, as we have seen, was in proportion to his rare powers and favourable opportunities. For a long time nobody else was willingly heard on the stage; and during the whole of the forty or fifty years that he wrote for it, he stood quite unapproached in general popularity. His unnumbered plays and farces, in all the forms that were demanded by the fashions of the age, or permitted by religious authority, filled the theatres both of the capital and the provinces; and so extraordinary was the impulse he gave to dramatic representations, that, though there were only two companies of strolling players at Madrid when he began, there were, about the period of his death, no less than forty, comprehending nearly a thousand persons.

"Abroad, too, his fame was hardly less remark-able. In Rome, Naples, and Milan, his dramas were performed in their original language; in France and Italy his name was announced in or-der to fill the theatres when no play of his was to be performed; and once even, and probably often-er, one of his dramas was represented in the se-raglio at Constantinople. But perhaps neither all this popularity, nor yet the crowds that followed him in the streets and gathered in the balconies to watch him as he passed along, nor the name of Lope, that was given to whatever was esteem-ed singularly good in its kind, is so striking a proof of his dramatic success, as the fact, so often com-plained of by himself and his friends, that multi-tudes of his plays were fraudulently noted down as they were acted, and then printed for profit throughout Spain; and that multitudes of other plays appeared under his name, and were repre-sented all over the provinces, that he had never heard of till they were published and performed.

"A large income naturally followed such pop-ularity, for his plays were liberally paid for by the actors; and he had patrons of a munificence un-known in our days, and always undesirable. But he was thriftless and wasteful; exceedingly char-itable; and, in hospitality to his friends, prodigal. He was, therefore, almost always embarrassed. At the end of his 'Jerusalem,' printed as early as 1609, he complains of the pressure of his domes-tic affairs; and in his old age he addressed some

4   3 K

verses, in the nature of a petition, to the still more
thriftless Philip the Fourth, asking the means of
living for himself and daughter. After his death,
his poverty was fully admitted by his executor;
and yet, considering the relative value of money,
no poet, perhaps, ever received so large a compensation for his works.

"It should, however, be remembered, that no
other poet ever wrote so much with popular effect.
For, if we begin with his dramatic compositions,
which are the best of his efforts, and go down to
his epics, which, on the whole, are the worst, we
shall find the amount of what was received with
favour, as it came from the press, quite unparalleled. And when to this we are compelled to add
his own assurance, just before his death, that the
greater part of his works still remained in manuscript, we pause in astonishment, and, before we
are able to believe the account, demand some explanation that will make it credible; an explanation which is the more important because it is the
key to much of his personal character, as well as
of his poetical success. And it is this. No poet
of any considerable reputation ever had a genius
so nearly related to that of an improvisator, or ever
indulged his genius so freely in the spirit of improvisation. This talent has always existed in
the southern countries of Europe; and in Spain
has, from the first, produced, in different ways, the
most extraordinary results. We owe to it the
invention and perfection of the old ballads, which

were originally improvisated and then preserved by tradition; and we owe to it the *seguidillas*, the *boleros*, and all the other forms of popular poetry that still exist in Spain, and are daily poured forth by the fervent imaginations of the uncultivated classes of the people, and sung to the national music, that sometimes seems to fill the air by night as the light of the sun does by day.

"In the time of Lope de Vega, the passion for such improvisation had risen higher than it ever rose before, if it had not spread out more widely. Actors were expected sometimes to improvisate on themes given to them by the audience. Extemporaneous dramas, with all the varieties of verse demanded by a taste formed in the theatres, were not of rare occurrence. Philip the Fourth, Lope's patron, had such performed in his presence, and bore a part in them himself. And the famous Count De Lemos, the viceroy of Naples, to whom Cervantes was indebted for so much kindness, kept, as an *apanage* to his viceroyalty, a poetical court, of which the two Argensolas were the chief ornaments, and in which extemporaneous plays were acted with brilliant success.

"Lope de Vega's talent was undoubtedly of near kindred to this genius of improvisation, and produced its extraordinary results by a similar process, and in the same spirit. He dictated verse, we are told, with ease, more rapidly than an amanuensis could take it down; and wrote out an entire play in two days, which could with difficulty be transcribed by a copyist in the same time.   He was not absolutely an improvisator, for his education and position naturally led him to devote himself to written composition; but he was continually on the borders of whatever belongs to an improvisator's peculiar province; was continually showing, in his merits and defects, in his ease, grace, and sudden resource, in his wildness and extravagance, in the happiness of his versification and the prodigal abundance of his imagery, that a very little more freedom, a very little more indulgence given to his feelings and his fancy, would have made him at once and entirely, not only an improvisator, but the most remarkable one that ever lived."

We pass over the long array of dramatic writers who trod closely in the footsteps of their great master, as well as a lively notice of the satirist Quevedo, and come at once to Calderon de la Barca, the great poet who divided with Lope the empire of the Spanish stage.

Our author has given a full biography of this famous dramatist, to which we must refer the reader; and we know of no other history in English where he can meet with it at all.   Calderon lived in the reign of Philip the Fourth, which, extending from 1621 to 1665, comprehends the most flourishing period of the Castilian theatre.   The elegant tastes of the monarch, with his gay and gracious manners, formed a contrast to the austere temper of the other princes of the house of Austria.

He was not only the patron of the drama, but a professor of the dramatic art, and, indeed, a performer. He wrote plays himself, and acted them in his own palace. His nobles, following his example, turned their saloons into theatres; and the great towns, and many of the smaller ones, partaking of the enthusiasm of the court, had their own theatres and companies of actors, which altogether amounted, at one time, to no less than three hundred. One may understand that it required no small amount of material to keep such a vast machinery in motion.

At the head of this mighty apparatus was the poet Calderon, the favourite of the court even more than Lope de Vega, but not more than he the favourite of the nation. He was fully entitled to this high distinction, if we are to receive half that is said of him by the German critics, among whom Schlegel particularly celebrates him as displaying the purest model of the romantic ideal, the most perfect development of the sentiments of love, heroism, and religious devotion. This exaggerated tone of eulogy calls forth the rebuke of Sismondi, who was educated in a different school of criticism, and whose historical pursuits led him to look below the surface of things to their moral tendencies. By this standard, Calderon has failed. And yet it seems to be a just standard, even when criticising a work by the rules of art; for a disregard of the obvious laws of morality is a violation of the principles of taste, on which the beautiful

4   3 K *

must rest. Not that Calderon's plays are chargeable with licentiousness or indecency to a greater extent than was common in the writers of the period. But they show a lamentable confusion of ideas in regard to the first principles of morality, by entirely confounding the creed of the individual with his religion. A conformity to the established creed is virtue, the departure from it vice. It is impossible to conceive, without reading his performances, to what revolting consequences this confusion of the moral perceptions perpetually leads.

Yet Calderon should not incur the reproach of hypocrisy, but that of fanaticism. He was the very dupe of superstition ; and the spirit of fanaticism he shares with the greater part of his countrymen—even the most enlightened—of that period. Hypocrisy may have been the sin of the Puritan, but fanaticism was the sin of the Catholic Spaniard of the sixteenth and seventeenth centuries. The one quality may be thought to reflect more discredit on the heart, the other on the head. The philosopher may speculate on their comparative moral turpitude ; but the pages of history show that fanaticism armed with power has been the most fruitful parent of misery to mankind.

Calderon's drama turns on the most exaggerated principles of honour, jealousy, and revenge, mingled with the highest religious exaltation. Some of these sentiments, usually referred to the influence of the Arabs, Mr. Ticknor traces to the ancient

Gothic laws, which formed the basis of the early Spanish jurisprudence. The passages he cites are pertinent, and his theory is plausible; yet, in the relations with woman, we suspect much must still be allowed for the long contact with the jealous Arabian.

Calderon's characters and sentiments are formed, for the most part, on a purely ideal standard. The incidents of his plots are even more startling than those of Lope de Vega, more monstrous than the fictions of Dumas or Eugène Sue. But his thoughts are breathed forth in the intoxicating language of passion, with all the glowing imagery of the East, and in tones of the richest melody of which the Castilian tongue is capable.

Mr. Ticknor has enlivened his analysis of Calderon's drama with several translations, as usual, from which we should be glad to extract, but must content ourselves with the concluding portion of his criticism, where he sums up the prominent qualities of the bard.

"Calderon neither effected nor attempted any great changes in the forms of the drama. Two or three times, indeed, he prepared dramas that were either wholly sung, or partly sung and partly spoken; but even these, in their structure, were no more operas than his other plays, and were only a courtly luxury, which it was attempted to introduce, in imitation of the genuine opera just brought into France by Louis the Fourteenth, with whose court that of Spain was now intimately connected. But this was all. Calderon has added to the stage no new form of dramatic composition. Nor has he much modified those forms which had been already arranged and settled by Lope de Vega. But he has shown more technical exactness in combining his incidents, and arranged everything more skillfully for stage effect. He has given to the whole a new colouring, and, in some respects, a new physiognomy. His drama is more poetical in its tone and tendencies, and has less the air of truth and reality, than that of his great predecessor. In its more successful portions—which are rarely objectionable from their moral tone—it seems almost as if we were transported to another and more gorgeous world, where the scenery is lighted up with unknown and preternatural splendour, and where the motives and passions of the personages that pass before us are so highly wrought, that we must have our own feelings not a little stirred and excited before we can take an earnest interest in what we witness or sympathize in its results. But even in this he is successful. The buoyancy of life and spirit that he has infused into the gayer divisions of his drama, and the moving tenderness that pervades its graver and more tragical portions, lift us unconsciously to the height where alone his brilliant exhibitions can prevail with our imaginations—where alone we can be interested and deluded, when we find ourselves in the midst, not only of such a confusion of the different forms of the drama, but of such a confusion of the proper limits of dramatic and lyrical poetry.

"To this elevated tone, and to the constant effort necessary in order to sustain it, we owe much of what distinguishes Calderon from his predecessors, and nearly all that is most individual and characteristic in his separate merits and defects. It makes him less easy, graceful, and natural than Lope. It imparts to his style a mannerism which, notwithstanding the marvellous richness and fluency of his versification, sometimes wearies and sometimes offends us. It leads him to repeat from himself till many of his personages become standing characters, and his heroes and their servants, his ladies and their confidants, his old men and his buffoons, seem to be produced, like the masked figures of the ancient theatre, to represent, with the same attributes and in the same costume, the different intrigues of his various plots. It leads him, in short, to regard the whole of the Spanish drama as a form, within whose limits his imagination may be indulged without restraint; and in which Greeks and Romans, heathen divinities, and the supernatural fictions of Christian tradition, may be all brought out in Spanish fashions and with Spanish feelings, and led, through a succession of ingenious and interesting adventures, to the catastrophes their stories happen to require.

"In carrying out this theory of the Spanish drama, Calderon, as we have seen, often succeeds, and often fails. But when he succeeds, his success is sometimes of no common character. He then sets before us only models of ideal beauty, perfection, and splendour; a world, he would have it, into which nothing should enter but the highest elements of the national genius. There, the fervid, yet grave, enthusiasm of the old Castilian heroism; the chivalrous adventures of modern, courtly honour; the generous self-devotion of individual loyalty; and that reserved but passionate love, which, in a state of society where it was so rigorously withdrawn from notice, became a kind of unacknowledged religion of the heart; all seem to find their appropriate home. And when he has once brought us into this land of enchantment, whose glowing impossibilities his own genius has created, and has called around him forms of such grace and loveliness as those of Clara and Doña Angela, or heroic forms like those of Tuzani, Mariamne, and Don Ferdinand, then he has reached the highest point he ever attained, or ever proposed to himself; he has set before us the grand show of an idealized drama, resting on the purest and noblest elements of the Spanish national character, and one which, with all its unquestionable defects, is to be placed among the extraordinary phenomena of modern poetry."

We shall not attempt to follow down the long file of dramatic writers who occupy the remainder of the period. Their name is legion; and we are filled with admiration as we reflect on the intrepid diligence with which our author has waded through this amount of matter, and the fidelity with which he has rendered to the respective writers literary justice.   We regret, however, that we have not space to select, as we had intended, some part of his lively account of the Spanish players, and of the condition of the stage.   It is collected from various obscure sources, and contains many curious particulars.   They show that the Spanish theatre was conducted in a manner so dissimilar from what exists in other European nations as perfectly to vindicate its claims to originality.

It must not be supposed that the drama, though the great natural diversion, was allowed to go on in Spain, any more than in other countries, in an uninterrupted flow of prosperity.   It met with considerable opposition more than once in its career ; and, on the representations of the clergy, at the close of Philip the Second's reign, performances were wholly interdicted, on the ground of their licentiousness.   For two years the theatre was closed.   But, on the death of that gloomy monarch, the drama, in obedience to the public voice, was renewed in greater splendour than before.   It was urged by its friends that the theatre was required to pay a portion of its proceeds to certain charitable institutions, and this made all its performances in some sort an exercise of charity.   Lope de Vega also showed his address by his *Comedias de Santos*, under which pious name the life of some saint or holy man was portrayed. which, however edifying in its close, afforded, too often, as great a display of profligacy in its earlier portions as is to be found in any of the secular plays of the *capa y espada*. His experiment seems to have satisfied the consciences of the opponents of the drama, or at least to have silenced their opposition. It reminds us of the manner in which some among us, who seem to have regarded the theatre with the antipathy entertained by our Puritan fathers, have found their scruples vanish at witnessing these exhibitions under the more reputable names of "Athenæum," "Museum," or "Lyceum."

Our author has paid due attention to the other varieties of elegant literature which occupy this prolific period. We can barely enumerate the titles. Epic poetry has not secured to itself the same rank in Castile as in many other countries. At the head stands the "Araucana" of Ercilla, which Voltaire appears to have preferred to "Paradise Lost!" Yet it is little more than a chronicle done in rhyme; and, notwithstanding certain passages of energy and poetic eloquence, it is of more value as the historical record of an eyewitness than as a work of literary art.

In Pastoral poetry the Spaniards have better specimens. But they are specimens of an insipid kind of writing, notwithstanding it has found favour with the Italians, to whom it was introduced by a Spaniard—a Spaniard in descent—the celebrated author of the "Arcadia."

In the higher walks of Lyrical composition they

have been more distinguished. The poetry of Herrera, in particular, seems to equal, in its dithyrambic flow, the best models of classic antiquity; while the Muse of Luis de Leon is filled with the genuine inspiration of Christianity. Mr. Ticknor has given a pleasing portrait of this gentle enthusiast, whose life was consecrated to Heaven, and who preserved a tranquillity of temper unruffled by all the trials of an unmerited persecution.

We cannot deny ourselves the pleasure of quoting a translation of one of his odes, as the last extract from our author. The subject is, the feelings of the disciples on witnessing the ascension of their Master.

"And dost thou, holy Shepherd, leave
    Thine unprotected flock alone,
Here, in this darksome vale, to grieve,
    While thou ascend'st thy glorious throne?

"O, where can they their hopes now turn,
    Who never lived but on thy love?
Where rest the hearts for thee that burn,
    When thou art lost in light above?

"How shall those eyes now find repose
    That turn, in vain, thy smile to see?
What can they hear save mortal woes,
    Who lose thy voice's melody?

"And who shall lay his tranquil hand
    Upon the troubled ocean's might?
Who hush the wind by his command?
    Who guide us through this starless night?

"For Thou art gone!—that cloud so bright,
    That bears thee from our love away,
Springs upward through the dazzling light,
    And leaves us here to weep and pray!"

A peculiar branch of Castilian literature is its Proverbs; those extracts of the popular wisdom—

"short sentences from long experience," as Cervantes publicly styles them. They have been gathered, more than once, in Spain, into printed collections. One of these, in the last century, contains no less than twenty-four thousand of these sayings! And a large number was still left floating among the people. It is evidence of extraordinary sagacity in the nation, that its humblest classes should have made such a contribution to its literature. They have an additional value with purists for their idiomatic richness of expression —like the *riboboli* of the Florentine mob, which the Tuscan critics hold in veneration as the racy runnings from the dregs of the people. These popular maxims may be rather compared to the copper coin of the country, which has the widest circulation of any, and bears the true stamp of antiquity—not adulterated, as is too often the case with the finer metals.

The last department we shall notice is that of the Spanish Tales—rich, various, and highly picturesque. One class—the *picaresco* tales—are those with which the world has become familiar in the specimen afforded by the " Gil Blas" of Le Sage, an imitation—a rare occurrence —surpassing the original. This amusing class of fictions has found peculiar favour with the Spaniards, from its lively sketches of character, and the contrast it delights to present of the pride and the poverty of the *hidalgo*. Yet this kind of satirical fiction was invented by a man of rank, and one of the proudest of his order.

Our remarks have swelled to a much greater compass than we had intended, owing to the importance of the work before us, and the abundance of the topics, little familiar to the English reader. We have no room, therefore, for farther discussion of this second period, so fruitful in great names, and pass over, though reluctantly, our author's criticism on the historical writings of the age, in which he has penetrated below the surface of their literary forms to the scientific principles on which they were constructed.

Neither can we pause on the last of the three great periods into which our author has distributed the work, and which extends from the accession of the Bourbon dynasty in 1700 to some way into the present century. The omission is of the less consequence, from the lamentable decline of the literature, owing to the influence of French models, as well as to the political decline of the nation under the last princes of the Austrian dynasty. The circumstances which opened the way both to this social and literary degeneracy are well portrayed by Mr. Ticknor, and his account will be read with profit by the student of history.

We regret still more that we can but barely allude to the Appendix, which, in the eye of the Spanish critic, will form not the least important portion of the work. Besides several long poems, highly curious for their illustration of the ancient literature, now for the first time printed from the original manuscripts, we have, at the outset, a dis-

cussion of the origin and formation of the Castilian tongue, a truly valuable philological contribution. The subject has too little general attraction to allow its appearance in the body of the
text; but those students who would obtain a thorough knowledge of the Castilian and the elements
of which it is compounded, will do well to begin
the perusal of the work with this elaborate essay.

Neither have we room to say anything of our
author's inquiry into the genuineness of two works
which have much engaged the attention of Castilian scholars, and both of which he pronounces
apocryphal. The manner in which the inquiry is
conducted affords a fine specimen of literary criticism. In one of these discussions occurs a fact
worthy of note. An ecclesiastic named Barrien-
tos, of John the Second's court, has been accused
of delivering to the flames, on the charge of necromancy, the library of a scholar then lately deceased, the famous Marquis of Villena. The good
bishop, from his own time to the present, has suffered under this grievous imputation, which ranks
him with Omar. Mr. Ticknor now cites a manuscript letter of the bishop himself, distinctly ex-
plaining that it was by the royal command that
this literary *auto da fé* was celebrated. This incident is one proof among many of the rare character of our author's materials, and of the careful
study which he has given to them.

Spanish literature has been until now less thoroughly explored than the literature of almost any

other European nation. Everybody has read " Gil Blas," and, through this foreign source, has got a good idea of the social condition of Spain, at the period to which it belongs ; and the social condition of that country is slower to change than that of any other country. Everybody has read " Don Quixote," and thus formed, or been able to form, some estimate of the high value of the Castilian literature. Yet the world, for the most part, seems to be content to take Montesquieu's witticism for truth—that " the Spaniards have produced one good book, and the object of that was to laugh at all the rest." All, however, have not been so ignorant; and more than one cunning adventurer has found his way into the pleasant field of Castilian letters, and carried off materials of no little value for the composition of his own works. Such was Le Sage, as shown in more than one of his productions ; such, too, were various of the dramatic writers of France and other countries, where the extent of the plunder can only be estimated by those who have themselves delved in the rich mines of Spanish lore.

Mr. Ticknor has now, for the first time, fully surveyed the ground, systematically arranged its various productions, and explored their character and properties. In the disposition of his immense mass of materials he has maintained the most perfect order, so distributing them as to afford every facility for the comprehension of the student. We are everywhere made conscious of the abun

4   3 L *

dance, not merely of these materials—though one third of the subjects brought under review, at least, are new to the public—but of the writer's intellectual resources. We feel that we are supplied from a reservoir that has been filled to overflowing from the very fountains of the Muses; which is, moreover, fed from other sources than those of the Castilian literature. By his critical acquaintance with the literatures of other nations, Mr. Ticknor has all the means at command for illustration and comparison. The extent of this various knowledge may be gathered from his notes, even more than from the text. A single glance at these will show on how broad a foundation the narrative rests. They contain stores of personal anecdote, criticism, and literary speculation, that might almost furnish materials for another work like the present.

Mr. Ticknor's History is conducted in a truly philosophical spirit. Instead of presenting a barren record of books—which, like the catalogue of a gallery of paintings, is of comparatively little use to those who have not previously studied them —he illustrates the works by the personal history of their authors, and this, again, by the history of the times in which they lived; affording, by the reciprocal action of one on the other, a complete record of Spanish civilization, both social and intellectual. It would be difficult to find a work more thoroughly penetrated with the true Castilian spirit, or to which the general student, or the student of civil history, may refer with no less advantage than one who is simply interested in the progress of letters. A pertinent example of this is in the account of Columbus, which contains passages from the correspondence of that remarkable man, which, even after all that has been written on the subject—and so well written—throw important light on his character.

The tone of criticism in these volumes is temperate and candid. We cannot but think Mr. Ticknor has profited largely by the former discussion of this subject in his academic lectures. Not that the present book bears much resemblance to those lectures—certainly not more than must necessarily occur in the discussion of the same subject by the same mind, after a long interval of time. But this interval has enabled him to review, and no doubt in some cases to reverse his earlier judgments, and his present decisions come before us as the ripe results of a long and patient meditation. This gives them still higher authority.

We cannot conclude without some notice of the style, so essential an element in a work of elegant literature. It is clear, classical, and correct, with a sustained moral dignity that not unfrequently rises to eloquence. But it is usually distinguished by a calm philosophical tenor that is well suited to the character of the subject. It is especially free from any tendency to mysticism—from vagueness of expression, a pretty sure indication of vague conceptions in the mind of the author, which he is apt to dignify with the name of philosophy.

In our criticism on Mr. Ticknor's labours, we may be thought to have dwelt too exclusively on his merits. It may be that we owe something to the contagion of his own generous and genial tone of criticism on others. Or it may be that we feel more than common interest in a subject which is not altogether new to us; and it is only an acquaintance with the subject that can enable one to estimate the difficulties of its execution. Where we have had occasion to differ from our author, we have freely stated it. But such instances are few, and of no great moment. We consider the work as one that does honour to English literature. It cannot fail to attract much attention from European critics who are at all instructed in the topics which it discusses. We predict with confidence that it will be speedily translated into Castilian and into German; and that it must become the standard work on Spanish literature, not only for those who speak our own tongue, but for the Spaniards themselves.

We have still a word to add on the typographical execution of the book, not in reference to its mechanical beauty, which is equal to that of any other that has come from the Cambridge press, but in regard to its verbal accuracy. This is not an easy matter in a work like the present, involving such an amount of references in foreign languages, as well as the publication of poems of considerable length from manuscript, and that, too, in the Castilian. We doubt if any similar work of erudition has been executed by a foreign press with greater accuracy. We do not doubt that it would not have been so well executed, in this respect, by any other press in this country.

THE END